Policy-making Proc
European Constitution

MW01717212

This new book presents a wealth of new data documenting and analyzing the different positions taken by European governments in the development of the European constitution.

Understanding how constitutional decisions are taken in the EU is of great societal and scientific relevance. This volume examines how these decisions have substantial effects on the sovereignty of nation states and on the lives of citizens, independent of the ratification of a constitution.

Few efforts have been made to document constitution building in a systematic and comparative manner, including the different steps and stages of the process. This book examines European constitution building by tracing the two-level policy formation process from the draft proposal of the European Convention until the Intergovernmental Conference, which finally adopted the document on the constitution in June 2004. Following a tight comparative framework, it sheds light on reactions to the proposed constitution in the domestic arena of all the actors involved. The volume includes a chapter on each of the original 15 member states and the ten accession states, plus chapters on the European Commission and European Parliament.

Building a clear understanding of the affects of constitutional decisions, the book will be of strong interest to scholars and researchers of European Union politics, comparative politics and policy making.

Thomas König is Professor of Political Science at the German University of Administrative Sciences, Speyer. **Simon Hug** is Professor of Political Science at the University of Zurich, Switzerland.

Routledge/ECPR studies in European political science

Edited by Thomas Poguntke

University of Birmingham, UK, on behalf of the European Consortium for Political Research

The Routledge/ECPR Studies in European Political Science series is published in association with the European Consortium for Political Research – the leading organization concerned with the growth and development of political science in Europe. The series presents high-quality edited volumes on topics at the leading edge of current interest in political science and related fields, with contributions from European scholars and others who have presented work at ECPR workshops or research groups.

1 **Regionalist Parties in Western Europe**
Edited by Lieven de Winter and Huri Türsan

2 **Comparing Party System Change**
Edited by Jan-Erik Lane and Paul Pennings

3 **Political Theory and European Union**
Edited by Albert Weale and Michael Nentwich

4 **Politics of Sexuality**
Edited by Terrell Carver and Véronique Mottier

5 **Autonomous Policy Making by International Organizations**
Edited by Bob Reinalda and Bertjan Verbeek

6 **Social Capital and European Democracy**
Edited by Jan van Deth, Marco Maraffi, Ken Newton and Paul Whiteley

7 **Party Elites in Divided Societies**
Edited by Kurt Richard Luther and Kris Deschouwer

8 **Citizenship and Welfare State Reform in Europe**
Edited by Jet Bussemaker

9 **Democratic Governance and New Technology**
Technologically mediated innovations in political practice in Western Europe
Edited by Ivan Horrocks, Jens Hoff and Pieter Tops

10 **Democracy without Borders**
Transnationalization and conditionality in new democracies
Edited by Jean Grugel

11 **Cultural Theory as Political Science**
Edited by Michael Thompson, Gunnar Grendstad and Per Selle

12 **The Transformation of Governance in the European Union**
Edited by Beate Kohler-Koch and Rainer Eising

13 **Parliamentary Party Groups in European Democracies**
Political parties behind closed doors
Edited by Knut Heidar and Ruud Koole

14 **Survival of the European Welfare State**
Edited by Stein Kuhnle

15 **Private Organizations in Global Politics**
Edited by Karsten Ronit and Volker Schneider

16 **Federalism and Political Performance**
Edited by Ute Wachendorfer-Schmidt

17 **Democratic Innovation**
Deliberation, representation and association
Edited by Michael Saward

18 **Public Opinion and the International Use of Force**
Edited by Philip Everts and Pierangelo Isernia

19 **Religion and Mass Electoral Behaviour in Europe**
Edited by David Broughton and Hans-Martien ten Napel

20 **Estimating the Policy Position of Political Actors**
Edited by Michael Laver

21 **Democracy and Political Change in the "Third World"**
Edited by Jeff Haynes

22 **Politicians, Bureaucrats and Administrative Reform**
Edited by B. Guy Peters and Jon Pierre

23 **Social Capital and Participation in Everyday Life**
Edited by Paul Dekker and Eric M. Uslaner

24 **Development and Democracy**
What do we know and how?
Edited by Ole Elgström and Goran Hyden

25 **Do Political Campaigns Matter?**
Campaign effects in elections and referendums
Edited by David M. Farrell and Rüdiger Schmitt-Beck

26 **Political Journalism**
New challenges, new practices
Edited by Raymond Kuhn and Erik Neveu

27 **Economic Voting**
Edited by Han Dorussen and Michael Taylor

28 **Organized Crime and the Challenge to Democracy**
Edited by Felia Allum and Renate Siebert

29 **Understanding the European Union's External Relations**
Edited by Michèle Knodt and Sebastiaan Princen

30 **Social Democratic Party Policies in Contemporary Europe**
Edited by Giuliano Bonoli and Martin Powell

31 **Decision Making within International Organisations**
Edited by Bob Reinalda and Bertjan Verbeek

32 **Comparative Biomedical Policy**
Governing assisted reproductive technologies
Edited by Ivar Bleiklie, Malcolm L. Goggin and Christine Rothmayr

33 **Electronic Democracy**
Mobilization, organization and participation via new ICTs
Edited by Rachel K. Gibson, Andrea Römmele and Stephen J. Ward

34 **Liberal Democracy and Environmentalism**
The end of environmentalism?
Edited by Marcel Wissenburg and Yoram Levy

35 **Political Theory and the European Constitution**
Edited by Lynn Dobson and Andreas Follesdal

36 **Politics and the European Commission**
Actors, interdependence, legitimacy
Edited by Andy Smith

37 **Metropolitan Governance**
Capacity, democracy and the dynamics of place
Edited by Hubert Heinelt and Daniel Kübler

38 **Democracy and the Role of Associations**
Political, organizational and social contexts
Edited by Sigrid Roßteutscher

39 **The Territorial Politics of Welfare**
Edited by Nicola McEwen and Luis Moreno

40 **Health Governance in Europe**
Issues, challenges and theories
Edited by Monika Steffen

41 **Republicanism in Theory and Practice**
Edited by Iseult Honohan and Jeremy Jennings

42 **Mass Media and Political Communication in New Democracies**
Edited by Katrin Voltmer

43 **Delegation in Contemporary Democracies**
Edited by Dietmar Braun and Fabrizio Gilardi

44 **Governance and Democracy**
Comparing national, European and international experiences
Edited by Yannis Papadopoulos and Arthur Benz

45 **The European Union's Roles in International Politics**
Concepts and analysis
Edited by Ole Elgström and Michael Smith

46 **Policy-making Processes and the European Constitution**
A comparative study of member states and accession countries
Edited by Thomas König and Simon Hug

47 **Democratic Politics and Party Competition**
Edited by Judith Bara and Albert Weale

48 **Participatory Democracy and Political Participation**
Can participatory engineering bring citizens back in?
Edited by Thomas Zittel and Dieter Fuchs

Also available from Routledge in association with the ECPR:
Sex Equality Policy in Western Europe, *Edited by Frances Gardiner*; **Democracy and Green Political Thought**, *Edited by Brian Doherty and Marius de Geus*; **The New Politics of Unemployment**, *Edited by Hugh Compston*; **Citizenship, Democracy and Justice in the New Europe**, *Edited by Percy B. Lehning and Albert Weale*; **Private Groups and Public Life**, *Edited by Jan W. van Deth*; **The Political Context of Collective Action**, *Edited by Ricca Edmondson*; **Theories of Secession**, *Edited by Percy Lehning*; **Regionalism across the North/South Divide**, *Edited by Jean Grugel and Wil Hout.*

Policy-making Processes and the European Constitution

A comparative study of member states and accession countries

Edited by Thomas König and Simon Hug

Routledge
Taylor & Francis Group
LONDON AND NEW YORK

First issued in paperback 2011

First published 2006
by Routledge
2 Park Square, Milton Park, Abingdon, Oxon OX14 4RN

Simultaneously published in the USA and Canada
by Routledge
270 Madison Ave, New York, NY 10016

Routledge is an imprint of the Taylor & Francis Group, an informa business

Typeset in Baskerville by Wearset Ltd, Boldon, Tyne and Wear

British Library Cataloguing in Publication Data
A catalogue record for this book is available from the British Library

Library of Congress Cataloging in Publication Data
A catalog record for this book has been requested

ISBN10: 0-415-38507-5 (hbk)
ISBN13: 978-0-415-38507-7 (hbk)

ISBN10: 0-415-66374-1 (pbk)
ISBN13: 978-0-415-66374-8 (pbk)

Contents

Figures

Tables

About the contributors

Christine Arnold is a postdoctoral researcher in the Department of Political Science, Vrije Universiteit Amsterdam (c.arnold@fsw.vu.nl) and Assistant Professor of European Studies at Universiteit Maastricht.

Giacomo Benedetto is Lecturer in Politics, School of Social Sciences, University of Manchester (giacomo.benedetto@manchester.ac.uk).

Kenneth Benoit is Lecturer in the Department of Political Science, Trinity College Dublin (kbenoit@tcd.ie).

Spyros Blavoukos is a PhD candidate in the Department of Government at the University of Essex and a Research Fellow at Athens University of Economics and Business (sblavo@aueb.gr).

Simone Burkhart is a Research Fellow and PhD candidate at the Max Planck Institute for the Study of Societies, Cologne (burkhart@mpifg.de).

Annemieke Burmeister is a student Research Assistant in the Department of Political Science, Leiden University.

Martina Chabreckova is a student Research Assistant in the Department of Political Science, University of St Gallen.

Raj S. Chari is Lecturer in the Department of Political Science, Trinity College Dublin (charir@tcd.ie).

Christophe Crombez is Professor in the Department of Applied Economics, Catholic University Leuven, and Visiting Professor at the Institute for International Studies, Stanford University (crombez@stanford.edu).

Stephanie Daimer is a Research Fellow and PhD candidate in Political Science, Research Institute for Public Administration, Speyer (daimer@foev-speyer.de).

Han Dorussen is Senior Lecturer in the Department of Government, University of Essex, Colchester (hdorus@essex.ac.uk).

Alfonso Egea-de Haro is a PhD candidate at the Juan March Institute, Madrid (aegea@ceacs.march.es).

Daniel Finke is a Research Fellow and PhD candidate in Political Science, Research Institute for Public Administration, Speyer (finke@foev-speyer.de).

Anna Gwiazda is a postdoctoral researcher at the Dublin European Institute, University College Dublin (anna.gwiazda@ucd.ie).

Madeleine O. Hosli is Associate Professor in the Department of Political Science, Leiden University (hosli@fsw.leidenuniv.nl).

Simon Hug is Professor of Political Science at the Institute of Political Science, University of Zurich (hug@pwi.unizh.ch).

Thomas König is Professor of Political Science at the German University of Administrative Sciences, Speyer (tkoenig@dhv-speyer.de).

Jan Lebbe is Research Fellow in the Department of Applied Economics, Catholic University Leuven.

Hartmut Lenz is Research Fellow and PhD candidate at the University of Essex, Colchester (hlenz@essex.ac.uk).

George Pagoulatos is Assistant Professor in the Department of International and European Economic Studies, Athens University of Economics and Business (gpag@aueb.gr).

Paul Pennings is Associate Professor in the Department of Political Science, Vrije Universiteit Amsterdam (pjm.pennings@fsw.vu.nl).

Tobias Schulz is a postdoctoral researcher at the Institute of Political Science, University of Zurich (schulz@pwi.unizh.ch).

George Tsebelis is Professor in the Department of Political Science, University of California, Los Angeles (tsebelis@ucla.edu).

Andreas Warntjen is PhD candidate in the Department of Government, London School of Economics and Political Science (a.k.warntjen@lse.ac.uk).

Series editor's preface

Writing in Britain one is tempted to question the editors' claim made in their introduction that the drafting of the European constitution is paralleled only by the creation of the US constitution in 1776. In fact, some may argue that it was exactly a somewhat exaggerated significance attached to this document that made ratification by the UK electorate seem highly unlikely and must have made the Labour government secretly grateful to Dutch and French voters who voted against ratification.

Nevertheless, there is much academic mileage in analyzing the intricate policy process that finally led to the adoption of the constitution by the Intergovernmental Conference in October 2004. Not only is it very likely that important elements of the constitution will be put into force through other mechanisms. By choosing a comprehensive approach and including all 25 states, the European Parliament and the European Commission, this study can offer unique insights into the internal logic of the European decision-making process. The main focus of this volume is on the preference formation in national political systems once the Convention had delivered its draft. Who were the main players involved? What were the main issues at stake? How were the discussions coordinated on the national levels? How much agreement was there between the national players?

In order to answer these questions, key experts were interviewed in all old and new EU members states, the Commission and the European Parliament. Their answers provide a comprehensive landscape of those issues that were considered to be important, or even vital, by all relevant players. The analysis also shows some interesting differences between the policy-making models of EU members states: except for the Nordic countries, where national parliaments played an important role, preference formation took place mainly within the executive, mostly under the control of the foreign office (and sometimes the prime minister's office). The editors attribute this to the desire of most governments to prepare for the Intergovernmental Conference instead of opening up "a national debate on constitutional issues."

George Tsebelis draws our attention to the fact that, in a way, the EU constitution is just one in a long series of constitutional arrangements, each of which changing the rules of the game more or less fundamentally. Applying a veto player analysis to the outcomes of the Convention and the Rome and Brussels Intergovernmental Conferences, he shows that when it comes to decision-making rules, "the final compromise is exactly between Nice and the Convention." The constitution had changed the decision rules by reducing the threshold against winning coalitions in order to make the EU a potentially more politically active structure. While it is not always preferable to design institutions in a way that facilitates political change, he argues that in an environment of economic and physical insecurity the EU needs to enhance its ability to act politically, and therefore the failure to implement the constitution may be detrimental to European political development.

The next chapter by Thomas König, Andreas Warntjen and Simone Burkhart reports results form a survey of Convention delegates and shows that "unsurprisingly, small countries' delegates favour the current appointing system of at least one commissioner per country." Similarly, a number of additional cleavages can be empirically documented, including differences between old and new member states and between actors of different institutional backgrounds. The following 27 chapters document the process of preference formation within all 25 member states and the Commission and the European Parliament. By following a rigid outline, theses chapters are easily comparable and provide rich insights into the political processes leading up the final compromise of October 2004. The editors subject this rich empirical material to a comparative analysis in their concluding chapter. Their findings indicate that European politics, on the whole, may be more responsive to what citizens want than is often assumed. While the national institutional design hardly affects the divergences of opinions among domestic actors and the same is true of economic variables (like inflation, unemployment, growth rates) the prevalence of pro-European attitudes in mass publics has a strong effect.

At the time of writing the future of the European constitution is uncertain. After the failed referenda in France and the Netherlands, the British government would be ill advised to embark on what would seem to be a lost cause and hold a referendum in the UK. Even in the best of times, this would have meant sailing close to the wind in a country which is notoriously Eurosceptic. Nevertheless, it is safe to assume that important elements of the constitution will eventually become operative. Furthermore, other important European issues will be processed by national institutions in a similar, if not identical way, and we can learn a lot about this in this timely study.

Thomas Poguntke

Abbreviations

AFSJ	Area of Freedom, Security and Justice
CAP	Common Agricultural Policy
CFSP	Common Foreign and Security Policy
COREPER	Comité des représentants permanents/Committee of Permanent Representatives
DOSEI	Domestic Structures and European Integration
EC	European Community/ies
ECJ	European Court of Justice
ECOFIN	Economic and financial affairs (Council)
EEC	European Economic Community
EFTA	European Free Trade Association
EMU	European Monetary Union
ENP	Effective Number of Parties
EP	European Parliament
ESDP	European Security and Defense Policy
EU	European Union
Euratom	European Atomic Energy Community
GDP	Gross domestic product
IGC	Intergovernmental Conference
MFA	Ministry of foreign affairs
NATO	North Atlantic Treaty Organization
NP	(Official) national position
PM	Prime minister
PO	Prime minister's office
QMV	Qualified majority voting
SEA	Single European Act
SGP	Stability and Growth Pact
US	United States (of America)

Introduction

Thomas König and Simon Hug

This book is about one of the most important real scale policy-making processes of our time: the formation of positions on the constitution of the second biggest economic power. In scope and significance there is perhaps only one parallel in history to the policy-making process for the "Treaty Establishing a Constitution for Europe," namely the creation of the American constitution in 1776. This process has been characterized by a number of critical events, the most recent being the negative referendum outcome in France and the Netherlands. Independent of the outcome – whether the constitution will be ratified or not – understanding how this treaty emerged and how this policy-making process has been carried out is of great societal and scientific relevance. The decision on the constitution affects a growing number of countries and the lives of their citizens. In case of ratification, Europe will have a constitution which defines the "rules of the game" for at least 25 member states. However, if ratification should fail, the Treaty of Nice (2003) will remain in force, leading, according to some authors, to a high risk of gridlock. Exploring and explaining the process having led to the elaboration and decision on the "Constitution for Europe" is thus an important task of political scientists in our days. The current political science literature on the EU – whether the intergovernmentalist, the two-level game, the constructivist or the (multilevel) governance school of thought – makes claims about the nature of this process, but few efforts have yet been made to document this process in a systematic and comparative manner, covering the different steps and stages.

The most cited intergovernmentalist work suggests a one-shot process, in which the three largest member states dominate inter-state bargaining at Intergovernmental Conferences, which transform their political-economic interests into the most efficient institutional structure (Moravcsik 1998). It is our contention that understanding EU constitutional policy making can be improved only by taking into account all the relevant actors involved and by considering the particular nature of this process, which combines the domestic and European level across multiple stages. This book is the first attempt to trace the two-level policy formation process from the draft proposal of the European Convention until the Intergovernmental Conference, which finally adopted the document on the constitution in October 2004. The authors of this book try to make a substantial contribution to this process by shedding light on reactions on the proposed draft text in the domestic arena of all the actors involved, namely the 15 member states and former ten accession countries plus the Commission and the European Parliament. At the time of writing (August 2005) more than half of the member states have already ratified the constitutional text, and each chapter describes how the respective governments formed their positions, which domestic actors were involved in this preference formation process, and whether they were able to develop coherent positions on the European constitution. Although this book does not examine the ongoing ratification stage, the insight into the policy formation and coordination stage might already improve our understanding of the outcome of the final stage.

After the revisions of the treaties at the Intergovernmental Conferences in Amsterdam (1997) and Nice (2000) and the accession of ten countries from eastern and southern Europe in May 2004, this process of constitution building has already achieved important goals. Under the presidency of Valéry Giscard d'Estaing, the European Convention drafted a proposal for constitutional reform that contained the key reform issues for a constitutional treaty including the basic principles of the EU, the regulation of material policy competencies and a reform of the institutional framework. This draft was sent to the 25 member and accession states, the Commission and the European Parliament, which coordinated their positions on the constitutional text in preparation for the summit negotiations of the Intergovernmental Conference in December 2003. They circulated the draft text among core (domestic) actors, held hearings and discussions on particular topics, and evaluated strategies for the upcoming summit. But how did the countries carry out their preferences on the constitutional text? How did they organize this preparatory process, and which domestic actors were involved? How contested were the specific issues among these actors, and did they make claims for vital issues, which would signal a threat against member state sovereignty? This book explains how these issues came on the domestic agenda, how the 27 institutional actors coordinated their positions in reaction to the Convention proposal, how cohesive the preferences were in the domestic arena, and which of the issues were particularly contested.

Outline of the book

This book provides detailed comparative insights into these coordination processes in the 25 member states (from which ten were still accession countries during the period under study), the Commission and the European Parliament. After introducing the theoretical framework of veto players, which explains why a constitutional reform of the institutional rules was necessary and which dangers will exist in case of ratification failure, and after providing empirical evidence that these reform issues were the most contested ones at the European Convention, each of the remaining country chapters introduces the formal coordination procedure, outlines the most contested issues in the domestic arena and studies the coherence of the national positions depending from the positions of the domestic actors involved. From a comparative perspective, the book considers not only the 27 institutional actors (25 countries plus Commission and European Parliament) involved at the European level, but it also relaxes the assumption that these actors are unitary in nature. In almost every case, we find multiple relevant domestic actors with divergent positions from the official (national) position. Their divergence indicates how contested the draft and specific issues are in the preparatory stage of the summit. Can we ignore these diverging positions, or should one even disregard countries which make claims for vital issues?

We believe that the inclusion of all relevant actors and issues is an important step forward in political analysis in general, and in the analysis of the policy-making process on the European constitution in particular. In our view, the exclusion of (signatory) actors risks bias in the findings, because smaller countries might have a decisive say in the constitutional negotiation and ratification processes. In addition to the unitary actor assumption of earlier studies on member state treaty formation, the absence of coherence of domestic actors might also explain why some member states changed their views during this process, and why some actors were more successful in determining the outcome, the constitutional draft text. The most prominent example during the constitution-building process is certainly the shift in the Spanish position due to the conservative government's electoral defeat. Similar events can be found in Poland where the unpopular Miller government blocked an agreement in December 2003. Without these governmental changes, we could hardly explain the compromise found in the June 2004 declaration of the Irish presidency on the constitutional agreement among the current 25 member states.

Comparing these characteristics requires a systematic collection of detailed information on preference formation. The combination of systematic and empirical rigour means that the present study should be of interest to both theorists and more empirically oriented social scientists. The empirical focus of this study consists of the stage of policy making after the presentation of the draft proposals by the European Convention. Most chapters examine the policy debates that took place on a large range of issues, both within the member states and accession countries and within the two main institutional actors: the Commission and the European Parliament. The authors of this book avoid the temptation of exploring these processes only on the basis of anecdotal evidence, practitioners' reports of the extent to which actual processes correspond with those postulated in theories, or easily quantifiable aspects, such as percentages of accepted or rejected convention amendments. Instead, with the help of key informants who were involved in the policy-making process, each chapter painstakingly reconstructs what were the main elements: the constitutional issues at stake and the positions of the relevant political actors involved.

Today we know that some actors – such as the Spanish and Polish governments – have changed part of their positions over time, others revealed different positions at the domestic and the European level (König 2005). This points to the collective and strategic nature of policy making of actors having participated in the following summit negotiations. Instead of stimulating a constitutional debate in their domestic arena, they focused on preparation for the summit. They coordinated their national positions and were able to find agreement on the constitutional text in June 2004. The Commission and the European Parliament played a significant role in the process of constitution building by providing information and preparing the agenda. Since the entry into force depends on ratifying parliamentarians and populations in all countries, which can lead to "involuntary defection" (Schelling 1960, Iida 1996), the ratification has to succeed in all member states. In so far, the coherence of the positions in each country might also indicate the likelihood for negotiation success and involuntary defection in the ratification process. Another indicator of the ratification outcome might be what kind of domestic actors were involved in the coordination process. Although an unprecedented number of ten referendums have been announced before and after the summit negotiations, few domestic actors participated in the debate on constitution building. The relatively small number of actors mostly comprised ministries and certainly facilitated domestic preference formation but it also risked excluding major societal interests. The French and the Dutch popular votes with their negative outcome may have demonstrated this deficit.

The research design: a multi-stage and two-level analysis

The authors of this book collaborate in the research project "Domestic Structures and European Integration" (DOSEI) which has been designed to enhance our understanding of the interplay between domestic and European constitutional actors on the major reform issues. At the domestic level, these actors included national ministries, political parties and a few other relevant actors, while governmental and supranational delegates dominated this process at the European level. Another feature of this process is its multi-stage nature: The Nice Treaty (2002) defines the current status quo, which served as starting point at the European Convention and will be the outcome in the event of ratification failure.

In particular, the institutional issues which proposed to change the balance of power among member states in the Council, their access to the Commission and the modus of the Council presidency raised concerns among smaller member states, which feared losing their influence on European integration. However, the delegates of the European Convention adopted a draft text in June 2003 which had to overcome the hurdles of the following stages, the summit in December 2003 (and June 2004) before ratification could begin in all 25 member states and in the European Parliament. This combination of a two-level and multi-stage constitution-building process, which intends to reform the EU's current institutional framework, also structures the outline of this book.

Tsebelis's analysis provides the theoretical framework for constitutional reform by examining the legislative procedures adopted at Nice, at the European Convention and in Rome in 2004 in light of veto players theory. He argues that EU was characterized by a plethora of veto players, which made decision making very difficult. In addition, the Nice arrangements – which gave most of the decision-making authority to the Council – had increased the powers of the judiciary and the bureaucracies. The European Convention under the presidency of Valérie Giscard d'Estaing was able to reverse all these elements, but (smaller) member states had different interests in constitutional reform. This configuration of diverging and sometimes opposing interests is outlined in the following chapter on the European Convention by König *et al.* These authors analyze the entire set of the Laeken reform issues and ask whether the traditional cleavages in European integration – based on population size (smaller versus large countries), institutional affiliation (governmental versus parliamentarian origin) and membership status (members versus accession countries) – also appeared in the Convention's debates among the 102 delegates from the 15 member states, 13 accession states[1] plus Commission and European Parliament. Their empirical analysis of the delegates' reform positions provides strong evidence for Tsebelis's argument that the institutional issues were decisive for constitutional reform. According to their findings, the traditional cleavages existed on these reform issues and the conflicting groups had opposite interests in their solution.

The following chapters introduce the coordination processes of the 27 actors, namely the 25 member states plus the Commission and the European Parliament. Each chapter briefly describes the situation in these countries, respectively supranational actors, before outlining the organizational structure of the coordination procedure. These procedures are important to understanding the access of specific actors. In most countries we find that the foreign office was in charge of the coordination, while the prime minister's office took the lead in countries with strong presidential features. In most countries governmental actors dominated the internal coordination process but there exist differences with regard to the structure of the process, the number of actors involved and their institutional affiliation. Note that parliamentary actors rarely participated in these coordination processes, and mostly only in the Nordic countries was parliament formally included in the preference formation process.

A major innovation of this book is using the preferences of the actors involved to describe the policy-formation process in the community. The data gathering was prepared in several steps. First, we had to define the boundaries of the constitutional space and decided to consider every issue which was contested between at least two actors during the Convention deliberations. For their identification, we studied the Convention documents, and in particular the amendments were used to extract the set of contested issues and their alternatives. We applied three criteria to determine the final set of issues for our questionnaire:

1 thematic classification (*synthesis*);
2 number of amendments proposed (*prominence*);
3 number of alternatives proposed (*thematic variety*).

This procedure produced a set of 65 issues which contain general issues (charter of fundamental rights, subsidiary, etc.), issues on institutions and procedures (presidency of the Council, etc.), on legal instruments (right of initiative, etc.) and on various policy fields. A broader classification lists 25 issues as substantial and 40 issues as institutional topics. The ordinal scales of their alternatives range from two to five possible alternatives. Finally, the construct validity of the questionnaire listing these issues and alternatives was examined in a pre-test done with the German scientific adviser of a German Convention member, Professor Dr. Oppermann. The questionnaire listed the issues and alternatives, and we ordered the alternatives according to their integrationist degree, understood as a transfer of sovereignty from the national to the European level. Interviewees were also asked to mention those issues which were vital for an actor.[2] Vital issues are defined as decisive issues for which the outcome is crucial for an actor to sign the treaty. It turned out that about half of the 65 issues (33) were vital for at least one of the actors.

To identify the domestic actors and the positions of the national position, of the leading ministry and of the relevant domestic actors, we carefully selected a number of experts in each country. Each DOSEI team used its own contacts with experts in the member and former accession states. Furthermore, we were able to operate in almost any EU-speaking language, which helped us to contact the experts and to conduct the interviews in the 25 countries. The DOSEI interviewers were also trained in a workshop before the fieldwork was conducted. To increase reliability we agreed to interview more than one expert per country, and at least one of the experts interviewed should be from inside the government. Moreover, we tried to collect this information before the end of the summit. For gathering data on the policy-making process of the 27 actors

(25 member states, European Parliament, Commission), we interviewed 82 experts, of whom 47 (57 percent) were from inside government. The majority of these interviews was finished before Christmas 2003 (83 percent). The remaining interviews were completed until February 2004 with the notable exception of the three additional interviews conducted with experts of the new Spanish government[3] in May 2004.

An additional indication for the validity is certainly the high response rate by the experts. We interviewed 3.05 experts on average, and the adjusted cross-validity of the experts was about 85 percent in the entire data set, ranging from 66.8 percent for each of the actors in the Commission to 95.1 percent in the case of the Irish national position. The experts were instructed to describe the national positions, the positions of the leading ministry and other relevant actors when they diverged from the national positions. The experts mentioned a total of 110 relevant domestic actors, 73 (67 percent) thereof are governmental actors, the remaining actors come from parliamentary committees and interest groups. Only 3.3 percent of the cells in the remaining actors–times–issue matrix remained empty.[4] Due to our research design, we could reduce the number of missing positions to about 1.2 percent, which can still be imputed by different methods (König *et al.* 2005).

Some experts, however, differed in their evaluation of a given actor's position. In order to determine the position of an actor having been evaluated differently by several experts, the interviewers ranked the experts according to their view of the experts' competence.[5] This allowed us to select between the different indications with regard to the most competent expertise. In case of any missing value, the indication of the second most competent expert has been used, etc. Since we asked only for relevant domestic actors deviating from the national position, we could replace the non-indication of an actor with the respective national position. This procedure reduced the percentage of lacking information from about 3.3 percent to 1.4 percent. Finally, we completed the data set by adding information on the alternative proposed by the draft constitution, the location of the status quo according to the Nice Treaty and – at a later stage – the outcome[6] of the summit agreed in June 2004.

These data are used in each chapter which offers an empirical evaluation of the coherence of actors' positions and points to the vital issues mentioned by the actors involved. In addition to finding reliable estimators for the national positions of the 27 actors, the literature on two-level games reminds us of the importance of including the views of the domestic actors, in particular if those actors must ratify the final agreement. This is also essential in the study of the bargaining outcome and negotiation success. Because ratification often faces higher institutional hurdles than those for government formation and delegation, actors can make credible claims for receiving concessions with respect to their ratification problems at home (König and Hug 2000, Hug and König 2002,

Schneider and Cederman 1994, Pahre 2001). In so far as the actors' empirical coherence not only informs about the intensity of the debates in the domestic arena, but it also provides a measure for bargaining and ratification success in the following stages of the constitution-building process. Note that these data do not contain information about the public which will vote on the constitution in 10 referendums (Hug and Schulz 2005).

Most of the data presented in this volume were gathered before completion of the following stage right until February 2004. At the first summit on 12–13 December under Italian presidency, Spain and Poland blocked the adoption of the text. In Poland, the *Sejm* had tied the hands of the unpopular minority government, which was forced to vote for the status quo regulations of the Nice Treaty. However, after the surprising electoral loss of the Spanish conservative government in the aftermath of the Madrid terrorist attacks, Poland could no longer withstand the pressure on its own, and the Irish presidency presented a compromise that was accepted in Dublin on 17–18 June 2004, and the "Treaty establishing a Constitution for Europe" was signed in Rome on 29 October 2004 (König 2005). In these days, this compromise has to be ratified in all 25 countries, with various ratification hurdles, including ten referendums (Hug and Schulz 2005). The diversity of interests and the large number of vital issues indicate that the constitution is not favored by all actors involved. Moreover, the exclusion of societal actors from the European Convention and domestic preference formation suggests that referendums will contain a higher risk of failure than parliamentary ratification will have. Whether these indicators matter in the ratification process will be seen in the near future.

Notes

1 Three accession candidate countries, namely Bulgaria, Romania and Turkey, have not yet become member states of the EU.
2 Vital interests vary at the level of international actors and not for each domestic actor. The reason is straightforward: Domestic actors do not sign the resulting treaty in the first place.
3 It took about a month to identify the experts of the new socialist Spanish government which was elected to office on 14 March 2004.
4 This number refers to the final, aggregated data set, including 142 actors and national positions and 65 issues. The five issues which have been dropped for this calculation were "other issues" without a more precise definition.
5 In a few cases these orders of competence varied by issues or groups of issues. This has been accounted for in the aggregation process.
6 For two issues (the voting rule and the role of the European Parliament in the adoption of the budget) we had to amend the scale because the compromise agreed upon in June 2004 was not an option offered by the DOSEI questionnaire.

1 The European Convention and the Rome and Brussels IGCs

A veto players analysis

George Tsebelis

The European Union (EU) is in the process of adopting a constitution. A European Convention under the Presidency of Valéry Giscard d'Estaing elaborated the document, which was presented at the Intergovernmental Conference of Rome at the end of 2003 and was rejected. The rejection led to a new text adopted at the Brussels IGC which from the point of view of this analysis is close to a 50–50 split between the Nice and the Convention texts.

This is not a new situation for the EU. After a period of constitutional and policy inertia, the EU adopted new constitutional arrangements in 1987, 1991, 1997, and 2001, all before the Convention. This means that each EU constitution has lasted for three to four years on average. Debate over the functioning of political institutions has preceded each new constitutional arrangement. In effect, the EU has been in a process of continuous constitutional design (and redesign) for about 15 years.

What was the response of the institutional literature to all these changes? For a long period of time, these changes were ignored because the literature (an off-shoot of the International Relations literature) was embroiled in a paradigmatic war that left the study of political institutions ignored: intergovernmentalists neglected the study of institutions because of major developments at intergovernmental conferences, and neofunctionalists ignored institutions altogether in favor of spillover processes (for a discussion see Garrett and Tsebelis 1996 and Tsebelis and Garrett 2001). The institutional descriptions of the EU were based on neologisms like: It is "neither a state nor an international organization" (Sbragia 1992: 257); "less than a Federation, more than a Regime" (Wallace 1983: 403); "stuck between sovereignty and integration" (Wallace 1982: 67); "institutionalized Intergovernmentalism in a supranational organization" (Cameron 1992: 66); the "middle ground between the cooperation of existing nations and the breaking of a new one" (Scharpf 1988: 242). Some scholars even took advantage of the lack of theoretical grounding: Sbragia (1992: 258) approvingly quotes Krislov, Ehlermann, and Weiler claiming: "The absence of a clear model, for one thing, makes ad hoc analogies more appropriate and justifiable. If one may not specify what are clear analogies, less clear ones may be appropriate."

Instead of using analogies (appropriate or inappropriate), I examine legislative procedures adopted at Nice in 2001 and at the European Convention in 2003 and in Brussels in 2004 in light of veto players theory (Tsebelis 2002). I analyze the outcomes of decision making generated by these procedures and discuss the policy, political and structural implications of the different arrangements. My argument is that the procedures proposed in the Convention text resolved a series of problems facing the EU, and the final compromise is exactly in the middle between Nice and the Convention.

More specifically, I argue that the EU was characterized by a plethora of veto players, which made decision making very difficult. In addition, the Nice arrangements – which gave most of the decision-making authority to the Council – had reduced the legislative powers of the Commission, and increased the powers of the judiciary and the bureaucracies.[1] Giscard was able to reverse all these features with one stroke of the pen: he had the power to eliminate the qualified majority decision-making rule in the Council. As a result, he could have made political decisions easier to adopt by reducing the power of the Council, increasing the legislative role of the Commission, and reducing the power of the bureaucracy and the judiciary. The final compromise is certainly better than Nice but not as good as the Convention solution particularly since the EU enlargement introduces increasingly politically heterogeneous players into the Union.

Veto players and their policy and institutional implications

According to Tsebelis (2002), veto players are individual or collective decision makers whose agreement is necessary for a change of the legislative status quo. From this definition follows that the higher the number of veto players, the more difficult it is to change the status quo.[2] Tsebelis calls the "difficulty of changing the status quo" *policy stability* and in addition to the effect of the number of veto players on policy stability he demonstrates that the larger the ideological distances among veto players, the higher policy stability is.

Here I will extract some ideas from the book that will help us understand the EU institutions.

Changing the qualified majority requirements. Tsebelis (2002) demonstrates that as the required majority for a decision increases, policy stability increases. This is the basic property that we will use in the article. I will argue that the Treaty of Nice produced institutions with exceptionally high policy stability, making political decision making practically impossible, while the agreements proposed at the Convention would have rectified the problem. Again, the final solution lies somewhere in between.

Bicameralism and changing qualified majorities. What happens if decisions are made by the congruent position of two distinct chambers, as is the case in the EU? In particular, what are the effects of changing the threshold of qualified majority decision making in one chamber? Tsebelis (2002) has identified two different effects of such a change. First, the power shifts in favor of the chamber whose threshold *increases*. Second, the overall policy stability of the system increases.

Policy stability and role of agenda setter. The player who makes a legislative proposal to the others for their discussion and adoption has a significant power: it can select among all the possible outcomes the one that (s)he prefers. Tsebelis (2002) studies the advantages of agenda setting which stem from the fact that an astute selection of the proposal may lead to its adoption without any modifications. The Commission plays the institutional role of the agenda setter in the co-decision procedure (called "ordinary legislative procedure" in the draft constitution). This implies two things, first, that the composition of the Commission (selection of its president, role of this president in the selection of commissioners, size of the institution) is significant; second that the significance increases when there are many possible compromises among the other institutions, because the choice set for the Commission proposal expands. In other words, the Commission plays an important legislative role in the EU, but this role is inversely related to policy stability.

Effects on judiciary and bureaucracies. Tsebelis (2002) argues that bureaucracies and the judiciary are involved with legislatures in a sequential game: Bureaucracies and the judiciary interpret the law and then the legislature can decide to overrule their statutory interpretation or not. This is a standard argument in the literature on judges and bureaucrats. The implication is that as policy stability increases the role of judges and bureaucrats increases, because they can make decisions without concern of being overruled.

Qualified majority in the Council: to what extent does it impede decision making?

In the previous section I argued that, in principle, increasing the qualified majority threshold makes decisions more difficult. The argument is simple and straightforward, but the actual differences between the sets of procedures introduced at Nice in 2001 and at the Convention in 2003 may have been inconsequential. In this paper, I will argue quite the opposite: the differences between the proposals put forth at Nice and the Convention are significant and consequential. The Brussels IGC adopted an intermediate solution.

Tsebelis and Yataganas (2002) analyzed the dynamics of bargaining in Nice, and argued that it was the first time that the three criteria (qualified majority of weighted votes, majority of states, and qualified majority of populations (62 percent)) did not coincide, and that different countries were attached to different principles. As a result, the conferees in Nice adopted the detrimental strategy of including all three criteria for valid decision making. In other words, the countries bargaining in Nice were involved in a collective prisoners' dilemma game and it was individually rational to insist on their own preferred criterion. As a result, they became collectively worse off by their inability to strike a compromise.

In the remainder of this section I will use the number of winning coalitions in the Council to represent the different decision-making rules. This methodology has been used by power index analysis of EU institutions in order to infer the "power" of different countries.[3] I have argued against this methodology (see Garrett and Tsebelis 1996, Tsebelis and Garrett 2001) because it ignores both the preferences of the different actors, as well as the institutions of the EU. Here I use this method for two reasons: First, I cannot take into account the actors' preferences. It is impossible to know the preferences of actors who have thus far not participated in the EU, or to consider the coalitions they would be willing to form. It is theoretically possible that winning coalitions are a very small percentage of the overall number of coalitions, and yet, these coalitions form with extremely high frequency because a certain number of countries have almost identical preferences. However, numerical comparisons are the only feasible strategy at this point. Second, I am not interested in the "power" of different actors, which is a function of votes in the Council as well as preference configurations, but rather on what the Council can or cannot do on the basis of its decision-making rule. However, the analysis that follows can be criticized since it does not take into account the preferences of the different actors; I would love to be able to do so, but will have to wait until more data is available on coalition formation in the 25 member EU.

As Table 1.1 demonstrates, the short-term effects of Nice were minor. Indeed, under the 62/87 qualified majority rule in effect before the Treaty of Nice the number of winning coalitions with the single qualified majority criterion before Nice was 2,549 out of 32,768 possible coalitions, resulting in a decision frequency of 7.78 percent. Had the weighting of the votes been preserved, this number would have been slightly restricted by the triple majority principle to 2,513 out of 32,768 coalitions (the table indicates that the first three decimal points of the decision frequencies are practically the same).

The effects of the triple majority become even smaller in an EU of 15 members with the weighting system adopted by the Nice Treaty itself. Now with the simple qualified majority criterion (169/237) the number of winning coalitions is 2,707 out of 32,768, while with the triple one, it is reduced to 2,692 out of 32,768 (now the first three decimal points are identical). In short, the decision frequency increased only slightly from 7.78 percent to 8.22 percent with the Nice triple majority principle.

Table 1.3 indicates that after the expansion to 25 members the difference between the simple qualified majority criterion (232/321) and the triple majority criterion remains insignificant (the number of winning coali-

Table 1.1 Effects of the Nice Treaty for EU-15 with old weighting system

EU15/Pre-NICE	*Votes*	*Qualified majority voting (62/87)*	*QMV + Majority of MS + 62%*
		winsets	*winsets*
Germany	10	2,199	2,199
UK	10	2,199	2,175
France	10	2,199	2,175
Italy	10	2,199	2,175
Spain	8	2,040	2,004
Netherlands	5	1,761	1,728
Greece	5	1,761	1,728
Belgium	5	1,761	1,728
Portugal	5	1,761	1,728
Sweden	4	1,671	1,638
Austria	4	1,671	1,638
Denmark	3	1,572	1,542
Finland	3	1,572	1,542
Ireland	3	1,572	1,542
Luxembourg	2	1,462	1,435
Winning coalitions	–	2,549	2,513
Decision frequency	–	0.0778	0.0767

Table 1.2 Effects of the Nice Treaty for EU-15 with new weighting system

EU 15/NICE	*Votes Nice*	*Qualified majority voting (169/237)*	*QMV + Majority of MS + 62%*
		winsets	*winsets*
Germany	29	2,348	2,348
UK	29	2,348	2,338
France	29	2,348	2,338
Italy	29	2,348	2,338
Spain	27	2,280	2,265
Netherlands	13	1,816	1,801
Greece	12	1,788	1,773
Belgium	12	1,788	1,773
Portugal	12	1,788	1,773
Sweden	10	1,714	1,702
Austria	10	1,714	1,702
Denmark	7	1,614	1,602
Finland	7	1,614	1,602
Ireland	7	1,614	1,602
Luxembourg	4	1,523	1,508
Winning coalitions	–	2,707	2,692
Decision frequency	–	0.0826	0.0822

Table 1.3 Effects of different QMV thresholds for EU-25

EU25	*Votes*	*Pre-Nice: QMV (232/321)*	*Treaty of Nice: QMV + Majority of MS + 62% pop.*	*Convention: Majority of MS + 60%*	*Constitution: 55% of MS + at least 15 MS + 65% pop. + 4 MS in block. minority*
		winsets	*winsets*	*winsets*	*winsets*
Germany	29	1,064,341	1,063,676	6,358,510	3,023,749
UK	29	1,064,341	1,063,648	5,616,196	2,667,807
France	29	1,064,341	1,063,646	5,611,025	2,665,472
Italy	29	1,064,341	1,063,646	5,573,809	2,650,049
Spain	27	1,040,713	1,040,022	5,099,561	2,419,575
Poland	27	1,040,713	1,040,022	5,089,235	2,411,881
Netherlands	13	830,464	829,972	4,468,862	2,171,443
Greece	12	813,299	812,813	4,338,580	2,117,939
Czech Republic	12	813,299	812,813	4,333,723	2,115,828
Belgium	12	813,299	812,813	4,331,262	2,114,753
Hungary	12	813,299	812,813	4,328,804	2,113,666
Portugal	12	813,299	812,813	4,326,393	2,112,605
Sweden	10	778,735	778,408	4,299,335	2,100,886
Austria	10	778,735	778,406	4,279,914	2,092,228
Slovak Republic	7	726,659	726,496	4,212,480	2,063,573
Denmark	7	726,659	726,496	4,210,034	2,062,482
Finland	7	726,659	726,495	4,207,565	2,061,446
Ireland	7	726,659	726,495	4,170,431	2,045,426
Lithuania	7	726,659	726,495	4,170,431	2,045,426
Latvia	4	673,651	673,573	4,137,357	2,031,764
Slovenia	4	673,651	673,573	4,127,676	2,027,612
Estonia	4	673,651	673,573	4,112,608	2,021,275
Cyprus	4	673,651	673,573	4,097,781	2,015,011
Luxembourg	4	673,651	673,573	4,087,618	2,010,689
Malta	3	655,519	655,451	4,087,618	2,010,689
Winning coalitions	–	1,204,448	1,203,736	7,543,799	3,393,499
Decision frequency	–	0.0359	0.0359	0.2248	0.1011

Note
The weighting of the votes for the EU with 25 member states (first two columns) is based upon the provisions of the Accession treaty (*Official Journal* L 236 of 23 September 2003).

tions goes down from 1,204,448 to 1,203,736, but what is significant is that these numbers identify 3.6 percent of winning majorities in the Council).

It is to the great credit of the Convention and its leader Valéry Giscard d'Estaing that they correctly identified the source of the high policy stability generated by the Nice Treaty: two of the decision-making requirements (majority of countries and qualified majority (60 percent) of population) impose fewer restrictions on the decision-making process. The key restriction comes from the qualified majority requirement of weighted votes. As a result, the convention leadership introduced the much more permissive double criterion. The frequency of valid decisions increases by a factor of 6: from 3.6 percent to over 22 percent.

So, the frequency of valid decisions went from 8 percent in an EU of 15 (before or after Nice) to 3.6 percent in an EU of 25 (after Nice) to 22.5 percent under the Convention proposal. After the failure of the Rome summit, this number drops back down to 3.6 percent. These numbers have significant implications on the legislative powers of the Commission. Under the Giscard proposal the Commission had a wide range of options to propose, while the Nice Treaty significantly reduces its legislative impact. Why did the Rome IGC reject the Giscard proposal?

Most of the negotiations were shrouded in secrecy, but some accounts were published in the press, and I will try to focus on these reports. First, we know that Poland and Spain vetoed the Convention proposal, leading to the failure of the summit. Official statements (particularly the one by former German chancellor Schröder criticizing Poland – which began its participation to the EU with a veto) made that point amply clear. Second, while we do not know for certain, there is some information regarding the counter proposal put forth by these countries. Here is a quote from the *Süddeutsche Zeitung*:

> According to many EU diplomats, there is evidence that Rome is seeking a solution on the basis of the double majority principle. As a concession to Poland and Spain, Prime Minister Silvio Berlusconi could make the offer to have the reform take effect in 2014 instead of 2009. It would also be possible to increase the population threshold of 60 per cent. It is said that Spanish delegates had floated the idea of 66 per cent, since Madrid would then have similar chances of building blocking coalitions in the Council as in the present situation. Berlin and Paris seem to be ready to go along only with 62 per cent though.
>
> (*Süddeutsche Zeitung*, 12 December 2003, own translation)

This quotation clearly demonstrates the effect of the delay: it keeps the Nice Treaty in place. The effects of different majorities, however, are less obvious. The only thing we know on the basis of the previous analysis is that increasing the required majorities makes decisions more difficult, and consequently shifts powers to the Council, and increases the role of bureaucracies and the judiciary. The question remains: by how much? What difference will it make for the EU if the required majority is 60, or 65 as in the final document adopted in Brussels? And what if a simple majority of countries is required (as Giscard suggested) or 55 percent is necessary as Brussels decided? We now turn to this issue.

The last column of Table 1.3 presents the outcomes of the decision-making rule adopted in Brussels: a 65 percent majority of the population of the EU, a 55 percent majority of the countries, and the requirement that in order to block a decision four countries are required (in order to eliminate the possibility of three major countries blocking EU decision making).

As the last column indicates the overall frequency of winning coalitions is around 10 percent. Compare this number to the 3.6 percent of the Nice Treaty and the 22.5 percent of the Giscard proposal. The final solution adopted is about 50–50 split between the two previous proposals. Why did Spain and Poland fight so hard in Rome, and is the solution adopted to their satisfaction?

The Spanish proposal (and I repeat here the confidentiality of negotiations makes it impossible to assert that this proposal was made) is similar to the results of the Nice Treaty: it makes Spain and Poland participate in most winning coalitions, or to put it differently it made participation of Spain or Poland a necessary condition for most coalitions to succeed. Spain and Poland pushed the outcome back to Nice. But what was so attractive about that treaty for these two countries?

Figure 1.1 provides the answer. The figure depicts the population and the number of votes that each country received in the Nice Treaty. I have fitted these points with a linear and a square root curve. According to different theories these two curves provide the "best" way of representation of different countries.

There are five countries that are outliers with respect to both curves: Italy, France, the UK, Spain and Poland. It is well known that the French presidency in Nice did not want France to have fewer votes in the Council than a unified Germany (Tsebelis and Yataganas 2002). In fact, Germany introduced the 62 percent of population clause in order to get some advantage over the other three large countries (France, Italy and the UK). Yet, Germany has a population of 80 million while the other three countries have approximately 60 million each. Given this French position, it was difficult to deny Spain and Poland (with around 40 million each) an advantage similar to the other large countries. If 20 million people do not count for a difference in representation between France and Germany, why should they count for a difference in representation between France and Poland?

The result of this logic was that these five countries are way above the curves that the others form. In fact, Poland and Spain are even more obvious outliers than the other large countries. The implication is that no

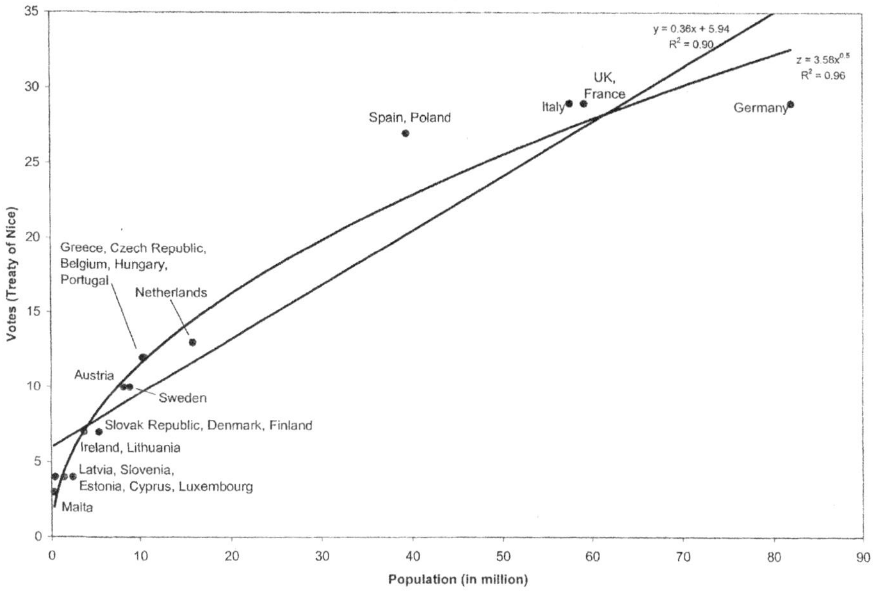

Figure 1.1 Population and number of votes (according to the Nice Treaty).

voting scheme based on population can ever provide Spain and Poland the same advantages that they had under Nice.

There may be additional reasons for Spain and Poland to have this intransigent position. Elections were upcoming more (in Spain) or less (in Poland) and it would be difficult to explain why the representatives of these countries gave up the advantages they enjoyed under Nice. Statements were made by the American administration implying that France and Germany are the "old Europe," implying that the "new Europe" (Poland and Spain, both American allies in the Iraqi war) have moral justification to block the other EU countries.

But Poland and Spain were not able to turn back the clock to Nice for a long time. The IGC in Brussels abandoned the weighted voting scheme of Nice but at the price of adopting a decision-making scheme that is located exactly in the middle between Nice and the Convention. This was a strategic choice, because it involved the second issue of contention, the composition of the Commission as well. Regarding the Commission there were three different decisions, two of which were contentious. The first was the size of the institution, that is, whether the member states would have one commissioner each (as the small and new countries wanted) or, whether it would be a smaller and more flexible body (as the larger and older countries wanted). The status quo was in the position the small countries liked it, the Giscard proposal adopted a smaller commission, and the final outcome was a 27 member Commission the first time, to be reduced to 18 members subsequently (unless there is a unanimous decision of member states otherwise).[4] The second was the appointment of the Commission president which remained the same (proposal by the Council to the Parliament by qualified majority, adoption by the Parliament), despite some alternative proposals giving more powers to the Parliament that were proposed by the Commission, and some smaller countries. The third was whether the composition of the Commission, would be selected by the member states (status quo), or the Commission president (Giscard proposal). The final outcome was again in the middle, the composition of the Commission would be decided by the Council in agreement with the president-elect of the Commission, and would be approved by the EP.

The effects on policy making, democratic deficit, and impact of the judiciary and bureaucracies

As demonstrated in the first part, introducing greater constraints in decision making in the Council is not a simple inconvenience. It has profound policy, political, and structural implications. I will discuss each of these issues in turn.

Policy implications

In the first part of this section I demonstrated that imposing constraints on the decision making of the Council (or the Parliament) leads to further difficulties in EU decision making since when the core of the Council increases the core of the EU either increases or remains the same. In the second part I explained that the restrictions imposed by the Nice Treaty were very significant, and that the proposals made at the Convention would have resulted in dropping one of the requirements, increasing by a factor of 6 the number of decisive coalitions in the Council, thus making changes to the status quo ten times easier than before. This is a numerically significant difference, but why should one care whether the EU is able to make political decisions or not? Could we say that an EU which is unable to decide politically is a better institution than a politically active EU?

In fact, the whole debate about political versus "other" issues in the EU is based on whether it is better for the EU to be able to make decisions that overrule the positions of any individual member country or not. It used to be that all decisions needed unanimity in the Council (Luxembourg compromise). Then, economic issues became part of the EU jurisdiction (Single European Act). Over the years, the environment was added to the areas of European jurisdiction, then issues of security introduced immigration and the free movement of people in the EU and currently only the issues of taxation and foreign policy remain exclusively in the hands of the member countries.

While there is no general "philosophy" about which issues should or should not be in what jurisdiction (why is it better for countries to have fiscal but not monetary discretion as determined by the Maastricht Treaty?) the ability of political decision making by the EU is directly linked to which decisions will be made, de facto, by the political institutions of the EU and which will be made by other institutions (national or supranational). We will focus on the national ones here.

Policy stability in any political system enables the citizens to know the rules of the game and undertake initiatives that will be beneficial to them on the basis of these rules. On the other hand, the ability to make changes to policy enables a political system as a whole to adapt to a changing environment. Let me use two examples to make the point clear: Having a taxation system that remains stable will enable people to make investment decisions that are as profitable as possible and, therefore, lead to higher levels of growth. This is a standard economic argument ("rules rather than discretion," Kydland and Prescott 1977) and empirical analyses have corroborated this line of reasoning (Henisz 2000). On the other hand, an exogenous shock (like an increase in the price of oil) may lead different political systems to adopt some kind of response, like increased taxation on oil in order to reduce consumption, or decreased taxation in order to keep prices stable in other areas, or the study or exploration of alternative energy resources.

Is it better for a political system to have more or less policy stability? As I have argued elsewhere there is no general answer, unless a political system occupies some kind of extreme position (if, for example, unanimity is required for decision making in a parliament like the Polish *Sejm*,[5] or decisions on human rights are made by simple majority in which case a majority can decide to oppress the human rights of a minority).

Obviously the EU does not fall into an extreme category like the ones described. However, will it be facing an economic and political environment with lots of shocks (and therefore, high variance of external conditions)? The developments of terrorism, potential trade conflict with the US, globalization and the opening of new markets, are all external shocks that may leave the European nation states ill-equipped to confront problems. Consequently decisions by the EU will become more necessary not less. So, restricting the Council's decision-making capabilities undermines the EU today more than it did in the past.

As a result of this analysis, I have argued that the steps taken in Nice were negative, and the failure of the IGC in Rome (which preserves the Nice rules) had been a further unfortunate development. The insistence of countries on their own rights and the lack of focus to the collective consequences would have inevitably led to an inability of the EU to address new issues; ultimately, this would have left each country to make its own decisions, but with only its own forces, facing situations where its own weight may not be enough to confront difficult conditions.

Democratic deficit

Scholars continue to discuss the issue of a "democratic deficit" connected with EU institutions. It is not clear what the discussion is about. It may be that political decisions do not reflect the wishes of the public. Or, it may be that information about the decisions made by the political system is not disseminated to the public. In all cases, there is a statement about the reduced role that the Parliament plays in political decision making. Let us analyze these issues separately.

If one uses the term "democratic deficit" to describe a discrepancy between public opinion and decisions made by the political system, this is a feature common in all political systems. Given the volatility of public opinion it is not possible to have measures reflecting public opinion all the time. In fact, it is not clear that we should, and probably mediated democracy is adopting a different model where important decisions are delegated to political elites who will be accountable in the subsequent election, when the consequences of the decisions will be clearer.

If "democratic deficit" implies the ignorance of the public about decision making "in Brussels," then it is a factually correct characterization, although it covers decision making in Strasburg (the location of the plenary sessions of the European Parliament) as well as decision making in Luxembourg (the location of the European Court of Justice). In fact, the average European is disinterested in European decision making, and is irritated by specific decisions (whenever he or she hears about them). This phenomenon does not reflect the intention of supranational elites (the EP is always trying to communicate its decisions to national parliaments and the public) but rather the predisposition of the EU population. When it becomes clearer that EU decisions are transposed to the national level, and a series of national decisions are taken unanimously *because* they reflect European legislation, and as a result individual countries have to adopt the specific policies, the attention of the public may increase.

The reduced role of the European Parliament is an inaccurate perception. As I have argued elsewhere, there is a difference in the role and importance of parliament greater than one would expect from presidential and parliamentary systems: the titles of these systems are misleading. It is parliaments in Europe that complain that they are little more than a rubberstamp for government decisions, and it is the President of the United States who complains that he cannot restrict the initiatives undertaken by the US Congress. The reason for this discrepancy between titles and reality is that the parliament makes proposals to the executive in presidential systems, while the government makes proposals to the parliament in parliamentary ones. The institution that makes the proposal enjoys greater discretion than the one that accepts or rejects the proposal.

Looking at EU institutions, the EP is able to make its own proposals to the Council, and according to the rules currently in place it shares agenda setting powers with the other policy-making institutions (Commission and Council). In fact, the Commission has stated that:

> Since the Single European Act came into force on July 1 1987, over 50 percent of Parliament's amendments have been accepted by the Commission and carried by the Council. No national Parliament has a comparable success rate in bending the executive to its will.
>
> (Commission Press release, 15 December 1994, quoted in Earnshaw and Judge 1996: 96)

So, the term "democratic deficit" is not an accurate characterization if it is meant to reflect the power of the European Parliament. However, as I demonstrated in the first section of this chapter, this influence declines when one imposes decision-making constraints on the Council as the Nice Treaty did.

Power of judges and bureaucrats

Another consequence of the failure of Rome would have been the increased role of bureaucrats and judges. While most analysts think that increasing the power of bureaucrats is a nightmare, the same assessment is not made with respect to judges. The latter are supposed to have the welfare of citizens in mind while the former are not.

It is not clear why judges are considered under a different lens than bureaucrats by the literature: they both interpret legislation, and there is no compelling analysis that tells us that they have different goals from each other (neither the arguments that the judges care for the "common good" are compelling, nor any argument has been made that bureaucrats do *not* care). But no matter what the interests and or preferences of these institutions, the real question is: should political decisions be made by the elected representatives of the people of the EU, or should these decisions be left to non-elected agents?

The question may seem provocative and the answer obvious. I just want to clarify that I do not share this belief. There are decisions that are better left to judges than to elected representatives: for example issues of human rights are better left to the courts. Similarly, there are decisions that are better left to independent agencies (like an ombudsman) than to governments. However, these arguments cannot be made for the majority of political decisions, and reducing the capacity of a political body to make these decisions increases the likelihood that these decisions will be made by non-elected (and non-politically accountable) agents. I am not sure that this was the intention of national governments (including the ones of Spain and Poland) at the IGC in Rome, but it would have been the consequence of the Treaty of Nice if the IGC in Brussels had not partially rectified the failure of the Rome meetings.

Conclusion

It is ironic that what happened under the presidency of one President of France was repealed under the presidency of another President of France: Jacques Chirac was the President of the EU in 2001 when the Nice Treaty was accepted and as such was responsible for the acceptance of the triple majority requirement that seriously undermines the decision-making abilities of the Council. Valéry Giscard d'Estaing (and ex-President of France) was the president of the Convention, which repealed the most restrictive clause of a qualified majority of weighted votes in the Council, a proposal which would have unblocked the Council and enabled it to make political decisions.

This decision to decrease policy stability in the EU was an important one, because under the Nice rules the EU would be unable to function. As I demonstrated, the difference between the two sets of rules on policy stability is overwhelming, and policy stability (or in the case of Europe political immobilism) affects not only policies, but also the democratic deficit and the role of the judiciary and bureaucracies as well. The final outcome was a Solomonic judgment: select a decision-making scheme that was located midway between the two. So, the EU will be able to make some decisions, not as few as under Nice and not as many as under the Convention proposal. The Commission will have more legislative (and less bureaucratic) powers under the final outcome than under Nice and less legislative (more bureaucratic) powers than under the Convention proposal. The Parliament will be more powerful under the compromise than under Nice, but less than under the Convention proposal. The judiciary will see more power under the compromise than under the Convention, but less than under Nice. If one believes in some intrinsic value of compromise, this person should be happy with the outcome of EU institutional design.

Acknowledgments

I would like to thank Sven-Oliver Proksch and Thomas König and Thomas Bräuninger for their help. The first calculated the frequencies of decision making under different EU rules by using a computer program generated by the other two. I also thank Lisa Blaydes and Sven-Oliver Proksch for their assistance.

Notes

1 In this respect, the Commission saw its legislative role reduced, but its role as head of EU bureaucracy increased. I explain below how these effects were produced.
2 Actually, increasing the number of veto players will *not decrease* the difficulty of changing the status quo, since as we shall see the addition of some veto players may have no impact.
3 Estimation based on Bräuninger and König's (2001) computer program IOP.
4 This assumes that Romania and Bulgaria join the EU before the constitution enters into force.
5 This refers to the tradition of *liberum veto* in Poland.

2 The European Convention

Consensus without unity?

Thomas König, Andreas Warntjen and Simone Burkhart

From the European Convention to constitutional reform?

The European Convention is a new agenda-setting method for drafting reform proposals of a widening and deepening European Union (EU), which encompasses 25 member states and has jurisdiction in vital policy areas, such as social, labor, monetary and defense policies (Dinan 2002). However, the obsolete institutional framework of the EU, originally designed for six founding members, risks gridlock in decision making (König and Bräuninger 2004, Tsebelis in this volume). Without having used the conventional agenda-setting method, previous reform attempts at the Amsterdam (1996) and Nice (2000) summits failed due to incommensurate conflicts between large and smaller, rich and poorer countries, more and less integrationists actors. After marathon summit negotiations, the governmental delegates always postponed institutional reform and revised the treaties on the lowest common denominator (Gray and Stubb 2001). Furthermore, summit outcomes sometimes failed to receive sufficient approval in the domestic arena, such as recently in the Irish referendum on the Nice Treaty (2001). The Convention agenda-setting method attempts to anticipate the constraints of the following stages of constitution building by the inclusion of the preferences of governmental and parliamentary delegates. While the governments have to agree on a text at the following summit, parliamentary actors must ratify the proposal in the member states. This anticipatory intention is also indicated by the incorporation of the accession countries, which became members after the completion of the Convention in May 2004. However, popular views were excluded, even though an unprecedented number of ten referenda were announced before the end of the process.

In this chapter, we examine whether the European Convention was characterized by the expected cleavages between large and smaller countries as well as between parliamentarian and governmental delegates in EU constitution building by investigating the preferences of the Convention's delegates. These cleavages are observed in day-to-day Council decision making (Mattila 2004) and were decisive for the failure of previous reform attempts. In addition to these traditional cleavages, Vaubel (2002) expects that the supranational delegates of the European Convention will have a strong interest in further European centralization, while König (2002) suspects a split between old and new members because accession countries did not have a voting right about the Convention's draft proposal.

Using data on the delegates' reform positions and saliencies, we are able to investigate whether the Convention's policy space reveals the suggested conflicts between delegates from large and smaller countries, old and new member states, parliamentarian, governmental or supranational background. We examine actors' positions to reveal the most controversial issues. Furthermore, our analysis of actors' saliencies can shed light on the resolvability of their conflicts on constitution building. We argue that differences in the delegates' positions indicate a cleavage between these groups, but their resolvability crucially depends on similar levels of saliency that actors attach to them. Before presenting our findings, we introduce into the issues and organization of the European Convention, derive hypotheses on delegates' reform preferences and cleavages, and present our data on delegates' positions and saliencies.

The European Convention: issues and organization

The Laeken Declaration of 15 December 2001 was the legal basis for the work of the Convention on the future of Europe and the first step toward a European constitution. The Convention was provided with an open mandate to review the key reform issues arising for the EU's future development and submit proposals in this respect. The final decision on a constitution has however been left to the adoption of a text by the member states and parliamentary ratification plus an unprecedented number of ten referenda. To meet the challenges of the future EU and to make the EU attractive to the European citizens, the Declaration specifies 57 questions regarding the simplification of the EU's instruments, democracy, transparency and efficiency in the EU, and it finally proposes different possibilities for a way toward a constitution. This list includes highly controversial institutional reform issues, such as the rules for the Council presidency, the size and election of the Commission, the voting procedure among member states, and the balance of power between the EU institutions. It also proposes the modification of the system of overlapping treaties, referring for the first time to a fully fledged constitution.

The Convention began its deliberation in February 2002 and submitted a draft constitutional treaty in June 2003. During the first phase, which has been called the *listening* phase by the Convention's president, Valéry Giscard d'Estaing, the delegates presented their views about the future of the EU. A relatively short amount of time was spent on discussing the topic of institutional reform (Maurer 2003a: 28). In September 2002, the presidency initiated a second phase, the so-called *study* phase, by establishing a system of eleven working groups. These groups discussed the issues of subsidiarity, the inclusion of the Charter of Fundamental Rights of the European Union, legal personality, the role of national parliaments, complementary competencies, economic governance, external action, defense, simplification of treaties, the area of freedom, security and justice, and the social dimension of Europe. In spring 2003, the Convention came into the decisive phase, which was called the *drafting* period. In the end, the delegates adopted a draft constitutional treaty after hectic and intensive debates on 13 June 2003 (CONV 850/03).

One week after the adoption of the text, Giscard d'Estaing presented the draft to the European Council in Thessaloniki. Under the Italian presidency, the European Council agreed upon the text as a good working basis for the following summit, which was to decide about the adoption of a constitution for Europe (*Financial Times*, 21 June 2003; Thessaloniki Council Presidency Conclusions). A majority of governments praised the final text as a good compromise. However, even though their delegates had participated in the drafting of the constitutional text, some member states immediately called the finality of the Convention's proposal into question and announced their intention to renegotiate several provisions at the Brussels summit on 12–13 December 2003. Between mid-June and mid-December 2003 the participants of the summit had time to coordinate their positions on the proposed European constitution.

Reform preferences and cleavages

The Convention was composed of 207 members and 13 observers, of which only 66 had the right to vote (from each country one governmental and two parliamentary representatives) on the final document (Article 6, Working Methods of the Convention).[1] Vaubel (2002) criticized the composition of the European Convention early on and predicted conflicts between certain groups due to their institutional background, in particular between governmental and parliamentary delegates, members from European and domestic institutions, and between members with different partisan affiliations.[2] Similar cleavages have been observed during previous summit negotiations, where the EP tried to strengthen parliamentary power against the Council (Hix 2002, Christiansen 2002).

Vaubel (2002) argues that the supranational delegates of the European Convention will have a strong interest in further European centralization and delegating powers to the European level, referring to the Commission, which proposed a strengthening of the "Community method" in its White Paper on Governance (Wincott 2001). Wessels (2002, 1999) points to another institutional cleavage between governmental and parliamentary preferences, the latter favoring to delegate powers to parliamentary institutions. This suggests the following hypothesis: *Reform preferences vary significantly between delegates to the Convention owing to their institutional background (national parliamentarians, governmental representatives, supranational actors).*

The delegates of the 13 accession and candidate countries were officially not entitled to vote on the Convention's final proposal. This suggests a split between old and new members because accession countries did not have a voting right about the Convention's draft proposal, even though these countries became members before the coming into force of a constitution (König 2005). Besides their similar voting status, accession/candidate countries face similar economic and political problems, and opinion polls show that the main concern of their citizens is loosing their national identity and sovereignty after joining the EU (e.g., *The Economist*, 7 June 2003 and 19 April 2003). The ten accession (Cyprus, Czech Republic, Estonia, Hungary, Latvia, Lithuania, Malta, Poland, Slovenia and Slovakia) and the three applicant countries (Bulgaria, Romania and Turkey) are all relatively poor and most have important agricultural sectors, which will change decision making and budgetary politics in the EU (König and Bräuninger 2004). This might induce similar constitutional preferences, which differ from the constitutional preferences of rich member states (Hosli 1996). Due to the cleavage between old, comparatively affluent countries and new, relatively poor countries (Peirce 1991, Carrubba 1997, Rodden 2002), we expect: *Reform preferences vary significantly between delegates of accession countries and delegates of current member states.*

Since the foundation of the European Communities smaller countries have worried about the dominance of the large member states, Germany, Great Britain, France and Italy. Compared to their population size, smaller countries are over-represented in terms of voting weights and access to European organizations. Mattila's (2004: 34) analysis of voting behavior in the Council reveals this cleavage between smaller and large member states in day-to-day decision making. Since smaller (and highly regulated) countries benefit from receiving access to the big markets, they might have preferences different from large countries (Moravcsik 1993: 492). Smaller countries were interested in a new mechanism because they were disappointed with the handling of intergovernmental conferences by large member states (Dinan 2002: 31). Our third hypothesis is: *Reform preferences vary significantly between delegates of small and large countries.*

Finding evidence for these preference patterns does not necessarily call the constitution-building process into question. It may only reveal the persistence of conflicts and cleavages, which blocked previous reform attempts of the EU's institutional framework. If these groups attach different saliencies to the issues at stake, they can find a compromise or make a package deal on a constitutional text. But if these groups have similarly saliency patterns on to the contested issues, it will make it difficult to reach consensus. For this reason, we additionally investigate whether these groups differ in the saliencies attributed to contested issues (Humphreys and Garry 2000, Laver 2001). This requires the identification of the issues at stake and the preferences of the delegates involved.

The European Convention: issues, positions and saliencies

The Convention draft consolidates all previous treaties into a single document. Part One comprises the division of competencies, the institutional structure, legislative procedures and voting rules. Part Two includes the Charter of Fundamental Rights, Part Three lists EU policies and Part Four concludes with general and final provisions, including treaty revision and withdrawal procedures. The draft proposes a number of contentious issues, such as the election of a president of the European Council for two and a half years, the election of the Commission president by the European Parliament and the modification of Commission's composition and the Council's voting rules.[3] Other reform issues relate to the inclusion of further policy fields.

To provide a systematic view on the issues and preferences of the Convention delegates we used a survey with a standardized questionnaire. For constructing the questionnaire, we extracted the topics and alternatives of the Convention's deliberations by document analysis of the Laeken European Council Summit.[4] These topics addressed the delimitation of competencies, the Common Foreign and Security Policy (CFSP), the institutional balance, the decision-making system, and the form of the final recommendation by the Convention. The questionnaire covers these areas by 23 questions on particular issues and lists the proposed alternatives.[5] For every issue, we asked the delegates to indicate their position and the importance which they attach to each issue.

Questionnaires were sent to all 102 full members of the Convention, their alternates, the observers, the president and two vice-presidents.[6] Our data set covers 84.5 percent ($n = 90$) of all 102 full members' positions.[7] For the governments of the 15 member states, the response rate is 88.9 percent, and for the accession country governments 79.5 percent. 92.9 percent of the countries include answers from one governmental and one parliamentarian delegate, which means that we can account for the two institutional affiliations from all 15 member states, and from 84.6 percent of the accession countries. Furthermore, our data contain 50 percent of the Commission's delegates, and 81.2 percent of the positions of the European Parliament, including members from all political parties.

We use these data to first assess the divergent reform positions indicating latent cleavages along the lines discussed in our theoretical part. Second, we focus on the saliency pattern to see whether or not contested issues exhibit convergent (and high) saliencies. We propose to uncover the cleavages over the 23 key issues by looking for the significance in the association between group affiliation and the reform positions of the delegates.[8] Table 2.1 lists the significance levels for chi square and tau-b statistics at the issue level.[9]

Table 2.1 P-values testing for group differences

Question	*Issue*	*Size of population*		*Membership EU-15*		*Inst. background*	
		Chi square	*Tau-b*	*Chi square*	*Tau-b*	*Chi square*	*Tau-b*
Q1a	Division of jurisdiction	0.201	0.286	0.494	0.243	0.714	0.487
Principles regulating jurisdiction							
Q2a_1	Subsidiarity	0.374†	0.372	0.253	0.205	0.695	0.503
Q2a_2	Proportionality	**0.079†**	**0.068**	0.230	0.141	0.820	0.529
Q2a_3	Responsibility of MS	0.103†	0.119	**0.020**	**0.010**	**0.085**	**0.032**
Q2a_4	Flexibility	0.329†	0.295	0.245	0.189	0.232	0.311
Q2a_5	Limited single authority	0.133†	0.156	0.473	0.258	0.370	0.296
Relegation of jurisdiction							
Q3a_1	European foreign policy	0.807	0.956	0.991	0.902	0.207	0.387
Q3a_2	Defence and security	0.570	0.319	0.150	0.991	0.131	0.497
Q3a_3	Development	0.259	0.162	0.974	0.856	0.283	0.689
Q3a_4	Protection of human rights	0.367	0.373	0.277	0.378	0.369	0.614
Q3a_5	(Im)migration	0.165	0.484	**0.013**	**0.063**	0.355	0.459
Q3a_6	Asylum	0.943	0.742	**0.082**	**0.033**	0.620	0.219
Q3a_7	International security	0.201	0.771	0.692	0.717	0.236	0.504
Q3a_8	Judiciary cooperation	0.631	0.316	0.659	0.377	0.205	0.293
Q3a_9	Fighting drugs	0.990	0.890	0.777	0.940	**0.057**	**0.037**
Q3a_10	Social policy	0.422	0.688	**0.093**	**0.027**	0.765	0.897
Q3a_11	Employee rights	0.474	0.250	0.655	0.463	0.994	0.835
Q3a_12	Fighting unemployment	0.486	0.230	0.626	0.368	0.777	0.936
Q3a_13	Economic policy	0.764	0.808	0.698	0.976	0.127	0.256
Q3a_14	Taxes	0.667	0.413	**0.093**	**0.054**	0.230	0.846
Q3a_15	Farming and fishing	0.663	0.975	0.430	0.186	0.260	0.470
Q3a_16	Environment	0.237	0.284	0.586	0.382	0.175	0.452
Q3a_17	Regions/infrastructure	0.816	0.692	**0.021**	**0.004**	0.132	0.158
Q3a_18	Education	0.608	0.438	0.104	0.125	0.122	0.353
Q3a_19	Research	0.261	0.098	0.475	0.235	0.610	0.772

Q3a_20	Health care	0.272	0.811	0.592	0.526	0.441	0.870
Q3a_21	Consumer protection	0.914	0.756	0.352	0.346	0.942	0.642
Q3a_22	Traffic and transportation	0.176	**0.058**	**0.033**	**0.005**	0.291	0.620
Q3a_23	Basic rights of the media	0.636	0.421	0.455	0.205	0.792	0.651
Q3a_24	Privacy in electronic com.	0.747	0.608	0.365	0.155	0.832	0.764
Q3a_25	Industrial policy	0.581	0.834	0.873	0.604	0.649	0.795
Common Foreign and Security Policy							
Q4a	Responsibility	**0.041**	**0.039**	0.236	0.442	0.701	0.500
Q5a	Concerted action	0.202	0.269	0.400	0.909	0.391	0.575
Q6a	Voting threshold	**0.054**	0.444	**0.092**	0.620	0.858	0.272
Q7a	EP – Council	0.320	0.387	0.973	0.817	0.191	0.015
Council							
Q8a	Veto right	**0.075**†	**0.062**	**0.020**†	**0.010**	**0.069**	**0.014**
Q9a	Voting weights	**0.019**	**0.002**	**0.061**	**0.022**	0.122	0.806
Q10a	Voting threshold	0.954	0.951	0.307	0.407	0.317	0.129
European Parliament							
Q11a	Distribution of seats	**<0.001**	**<0.001**	0.315	0.305	**0.017**	**0.016**
Q12a	Uniform voting regulation	0.570	0.734	0.643	0.369	0.843	0.645
Q13a	Election of Commission	0.356	0.109	0.262	0.371	0.270	**0.060**
Q15a	Right to initiate legislation	0.580	0.310	0.323	0.626	0.130	0.195
Q16a	Legislative procedures	0.357	0.709	0.312	0.715	**0.010**	**0.006**
Council							
Q17a	General reform	**0.038**	**0.025**	**0.083**	**0.031**	0.149	**0.180**
Q18a	Council Presidency	**<0.001**	**<0.001**	0.173	**0.077**	0.764	0.307
Other							
Q19a	Number of Commissioners	**0.002**†	**0.001**	**0.001**†	**<0.001**	0.466	0.662
Q19a_2	Commission President	**0.015**	**0.028**	0.175	0.178	**0.057**	**0.042**
Q20a	Scope of treaty reform	0.220	**0.013**	0.363	0.302	0.129	**0.067**
Q21a	Unanimity	0.739	0.710	0.537	0.759	0.523	0.541
Q22a	Constitution	0.186	0.319	**0.089**	**0.015**	0.630	0.378

Note
Fisher's exact test (two-sided) was used when one cell had an expected frequency of less than five. These occasions are marked by a dagger.

The findings show that group differences in positions are clearly pronounced with respect to institutional issues, such as the voting weights in the Council, the number of commissioners, and the distribution of seats in the Parliament. The hypothesized cleavages also exist with regard to the principles ruling the jurisdiction of competencies and their relegation in some areas (asylum, immigration, regional policy, social policy, taxes, and transportation), which is particularly relevant for old and new member states. Furthermore, delegates from smaller and large countries differ in their positions regarding the responsibility for the Common Foreign and Security Policy. On closer inspection, Table 2.2 exhibits the different reform positions across all group cleavages for some of the most contested issues.

Unsurprisingly, small countries' representatives favor the current appointing system of one commissioner at least per country, while large countries' representatives prefer to lower the number of commissioners (Table 2.2). Delegates from old member states tend to favor a smaller Commission compared to delegates from new member states. Finally, a majority of national parliamentarians supports to keep one commissioner per country. Delegates of national governments and supranational institutions, however, prefer to restrict the number of commissioners, too.

The reform of the Council is particularly contested. At least two, if not all, of the hypothesized cleavages matter for the general reform of the Council (public sessions, introduction of a legislative Council), the distribution of the voting weights, and the question of veto rights for individual member states. Independent from their governmental or parliamentarian status, a majority of representatives from smaller countries as well as from accession/candidate countries favor the status quo arrangements of the Nice Treaty, but delegates from large countries and old member states prefer changing the voting weights to population size by introducing a double majority criterion of states and population quota. This clearly confirms the theoretical expectation on the power redistribution of the new voting procedure, which will decrease the power of the smaller countries.

Finally, supranational actors prefer giving more weight to population size in Council voting, whereas a majority of national delegates, governmental representatives and parliamentarians favor the status quo. We observe similar cleavages regarding the topic of the Council presidency. The majority of delegates from large member states supports the election of a Council president, while an overwhelming number of delegates from smaller countries prefers either to keep the status quo of a rotating presidency or to introduce team presidencies. Most delegates from accession/candidate countries advocate the status quo, but delegates from old member states favor team presidencies.

In sum, our empirical results confirm the existence of the hypothesized cleavages between old and new member states, small and large countries and actors with different institutional backgrounds, in particular for

Table 2.2 Reform preferences and cleavages

Reform	*Size of population*		*Membership EU-15*		*Institutional background*		
	Small	*Large*	*New*	*Old*	*Government*	*Parliament*	*Supranational*
Voting in the Council							
Favoring large states	1 (1.7%)	1 (3.8%)	1 (3.2%)	1 (1.9%)	1 (4%)	0 (0%)	1 (6.7%)
Double majority/based on population	14 (24.1%)	**15 (57.7%)**	5 (16.1%)	**24 (45.3%)**	8 (32%)	14 (31.8%)	**7 (46.7%)**
Nice Treaty	**32 (55.3%)**	8 (30.8%)	**19 (61.3%)**	21 (39.6%)	**15 (60%)**	**22 (50%)**	3 (20%)
Favoring small states	11 (19.0%)	2 (7.7%)	6 (19.4%)	7 (13.2%)	1 (4%)	8 (18.2%)	4 (26.7%)
Total	58 (100%)	26 (100%)	31 (100%)	53 (100%)	25 (100%)	44 (100%)	15 (100%)
Council presidency							
Rotating presidency	**26 (42.6%)**	2 (8%)	**15 (44.1%)**	13 (25%)	–	–	–
Team presidency	**26 (42.6%)**	9 (36%)	12 (35.3%)	**23 (44.2%)**	–	–	–
Elected president	9 (14.8%)	**14 (56%)**	7 (20.6%)	16 (30.8%)	–	–	–
Total	61 (100%)	25 (100%)	34 (100%)	52 (100%)	–	–	–
Number of commissioners							
One per country	**36 (64.3%)**	5 (23.8%)	**24 (77.4%)**	17 (37%)	12 (46.2%)	**24 (60%)**	5 (45.5%)
Restricted number	20 (35.7%)	**16 (76.2%)**	7 (22.6%)	**29 (63%)**	**14 (53.8%)**	16 (40%)	**6 (54.5%)**
Total	56 (100%)	21 (100%)	31 (100%)	46 (100%)	26 (100%)	40 (100%)	11 (100%)

institutional issues. However, whether these cleavages matter for constitution building might also depend on the actors' saliency. Gridlock and failure are particularly likely when cleavages emerge for issues which are similarly important to both sides.[10] To control for these configurations, we use the standardized saliency across issues for each actor (z-scores). This allows us to run one-way statistics of variance for each cleavage and issue testing the significance in the levels of salience. Table 2.3 lists the areas and cleavages for which (1) preferences differ significantly (2) the mean level of salience for the groups is above average, and (3) the mean level of salience does not differ significantly across groups.

The findings show that the hypothesized cleavages remain virulent for specific reform issues (principles regulating jurisdiction, CFSP, number of commissioners, scope of treaty reform). In particular, the cleavage between small and larger countries exists for several reform issues on which both groups of countries attach similarly high levels of saliency. This suggests that the Convention method could not settle all conflicts but perhaps overcome these cleavages by using its agenda-setting power. Although the delegates adopted a draft proposal in June 2003, the results raise the expectation of renegotiation, at least for some of the contested issues.

Table 2.3 Potential areas of gridlock

Issue	*Size of population*	*Cleavage*	
		Membership EU-15	*Institutional background*
Division of jurisdiction	–	–	–
Principles regulating jurisdiction	•	–	–
CFSP, responsibility	•	–	–
Concerted action	–	–	–
CFSP, voting threshold in the Council	–	•	–
EP – Council	–	–	–
Veto right	–	–	–
Voting weights	–	–	–
Voting threshold	–	–	–
EP, distribution of seats	–	–	–
Uniform voting regulation	–	–	–
Election of Commission	–	–	–
National parliaments	–	–	–
Right to initiate legislation	–	–	–
Legislative procedures	–	–	–
Council, general reform	–	–	–
Council presidency	–	–	–
Number of commissioners	•	–	–
Scope of treaty reform	•	–	•
Unanimity	–	–	–
Constitution	–	–	–

Conclusion

The European Convention on the Future of Europe was a new instrument to find solutions for institutional arrangements of a widening and deepening EU. After the prior reform failures of intergovernmental conferences at the Amsterdam and Nice summits, the European Convention was established to increase transparency and legitimacy to the process of European integration and to propose solutions for institutional reform. In contrast to secret marathon negotiations at intergovernmental conferences, most of the Convention's deliberations were held in public, and the number of parliamentarian delegates was higher than those of governmental representatives. Moreover, accession and candidate countries were included, even though they had no right to vote on the final text. Under the President Valéry Giscard d'Estaing, the European Convention adopted a draft proposal for a European constitution, which proposes to reform the power distribution in the EU, to increase the competencies of the EU and simplify the existing treaties.

Previous reform attempts failed due to cleavages between large and smaller, rich and poorer countries, more and less integrationists as well as between old and newer members. Our findings show that many of these cleavages are also found to be significant. Reform preferences differ between delegates from member states and accession countries, smaller and large countries, and for delegates from different institutions (national parliaments, national governments, supranational actors). The results also confirm Tsebelis's analysis on the significance of the institutional changes proposed by the Convention. The cleavages are particularly relevant for institutional topics: The reform of the Council and its decision-making process seems to remain contested. Furthermore, some of the cleavages are salient. Today we know that the subsequent modification at the intergovernmental conference confirms our findings and Tsebelis's analysis. How the actors reacted on the Convention draft and how the governments prepared their positions in reaction on the Convention draft in the member states, accession countries as well as in the Commission and the European Parliament will be subject to the following chapters.

Notes

1 Members with voting rights were the President of the Convention, the two Vice-presidents, Giuliano Amato and Jean-Luc Dehaene, 15 representatives of the member state governments (one from each country), 30 representatives of the national parliaments of the member states (two from each member state), 16 members of the European Parliament, and two representatives of the Commission.

2 Formal analyses of the institutional interplay between the three legislative relevant institutional actors – the Council, EP and Commission – also stress that the EP and the Commission advocate a stronger position on European integration as the member states in the Council do (Tsebelis and Garrett

2000, Garrett 1992; for counter-arguments see Crombez *et al.* 2000, Crombez 1996).

3 The draft proposes that 13 member states (determined by a system of rotation) should nominate three qualified persons for commissioner. Subject to approval by the European Parliament, the president of the Commission selects one person of them for the college, the voting members of the Commission (Article 26). The Commission president also appoints non-voting commissioners from the other member states. This provision will, however, not be implemented before 2009 (Article 25). The text also simplifies the complicated QMV procedure by a simplified "double" majority: a majority of member states, which represents at least three-fifths of the EU's population votes can adopt legislative initiatives (Article 24). In cases where the Council is not acting on a proposal by the Commission or the Union minister for foreign affairs, a qualified majority consists of two-thirds of the member states, representing at least three-fifths of the population.

4 We checked the construct validity of our questions by interviewing the scientific advisor of a German Convention member, Professor Dr Oppermann.

5 The last question refers to the favored form of the recommendation made by the Convention, which we did not include in the analysis. The third question consisted of a catalogue of 25 issue areas. For coding purposes questions 2 and 19 have been divided into several items.

6 In addition to these 207 individuals, the Economic and Social Committee (three representatives), the Committee of the Regions (six representatives), the social partners (three representatives) and the European Ombudsman were invited to attend the meetings as observers. In sum, 220 persons participated in the deliberations of the Convention.

7 We received 127 (57.7 percent) responses from the 220 persons addressed. We excluded anonymous answers and all observers from the data set. To avoid a disproportionate representation of a few groups we reduced the data set to one governmental delegate per country, two parliamentary representatives per country and one delegate per position from the European Parliament and Commission. Furthermore we replaced missing members with their alternates.

8 We coded the delegates by the country's size (small versus large with France, Germany, Italy, Poland, Spain, Turkey and the United Kingdom being large countries), membership status (current member versus accession/candidate country), and according to their institutional background (national parliament, government, supranational actor). Delegates of the European Parliament and of the Commission represent supranational institutions. The codebook is available at http://personal.ac.uk/warntjen. Due to the exploratory nature of this study we use the 0.1 level for either of the tests.

9 Whereas chi square tests only use the information given by nominal categories, tau-b statistics assume an ordinal level. Due to the loss of information by treating the data as nominal, tau-b statistics prove to be more powerful (Agresti and Finlay 1997: ch. 8; cf. Signorino and Ritter 1999). For the analysis at the ordinal level the alternatives were ordered along a single dimension, where one extreme refers to national arrangements (i.e., empowering the Council) and the opposite extreme indicates supranational arrangements (i.e., empowering the EP).

10 Two actors did not give any response and another one only answered a few questions. These were excluded from this analysis. Due to missing data we had to drop the responses for question 3 from our analysis. For comparative purposes, we standardized the importance for each actor across the reform issues.

3 Austria

The coordination of the national position regarding the constitution

Christine Arnold and Annemieke Burmeister

Austria became a member of the EU in 1995. A very strong majority 66 percent of Austrians voted in favor of joining the EU.[1] In the past, Austria's relationship with the EU has been strongly influenced by its preference for neutrality. In 1955, in order to end the occupation by the allies, Austria agreed to refrain from joining a military alliance. Additionally, the SPÖ for a long time was reluctant to join what it considered to be a "bourgeois bloc" (Luif 2003: 97) and was only willing to participate in the European Free Trade Association (EFTA), yielding to demands of the ÖVP.

Concerning public support for the draft constitution, a Eurobarometer survey in January 2004 found that 68 percent of Austrians agree with the statement that the European Union must adopt a constitution, while 23 percent disagree and 9 percent did not know (Eurobarometer 2004a). This perception is very close to the EU average of 78 percent, 15 percent and 7 percent. As argued below, the public opinion concerning the constitutional treaty gained importance once Austria's neutrality and an atomic free Europe were at stake. During the later phase of the Convention, and also during the IGC, the government negotiator faced a constant threat of a popular referendum. The opposition parties and the FPÖ were aware of the executive dominance during the negotiations and saw the threat of a referendum as a means by which to influence the government's position.

Domestic structures in a comparative perspective

The Austrian political system is a federal republic of nine states.[2] Although most authority rests with the federal government, the states have considerable responsibility for welfare matters and local administration. According to Lijphart (1999: 312), Austria is an example of the consensual model of democracy. "One expression of this political system was the huge delegation on the Austrian side during the membership negotiations. Not only ministers and high-ranking civil servants participated in these delegations, but also representatives of the provincial government and from social partners" (Luif 1998: 120).

During most of the twentieth century, the government in Austria was dominated by a grand coalition of the conservative ÖVP and the socialist SPÖ.[3] Political appointments were proportionately shared between these two ruling parties (Neuhold 2002: 24). Since 4 February 2000, Chancellor Wolfgang Schüssel (ÖVP) has been head of the federal government. His government consists of a coalition by the ÖVP and the FPÖ.[4]

The current head of state is President Heinz Fischer (since 25 April 2004) who belongs to the SPÖ and who was elected by 52.41 percent of votes. The Federal Assembly (parliament) consists of two houses, the National Council (*Nationalrat*), or lower house, and the Federal Council (*Bundesrat*), or upper house. Legislative authority resides in the National Council. Its 183 members serve a maximum of four years. The electoral system is a closed party-list system with proportional representation according to the Hagenbach–Bischoff method and preferential vote. There is a 4 percent threshold for parties to gain representation. The last election was conducted on 24 November 2002.[5]

The 62 members of the Federal Council are elected by the legislatures of the nine states for five to six year terms. The Federal Council only reviews legislation passed by the National Council and can delay but not veto its enactment. The constitutional treaty had to be ratified by two-thirds majorities in both houses of parliament, namely the *Nationalrat* and the *Bundesrat*, which happened on 11 May 2005 respectively 25 May 2005.

The economic system of Austria is characterized by a well developed social market economy with a relatively even distribution of wealth in which the government has played an important role.[6] Luif argues that the years of allied occupation not only caused neutrality, but they also "laid the foundations for a democratic 'corporatist' structure of the Austrian political and economic system" (Luif 2003: 97). The Austrian system of economic and social consensus, characterized by strong social partnership, has functioned effectively to permit a high standard of living.[7]

Constitutional policy coordination

The formal coordination process through which the Austrian government arrived at its position on the European constitution was not considerably different during the Convention and the IGC. As can be seen in Figure 3.1, the two most important organizational units in this policy coordination process are the chancellor's office and the ministry of foreign affairs (MFA). The reason both organizational units are involved in the process can be explained by the historical fact that the two governing parties, ÖVP and SPÖ, in the past had been successful in asserting their interests. For the most part, the SPÖ was prominent in the chancellor's office, while the foreign minister would be from the ÖVP (Müller 2000: 205). One should note that since elections in 1999 the chancellor has also been from the ÖVP, thus one and the same party now controls both ministries (Neuhold 2002: 26).

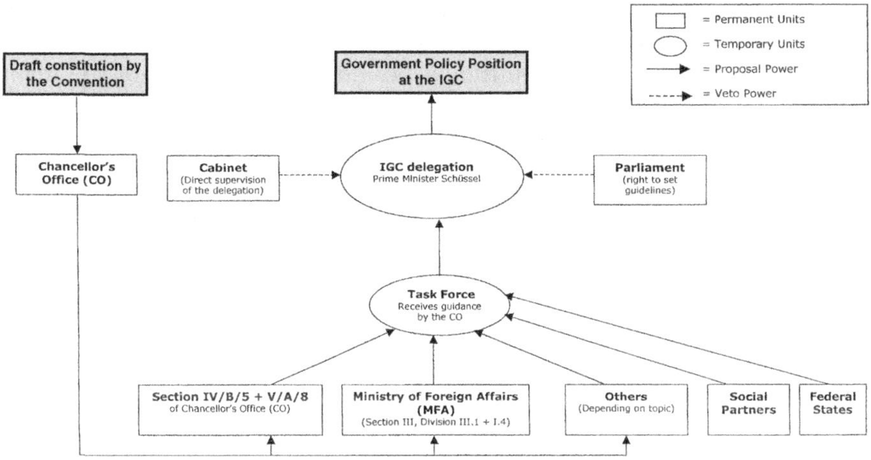

Figure 3.1 Austria: domestic policy coordination for the IGC 2003–4.

During the expert interviews, all respondents confirmed that the federal chancellery and the MFA are the most important actors that influenced the final negotiation position. Three respondents identified parliament as a relevant actor, and one also named the social partners and the *Länder*.

The Austrian national position during the Convention, voiced by government representative Mr Hannes Farnleitner (conservative People's Party) was coordinated through a task force.

The policy preferences presented by Mr Farnleitner were the result of the interdepartmental domestic coordination process in the task force. It consisted of members from the MFA of which the sections IV/5 and V/A/8 are predominantly important, as marked on the chart.[8] However, the task force was very much guided by the preferences of the Austrian chancellor and received guidance from the chancellor's office, which has since 2000 created a central coordination unit (*Stabstelle für die Koordinierung der allgemeinen Regierungspolitik*). During the IGC, the chancellor was equally involved in the negotiations, and if anything in fact gained more prominence.

Furthermore, the task force informed all Austrian participants in the Convention of policy preferences of the Austrian government. Not only members of the Austrian parliament, which participated in the Convention, but also Austrian members of the European Parliament were able to attend meetings of the task force and were informed of policy developments. Parliament was represented by two members of the *Nationalrat*: Mr Caspar Einem (SPÖ) and Mr Eugen Bösch (FPÖ).[9]

Although parliament in practice does not exercise a direct influence on the Austrian policy position during the Convention and the IGC, the formal right enjoyed by parliament pressures the coalition parties in the cabinet to reach a common position. This common position (*Österreichische Grundsatzposition, Regierungskonferenz 2003*) was approved by the main committee.[10] The Austrian minister is bound by the position of the main committee (*Hauptausschuss*) of the *Nationalrat* (Luif 1998: 123).

Constitutionally, the Austrian parliament now has far-reaching powers to control government position taking in EU affairs (Müller 2000: 211). The Austrian model even exceeds the Danish one in this respect (Falkner 2000: 228). In practice parliament's control over the government is further strengthened by a political culture which strives to accommodate diverse interests.

Furthermore, the Austrian parliamentary system has another committee, the so-called "fire-brigade committee" which is smaller and more flexible than the main committee. It consists of one representative of every party and functions as a consultative body with the aim of ensuring flexibility for ministers during negotiations in the EU (Pollak and Slominski 2003: 723). This committee was in direct contact with Mr Schüssel during the final stages of the negotiations.

Coordination during the Convention was characterized by a strong orientation toward consensus that is inherent in the Austrian political and administrative system. During the IGC the chancellor and the MFA became increasingly dominant. Essentially it can be said that during the preparatory phase the chancellor's office and the MFA possessed veto power but many other actors were involved in the preliminary coordination and could bring forward their proposals. During the IGC the chancellor retained most of this power and the decision-making process was further centralized during the final negotiations.

Data and empirical analysis of forming positions on the constitution for Europe

The Austrian national position during the Convention and the IGC was characterized by four preferences. First, a key concern of the Austrian government was the composition of the Commission. Chancellor Schüssel insisted during the IGC that every member state should be represented with one commissioner who was to be guaranteed full voting rights.[11] Nevertheless, domestically, this position created some controversy. Mr Voggenhuber, a member of the European Parliament and his colleague Mr Lichtenberger (Greens) openly criticized this standpoint. Furthermore, the SPÖ spokesperson for EU affairs, Mr Einem, suspected that Chancellor Schüssel only took this position to gain advantage in national politics and in the process was willing to carelessly risk damaging the Union (*Die Presse*, 30 October 2003).

Second, the government did not see a need to create a permanent president of the European Council, but instead favored the current system of making appointments on a rotating basis. This arrangement Austria viewed as a guarantee that even small countries will continue to have the right to take over the responsibility of the Council presidency, albeit for a short period of time.

Third, Austria had a strong preference for an atomic energy free Europe. The common position adopted by the Austrian government (*Grundsatzposition*) for the negotiations in the Council supported a reform of the Euratom treaty. However, during the debate with the *Hauptausschuss*, Mr Schüssel regretted the fact that he would not be able to achieve a revision of the treaty, since this treaty was not part of the convention proposal and thereby was not amendable.[12] The chancellor only promised to initiate a conference for the revision of the treaty, should the matter not be addressed satisfactorily during the IGC. Greenpeace in Austria, unhappy with just a promise, hoped to influence the position of the government by collecting signatures for a popular referendum. Although it failed to get a referendum to be held, since it only collected 130,000 signatures, it managed to force the government to discuss the issue in parliament after it garnered additional support from the SPÖ and the Greens.

Fourth, the Austrian government favored participation in a common European security and defense system (*Die Presse*, 5 December 2002). However, to meet the demands of joining, Austria would have to give up its neutrality. Mr Voggenhuber encouraged the discussion on Austria's neutrality and thereby broke what was until then a taboo among the Greens (*Die Presse*, 16 November 2002a). The ÖVP and FPÖ for a long time have been in favor of reconsidering Austria's neutrality. However, the two opposition parties (SPÖ and Greens) in the past had prevented such a change. Given the fact that a two-thirds majority in parliament is needed to change the constitution and the SPÖ alone only held approximately one third of the seats there was a deadlock on the issue for a long time (Luif 2003: 105). During the deliberations of the Convention the Greens became supportive of reconsidering neutrality and were also in favor of the inclusion of a mutual defense obligation for all EU member states.[13] The tensions surrounding this issue increased with the progression of the IGC. As a last resort to make its preferences prevail, the FPÖ championed a referendum on neutrality. This initiative, however, ultimately was blocked by the ÖVP and SPÖ.

Finally, during the IGC the Austrian government steered toward consensus when it joined Finland, Sweden and Ireland for a common proposal (CIG 62/03). While this move was not fully welcomed by all participants in the IGC, since it was seen as a weakening of the military assistance obligation, it helped the Austrian government to find a compromise solution which was domestically more likely to be acceptable. Together with Finland, Sweden and Ireland, Austria opted for a voluntary assistance scheme in case of an emergency, and thereby rejected the military assistance obligation.

Empirical data gathered during expert interviews confirm both the policy priorities discussed above and the tensions between the government position and preferences of national parliamentarians.[14] As can be seen in Table 3.1, interviewees identified the following issues as vital interests of the Austrian government: reform of the Council presidency and Commission appointment, Euratom, Common Foreign and Security Policy, economic objectives, and issues relating to voting rules in the area of freedom, security and justice, and defense policy in the Council. This table also demonstrates that the preferences of the Austrian actors were fairly close. Out of a total of 260 observations, 2.6 percent of answers indicated that the national actors differed from the national position. These deviations can be found in the parliament's position while the leading unit (PO) and the other governmental actors are completely in line with the national position. In other words, in five answers, national parliamentarians provided a deviating preference from the national position. The average percentage of deviating positions mentioned for institutional issues is slightly higher (3.1 percent) than for policy related questions (1.5 percent). The institutional issues on which there were differences among the actors were the following: voting rule in the Council and decision rule in the European Parliament concerning the policy areas of freedom, security and justice and defense policy. The policy issue on which there was a difference among the actors was the question of the religious reference in the constitution. Also it should be noted that the number of deviations are about equally spread in the direction of less integration and more integration, and thus the disagreement with the national position does not appear to be indicative of a more pro- or anti-European attitude.

Conclusion

Austria has based its policy coordination toward position taking in the IGC on a centralized consensus approach. A task force was created to facilitate a broad base of participants in the preliminary phase. The chancellor's office and the MFA, however, dominated the final position taking. Furthermore, the Austrian coordination procedure followed the national patterns of policy making to arrive at outcomes presented at the European level. Overall a large degree of coherence amongst the actors could be observed. The ÖVP controlled both veto power positions and the main committee in parliament approved the *Grundsatzposition* paper brought forward by the government.

Concerning the vital interests of the government, Austria insisted that every member state should be able to appoint one commissioner, and that the president of the European Council should be appointed on a rotating basis. The modification of the enhanced cooperation procedure in the area of Common Foreign and Security Policy (CFSP) and the inclusions of the Euratom treaty were controversial in the domestic debate.

Table 3.1 Cohesiveness of actors' positions in the Austrian coordination process

National position comparison	*Actor(s) (No. or type)*	*Observations (No.)*	*Deviations*									
			from national position		*on integration*				*related to*			
					toward less		*toward more*		*institutional issues*[a]		*policy fields*[a]	
			No.	*%*	*No.*	*%*	*No.*	*%*	*No.*	*%*	*No.*	*%*
All actors	3	195	5	2.6	3	1.5	2	1.0	4	3.1	1	1.5
Subset												
Lead unit	PM	65	0	–	0	–	0	–	0	–	0	–

Deviations related to institutional issues
Voting rule (Council) for Area of Freedom, Security and Justice, and for defense policy; Decision rule (EP) for foreign and for defense policy

Deviations related to policy fields
Religious reference

Vital interests
Economic objectives; Rotation of the presidency in the Council; European commission; External policy; Reform Euratom

Notes

a Percentage shares refer to subsets of institutional (43) and policy (22) issues. *Lead Unit* Leading unit in domestic coordination: Prime Minister's Office (PM) or Ministry of Foreign Affairs (MFA).

While the Austrian delegates to the Convention supported the idea of a consultative referendum, Chancellor Schüssel has strongly opposed the idea. It was feared that a referendum about the constitution will turn out as a vote against atomic energy or neutrality, instead of a referendum on the constitution of the European Union. A parliamentary ratification process can be expected to take place without any problems given the fact that the majority of parties have clearly signaled their willingness to support the new constitutional treaty.

Notes

1 In Sweden and Finland, 52.2 percent and 57 percent, respectively, voted in favor of EU membership. In Norway, 52.5 percent of the people were against EU accession (Neuhold 2002: 23).

2 Burgenland, Kärnten, Niederösterreich, Oberösterreich, Salzburg, Steiermark, Tirol, Vorarlberg, Wien.

3 *Österreichische Volkspartei* and *Sozialistische Partei Österreichs.*

4 *Freiheitliche Partei Österreichs.*

5 For details see Parline Database www.ipu.org/parline-e/parlinesearch.asp. The distribution of votes and seats in the most recent elections for parliament and the 2004 elections for the European Parliament, including the EP bloc affiliation of the parties, can be downloaded from the projects' website at dosei.dhv-speyer.de.

6 Austria had a Gini coefficient of 30.0 in 1997, the latest year for which data is available (World Bank 2004).

7 In 2003 the unemployment rate was 4.1 percent and the employment rate was 69.2 percent (Eurostat 2003).

8 Division III.1 and Division I.4 and the chancellor's office (*Bundeskanzleramt*). The official title of this section IV is *Abteilung IV/B/5: Angelegenheiten der Mitgliedschaft Österreichs bei der EU.* The official title of section V is *Rechtliche Angelegenheiten der Europäischen Integration, Angelegenheiten der Internationalen Wirtschaftsrechtes und andere Verwaltungsangelegenheiten.*

9 Formerly he was Federal Minister for Economic Affairs.

10 IV-4 der Beilagen zu den Stenographischen Protokollen des Nationalrates XXII. GP, Beratung des Hauptausschusses in Angelegenheiten der Europäischen Union, Dienstag, 30. September 2003. (Auszugsweise Darstellung), 15427/EU XXII.GP.

11 Ibid.

12 Ibid.

13 "Diskussion im Hauptausschuss zum EU-Konvent. Die Positionspapiere der Österreichischen Konvents-Mitglieder" Ausschusssitzung des NR, Parlamentskorrespondenz/02/19.06.2002/Nr. 458. And "Hauptausschuss befasst sich erneut mit Konvent zur Zukunft der EU" Ausschusssitzung des Nationalrates, Parlamentskorrespondenz/02/19.06.2002/Nr.457. Also see *Die Presse*, 16 November 2002b.

14 The discussion of this section is based on four standardized interviews conducted between mid-November and mid-December 2003. The results of the interviews give a sense of the degree to which the data of the four interviews are coherent. Our data suggest that there was quite a high degree of congruence between them. If one takes into account the numbers of experts interviewed and modifies the coherence accordingly, we get a mean adapted coherence of 0.94, which is above the average coherence of the countries examined in this volume, which is 0.85.

4 Belgium, the Convention and the IGC

Consensus and coalition politics

Christophe Crombez and Jan Lebbe

Belgium is a constitutional monarchy with a parliamentary system. Its population stands at more than ten million. Belgium is a federal state consisting of three regions (Flanders in the north, Wallonia in the south, and Brussels in the center), and three linguistic communities (the Dutch-speaking community in Flanders and Brussels, the French-speaking community in Wallonia and Brussels, and the German-speaking community in the eastern part of Wallonia).

The federal parliament is bicameral, consisting of a senate and a chamber of representatives. Most legislation only requires chamber approval. The 150 members of the chamber are elected from 11 electoral districts. The 40 directly elected senators are elected from two districts. A further 31 senators are indirectly elected. Elections to the chamber and the senate are held every four years, the last election having been held in May 2003.[1] Belgium uses the d'Hondt electoral system.

Belgium is one of the founding members of the EU, and there is a wide consensus among political parties, except for the extreme right, in favor of more European integration. Ratification of the constitution is therefore very likely, even though it requires the approval of both houses of the federal parliament as well as the parliaments of the regions and communities. By 19 July 2005 all chambers had ratified the constitution except the Flemish regional parliament.

Belgium is a member of the Benelux and the Belgium–Luxembourg Economic Union. It is also part of the euro zone. Its economy is expected to grow by 2.1 percent in 2005. Belgium is a net contributor to the EU budget, to the amount of €75 per capita in 2003.

Domestic structures in a comparative perspective

Historically Belgium can be considered as an example of a consociational state (Lijphart, 1980). Society consists of different segments, often referred to as pillars, separated along ethnic, religious and economic lines. The different pillars share power in the various political institutions. The three principal pillars are the Catholic, socialist and liberal pillars.

They exist both in the Dutch- and French-speaking parts of the country. This structure is mirrored in the party landscape. The principal political "families" are the Christian democrats, CD&V in Flanders and CDH in Wallonia, the socialists, SP.A in Flanders and PS in Wallonia, and the liberals, VLD and MR.[2]

The pillar system is disintegrating, however, mainly due to the decrease in religious practice, which has eroded support for the Christian democrats, and the economic decline in the old industrial areas, which has dented the support for the socialists. In general party loyalty has diminished over the past decades. Meanwhile, the extreme-right Vlaams Belang, the only major party that can be considered as Euro-skeptic, is flourishing in Flanders. Regional parties that were strong during the 1960s and 1970s have all but disappeared, and the green parties, Groen! and Ecolo, are struggling for survival.

The current federal government is formed by the two liberal and the two socialist parties. It is led by the Flemish liberal Prime Minister Guy Verhofstadt. The approval of major policy initiatives requires agreement amongst the coalition parties. The current coalition parties have widely divergent views on economic issues, having formed a government together in 1999 to keep the Christian democrats out of power for the first time in 40 years, rather than to pursue consistent economic policies. The next federal elections are scheduled for spring 2007. The strong showing of the Christian democrats at the regional and European elections in June 2004 may well pave the way for their return to the federal government prior to the next federal elections, however. At the regional level, the Christian democrats lead the government of Flanders, which has traditionally been their stronghold, whereas the other regional governments are socialist-led. The regional elections coincide with the European elections. The next regional elections are thus to be held in June 2009.

The three principal political families are staunchly pro-EU and favor further integration. This reflects Belgium's dependence on foreign trade, the near absence of Belgian nationalism, and the fact that Belgium is the host country for most of the EU institutions.

Constitutional policy coordination

To prepare for the Convention and IGC the Belgian government set up an elaborate system of domestic policy committees. In addition the Belgian approach provided for considerable coordination with the other two Benelux countries. The ministry of foreign affairs (MFA) was the principal actor in the preparations for the Convention: it initiated the internal discussions and its representatives were present at every stage of the policy-making process.

After the conclusion of the Convention the prime minister's office took control of the policy process in preparation for the IGC. At the IGC the initiative thus lay with the prime minister rather than the foreign affairs minister. Furthermore, the policy process followed in preparation for the IGC required less involvement from the different committees. Figure 4.1 shows the process the Belgian government followed to determine its policy positions.

The internal debates would typically start at the prime minister's office (at the MFA during the Convention). It would first receive and gather information about the topics to be discussed. Next it would determine what ministries had an interest in the topics under consideration. The relevant ministries would then together prepare a first informal government position on the issue, which would serve as a basis for further discussion.

Subsequently, the discussion would move to a committee of experts, often referred to as the "Non-group," for lack of a better name. This committee was set up specifically for the Convention and IGC. It included academic and legal experts as well as diplomats. It met on a weekly basis to put together the principal policy documents that would serve as the basis for the government positions.

Next, the committee of experts would send its proposed government positions to another committee referred to as the *Groupe de Soutien* (support group). This committee consisted of the assistants and political advisors to the Belgian delegates. They would discuss the proposed positions and prepare the meetings of the delegation.

Finally, the discussion would reach the level of the delegation. The delegation, during the Convention often referred to as the *Groupe Dehaene–Nagy*, met on a regular basis. Experts and diplomats also attended the meetings. The work of the committee was closely followed by Prime

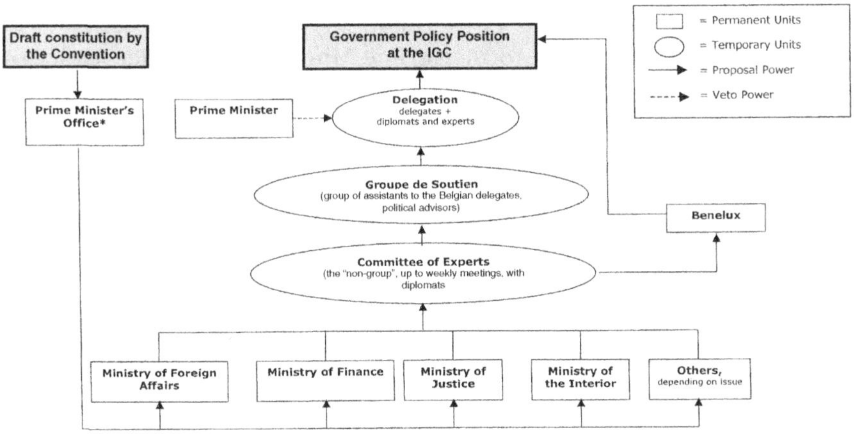

Figure 4.1 Belgium: domestic policy coordination for the IGC 2003–4.

Note
* For the Convention the foreign ministry led the discussions.

Minister Guy Verhofstadt. The delegation would determine the policy positions of the government in coordination with the prime minister. Involvement from other political institutions, such as the federal parliament or the regional governments, was minimal.

The government position on a limited number of specific issues, mainly related to the EU institutions, was determined in negotiations with the Benelux partners. In this case the *Groupe de Soutien* and the *Groupe Dehaene–Nagy* did not directly participate in the discussions.

During the Convention the Belgian government consisted of liberals, socialists and greens. The greens were no longer in government during the IGC. The two main actors within the government were the foreign affairs minister and the prime minister, the former having proposal rights during the Convention, the latter during the IGC. They were both liberals, and there were few, if any, disagreements between them. To obtain government approval, they needed the support of their principal coalition partners, the socialist parties. In party-political terms we can thus say that the liberal parties had proposal and veto rights in the policy process, the socialist parties had amendment and veto rights.

Data and empirical analysis of forming positions on the constitution for Europe

The experts we interviewed identified the following key actors in the coordination process: (1) Louis Michel, Deputy Prime Minister, Minister of Foreign Affairs, leader of the French-speaking Liberal Party and government representative at the Convention; (2) Guy Verhofstadt, Prime Minister and leader of the Flemish Liberals; (3) Elio Di Rupo, leader of the French-speaking Socialist Party and parliament representative at the Convention; and, during the Convention, (4) Jean-Luc Dehaene, Vice-president of the Convention, former Prime Minister and former leader of the Flemish Christian Democrats; and (5) Anne Van Lancker, Flemish socialist MEP and EP representative at the Convention. We interviewed three experts. Their adapted coherence was 0.85, which is at the average for the entire project (see Appendix 2).

According to the experts there was little policy disagreement amongst the actors involved in the constitution-building process in Belgium. This is illustrated in Table 4.1. The table shows the extent of the policy deviation between all relevant actors and the national position, and between the prime minister's office and the national position. In the table the percentages of policy disagreements, whether it be on further integration, institutional issues or policy issues are generally in the single digits. Most politicians strongly favor further EU integration. The little disagreement there was, arose mainly between the Liberals and the Socialists. Within these two political families there was no significant disagreement.

Table 4.1 Cohesiveness of actors' positions in the Belgian coordination process

National position comparison	*Actor(s) (No. or type)*	*Observations (No.)*	*Deviations*									
			from national position		*on integration*				*related to*			
					toward less		*toward more*		*institutional issues*[a]		*policy fields*[a]	
			No.	*%*	*No.*	*%*	*No.*	*%*	*No.*	*%*	*No.*	*%*
All actors	7	455	14	3.1	8	1.8	6	1.3	6	2.0	8	5.2
Subset												
Lead unit	PM	65	4	6.2	3	4.6	1	1.5	1	2.3	3	13.6

Deviations related to institutional issues
Right to withdraw from the Union; Presidency of the Council; Additional approval of the Foreign Minister by the EP; Legislative initiative for citizens

Deviations related to policy fields
Level of competence for tax harmonization, for employment policy, for environment policy; External borders; Migration and asylum

Vital interests
Enhanced cooperation; More QMV areas in general

Notes
a Percentage shares refer to subsets of institutional (43) and policy (22) issues. *Lead Unit* Leading unit in domestic coordination: Prime Minister's Office (PM) or Ministry of Foreign Affairs (MFA).

There was a broad consensus on most of the principal issues. We mention the agreement on a number of issues. All actors wanted to include the Charter of Fundamental Rights in the constitution. They were happy about the Amsterdam rules on subsidiarity. They initially wanted to maintain the rotating system for the Council presidency. They favored a new qualified majority rule that would require the support of a majority of member states and a majority of the population for approval of a legislative proposal. They were willing to give up the one commissioner per member state rule. They wanted enhanced cooperation in all areas. They favored extending the Parliament's role in the budgetary process. And, they wanted a common defense policy that would allow for mutual defense commitments.

The most heated discussions were related to the powers of the EU on economic and social issues. Specifically, the Socialists were striving for more EU powers, more qualified majority voting and more co-decision making in such areas as structural and cohesion policies, social and economic policies, employment, the environment and tax harmonization. The Liberals, by contrast, opposed such moves. On some of these issues the disagreements prevented the government from taking an official position, on others the Liberals and Socialists reached compromise solutions.

Opinions diverged also on a number of other issues. We distinguish four issues. (1) The Socialists were opposed to the right to withdraw from the EU, whereas the Liberals were in favor. The government position was a compromise. Countries would be allowed to withdraw if they failed to approve a treaty. (2) The Liberals wanted more direct voter involvement in EU politics. They favored the direct election of the Commission president and providing for voter initiatives in the legislative process. The Socialists were opposed. Again, the government position was a compromise. The government declared to be in favor of such voter involvement in EU politics in the long run. In the short run the government was in favor of appointing the Commission president by a qualified majority in the Council on a proposal by the Parliament. (3) The Socialists wanted the appointment of an EU foreign minister to be subject to approval by the Parliament, but had to give in on this point. (4) The Socialists favored the creation of an EU border guard, whereas the Liberals opposed this, mainly for economic reasons: Belgium has no external borders and the current system is thus cheaper. On this issue the Socialists prevailed.

This analysis shows that there was agreement on most issues within the Belgian government and Belgian delegation. Where there was disagreement, most often the Liberals and Socialists compromised. In a few cases, related to economic and social policies, they failed to determine a government position. Such outcomes are not surprising given the policy process analyzed in the previous section. The Liberals had proposal rights. They were the agenda setters, but had to take the opinions of their socialist coalition parties into account, because the Socialists had veto rights. In some cases the Liberals' ambitions were tempered as a result and they had to agree on less radical reforms, as in the areas of direct democracy and the right of withdrawal. In other cases there was bargaining across issues, with the Liberals getting their way on some issues, such as the appointment of the EU foreign minister, and the socialist parties on other issues, such as the EU border guard. In yet another set of cases, relating to social and economic policies, the opinions of Liberals and Socialists were too far apart and no government positions could be determined.

As mentioned above a number of institutional issues were discussed at the Benelux level. This led to three important changes in the government position. (1) Belgium agreed to a system of rotating commissioners, chosen by the Commission president and approved by the Council and the Parliament. (2) Belgium also altered its position on the qualified majority threshold. At the Benelux level it agreed to a simple majority of member states and three-fifths of the population, instead of the simple majority of member states and population that it favored. (3) Finally, it also compromised on the European Council presidency, accepting that a European Council president be appointed from among the members of the European Council, for a fixed term, elected by the European Council using qualified majority.

At the IGC the Belgian government defended the approval of the draft constitution. It was particularly concerned that the extension of qualified majority voting and the new rules on enhanced cooperation be preserved.

Conclusion

This analysis illustrates that Belgian policy toward the EU is consensus-oriented. There is widespread agreement amongst mainstream political parties on the issue of European integration and this consensus is reached in a political process that opens opportunities for all major parties to provide input.

The most prominent actors in Belgian politics are the political parties and their leaders. In general policies on major issues are set by the government and require the approval of all the coalition parties. During the Convention liberals, socialists and greens formed the federal government. The Greens played no significant role however, and they were ousted from the government at the end of the Convention. Thus determining the government position required the support of the two liberal and the two socialist parties.

From the outset the Belgian government took a well organized approach to the Convention and IGC. It set up an elaborate system of committees to formulate government policies. These committees consisted of experts, diplomats, political advisers and the Belgian delegates.

The consensus position of the government and delegation was staunchly pro-European, as is Belgian foreign policy in general. Disagreements occurred mainly on left–right economic issues.

On institutional issues, such as the composition of the Commission, the qualified majority rule, and the Council presidency, the Belgian government cooperated with its Benelux partners to establish a consensus at the Benelux level and determine joint positions.

The minister of foreign affairs led the policy formation process during the Convention, whereas the prime minister took control at the IGC. At the IGC Belgium favored the approval of the draft constitution. It was particularly concerned that qualified majority voting be extended and that enhanced cooperation be facilitated.

Ratification of the constitution requires the approval of both chambers of the federal parliament and of the parliaments of the regions and the communities. As all major parties, except for the extreme-right Vlaams Belang, are in favor, ratification is highly likely.

Notes

1 The distribution of votes and seats in the most recent elections for parliament and the 2004 elections for the European Parliament, including the EP bloc affiliation of the parties, can be downloaded from the projects' website at dosei.dhv-speyer.de.

2 A political family in Belgium refers to a Flemish political party and its Francophone counterpart.

5 Cyprus

Under the shadow of the inter-communal conflict

Spyros Blavoukos and George Pagoulatos

Cyprus's political trajectory is stigmatized by the political problem of the island, largely nested in the fragmented ethnic, historical, social and institutional foundations of the independent Cypriot state that came into being in 1960 institutionalizing the communal dualism into the state apparatus and the policy-making process (Joseph 1997). Since the *de facto* partition of the island in 1974, the unique security and political conundrum and the continuously unsuccessful mediating attempts for a just and functional solution to the problem have preoccupied almost exclusively the Cypriot polity (Evriviades and Bourantonis 1994 etc.). The most recent attempt, in 2004, to bring forward the reunification of the two communities was stalled following the rejection of the Annan plan – from the name of the Secretary General of the United Nations – by the Greek–Cypriot community in the Republic of Cyprus referendum. Despite the non-conducive security environment throughout the years, the recovery of the Cypriot economy following the 1974 imbroglio has been remarkable with the country ranking first among all new member countries in terms of economic performance.[1]

Domestic structures in a comparative perspective

The Republic of Cyprus has a presidential system of government with the executive power exercised through an 11 member council of ministers appointed by the directly elected president and the legislative power entrusted to a multi-party unicameral house of representatives elected under a system of simple proportional representation.[2]

Application for EU membership in 1990 was seen primarily as a political move with widespread expectations by the Greek–Cypriot side for accession to operate as a catalyst in the negotiation deadlock. Hence, accession negotiations were part of the broader negotiations for the political settlement of the issue and the strategic calculations of the two agendas were inexorably linked (Christou 2003, Brewin 2000, Demetriou 1998). The progress of the Cypriot application was troubled by the uncertainty of the political situation and the EU's strong preference for avoiding direct entanglement in the island's precarious political situation (Stavridis 1999, Tsardanidis and Nicolau 1999, Joseph 1996). During the accession negotiations there was a domestic political consensus in Cyprus that no derogation should be sought and no substantial reservations should be raised in order not to jeopardize membership prospects (Featherstone 2000). Hence, political considerations predominated in the accession negotiations and overshadowed calls for a more cautious approach to the adoption of the Communitarian economic, legislative and institutional *acquis*. Together with the inevitable asymmetry of power between the EU and any candidate country, these two parameters enhanced even further the EU's leverage on the domestic reform process. In that respect membership came to serve an additional function of secondary but gradually increasing importance as compared to the political one, namely that of the socioeconomic and institutional modernization of Cyprus (Agapiou-Josephides 2003, Featherstone 2000).

The externally induced economic modernization, which was bound to trigger also societal and political change, was assisted by the domestic political and public consensus as regards membership. This consensus was possible only after the repositioning of the powerful Communist Party AKEL (Progressive Party of the Working People) in the early 1990s. The other three main parties (two conservative: DHSY – Democratic Rally, DHKO – Democratic Party; and one socialist: KISOS – Social-democratic Movement) had always embraced European integration to one or the other extent. Charismatic personalities have characterized the Cypriot party system for a long time in a political culture favoring paternalism (Featherstone 2000). However, parties remain the dominant actors in the presidential political system of the island and party influence is founded not only on the personal appeal of the candidates but also on partisan support, identification and alignment (Katsourides 2003).

Binding popular voting is not foreseen in the Cypriot constitution and hence Cyprus is the only new EU member state not to have held a referendum on EU accession (Kurpas *et al.* 2005). Respectively, the house of representatives is responsible for the ratification of the constitution. Given the cross-party agreement and the pro-EU public support it is hardly surprising that the parliament ratified the constitution on 30 June 2005.

Constitutional policy coordination

The starting point of any discussion on administrative and institutional policy-making structures in Cyprus is the small size of the country and the limited available resources. In that respect, dealing simultaneously with accession negotiations and the European constitution-making process imposed severe constraints on the Cypriot public administration (Nugent 2003b). The need to reinforce administrative capacity was repeatedly stressed in the Commission Regular Progress Reports although in the last report prior to accession (November 2002) there was satisfaction with the achieved progress.[3] In addition to the size-related limited availability of resources, which is an inherent problem for any micro-state (cf. Thorhallson 2000, Archer and Nugent 2002), Cyprus faced the additional constraint of the settlement negotiations (toward the objective of the island's reunification), which absorbed an equally significant degree of available resources. These two factors have tested the efficiency and capacity of Cypriot EU policy-making structures to function under the most adverse conditions.

The accession negotiations were conducted by an *ad hoc* coordinating structure evolving around the chief negotiator.[4] In that process the involvement of civil society and interest groups was not substantial. The salient EU image as a potential contributor to the settlement of the island's political problem and the cross-partisan consensus on the country's accession have led to the embrace of the EU by all major actors and interest groups including media, trade unions, NGOs, the employers association, etc. (Katsourides 2003). Coupled by the government's intention to avoid any obstruction in the negotiating process, this positive disposition resulted in a rather hasty treatment of the accession negotiations by both government and the public without any significant protest.

Given the ongoing negotiations for the settlement of the political problem of the island and for accession and the resulting overstretching of domestic administrative and political resources, there is little wonder why the European Convention did not attract a lot of attention in the Cypriot public debate.[5] No particular structures were set up and to a large extent the burden was fully taken up by the government representative and his aide, who had a direct, mainly informal contact with the foreign minister.[6] The two-man team was based in the MFA and depended on administrative assistance from a special secretariat established in the MFA (Agapiou-Josephides 2004). Relevant ministries and authorities were invited to provide information and input on issues of their competence with rather limited response at least in the early phase of the Convention work, with the notable exception of the legal service on institutional affairs. No explicit coordination took place with the parliament representatives, who focused on various issues according to their political orientation without, however, the emergence of any substantial dissent.

In the period after the Convention deliberations intensified and there was a growing realization of the significance of the project, departmental studies were requested to the relevant ministries in view of the upcoming IGC. The legal service again showed the most enthusiastic reaction, with a growing responsiveness from the economic ministries on issues of economic governance. During the IGC, the Cypriot negotiating team, clustered around the MFA, established direct links with the most relevant ministries through the special appointment of a senior civil servant in each ministry to act as a ministerial "focal point." The urgent nature of

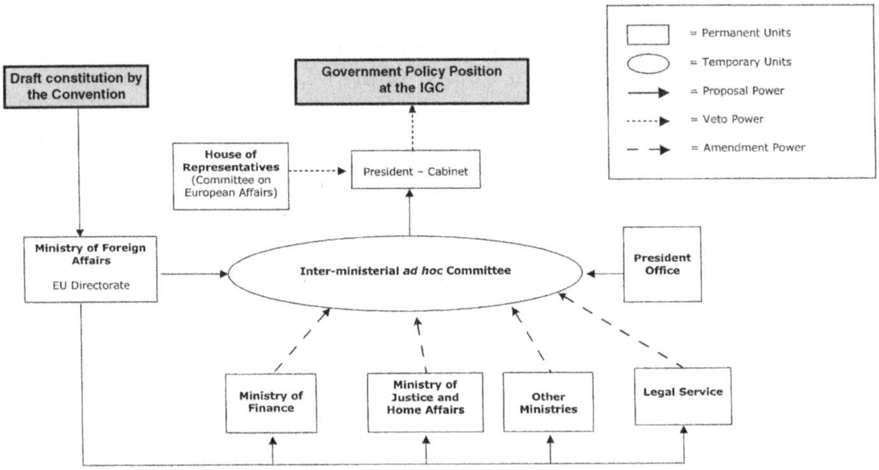

Figure 5.1 Cyprus: domestic policy coordination for the IGC 2003–4.

negotiations demanded a curtailment of bureaucratic inertia if national positions were to be coherently articulated and promoted. Hence the task of this "focal point" was to streamline flows of inputs to the negotiating team and ensure feedback to each ministry from the negotiations. Cooperation with the president's office was smooth and was facilitated by the appointment of the governmental representative in the Convention as presidential advisor to achieve continuity and coherence. In that respect the MFA was the primary interlocutor and coordinator in the domestic policy-making process with *ad hoc* participation of other ministries and the legal service according to the issue.

The IGC was discussed twice in the parliament with a large convergence of views, which comes as no surprise given the broad domestic political consensus. In general the parliament tried to seize the opportunity of the debate on the future of Europe to introduce some innovative interactive features in its consultation and rapport with civil society (Agapiou-Josephides 2004). The political educational dimension of the debate on the future of Europe did not pass unnoticed at least by the governmental and parliamentary representatives in the Convention. The Convention offered opportunities for acquaintance of the Cypriot public with the broader European demos through conferences and information campaigns.[7] This indirect socialization effect especially for the public in acceding countries might be an even more significant contribution of the Convention process than the draft constitution itself (Agapiou-Josephides 2003). However, this process had a clear top-down direction, civil society receiving information on the output of the Convention and IGC deliberations with little actual input in the process. Although it is difficult to have a clear view, it seems that socioeconomic interest groups failed to grasp the importance of the negotiations despite a special letter/invitation to come forward with suggestions and proposals. In contrast, non-governmental organizations especially those having transnational European links showed more interest and willingness to get involved in the process.[8]

Data and empirical analysis of forming positions on the constitution for Europe

The data for Cyprus was collected through two interviews with the government representative to the Convention and later advisor to the President of the Cypriot Republic during the IGC and a highly ranked diplomat in the Cypriot MFA. Both interviewees had a direct involvement in the Convention deliberations and the domestic position formation process, hence they were in a position to provide an authoritative record of the policy-making process and the contributions of the various domestic actors in it. One of the interviews was based on the structured questionnaire developed for the needs of the collaborative project whereas the second was more a rich-informative discussion whereby the answers provided were validated and cross-checked.[9]

Table 5.1 illustrates the high degree of homogeneity in Cyprus as regards the positions of the domestic actors involved in the process. An obvious justification of this homogeneity can be derived from the limited number of – almost exclusively governmental – actors involved, their mode of – continuous – interaction and the nature of the IGC agenda. Hence, on most institutional and EU-competence issues, there was little space for divergent positions and whenever minor disagreements did pop up they were trimmed down in the policy-making process.

The positions held by the Cypriot government in the IGC negotiations took into consideration the small size of the country as well as the island's political predicament. Hence, as regards the former concern, the main axis was the defense of appropriate representation in the institutional bodies of the EU be it the presidency of the European Council, the composition of the Commission or the minimum threshold in EP representation. The Commission composition and the EP representation were the two most salient issues for Cyprus in the IGC negotiations. The Cypriot government sided along the countries requiring the preservation of one commissioner per country with full voting rights and equal status. Sharing the concerns of other member states of roughly equal size and population, it also objected the suggested minimum threshold of four MEPs in the European Parliament considering that it constrained domestic political pluralism and did not allow for adequate representation of the country in this body. The Cypriot government endorsed the prospect of team presidencies suggesting a set of four countries per 18 months with internal rotation. Acknowledging in the process of the negotiations the

Table 5.1 Cohesiveness of actors' positions in the Cypriot coordination process

National position comparison	*Actor(s) (No. or type)*	*Observations (No.)*	*Deviations*									
			from national position		*on integration*				*related to*			
					toward less		*toward more*		*institutional issues*[a]		*policy fields*[a]	
			No.	*%*	*No.*	*%*	*No.*	*%*	*No.*	*%*	*No.*	*%*
All actors	2	130	0	–	0	–	0	–	0	–	0	–
Subset												
Lead unit	MFA	65	0	–	0	–	0	–	0	–	0	–

Deviations related to institutional issues
Nil

Deviations related to policy fields
Nil

Vital interests
Number of commissioners; Number and distribution of seats in the EP

Notes

a Percentage shares refer to subsets of institutional (43) and policy (22) issues. *Lead Unit* Leading unit in domestic coordination: Prime Minister's Office (PM) or Ministry of Foreign Affairs (MFA).

dynamic in favor of a single president of the European Council, it required more clarification about the mandate and the functions of this institutional innovation. The participation of the EP in the election of the president was considered a *sine qua non* condition to add visibility to the post and increase the legitimacy of the president.

In terms of decision rules, a simplification of the Nice QMV arrangements was acknowledged as necessary, with the double majority criterion being accepted although the exact level of the required majority remained to be further discussed. Cyprus supported the idea of a foreign minister for the EU, although it warned against the complications deriving from the "two hats" of the minister if accountable both to the Commission and the Council. Enhanced cooperation schemes were endorsed by the Cypriot government with extension of scope envisaged to all possible areas although more clarification was needed on how the "outs" could be linked with the "in" group.

As regards competence allocation in specific policy areas, the extension of EU's action scope was in general embraced. However, in particular fields like tax harmonization, foreign, economic and social policy this extension was conditional to the preservation of unanimity rule. Interministerial divergence of views occurred as regards defense integration, with military and political considerations pointing to different directions. Strong reservations were expressed in the ministry of defense about the potential implications of defense commitments, as a result of which no synthesis became possible with the official position being "not to have a position."

The political problem and prospects for solution weighed heavily on the national position held in the question of the religious reference on the preamble of the constitution. Although the Greek Orthodox Church did exercise some pressure to support inclusion of the reference in the preamble, the government had to consider the eventuality of a single federal state with the integrated Muslim Turkish Cypriot community. Hence a neutral position had to be adopted in the end with the reference neither rejected nor supported.

Conclusion

In sum, the Convention and the 2003–4 IGC coincided for Cyprus not only with the concluding stages of the accession negotiations but also with a critical period for the settlement of the political problem of the island. Hence intense pressure was exercised on the administrative and political resources of the state and the polity. Naturally, accession and the negotiations toward Cyprus's reunification prevailed over the Convention and the IGC attracting media and public interest. The level of stretching of the Cypriot administrative and political resources can be manifested by the absence of any institutional structure whatsoever dealing with the

Convention. In the course of the IGC, after accession negotiations had been successfully completed with the signing of the accession treaty in April 2003, more resources could be channeled in that direction. No particular institutional bodies emerged either, but a greater involvement of the legal service, economic ministries and the presidential office could be seen. Institutional continuity between the Convention and the IGC was secured with the appointment of the government representative in the Convention as presidential advisor during the IGC. There was an attempt to engage civil society and the public with some success as regards raising awareness but less so in the field of active participation in the policy-making process. Hence governmental actors dominated almost exclusively the position formation process with high degree of homogeneity as regards the embraced positions given the considerable limitations in the range of possible alternatives and Cypriot concerns more generally.

In that respect, Cyprus as a newcomer and having limited political capital in its disposal as a result of the settlement negotiations, adopted in general an accommodating attitude during the negotiations on most issues discussed. Institutional issues, in particular those related to the country's representation in the institutional bodies of the EU, were of particular sensitivity. Given the small size of the country, the Cypriot government sought to ensure maximum representation in the European Parliament and the Commission. Finally, the Convention and the IGC were the first opportunity for Cyprus (and all "new" member states) to participate on equal terms in EU policy making. They thus entailed a "political educational" value as well, raising public awareness over the exact modes of governance in the EU and the course of European integration more generally.

Notes

1 With GDP per capita amounting to 72 percent of EU-15 average (€17,400), all indicators suggest a balanced macroeconomic environment (inflation 2.8 percent; budget deficit around 3 percent; public debt below the 60 percent ceiling) coupled with a low unemployment rate (3.8 percent) and a dynamic and flexible entrepreneurship in particular in the services sector (European Commission 2003a).

2 The distribution of votes and seats in the most recent elections for parliament and the 2004 elections for the European Parliament, including the EP bloc affiliation of the parties, can be downloaded from the projects' website at dosei.dhv-speyer.de.

3 See Regular Reports of the Commission on Cyprus's progress from 1998 onwards. Online. Available at: www.mfa.gov.cy/mfa/mfa.nsf/DOCCyEU.

4 The chief negotiator convened and chaired a staff advising group composed of representatives of the planning bureau, the ministry of foreign affairs and the legal service together with the permanent secretaries of the planning bureau, the ministry of agriculture and the negotiator's own advisor (Featherstone 2000). He was the person in charge, on the political level, of the process of the accession negotiations and the general monitoring and coordination of the min-

istries in terms of harmonization with the *acquis communautaire* (see Office of the Coordinator for Harmonization at www.eu-coordinator.gov.cy). The ministry of foreign affairs tried to assert its leadership over the process in the initial stages but the establishment of this *ad hoc* structure somehow curtailed its overall control of the process. The MFA assumed primary responsibility on issues touching upon the second pillar of the EU, whereas the planning bureau did the same for pillar one. They worked together with the ministries of the interior and justice for pillar three. The planning bureau carried out the bulk of the domestic preparatory and monitoring work, with the MFA directing and coordinating flows of information internally and vis-à-vis the EU (Featherstone 2000).

5 This is a personal estimate by the government representative in the Convention, Professor Attalidis (interview, 24 November 2003). For a record of the relevant activities and the public debate on the Convention in Cyprus, see Agapiou-Josephides (2004).

6 Interview, deputy director of the EU affairs division in the ministry of foreign affairs and "focal point" in the MFA for IGC issues (25 November 2003).

7 Interview, Professor Attalidis, above.

8 Interview, deputy director MFA, above.

9 Hence, given the single questionnaire completed, the high degree of experts coherence should be expected by definition (see Appendix 2).

6 The Czech Republic

Sitting on the fence

Tobias Schulz and Martina Chabreckova

For quite some time, the Czech Republic had overestimated its prospects of entering the EU. Prime Minister Václav Klaus speculated on the persuasiveness of his early economic remedy reforms and did not invest in diplomatic institutions that would prepare negotiations and build up relations (Hanley 2002a). After the new government came to power with the 1996 election, the socialists managed to adopt the *acquis communautaire* and to negotiate the accession successfully. In the accession referendum of June 2003, 77 percent voted in favor, with a turnout rate of 55 percent.

The political elite is divided on the EU integration issue and accordingly Taggart and Szcerbiak (2004: 16) place the Czech Republic on a considerably higher rank in terms of Euro-skepticism than other new member states. The ultra-liberal ODS is strongly intergovernmentally oriented and rejects any tendency toward a federalization of the European Union.[1] Conversely, the elite of the KSČM (the communists) stands for "hard" Euro-skepticism, although in its party programs of the 1990s it is not rejecting the EU absolutely (Kopecký 2004: 243).

There is a consensus within the political elite that there must be a referendum on the constitutional treaty, although the most important precondition, a required amendment of the constitution,[2] is still not finally decided at the time of writing.

Although there is no reason to be overly confident of an approval of the constitutional treaty by the Czech voters, it is still quite plausible that the government has judged this option as being less risky than a pure parliamentary ratification, as speculated by Closa (2005).

Mistrust of European institutions is certainly related to some disappointments during the accession process. The early reforms introduced by the government of Prime Minister Klaus remained superficial, because they were merely directed toward competitiveness of the economy in the global markets but did not include administrative and legal reforms. Nevertheless, the Czech Republic had some economic difficulties in the recent past: the real GDP growth peaked in 1995 at around 5.5 percent but the ensuing period even led to negative growth rates and at the moment the country still lags behind the remaining new members of the

EU (OECD Economic Outlook 2002). On the other hand, the country does not depend on its agricultural sector very much, which amounts to only 4.3 percent of the GDP and unemployment is relatively low with about 7.8 percent. Since the Czech Republic is one of the larger new members, it has more difficulties in complying with the criteria that would allow the country to join the EMU, similar to Poland and Hungary. Hence, no accession before the end of the decade is expected.

Domestic structures in a comparative perspective

After the split with Slovakia, a parliamentary system was established with a president elected by the assembly who is entrusted with largely representative functions, but having limited power to dissolve the assembly and to veto legislation.

The assembly consists of two asymmetric and incongruent chambers, similar to the chambers in France (Morlino 2001: 82), with 200 and 81 seats respectively. Whereas the former holds the legislative powers and is elected according to a proportional rule, the second has no legislative power and every member represents his or her own electoral district. Hence, the high proportionality of the lower chamber is to some extent made up for by the majority principle for the upper chamber. With an effective number of parliamentary parties of about 3.7 (Armingeon and Careja 2004), the Czech Republic's party system is relatively stable and even comprises parties from the communist area.

Government majorities remained unstable, however. At the time of the preparation of the first IGC, the strong Social Democratic Party (ČSSD) that is positioned left of the center was forced into a somewhat problematic coalition with the *Koalice*, a grouping of two parties that stands right of the center. On the left, there are only the communists (KSČM) as one potential coalition partner. This party does in fact hold quite an important share of the seats in the assembly but the remaining parties ignore it because of its obstructive and isolationist program (*Economist*, 3 July 2004).

Before 1996 government dominance was apparent due to clear majorities and stable coalitions. In 1998 Prime Minister Miloš Zeman had to rely on a single party minority already (Blondel and Müller-Rommel 2001: 213). Governing was possible only because of a problematic agreement with the strong opposition party ODS, the party of former Prime Minister Klaus (Linek 2003). The government that was in power during the IGC negotiations was able to break this false "grand coalition."[3]

Similar to the French case, Article 63 of the constitution states that the president shall negotiate and ratify international treaties. However, it also states that he may transfer this right to the government or even to individual ministers, which usually is the case. Due to his international reputation and his contacts, the former president, Havel, insisted on and was able to establish some informal rules (Kopecký 2001), which, however, were by no means meant to be binding for the future. His successor, Klaus, was not able to follow in his footsteps.

As far as the administration was concerned, there had already been some experiences with self-administration at the local level but beginning with 2000, regional self-administration authorities with separate competencies, parliaments and party systems have been established. This ongoing development of decentralization is seen as an important support of political stability (Vodička 2004: 278, Kipke 2004: 296). However, the Czech Republic still remains a rather unitary political system.

Constitutional policy coordination

The number of main actors involved in the position formation process in the Czech government is quite limited. There has been some coordination between the European Integration Department of the Office of Government and the Section for European Integration of the State Secretary for European Integration of the ministry of foreign affairs (MFA) but the latter certainly played the leading role as our interviewees confirmed. On the other hand, the influence of the prime minister's office seems to be less important. The delegate of the government, Jan Kohout, is a state secretary in the MFA and also the first deputy of Foreign Minister Cyril Svoboda (Figure 6.1).

In addition, other ministries may have been consulted depending on the issue but according to our interview partners, they had no strong impact on the process. As in the case of Slovakia and Italy, the MFA did not oppose the foundation of a temporary and informal organization that provided an opportunity for a wide range of interested institutions and individuals to discuss the contents of the Convention. However, the National Forum was not assigned to the executive but to the Senate Committee of European Integration (Krotohvil 2003). Hence, it certainly was not formally incorporated into the position formation process. Nevertheless, the influence of think tanks on the government is seen as considerable and hence, the National Forum is also incorporated in Figure 6.1.

The opposition in the Czech Republic was very active in frustrating the efforts of the government. Former Foreign Minister Zahradil (ODS), who was the delegate of the parliament and acted as the "shadow foreign minister," received strong attention in public. As a result, he might have been able to impose some of his views and this was probably the reason why he had been mentioned by both of our interviewees.

In addition, President Klaus (ODS) also tried to influence the position formation process on several occasions. First, his signing of the accession treaty in Athens drew much media attention and gave him the opportunity to comment on the present government policy toward the EU.[4] Second, he invited the government to coordinate the position with him and all convention members (an initiative that escalated in a dispute with

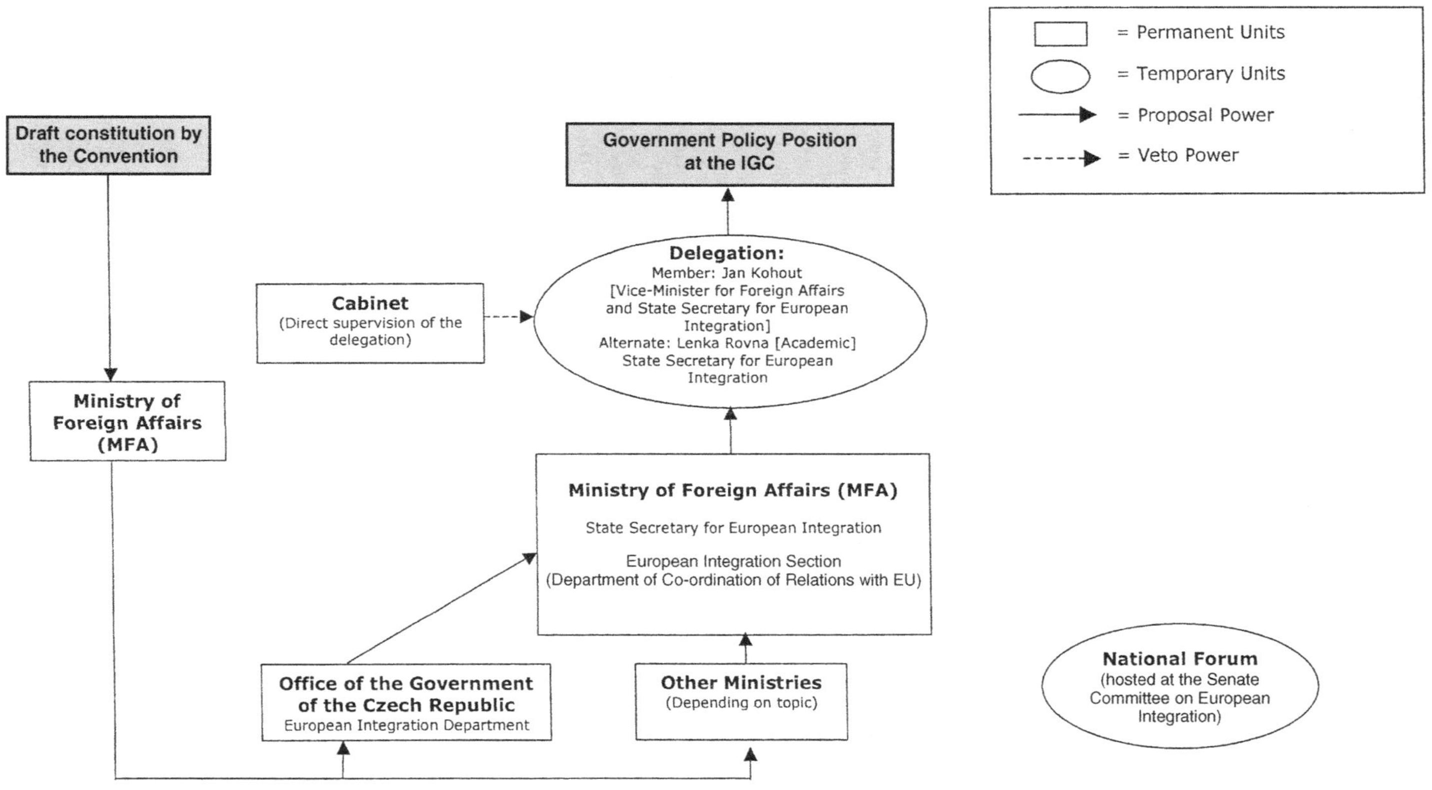

Figure 6.1 Czech Republic: domestic policy coordination for the IGC 2003–4.

Foreign Minister Svoboda). Third, he even invited members from both chambers of parliament as well as leaders from all major parties including the communists. This meeting was doomed, however, because of foreseeable, insurmountable differences between the government coalition and the communists (Král 2003b). The government strictly negated the president's responsibility in this area, and hence the ODS was not formally incorporated into the position formation process.

Data and empirical analysis of forming positions on the constitution for Europe

In the Czech Republic, two experts were interviewed in late November of 2003. Both of them are academics. One of them actually was a member of the delegation of the Czech government to the European Convention. The other had been working for one of the major think tanks that is well known for government consulting and is the author of an important publication in that field.

The main actors that had been identified by these interviewees were the government and the MFA[5] as well as the opposition party ODS and the National Forum.[6] This reflects the circumstance that the two prominent exponents of the ODS mentioned above managed to influence the public debate by their agitation.

In February 2003, the delegate of the government Jan Kohout presented a "Non-paper on the Reform of the EU Institutions" (Kohout 2003) that was the first policy paper outlining the position of the government in some detail. As an early reaction to the initiative by the French and Germans in January 2003 (Král 2003a), this contribution remained rather vague, however.

Whereas the "Non-paper" focused on the reform of the EU institutions, these had not been the only issues of importance to the Czech government. The KDU-CSL was eager to put the reference to the religious heritage on the agenda (*Ceska Tiskova Kancelar (CTK) and BBC Monitoring European*, 3 July 2003). Together with Austria, the Czech Republic initiated the group of 15 smaller countries criticizing the draft constitution (*Slovenska Tlacova Agentura*, 14 October 2003) and as a Visegrád member, it demanded a stronger reference to the Christian heritage in the preamble and expressed concerns against enhanced cooperation and that the voting rules of the Nice Treaty should be abandoned (*Neue Zürcher Zeitung*, 1 October 2003). Krotohvil (2003) mentions several additional topics like the incorporation of the Charter of Fundamental Rights, which he sees as being vital to the government coalition, further the role of national parliaments, the Common Foreign and Security Policy and the European Monetary Union. Zemanek (2003) mentions also the composition of the European Commission and transparency in decision making (notably the QMV rule), among others.

We did ask our experts about the "vital" issues and thus are able to weight the issues listed above. Not surprisingly, the issue that was raised by both experts was the number of commissioners. One expert mentioned also the QMV rule in the Council and the other the regulation of jurisdiction with respect to defense policy. All of these, except the mentioning of Christianity in the preamble, can be found in the above-mentioned list we have compiled from other sources.

Given the fact that the main conflict persisted between the government and its strongest counterpart, the strong ODS, most deviations should be found along this dividing line. If we compare the positions across the actors in the Czech Republic (Table 6.1), we are not able to find much variation. Deviations from the national position can only be found in 7.7 percent of the cases (issues), with 5.7 percent and 8.7 percent for the policy questions and the institutional questions respectively.

Not surprisingly, the opposition party ODS deviates most. Of the other actors, the think tanks and the government party ČSSD have a less integrationist position at only one point, related to the delegation of competencies regarding "research, technological development and space." All other deviations must be attributed to the ODS and they generally are less integrationist. This concerns the integration of the Charter of Fundamental Rights and the role of the national parliaments.

On four occasions, the ODS moves in the "more integration" direction: besides the preamble (reference to religious heritage), this is regarding such important institutional questions as the organization of the presidency of the European Council, the composition of the European Commission and the external representation of the EU. However, in many policy-related questions, the ODS is actually defending national sovereignty. Finally, it rejects majority voting in some policy fields (monetary policy, employment and social policy) and giving more power to the European Parliament in most areas.

Most important, the leading ministry (the MFA), deviates from the national position only once. It does so for the delegation of competencies in the field of "research, technological development and space," as is the case for the ČSSD and the think tanks. Therefore, this must be seen as a concession to the opposition, since the opposition did actually favor a more integrationist position in this area. However, the importance of the issue is only marginal.

Conclusion

To conclude, the position formation process in the Czech Republic cannot be judged to have been as representative as the one in Slovakia, for example. The parliament was not as strongly consulted by the government, which merely relied on traditional channels and also within the government administration merely on the MFA.

Table 6.1 Cohesiveness of actors' positions in the Czech coordination process

National position comparison	*Actor(s) (No. or type)*	*Observations (No.)*	*Deviations*									
			from national position		*on integration*				*related to*			
					toward less		*toward more*		*institutional issues*[a]		*policy fields*[a]	
			No.	*%*	*No.*	*%*	*No.*	*%*	*No.*	*%*	*No.*	*%*
All actors	4	260	20	7.7	16	6.2	4	1.5	15	8.7	5	5.7
Subset												
Lead unit	MFA	65	1	1.5	1	1.5	0	–	0	–	1	4.5

Deviations related to institutional issues
Subsidiarity (role of national parliaments); Presidency of the Council; Election/appointment of Council president; Number of commissioners; External representation of the EU (Foreign Minister); Voting rule (Council) for monetary policy, for social policy, for social security rights; Decision rule (EP) for structural and cohesion politics, for Area of Freedom, Security and Justice, for internal market, for monetary policy, for economic policy, for social policy, for social security rights

Deviations related to policy fields
Charter of Fundamental Rights; Religious reference in the preamble; Level of competence for research technological development and space

Vital interests
Qualified majority threshold; Number of commissioners; External policy

Notes
a Percentage shares refer to subsets of institutional (43) and policy (22) issues. *Lead Unit* Leading unit in domestic coordination: Prime Minister's Office (PM) or Ministry of Foreign Affairs (MFA).

Shortly after the last IGC, at the beginning of July 2004, Prime Minister Špidla had to resign because he lost the support of his party due to the landslide victory of the communists in the elections to the European Parliament. Although the political establishment agreed on a ratification of the constitutional treaty by popular referendum, the government and the ODS are still divided over the proper way to amend the constitution to allow for such a referendum. The trouble of the government with its new Prime Minister Gross and the prospect of having early elections bears the danger that the referendum will be abused for power struggles.

Acknowledgment

Our thanks go to Barbara Gähwiler, who was involved as an interviewer.

Notes

1 Taggart and Szcerbiak (2004) call the ODS one of the remaining major parties that represents *soft* Euro-skepticism, which is embodied in its foreign affairs spokesman Jan Zahradil. However, it seems that this "Euro-realistic" stance is not paying off any more, because of "the strong pro-EU membership views of Czech right wing voters" (Hanley 2002b: 8).

2 Article 39 (4) of the constitution requires a three-fifths majority in both chambers for ratification of international treaties. Article 10a holds that such an agreement shall be approved by parliament unless a *constitutional law requires approval from a referendum.* This means that the Czechs are not decided yet if there should be a *general* provision on referendums in the constitution or if it should be required to introduce an amendment of the constitution each time a referendum on a certain matter seems to be necessary. For the EU-accession referendum, a special amendment had been introduced and in the meantime, Prime Minister Špidla had announced to draft a constitutional amendment for a *general* referendum provision (*Ceska Tiskova Kancelar (CTK) Business News*, 7 October 2003), which would enable a referendum on the European constitution. For some time this issue seemed to be settled although the constitutional amendment is not decided at the time of writing.

3 The distribution of votes and seats in the most recent elections for parliament and the 2004 elections for the European Parliament, including the EP bloc affiliation of the parties, can be downloaded from the projects' website at dosei.dhv-speyer.de.

4 Klaus even planned to join the government at the IGC inaugural conference in October 2003 but in the end, refrained from doing so.

5 The higher-rated expert did not mention the foreign ministry explicitly in the first place. However, after checking up he confirmed that it actually should have been mentioned as a key player.

6 The second rated expert had given stronger pro-integration answers relative to the other expert. Besides the national position, the actors mentioned by both interviewees were the think tanks, the foreign ministry and the ODS. For the national position and the think tanks, expert coherence is not particularly high (0.84) but it is higher for the ODS (0.92). Thus, our experts were most in agreement with respect to the position of the opposition party, the ODS. It may be that the ODS's position had been communicated more effectively to the public.

The mean coherence (0.89) therefore is above the average (0.85). There are not many missing values and hence comparing the two experts should reveal a relatively clear picture: The highest agreement of our experts is in the area of "legal instruments" and high disagreement persists only for the general questions as well as the questions regarding the different policies, which, however, is usually the case also for other countries. Also, the only actor that had been mentioned by only one expert had been the ČSSD. But mentioning this actor was redundant, since its position did not deviate from the government position. Hence, we may conclude that we received a reasonably clear picture of the government position of the Czech Republic.

7 Denmark

The Nordic model as an effort to bridge elite Euro-optimism and popular Euro-skepticism

Hartmut Lenz and Han Dorussen[1]

In the 1992 referendum on the Maastricht Treaty, the Danes initially voted against the treaty. Following the successful negotiations for four exemptions – the so-called Danish opt-outs – the treaty was eventually accepted at the second attempt in 1993. The 1992 referendum was a watershed event in Denmark's EU membership. It has also clearly cast its shadow over the Danish attitude toward the EU constitution (Laursen 2003). The high threshold for ratification by parliament of any international treaty involving delegation of authority to a supranational organization – a five-sixth majority is required – makes a referendum nearly inevitable. Moreover, as the 1992 referendum revealed, broad support in parliament does not necessarily guarantee a popular mandate. Instead, the Danish public demonstrated its strong objections when a deepening of European integration impinges on the autonomy of the nation state (Taggart and Szcerbiak 2002).

The Danish delegation to the IGC 2003–4 was thus well aware that any deal on a future EU constitution only stands a chance to pass the Danish ratification hurdles if it meets several conditions. First of all, it requires broad support in parliament. Second, the Danish government had to retain its essential responsibilities. In particular, Danish exceptionalism codified in the "opt-outs" to the Maastricht Treaty had to be kept in place. A referendum on the EU constitution was planned for 27 September 2005, but the country postponed its referendum after the French and Dutch rejected the treaty.

Denmark (about 5.4 million inhabitants) has a modern market economy which is highly export-oriented. The service industry with 71 percent of GDP is its most important economic sector, while industry contributes 26 percent, and agriculture contributes 3 percent. Denmark is not a member of the EMU, but the Danish krona is pegged to the euro. Average economic growth between 1996 and 2003 was 2.1 percent but, reflecting the generally poor state of the European economy, growth in 2003 was only 1.1 percent. At 2.1 percent, the inflation rate on consumer prices is below the EU average. The Danish unemployment rate of 5.6 percent is also well below the EU average of 8 percent (Eurostat 2004).

Domestic structures in a comparative perspective

Denmark is a constitutional monarchy with a unicameral legislature. It consists of 14 counties including Greenland and the Faroe Islands.[2] The parliament, the *Folketing*, has 179 seats, including two seats for Greenland and two seats for the Faroe Islands. Members of parliament are elected by popular vote on the basis of proportional representation to serve a four-year term. Denmark joined the EEC in 1973.

After the most recent general election of February 2005, the incumbent minority government consisting of the Liberal Party, who provide the Prime Minister Anders Fogh Rasmussen, and the Conservative People's Party remained in power. Both governing parties as well as the Christian People's Party are pro-integrationist parties. The social democrats and social liberals are also generally in favor of integration, but contain skeptical minority groups. The Socialist People's Party and the Red–Green Unity List on the left and the Danish People's Party on the right are against further integration.[3]

Even though there is a comfortable majority in favor of European integration, the government does not always find it easy to attain political support on specific EU issues. The incumbent minority government relies on the support of some opposition parties on individual issues. On EU matters support has to come mainly from the Social Democratic Party, the largest opposition party, since the conservative Danish People's Party takes an outspoken anti-EU position. Moreover, ratification of an international treaty implying delegation of sovereignty to an international organization by parliament alone requires a five-sixths majority. Pro-EU parties control a maximum of 134 of the 146 seats needed for ratification by parliament. The government therefore depends on the outcome of a referendum for the ratification of the EU constitution (Gabel 2000).

The 2004 elections for the European Parliament provided a clear victory for the main opposition party, the Social Democrats. This result, however, should not be interpreted as either a pro- or anti-EU vote, but as opposition against the incumbent Liberal Party. However, opposition to European integration can be seen in the success of the June Movement and the People's Movement against the EU, who both gained one seat in the European Parliament (Ferrara and Weishaupt 2004).

Attitudes toward European integration are quite ambiguous in Denmark. A majority of Danish people appears to support economic integration as long as it does not affect the autonomy of the Danish state too much. The public supported four out of the five Danish referendums on EU matters – the first referendum on the Maastricht Treaty was the notable exception – but generally with a less than overwhelming majority (Siune and Svensson 1993). In contrast to the hesitation of the Danish population, its political leaders are more integrationist. Here, the exception to the pro-integrationist view was the ratification of SEA, where the conservative–liberal government failed to get a majority in parliament (Feldstein 1997). However, following a successful referendum, a sizable majority in parliament also favored the treaty (Petersen and Sjursen 1999).

Generally the Danish population is among the most Euro-skeptic. For example, a recent Eurobarometer poll shows that 29 percent of Danes were against the constitution (Eurobarometer 2004a). The political leaders are clearly in support of further EU integration. They are mainly concerned about maintaining the Danish opt-outs and, to some extent, the number of commissioners. The Danish government participated actively in the European Convention and the IGC 2003–4. Somewhat surprisingly, recent opinion polls show a clear majority in favor of the EU constitution. On 1 November 2004, a Catinet research poll showed 54 percent of voters in favor of the EU constitution (Catinet 2004), with only 17.4 percent against and 28.6 percent undecided. A Megafon survey (14 April 2005, Megafon 2005) for TV2 news showed that 49 percent of possible voters plan to support the constitution, with 32 percent against and 19 percent undecided.

Constitutional policy coordination

Formally, the most important actors involved in the national policy formation on the EU constitution are the government, the ministries, as well as parliament. The most significant feature of the Danish coordination process is that parliament has relatively tight control over the government's position on the IGC. The government and administrative procedures as well as the parliamentary procedures changed after the Maastricht Treaty, partly in response to demands for more transparency, and partly in response to the expanded agenda and increased majority voting in the EU (Thurner *et al.* 2002). The general outline of the formation process over the national position for the IGC 2003–4 in Denmark is visualized in Figure 7.1.

The Government's Presidency Committee, a non-standing body, collects initial policy positions as prepared by the relevant ministries. Here, proposals are discussed among experts of the ministry of foreign affairs (MFA), the relevant ministry and the key negotiator at the IGC. At this stage the European Affairs Committee, a standing body of parliament, has to be informed of all decisions made, and generally has to give its approval.

The responsibility for the IGC negotiations was mainly in the hands of the delegation sent to the final negotiation. However, the Danish government has the obligation to discuss positions with the European Affairs Committee. The parliamentary committee thus also keeps track of the negotiations itself, and the delegation remained in very close contact with the committee throughout the entire IGC.

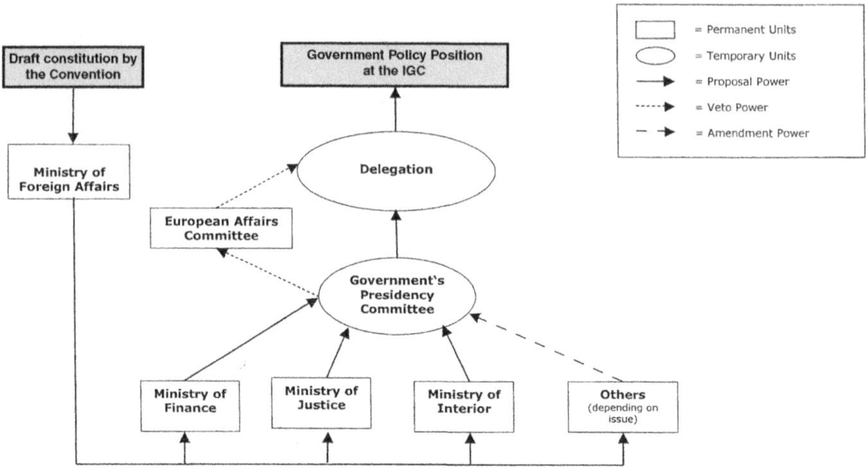

Figure 7.1 Denmark: domestic policy coordination for the IGC 2003–4.

The deep involvement of the parliament in the policy formation process is important for several reasons. First of all, it facilitates approval by parliament. The committee has already provided input prior to the actual negotiations, and therefore has been actively involved in the decision formation process. Second, since the mandate of the European Affairs Committee is binding, it gives the government stronger credibility at intergovernmental negotiations (Putnam 1988).

Participants perceive two major deficiencies in the organization of government–parliament relations on EU matters. First, the government's representative appears before the committee relatively late in the policy cycle. Second, the government provides primarily issue-specific information. In order to lessen the monopoly of the government on information, the committee also relies on outside sources of information. One such source of information is the close cooperation between the European Affairs Committee and the European Parliament, especially the Danish members. Other sources are various databases and documentation from other parliamentary bodies dealing with European affairs, notably those in other Nordic member states.

Data and empirical analysis of forming positions on the EU constitution

The empirical section relies on the interviews with experts held as part of the DOSEI project. The interviews took place between November and December 2003, just before the IGC 2003–4. The three experts who were interviewed were from slightly different backgrounds but all worked very closely with the government on the domestic decision-making process. To measure how closely the positions of the experts correlate, we calculated the coherence between their answers. The mean adapted coherence of the experts' answers is just slightly below mean adapted coherence in the DOSEI project.[4] Therefore we are confident that the information given by the experts is a reliable source.

The Danish position formation on the EU constitution has been quite transparent, since most issues are openly discussed in the European Affairs Committee, and we found only minor variations in the answers of the different experts. Apart from the government, the experts point out parliament as a key actor in shaping policy positions. Since the European Affairs Committee has indeed a quite powerful position in the policy formation process, this is not surprising. One of the experts also mentioned the ministry of finance as a third key actor. Its influence on the government was limited mainly to economic issues and issues of taxation.

The Danish opt-outs, concerning the EMU, defense, citizenship, and justice and home affairs, summarize the key issues for the Danish government. The government insisted on keeping the current status for Denmark on the opt-outs, and it publicly emphasized its independence on asylum and migration policies. It was more willing to compromise on other issues. Even though concerned about its envisioned number of commissioners – like most of the smaller countries, Denmark prefers one commissioner per member state – the Danish government supported the draft constitution at the IGC.

An overview of disputed issues is given in Table 7.1. Comparing the national position with the ideal policy positions of all actors, deviations toward less integration match the deviations toward more integration. However, both are low at 8.5 percent. Deviations on institutional issues are relatively low (9.3 percent) as well, whereas the deviation on political issues is considerably higher (31.8 percent). In Denmark, the foreign ministry is the leading unit in domestic coordination. We found that the MFA was somewhat more likely to prefer less integration than agreed upon in the national position. The MFA was also more likely to deviate on policy issues, compared to the other actors.

The Danish parliament held a different view on the issue of subsidiarity. The government's position was that the national parliament should monitor the division of competence, via a "subsidiarity early warning system." Parliament tended more to the opinion that national parliaments should have the right to veto a legislative proposal from the Commission. The qualified majority threshold in the Council was a further area of dispute. While the government was in favor of a simple majority of member states and three-fifths of the population, parliament preferred the solution of the Nice Treaty. The third most vivid issue of dispute was how much competence on policy areas should be given to the EU level. The government preferred the EU level in the issues of employment,

Table 7.1 Cohesiveness of actors' positions in the Danish coordination process

National position comparison	*Actor(s) (No. or type)*	*Observations (No.)*	*Deviations*									
			from national position		*on integration*				*related to*			
					toward less		*toward more*		*institutional issues*[a]		*policy fields*[a]	
			No.	*%*	*No.*	*%*	*No.*	*%*	*No.*	*%*	*No.*	*%*
All actors	2	130	22	16.9	11	8.5	11	8.5	8	9.3	14	13.8
Subset												
Lead unit	MFA	65	15	23.1	9	13.8	6	9.2	6	14.0	9	40.9

Deviations related to institutional issues
Subsidiarity (role of national parliaments); Right to withdraw from the Union; QMV threshold; External representation of the EU (Foreign Minister); ECJ jurisdiction; Enhanced cooperation; Rights of EP in the adoption of the budget

Deviations related to policy fields
Economic objectives: kind of market economy, employment; Level of competence for agriculture, for the Area of Freedom, Security and Justice, for foreign policy, for economic policy, for employment policy, for social policy, for health policy, for environment policy; Stability and Growth Pact; External borders

Vital interests
Role of national parliaments in monitoring the principle of subsidiarity; Number of commissioners; Council voting rule for immigration policy; Danish opt-outs

Notes

a Percentage shares refer to subsets of institutional (43) and policy (22) issues. *Lead Unit* Leading unit in domestic coordination: Prime Minister's Office (PM) or Ministry of Foreign Affairs (MFA).

social policy and health. In these issues, however, parliament was more in favor of a lower level of policy competence. Especially the center-right parties stressed the latter point. The ministry of finance disagreed with the government's position on the issue of tax harmonization. The ministry of finance definitely wanted to keep the national veto right on this issue, whereas the government was willing to accept qualified majority voting.

Conclusion

In the case of Denmark, we see a strong pro-European position of the government, whereas the general public is more critical of the process. Our research shows a high level of internal agreement of the political actors on the majority of policy positions. In this sense, it is meaningful to speak of the Danish *national* position on the EU constitution. However, this does not imply that domestic politics is unimportant in Denmark; quite the contrary. The government is acutely aware of the need of parliamentary and *public* approval to get any agreement ratified. Following the ratification problems of the Maastricht Treaty, parliament has acquired a powerful committee role in dealing with EU matters in 1994, which has made it easier to attain parliamentary approval.

The objective was also to make the policy process more public and less dominated by specialists, since it is nearly impossible for the Danish government to avoid a referendum on an international treaty related to the EU because of the five-sixths majority required in parliament. Broad parliamentary support for a treaty is thus not an alternative to a referendum but complementary to increasing the chances of ratification by referendum but the country indefinitely postponed its planned referendum after France and the Netherlands rejected the constitution.

The key issues for the government and parliament were to retain the opt-outs – gained in renegotiating the Maastricht Treaty – especially national independence on migration and asylum policies. The prioritization of these issues has been clearly influenced by the expectation that these issues also matter most for the general public. Concerns about its Euro-skeptic public have motivated the Danish government to give its domestic audience the impression of having successfully defended national interests throughout the negotiations on the EU constitution.

A referendum was planned to take place on 27 September 2005, but was postponed after the EU leaders agreed on a "period of reflection" after the failed referendums in France and the Netherlands. Nevertheless, opinion polls suggest that the Danish public is likely to support it. In parliament pro-EU parties have a clear majority and it is certain that parliament will support the constitution. We expect therefore that Denmark will support the EU constitution.

Notes

1 Equal authorship.
2 Greenland (since 1979) and the Faroe Islands (since 1943) are self-governing administrative divisions.
3 The distribution of votes and seats in the most recent elections for parliament and the 2004 elections for the European Parliament, including the EP bloc affiliation of the parties, can be downloaded from the projects' website at dosei.dhv-speyer.de.
4 The mean adapted coherence of the experts' answers for the national position equals 0.84 and for parliament 0.73. In both cases, this is slightly below the mean adapted coherence for all experts and actors in the DOSEI project (0.85). The coherence on the position of the ministry of finance has not been calculated since just one expert named it as relevant. See Appendix 2.

8 Estonia

A single voice in Europe's intergovernmental bargaining

Daniel Finke

Together with the other nine candidate member states Estonia got a fair and, in the history of EU integration, uncommon chance: It was invited to participate in the reform of the Union's political system before becoming a full-fledged member. In a referendum held in September 2003, 67 percent of Estonians voted for membership (64 percent turnout) (Toots and Vetik 2004).[1] By that time the Convention on the Future of Europe had already completed its work, and the IGC organized by the Italian presidency had already begun.

With this backdrop, an overwhelming majority of the Estonian parliament ratified the constitution in May 2006. Although the Estonian constitution foresees binding referendums for several occasions, Article 106 explicitly excludes a binding referendum for international treaties. None the less a facultative, non-binding referendum would have been possible, but the majority of the country's parties supported the government's position (*EUbusiness*, 22 April 2005). The government argued that when the Estonian accession referendum was held in September 2003, the result of the Convention and the prospect of an IGC were already known. Neither of the major parties has expressed any significant concerns about the constitution, although many of them can be characterized as mildly Euroskeptic.[2]

The Estonian public appears to have relatively little knowledge about the constitution. A recent poll showed that 36 percent of Estonians had not even heard of the constitutional treaty, 4 percent considered themselves "informed" of the contents of the constitution, 21 percent said to have knowledge "to some degree," and 37 percent had heard of it but did not know its content (Emor 2005). The Eurobarometer survey carried out in early 2005 revealed that 32 percent were in favor of the constitution, while only 11 percent opposed it (Eurobarometer 2005).

The Estonians' attitude toward the EU can only be understood in light of the country's Soviet history. Many Estonians see the EU both as an opportunity to strengthen their independence from Russia and as a potential threat of new foreign rule. The first point of view is emphasized by the prospective net benefits Estonia will receive from the EU.

Calculations by the EU Commission and the German federal ministry of finance predict that Estonia will receive approximately €680 million in the 2004–6 period (*Die Zeit*, 11 March 2004). Recent political conflicts between the Commission and the Estonian government were marked by criticism of the country's naturalization law (Ehin 2003a), which is the direct result of Russian domination during the Soviet era and the many Russians still living in Estonia (roughly 30 percent of the population), and on the other hand the economic infrastructure is still underdeveloped.

This chapter presents Estonia's position at the IGC and the way in which the government coordinated the few diverging positions between government and parliament. It demonstrates the high degree of consensus within the government as well as between the government and parliament.

Domestic structures in a comparative perspective

Estonia is still in a process of consolidation. As in other Baltic states, left-wing parties are still comparatively weak because they are associated with the former Communist Party (Lagerspetz and Mayer 2004: 89). In the general elections in March 2003, six out of the 12 parties that ran for office obtained seats in parliament. The party system is still changing, as is the voting behavior of Estonians. In general, the number of parties decreased during the 1990s (Roberts 2003: 4).

Since the 2003 general election (58.7 percent turnout), a right-centrist coalition of Res Publica, Reform Party and People's Union has governed the country (Mikkel 2003).[3] On 24 March 2005 Prime Minister Juhan Parts announced his resignation following a vote of no confidence in the Estonian parliament, the *Riigikogu*, against Minister of Justice Ken-Marti Vaher. At the end of 2004, the government nominated the conservative Siim Kallas as future commissioner. During the 1990s, the government was supported by either a minimum winning coalition or a single party 34.3 percent of the time (Blondel and Müller-Rommel 2001): roughly comparable to Germany in this period (Roberts 2003: 9).

Both Lennart Meri, who was Estonia's president from 1992 to 2001 and became the country's representative to the European Convention thereafter, and the current President Arnold Rüütel enjoy a high level of popularity. However, their office only fulfills a representative function. Estonia's political system is purely parliamentary with only one chamber, the *Riigikogu* (Roberts 2003: 7, Lagerspetz and Mayer 2004: 74). As is typical for transition democracies, the average duration of the government is with 1.34 years comparably low (ibid.).

Organized interests in the form of NGOs or trade unions, although still weak, are growing in importance, as may be observed in several young Central and Eastern European democracies (Ismayr 2004). Civil society is developing slowly due to the still uncomfortable economic conditions. The unions' position in the political system is designed to result in a low level of co-decision (Roberts 2003: 10, Lagerspetz and Mayer 2004: 84).

Although marked by a slightly lower unemployment rate than in the other Baltic states (10.1 percent in 2004), wealth is distributed highly unevenly in Estonia (Toots and Vetik 2004, Eurostat 2004).[4] The present government, and its predecessors, claim that the constant growth rates between 4 percent and 7 percent are a consequence of this liberal economic course. In any event, the recent growth rates are only slowly compensating for the losses of the drastic recession between 1990 and 1995 (negative growth rates down to −15 percent) (Dauderstädt 2004: 19). Divided by sectors in 2002, about 6.9 percent of employees work in the agricultural sector (slightly more than on EU average), 31.2 percent are employed in the industrial and 62 percent in the service sector (Eurostat 2004).

Constitutional policy coordination

In general the Estonian EU policy-making process is characterized by a small number of elites actively involved in the debate (Ehin 2003b). This small community appears to be networking across institutions and party borders. Although the liberal stance in economic policy appears to be particularly emphasized by the right-wing government, there is almost no discernible difference between the major parties on EU affairs (ibid.).

The coordination structure of the Estonian EU policy making is headed by the prime minister, who is advised by the EU Secretariat. All ministries work closely and flexible together on policy matters of their concern. Senior civil servants meet on a weekly basis to coordinate their position. The EU Affairs Committee of the parliament monitors the coordination process and must be involved in all matters that could result in domestic legislative changes. The ministry of foreign affairs (MFA) coordinates the positions at the level of COREPER.[5]

Domestic coordination during the European Convention is a slightly modified mirror image of this general EU policy coordination: Mr Hendrik Holelei, now the head of the Estonian EU Secretariat, and former president, Mr Lennart Meri, have been the Estonian representatives. The position that they presented at the Convention was conceived in a process headed and coordinated by the EU Secretariat which belonged to the state chancellery (office of the prime minister). They provided the ministries (most notably the MFA and the ministry of financial and economic affairs (MFE)) and the *Riigikogu* (here particularly the committee for EU affairs) with the latest information on the Convention. The public did not actively participate in the domestic coordination process during the European Convention, and neither did the few emerging NGOs or the trade unions.

Although the basic actors (institutions and people) remained the same, the domestic coordination process changed for the IGC. The MFA took the lead and informed the inter-ministerial working group (IMWG) including representatives of the EU Secretariat as well as the *Riigikogu* of the latest negotiations at the IGC. The working group was headed by the MFA and coordinated the positions of the *Riigikogu* and the government. During the negotiations at the IGC the delegates had to act in the shadow of the necessary ratification of the constitution by the parliament, which therefore became involved via the IMWG.

For the usual EU policy coordination the informal proposal and amendment power heavily depends on the policy field, which the EU Secretariat at the state chancellery most likely has an informal veto position on highly salient issues. With regard to the coordination process during the European Convention the same holds true as far as amendment is concerned. The proposal and veto powers were certainly more concentrated at the EU Secretariat. This is a consequence of the fact that instead of various policy directives a single package on institutional issues had to be negotiated. During the 2003–4 IGC the MFA got more proposal power and the EU Affairs Committee's veto power was formalized.

In any case, the discussion about the impact domestic actors in Estonia had on the final national position (NP) has to be qualified by (1) the high degree of interest homogeneity between the actors and (2) the small number of institutional actors and persons involved in the coordination process.

Data and empirical analysis of forming positions on the constitution for Europe

Two interviews with experts were conducted in mid-December 2003 in Tallinn. The interviewees were civil servants of the MFA and the EU Affairs Committee in *Riigikogu*, who both were heavily involved in the domestic and international coordination/negotiation process leading to the constitution as adopted under the Irish presidency in June 2004. Asked for the relevant domestic actors in the coordination process the two experts boiled the list of possible actors as displayed in Figure 8.1 down to three: the ministry of foreign affairs (MFA), the *Riigikogu* and the ministry of finance (MFE).

Considering the structure of domestic coordination it is not surprising that both experts mentioned the MFA as a relevant actor. The parliament was added by the expert working for the EU Affairs Committee. The ministry of finance was regarded as relevant by the civil servant in the MFA, although both ministries held completely identical positions on all issues. In general the high degree of interest homogeneity (see below) between the actors imposed a major problem for identifying additional relevant actors.[6]

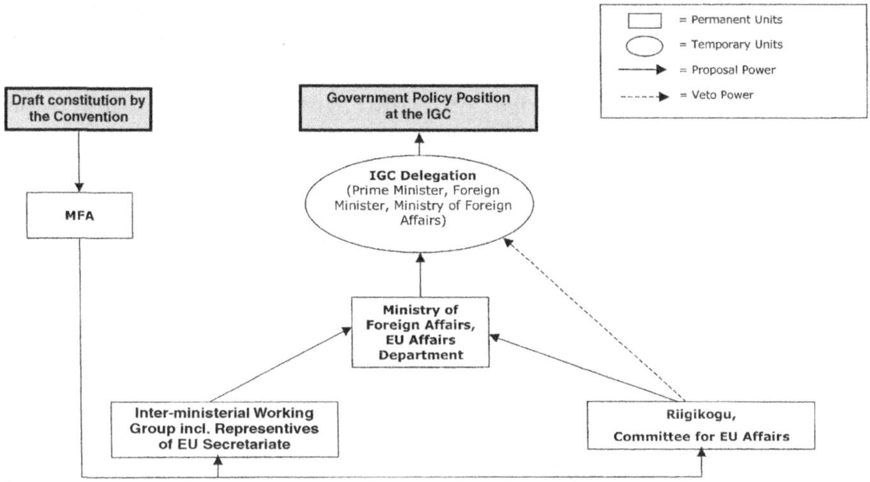

Figure 8.1 Estonia: domestic policy coordination for the IGC 2003–4.

The fundamental aspects of the Estonian positions in the constitutional debate, as revealed by the interviews, are reflected in the joint position paper of the small states that was presented to the Convention on 28 March 2003. "The main principles of the document include preserving and strengthening the Community Method, maintaining the existing institutional balance, and ensuring the equality of all member states" (Ehin and Veebel 2003: 41). This, for example, is reflected in the issue concerning the composition of the Commission (one commissioner per member state) or the presidency of the Council (rotating). Ehin and Veebel (2003) note that these positions often reveal a conflict of goals with respect to the government's demands for effective decision making which were raised by the Estonian government (ibid.: 45). The same criticism was mentioned by the parliamentary expert.

With regard to the policy fields, tax policy was of vital interest to the Estonian government because its low income taxes are one of the country's most important comparative advantages. Additionally, border control was of obvious salience, as it is in all future member states having an external eastern border.

As mentioned earlier, the Estonian case reveals a comparably high homogeneity of interests across the relevant domestic actors: On average about 1.21 positions were held per question by the three different actors. This equates to approximately 84.1 percent agreement. This number was slightly higher for substantial issues (18.2 percent) than for institutional issues (14.7 percent).

The interpretation of the domestic debate is comparably easy. The most important debate took place between the parliament and the government. This included a whole range of institutional issues: Council presidency, majority voting threshold, appointment of a Foreign Minister and Commission president, subsidiarity, right of initiative for citizens, decision rule on economic and structural policies and the European Parliament's position in the budget procedure. Interestingly this dimension of the domestic debate is basically characterized by the same bundle of institutional questions that described the distance between the parliament and government in Lithuania (in addition to the issue on the EP position in the budget procedure).

The national position is surprisingly close to the parliamentary position on most of the debated issues. This explains the government's comparably high number of deviations from the national position (21.5 percent: see Table 8.1). Counting the actors' deviations from the national position underlines this picture: The two ministries deviate from the national position on 14 questions and from the parliament on 13 questions, while the parliament deviates from the national position on only three questions.

This leads to the most surprising observation revealed by the DOSEI interviews. Within the rather limited existing conflict between parliament and the two ministries, the national position appears to be dominated by the preferences of the former actor. We can think of two possible explanations for this finding:

1 The government must formulate a position emphasizing national sovereignty in institutional questions, due to public pressure manifested via the parliament, even though it may believe that this position is unrealistic, and thus the government may retain a different position for itself. This explains the interest configuration for issues like enhanced cooperation and the majority voting rule, on which the parliament revealed a slightly less integrationist position than the government.
2 The parliament might be closer to the feasible international solution, and therefore the government adopts this as its national position, recognizing that its own position will be outvoted in both the international and domestic arenas. This might be more likely for issues like subsidiarity, the court of justice and the right of initiative.

Taking both possible explanations into account we end up with the typical ambiguity of a two-level analysis. It remains a challenge for future research to understand the impacts of either the domestic public or the international negotiation environment on the strategic formulation of the national negotiation position (König and Finke 2005).

Conclusion

This chapter began by embedding the Estonian government's decision not to hold a referendum in its unique historical and political context. It

Table 8.1 Cohesiveness of actors' positions in the Estonian coordination process

National position comparison	*Actor(s) (No. or type)*	*Observations (No.)*	*Deviations*									
			from national position		*on integration*				*related to*			
					toward less		*toward more*		*institutional issues*[a]		*policy fields*[a]	
			No.	*%*	*No.*	*%*	*No.*	*%*	*No.*	*%*	*No.*	*%*
All actors	3	195	31	15.9	14	7.2	17	8.7	19	14.7	12	18.2
Subset												
Lead unit	MFA	65	14	21.5	6	9.2	8	12.3	8	18.6	6	27.3

Deviations related to institutional issues
Subsidiarity (role of national parliaments); Presidency of the Council; QMV threshold; Appointment of commissioners; External representation of the EU (Foreign Minister); Appointment of Foreign Minister; Legislative initiative for citizens; Voting rule (Council) for Area of Freedom, Security and Justice, for internal market; Rights of EP in the adoption of the budget

Deviations related to policy fields
Economic objectives: kind of market economy, employment; Level of competence for structural and cohesion politics, for foreign policy, for economic policy for research, technological development and space

Vital interests
Qualified majority threshold
Number of commissioners
Regulation of jurisdiction with respect to tax harmonization; Voting rule (Council) for taxes

Notes
a Percentage shares refer to subsets of institutional (43) and policy (22) issues. *Lead Unit* Leading unit in domestic coordination: Prime Minister's Office (PM) or Ministry of Foreign Affairs (MFA).

demonstrated that some of the major institutions, the coordination style and the domestic debate adapted in EU policy making resemble those found in Finland and other small Baltic states. An obvious, though easy to explain, difference is the lower level of participation by interest groups and other parts of the developing civil society. For this reason and due to the country's small size and the homogeneous composition of the political elite, the positions held during the domestic debate on the EU's future are rather homogeneous.

The subsequent detailed analysis of the Estonian domestic policy coordination prior to and during the IGC 2003–4 revealed the following insights:

1 There exists a low level of conflict and interest heterogeneity between the domestic actors. Given the challenges of a country that is still in transition, the common interest of all actors is well defined.
2 The coordination process is highly structured, and there exist virtually no disputes within the government. The debate is carried out within a comparably small elite that additionally enhances the consistency and homogeneity of positions.
3 The only interest difference is found between the parliament and the MFA, although this difference is relatively small when compared to other countries. The parliament obtained its position as the national position for most of the issues.

Notes

1 Low support rates for EU membership characterized the debate in 2002 and 2003, but especially noticeable was a high level of indifference with regard to whether or not Estonia would benefit from EU membership (Ehin 2003b: 97).
2 According to Taggart and Szczerbiak (2004), six of the Estonian parties running for the 1999 elections can be characterized as Euro-skeptic, but the two mildly Euro-skeptic parties (Centre Party and Estonian Rural People's Party) gained the vast majority of Euro-skeptics' votes (30.68 percent of 33.1 percent).
3 The distribution of votes and seats in the most recent elections for parliament and the 2004 elections for the European Parliament, including the EP bloc affiliation of the parties, can be downloaded from the projects' website at dosei.dhv-speyer.de.
4 Gini coefficient: 0.37 for 2002 (IIES 2004).
5 Source: Estonian ministry of foreign affairs. Online. Available at: www.vm.ee/eng (accessed 12 October 2004).
6 The two expert interviews revealed about 66 percent agreement on the MFA and official national position as held during the IGC. Modifying the expert coherence with respect to the number of experts interviewed allows us to compare the adapted coherence of about 0.92 to the mean coherence across all countries in the DOSEI data set, which is slightly lower (0.85; see Appendix 2).

9 Finland

Centralized consensus on EU constitution building

Daniel Finke and Thomas König

Finland joined the EU in 1995. Membership was only opposed by farmers and the rural population who believed that the accession would threaten their sources of livelihood (Tiilikainen 2003: 150). Their fears are reflected in the accession protocol that grants special EU support to Finnish rural communities. Overall, Finland's financial relation with the EU is balanced (Auffermann 2003). Finnish public support to EU membership has remained relatively constant over time, varying between 55 percent and 60 percent. Eurobarometer polls show that 57 percent of the Finns support widening and deepening the EU (Eurobarometer 2003a). Successful parliamentary ratification of the constitutional text – although postponed due to the EU's "reflection period" – is highly likely. Traditional Euro-skeptic parties are the Green Party (Agrarian) (8.0 percent), the Leftist Alliance (9.9 percent) and the Christian League (5.3 percent) (Taggart 1998).

During the mid-1990s Finland experienced a rapid change, developing from an economy with a large primary sector at the north-eastern frontier of Cold War Europe to one of the world's leading economies in the high-tech sector. After a crisis in the early 1990s the Finnish economy annually grew by 6.3 percent since 1996. In spite of the worldwide recession Finland had still a moderate growth rate of 1.9 percent but increasing unemployment to 9.0 percent (Eurostat 2004).

The end of the Cold War had a decisive political impact on Finland. After the breakdown of the Soviet Union, Finland reformed the constitution in 1992–5, the first constitutional reform since 1919 (Auffermann 2003: 97 ff.). The majority requirements for legislation in the *Eduskunta* have been lowered to simple majority,[1] and nowadays the president is popularly elected (König and Bräuninger 1999, Mattila 1997).

Domestic structures in a comparative perspective

Finland is often called a consensus democracy with a strong president (semi-presidentialism).[2] The high number of political parties in parliament[3] is mirrored in the effective number of parties (ENP)[4] of 5.03

(Roberts 2003: 3). Before the constitutional reform the government was rarely built on a minimum winning coalition or a single party (12.8 percent of the time) (König and Bräuninger 1999: 43, Mattila 1997: 331). Governments were usually composed of a grand coalition including the major moderate right and left parties (Auffermann 2003). This tradition of oversized coalition building continued after the reform. Although the Social Democratic Party (SDP) and the Center Party (KESK) won 108 of the 200 seats in 2003, the Swedish People's Party (RKP) is included, with two ministers in the new government. The reformed constitution also strengthens the parliament, but the president remains powerful in many legislative areas (Nouisianen 2003).[5]

The Finnish electoral voting system is a pure proportional representation (PR) system (Roberts 2003: 9) which leads to comparatively low disproportionality in the representation of votes[6] (Lijphart 1999). Following the 2003 election the rainbow coalition[7] led by the Paavo Lipponen (SDP) has been replaced by a coalition of SDP (24.5 percent), KESK (24.7 percent) and RKP (4.6 percent) with Prime Minister Matti Vanhanen (KESK). Constitutional amendments usually require a simple majority in parliament which must be approved by a two-thirds majority in the new parliament after the following elections. For matters of urgency a five-sixths majority provide for a two-thirds majority decision (without waiting until the next general elections; Auffermann 2003: 205). A consultative referendum on the EU constitution is possible, but not necessary.[8] Typical for Scandinavian countries, the various Finnish interests are highly organized and incorporated in the legislative process (Auffermann 2003: 211 f.). After EU accession in 1995 many of these interest groups were also concerned about EU affairs. During the Convention and the following IGC they organized on nationwide NGO forum (Tiilikainen 2003: 168 f.).

Constitutional policy coordination

The key players in Finnish EU politics are the parliament (the Grand Committee of the *Eduskunta*), the president, the government (especially the prime minister's office, the Cabinet Committee on EU Affairs, Committee for EU Affairs) and via the government secretariat for EU affairs which heads the section meeting across all ministries, the entire government. The EU Secretariat was transferred from the MFA to the prime minister's office in July 2000. Its main task is to scrutinize EU affairs and prepare the Council meetings dealing with institutional questions.

In general the responsibility for the preparation and monitoring of EU-related affairs rests within the respective ministries. The ministers meet with the prime minister and the president (Council of the State) if no solution can be made at lower hierarchical levels. In addition, many NGOs are invited to participate in the governmental section meetings. The role of parliament in EU matters is especially important: the constitution requires parliamentary approval before international negotiations may be concluded (Tiilikainen 2003).[9]

The domestic coordination process that led to the Finnish national position on the issues discussed at the Convention and in preparation for the IGC 2003–4 followed the general structure described above. It has been characterized by a modestly more centralized coordination between the governmental organizations, the Grand Committee of the parliament and the Convention delegates: the prime minister's office set the agenda for the institutional affairs section where all 13 ministries were represented as well as representatives from the Aaland Islands. Issues discussed at this level were forwarded to the Cabinet Committee on EU affairs which met on a weekly basis, chaired by the prime minister. Before the matters were finally handed over to the Convention delegates, the Grand Committee of the Finnish parliament could modify the positions.

This coordination structure suggests that the prime minister's office (including the EU Secretariat) and the parliament via the grand committee had veto power. While usually the power to propose rests within the respective ministry, agenda-setting for the summit negotiations was done by the prime minister's office. All actors could amend the proposed positions.

Data and empirical analysis of forming positions on the constitution for Europe

For the study of the domestic coordination process, four interviews with experts have been carried out in Helsinki during December 2003. Two of the interviewed experts were senior civil servants working for the EU

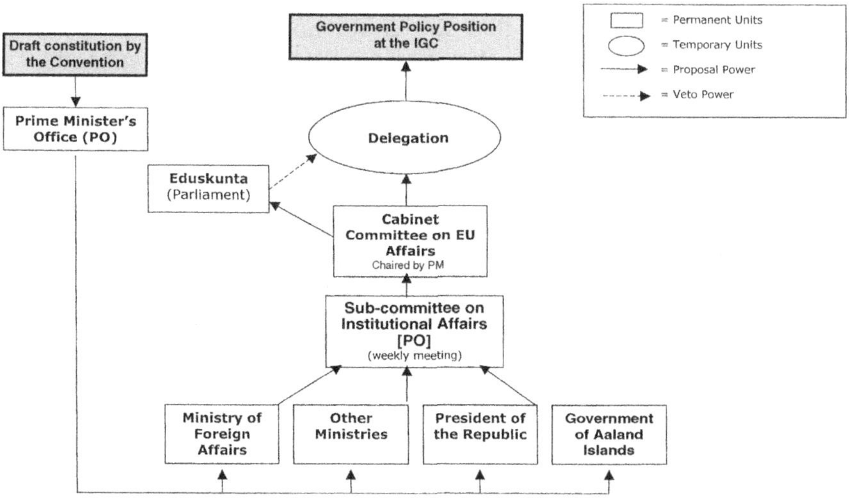

Figure 9.1 Finland: domestic policy coordination for the IGC 2003–4.

Secretariat and the EU Grand Committee. The other two were independent academics, one of them used to participate actively in EU-related negotiations.

Of all the actors involved in the coordination process the experts indicated four as particularly relevant: the prime minister's office, the *Eduskunta*, the MFA and the President of the Republic. While the first three were mentioned by all four experts, the latter two were only indicated by one each. Except for the president all of these actors held prominent positions according to the formal coordination chart.[10]

The most contested issues are listed in the joint position paper of the small states presented to the Convention on 28 March 2003. "The main principles of the document include preserving and strengthening the Community Method, maintaining the existing institutional balance, and ensuring the equality of all member states" (Ehin and Veebel 2003: 41). According to the interviewees this concerns the number of commissioners and the presidency of the Council. The Finnish government furthermore stressed the importance to revise the conventional text with respect to the structured cooperation in the field of defense and development of military capabilities (Secretariat for EU Affairs 2003: 1). Finland did not support the office of a EU Foreign Minister. Apart from this, the exceptions granted to Finland in the accession treaty should remain in place. In addition to the financial support to the certain rural regions in the Finnish periphery this referred to the special status of the Aaland Islands, which are governed by home rule.

As a general notion the Finnish government is very much pro-Europe and in favor of a constitution. Most of the topics mentioned above are either undisputed internationally or not salient enough to become a reason for the Finnish government to block a possible agreement. One of the interviewed experts said that she could not even imagine an issue which would lead to a credible threat of the Finnish government to block the adoption of the constitution.

Our results confirm this view: the average actor deviated only on 15 percent of the issues from the national position. The average percentage of deviating positions mentioned for policy-related questions is slightly higher (21.6 percent) than for institutional (11.6 percent) issues. The domestic debate has been characterized by moderate differences between either the government (MFA and prime minister's office) and the parliament and/or the government and the president. The issues on which the president held different positions from those of the government include a whole range of institutional questions, i.e., the right of withdrawal from the EU, Council presidency, appointment of commissioners, right of initiative, division of competencies in the fields of foreign, tax, health and environmental policies as well as the decision rule in the field of economic and security policies.

The dissimilarities between parliament and government concern

Table 9.1 Cohesiveness of actors' positions in the Finnish coordination process

National position comparison	*Actor(s) (No. or type)*	*Observations (No.)*	*Deviations*									
			from national position		*on integration*				*related to*			
					toward less		*toward more*		*institutional issues*[a]		*policy fields*[a]	
			No.	*%*	*No.*	*%*	*No.*	*%*	*No.*	*%*	*No.*	*%*
All actors	4	260	39	15.0	21	8.1	18	6.9	20	11.6	19	21.6
Subset												
Lead unit	PM	65	0	–	0	–	0	–	0	–	0	–

Deviations related to institutional issues
Right to withdraw from the Union; Appointment of commissioners; External representation of the EU; Legislative initiative for national parliaments, and for citizens; Voting rule (Council) for Area of Freedom, Security and Justice, for internal market, for monetary policy, for economic policy, for social policy, for social security rights, for foreign policy; Decision rule (EP) for economic policy, for social security rights; Rights of EP in the adoption of the budget

Deviations related to policy fields
Religious reference; Economic objectives: employment; Level of competence for structural and cohesion politics, for the Area of Freedom, Security and Justice, for foreign policy, for tax harmonization, for health policy, for environment policy; Stability and Growth Pact; Defense; External borders; Migration and asylum

Vital interests
Presidency in the Council; Number of commissioners; External policy/structured cooperation in defense; Council voting rule for Common Security and Defense Policy; Finnish Accession Treaty

Notes
a Percentage shares refer to subsets of institutional (43) and policy (22) issues. *Lead Unit* Leading unit in domestic coordination: Prime Minister's Office (PM) or Ministry of Foreign Affairs (MFA).

institutional issues as well as certain policy fields, including AFSJ, external borders, migration, foreign minister and the voting rules on monetary and social policy. Both sides included a couple of issues considered as vital in the Finnish debate, in particular the presidency of the European Council, the number of commissioners, etc.

The governmental positions were more "integrationist" than those of both other actors. One possible explanation is that the president and the parliament are more closely linked to the public, while the government has to face the power constellations at the summit and to make strategic but realistic proposals. Noteworthy exceptions were the issues of external border management and a possible common migration and asylum policy. On these two topics the parliament held a slightly less integrationist position than the government.

Due to the parliament's position, the crucial topics of the domestic debate were AFSJ, external borders, migration, foreign minister and the voting rules on monetary and social policy. Most of the issues in which either the president or the parliament or both held a different position than the government were of public interest. This demonstrates that these actors' major power resource is their stronger direct link to the public. The same holds true for the various topics on which the president and parliament had diverging opinions: migration and asylum, external representation of the Union, right to withdraw from the union and religious reference in the preamble.

The national position is identical to that of the governmental actors, which is – considering the coordination process – not surprising. These findings are confirmed at the level of particular questions: the positions on each issue for the MFA, the national position and the prime minister's office are identical, but the parliament deviates on 21 and the president on 18 issues from the national position. Nevertheless, with respect to the strong position of the parliament we would have expected less distance between the *Eduskunta* and the NP. This suggests that the MFA was more powerful either due to the international constellation or its extraordinary central position in the domestic coordination process. An indication in line with the former interpretation was the surprising shift of the Finnish MFA toward backing more possible cooperation in the area of foreign and security policy at the ministerial conclave in October 2003.

An example for the MFA's ability to anticipate and accept different domestic actors' positions early in the coordination process is shown by the inclusion of a binding charter of fundamental rights: While the MFA as well as the prime minister's office opposed this idea when the Convention had started, they accepted it later on, recognizing the will of the *Eduskunta* and several NGOs as well as the positions held by other delegates to the Convention.

Conclusion

The Finnish government is strongly pro-Europe. During the coordination process its mode of influence has been constructive dialogue rather than using threats to block a possible agreement. This mode of forming the national position in preparation for the IGC 2003–4 corresponds to the regular domestic coordination structure. It is characterized by an encompassing consensus approach, which allows for hierarchical control by the prime minister's office if necessary. The highly centralized and structured coordination process furthermore enables the government to anticipate the domestic reactions in an early phase of the deliberations.

One fundamental difference between general EU policy-making style and the negotiations on the future of Europe is the involvement of the president and the critical role of the parliament. Both could mobilize the public on the issues at stake. But due to its extraordinary central position in the coordination process the government finally managed to form internationally and domestically acceptable national positions. Parliamentary ratification in Finland initiated in May 2006 is – due to the broad based consensus across all parties and institutional actors – most likely to be successful.

Notes

1 Until the constitutional reform special majority requirements enabled one-third of the MEPs to delay a proposal in parliament (König and Bräuninger 1999: 43).
2 An analysis of the post-reform Finnish system reveals mixed results. Theoretically political scientists expected to observe a move toward parliamentarism and a potential move toward majoritarian democracy, but the empirics do not yet verify these expectations (König and Bräuninger 1999, Mattila 1997).
3 Following the March 2003 elections eight parties are represented in the *Eduskunta* (Auffermann 2003). The distribution of votes and seats in the most recent elections for parliament and the 2004 elections for the European Parliament, including the EP bloc affiliation of the parties, can be downloaded from the projects' website at dosei.dhv-speyer.de.
4 The ENP (Effective Number of Parties) was invented by Laasko and Taagepera (1979) and is calculated

by $1/1 - (\Sigma_{n}^{i=1} S_i)$

where S_i denotes the proportion of parliamentary seats of party *i*.
5 Another facet which – following Lijphart (1999) – is typically for consensual democracies is Finland's relatively short duration of government (1.24 years).
6 The average Gallagher index for Finland until 1998 was 2.98 (Lijphart 1999). The Gallagher index measures the average squared difference between party seats (percentage) and party votes (percentage).
7 The rainbow coalition has been formed under Paavo Lipponen in 1995 and comprised the following parties: Social Democrats, National Coalition, Left Alliance, Swedish People's Party and the Greens.
8 While the Finnish Prime Minister Matti Vanhanen stated that he did not expect his government to hold a referendum on the constitution (Convention website, 29 March 2004), the Conservatives and the Greens are in favor of holding a referendum (Kurpas *et al.* 2005).

9 Further information on the Finnish EU policy coordination. Online. Available at: www.valtioneuvosto.fi.

10 For the national position as well as for those actors mentioned by all four experts the coherence is about 58 percent, while it reaches 66 percent for the MFA, which was mentioned by two experts only. Modifying the coherence for the number of experts interviewed, we can compare the mean adapted coherence of the Finnish case (0.83) with the overall coherence in the DOSEI data set, which is slightly better (0.85, see Appendix 2).

10 France

The President takes all

Tobias Schulz

As a founding member of the EU and a leader with a strong vision in the early stages of the EU integration process, France continuously showed an exceptional commitment to European integration. It shares most of its border with Germany, the largest member country since its reunification. Not least because of its ability and willingness to form alliances with Germany, France had always been crucial to the process of European integration.

Although the political elite never left the "path of virtue" and serious Euro-skepticism (still) is a taboo in all major parties,[1] the pro-integration attitude of the French is also ambiguous to some extent. Of course, the French had been too closely involved and receive too many advantages from the project to reject it. Important advantages are the Common Agricultural Policy (CAP) as well as the fact that France utilizes the community as a vehicle to push through its ideas related to foreign and security policy (Dinan 2000). However, of the two referendums that allowed French voters to show their positive attitude toward a more integrated Europe, in 1972 and 1992, the latter had a rather close outcome which revealed that there are limits to the identification of the French with the project of European integration (Hainsworth *et al.* 2004, Milner 2004).

On 14 July 2004 (the national holiday), a few weeks after the governments had adopted the constitutional treaty in the final IGC, President Chirac officially announced the referendum.[2] It is hard to tell if it was foreseeable at that point in time that public support for the constitutional treaty would fall below 50 percent shortly before the referendum date, due to a general dissatisfaction with the performance of the government (*Libération*, 23 April 2005). Thus, it surprised more than one observer when on 29 May 2005 the French voters rejected the constitution by a 54.7 percent "no."

Spreading pessimism and unease is founded not least in economic problems. France shows the same symptoms as other highly developed and industrialized European countries, in particular Germany, that have been transformed into service economies: relatively moderate growth right below the European average and high unemployment (9.5 percent). Unsurprisingly, France supports the attempts of Germany to redefine the

Stability and Growth Pact that puts a heavy constraint on the domestic budget. Because the agrarian sector, relative to other countries, is small (approximately 3 percent of the GDP) but at the same time quite important economically and politically, the French net contribution to the EU budget has remained unimportant (Weise 2002). The country receives 22 percent of the EU's agricultural subsidies (European Commission 2003b: 49). Therefore, such maneuvers are even less appreciated by other member states.

Domestic structures in a comparative perspective

The two chambers of the French assembly are considered being asymmetric and incongruent. Every deputy of the lower house represents his or her own electoral district (there are 555 such districts in France altogether and another 22 overseas) and thus the electoral system is not based on a proportional representation rule. The number of effective parties has stayed at about seven since 1993 (Armingeon *et al.* 2004). It mirrors the growing competitiveness of the national political system (Schain 2004: 234). France has experienced a series of minimum winning coalitions and minority cabinets since the 1980s with one short phase of "cohabitation"[3] between 1986 and 1988. Since then, usually a simple majority coalition government ruled the country.

The political system of France is special in at least two respects. First, it is a highly unitary system. Second, it sometimes is called "semi-presidential," meaning that in principle it is a parliamentary democracy but with a directly elected and strong president, who does not only appoint the prime minister and may overturn the possible recall of the government by the assembly but has also some informally defined powers.

Parliament and government are clearly dominated by one party, the UMP.[4] It was founded, on the initiative of President Chirac, as an amalgamation of the RPR and the DL and as a third party also the UDF. It holds 62 percent of the seats in the lower house, which is a comfortable majority that nearly completely covers the political space on the right. The socialists only hold 24 percent of the seats.[5]

As mentioned in the beginning, the most salient characteristic of the French system is the strength of the president, who shares responsibility with the prime minister to a certain degree and definitely has the initiative and authority concerning foreign policy, except in times of divided government ("cohabitation"). This has not been the case during the Convention and the IGC 2003–4. However, with the creation of the UMP, the president has not only gained at least symbolic chairmanship over "nearly the whole conservative electorate" (Ysmal 2003: 953) but also a dominant influence in the cabinet. Most importantly, the initiative for foreign and hence European policy certainly is vested in the president.

The legislature, on the other hand, is quite weak and the cabinet as well as the president have a number of instruments to force parliament to accept their legislative initiatives. The assembly holds the initiative over law making only in some areas, but otherwise, the government is the agenda setter in both chambers (Schain 2004: 245 f.).

Compared to other European countries the French political and administrative authority is highly centralized and concentrated respectively (Schain 2004: 253 ff.). Although a decentralization reform in the 1980s reinforced the influence of local officeholders, France remains among the highly unitary and centralized countries of Europe.

Constitutional policy coordination

Beginning with November 2002, the position formation process in France involved the highest representatives of the state. Foreign Minister Dominique de Villepin took over the function of the former delegate Moscovici, whereas Pascale Andréani, the head of the SGCI (*Secrétariat Général du Comité Interministériel pour les questions de coopération économique européenne*), remained as the deputy.

The SGCI is the very heart of all inter-ministerial coordination regarding the European Union (Figure 10.1). It is affiliated to the prime minister's office. Foreign Minister Robert Schuman set up the SGCI in 1948 and it has a long tradition in and experience with position formation regarding international treaties. Its main tasks are the coordination between the ministries, the diffusion of information, the provision of expertise as well as the control over implementation of EU guidelines. It is

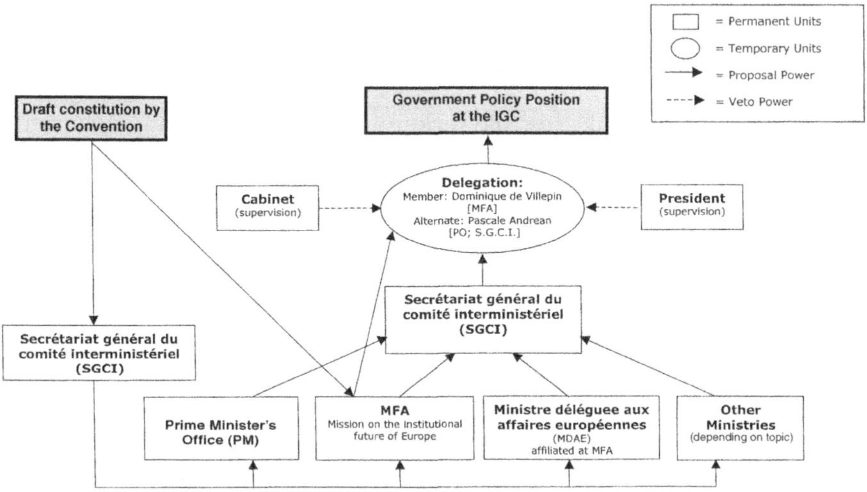

Figure 10.1 France: domestic policy coordination for the IGC 2003–4.

the explicit duty of the SGCI to assure that France is speaking with one voice at Brussels. To this end, the SGCI has permanent contacts with the institutions and the administration at the European level and regularly organizes inter-ministerial meetings to accomplish its tasks. Interestingly enough, within the ministry of foreign affairs at the Quai d'Orsay, a new sub-unit was formed to assist the foreign minister at the negotiation of the constitutional treaty and at coordinating the foreign ministry with the other ministries on this matter: the *Mission sur l'avenir institutional de l'Europe*. This mission received the same information from the European Union and the permanent representation as the SGCI. Obviously, some redundancy was desired, probably to enhance the efficacy of the foreign ministry.

Pascale Andréani is important not only because she is the head of the SGCI but also because she is at the same time acting as an advisor for EU politics to the prime minister. Furthermore, she already used to be the advisor of President Chirac in the field of European affairs when he still was prime minister. She therefore is widely acknowledged as being his confidant or as Quatremer puts it: "Pascale Andréani est sans conteste la pièce maîtresse du Président sur l'échiquier européen" (*Libération*, 22 January 2003).

Unquestionably, the president was the most important player. Not only because within the current constellation (absence of cohabitation) he was able to take the initiative for setting strategic guidelines but also because through Adréani, he seemed to have had strong influence on the coordination process itself. The position formation depended heavily on the president and had been relatively closed (Jabko 2004). In addition, the SGCI and the MFA were effective in deterring the resistance of single ministries. Therefore, it is plausible that the president and his longstanding diplomatic staff (Jabko 2004) constituted the very center of the position formation process as far as the impulses and new ideas are concerned.

The president did take his role seriously and decided to launch an initiative together with Gerhard Schröder, in January 2003, to introduce some new ideas on the institutional reform of the EU, most importantly the proposal of a double presidency (European Commission and Council of Ministers). According to our interviewees, it was clear to all actors involved that none of these issues had to be discussed within the government any further after this initiative had been launched.

Another actor that comes into play has, however, a somewhat ambiguous role: it is the *ministère délégué aux affairs européennes*, headed by Noëlle Lenoir. Although this position used to be more influential in the previous government and shortly before the Convention,[6] the role of Lenoir remains somewhat in the dark. Being an independent member of government, she is usually seen as belonging to the left, which may explain her failure to exert perceivable influence.

Data and empirical analysis of forming positions on the constitution for Europe

Two experts were interviewed in France. The interviews were conducted between mid- and late November 2003. The first is a member of the government administration, namely the SGCI. The second is an academic and a member of a think tank, working on European integration and the Convention.

Both interviewees mentioned the same key actors in the interviews: the prime minister, the president, the ministry of foreign affairs and the minister of European affairs.[7]

The public debate on the convention was explicitly launched by a joint declaration of the president and the prime minister. A special committee, that had been set up by the government, accompanied this process, which resulted in a report on the national debate (Groupe "Débat sur l'Avenir de l'Europe" 2001). The main issues raised in this report were the mobility of persons, social policy, environment, agricultural and economic policies, foreign and security policy as well as cooperation in the field of police and justice.

Since France is at the forefront of European integration, many aspects of the discussion at the Convention are of utmost importance to the country. However, the perhaps most salient issue that dominated the debate in France (and the whole of Europe) for some time had been the unveiling of the Franco-German proposal for a double presidency of the EU at 15 January 2003 (*Le Figaro*, 16 January 2003; *Le Monde*, 16 January 2003; *Libération*, 22 January 2003). This proposal contained also some other important institutional reforms and innovations like the *double casquette* of the new EU Foreign Minister.

Some other issues are, for example, the preservation of the veto right regarding policies affecting "culture," i.e., the trade in cultural and audiovisual services (*Le Monde*, 10 July 2003a). Furthermore, France was also concerned to set up rules that would protect the provision of the *service publique*, i.e., services of "general economic interest" (*Le Monde*, 10 July 2003b). President Chirac also repeatedly mentioned foreign policy as a salient issue (*Le Monde*, 3 September 2002). The references to Christianity or even God in the preamble of the constitution had also been a subject of debate (*Libération*, 2 March 2004), particularly since countries with opposing views raised this issue.

From our questionnaire, we can confirm some of these high salience issues. As the most salient issue appears the reference to religion in the preamble, since both experts mentioned it. Otherwise, one of our experts mentioned the organization of the presidency in the Council as well as the QMV principle and the appointment of the minister of foreign affairs. The other expert mentioned the regulation of jurisdiction with respect to external policy as well as co-decision of the European Parliament and Council voting rules with respect to the agricultural budget and culture (where he opted for unanimity and against co-decision).

The most dominant and important player in the domestic coordination game had been the president and it hence is no surprise that there is no difference to make out between the president and the national position. As Jabko (2004) shows, the president did take a rather progressive stance as compared with former positions and in addition, he had locked himself in by agreeing to the French–German alliance, which was reinforced with the upcoming war in Iraq. Hence, some disagreement with the other actors should be expected. However, comparing the positions of the remaining actors in France, almost no differences can be found (Table 10.1). On average, an actor deviated from the national position on only 3.7 percent of the issues (regarding the policy questions this amounts to 4.5 percent and for institutional questions to only 3.3 percent).

We received some information about deviating positions of some of the players. The minister of research (who would have delegated fewer competencies to the EU in the area of research and technology), the prime minister's office (revealing a less integrationist stance regarding the Stability and Growth Pact) and parliament (which had a more integrationist stance on the organization of the presidency). According to our data set, the strongest deviation can be found for the UMP.[8] Overall, the UMP (which could also be interpreted as an alternative position of the parliament) had a less integrationist position on many issues, mostly in the policies realm.

On the other hand, our experts unveiled minor differences between the national position and the ministry of foreign affairs, which is the leading ministry (apart from the SGCI). The only difference that was reported by one of our experts concerned the delegation of competencies in the area of research and technology, where the MFA obviously would have taken a more integrationist stance.

Conclusion

The analysis of the French position formation process does not reveal many surprises. In France, the process related to Intergovernmental Conferences is, in contrast to the ordinary organization of the relations to the EU, traditionally dominated by the president in a way that allows him rather obstinate appearances on the international level, since he does not have to form coalitions to find support for his ideas (Jabko 2004). Even if compared to earlier IGC preparation stages, the process was extremely closed. There certainly was not much leeway for the remaining governmental actors for strategic influence and actors outside the government (in particular the parliament) were virtually excluded from the process. By appointing a close advisor the head of the SGCI, it is likely that his influence grew even stronger. After Foreign Minister Villepin became the

Table 10.1 Cohesiveness of actors' positions in the French coordination process

National position comparison	*Actor(s) (No. or type)*	*Observations (No.)*	*Deviations*									
			from national position		*on integration*				*related to*			
					toward less		*toward more*		*institutional issues*[a]		*policy fields*[a]	
			No.	*%*	*No.*	*%*	*No.*	*%*	*No.*	*%*	*No.*	*%*
All actors	7	455	17	3.7	13	2.9	4	0.9	10	3.3	7	4.5
Subset												
Lead unit	PM	65	1	1.5	0	–	1	1.5	0	–	1	4.5

Deviations related to institutional issues
Subsidiarity (role of national parliaments); Presidency of the Council; Voting rule (Council) for Area of Freedom, Security and Justice, for employment policy, for social policy, for social security rights; Decision rule (EP) for agriculture, for Area of Freedom, Security and Justice, for employment policy, for social policy

Deviations related to policy fields
Charter of Fundamental Rights; Level of competence for health policy, for research, technological development and space; Stability and Growth Pact; Migration and asylum

Vital interests
Religious reference in the preamble; Presidency of the Council; Qualified majority threshold; Appointment of the Foreign Minister; Regulation of jurisdiction with respect to external policy; Application of legislative procedures and council voting rules to agricultural budget and culture; Budgetary procedure

Notes
a Percentage shares refer to subsets of institutional (43) and policy (22) issues. *Lead Unit* Leading unit in domestic coordination: Prime Minister's Office (PM) or Ministry of Foreign Affairs (MFA).

government's delegate to the Convention, a counterpart to the SGCI had been established within the foreign ministry. Although this might have strengthened the standing of the foreign minister, it certainly did not weaken the influence of the president.

Accordingly, we do find some deviating positions of parliamentary actors, although they do not amount to a serious disagreement. After the IGC, the president announced a referendum and since then, public support for the constitutional treaty has been on the decline. On 29 May 2005 the treaty was rejected by the French voters with about 55 percent negative votes.

Acknowledgment

I have to thank Renaud Dehousse for giving valuable input concerning the interrelation of the French actors depicted in Figure 10.1.

Notes

1 Of course, as Hainsworth *et al.* (2004) show, there is a tension within the governing party of President Chirac, because it tacitly had to redefine its traditional "Gaullist approach" to Europe. Openly and entirely Euro-skeptic parties are the *Front National*, the Communist Party as well as the Greens (Taggart 1998). However, only the *Front National* received slightly more than 10 percent of the votes at the last parliamentary election.

2 Article 52 of the French constitution states that the president shall negotiate and ratify international treaties and agreements. According to Article 11, upon proposal of the government or both chambers of the assembly, he may submit such a decision to a referendum, which would substitute parliamentary ratification. If a constitutional amendment is involved, this must not be subject to the referendum (Article 11) and shall be settled in advance. In this case, the parliament has to approve the amendment with a three-fifths majority in a joint meeting (Article 89).

3 This expression qualifies the division of government that is caused by the president and the prime minister not being members of the same party.

4 Union for a Popular Movement (*Union pour un Movement Populaire*).

5 The distribution of votes and seats in the most recent elections for parliament and the 2004 elections for the European Parliament, including the EP bloc affiliation of the parties, can be downloaded from the projects' website at dosei.dhv-speyer.de.

6 The predecessor of Lenoir, Moscovici, even acted as a negotiator at the IGC in Nice in 2000 (*Libération*, 14 February 2000).

7 We have calculated an index of expert coherence for every single actor mentioned, which controls for the number of experts interviewed. The French actors rate relatively low on this index (about 0.78 for actors that were mentioned by both experts; otherwise, the index is 1). The experts largely disagreed in their evaluation of the French position on the policies questions in about two-thirds of the questions. However, with 0.83, the mean coherence is about the same as the mean of the whole project (0.84). The number of actors that had been mentioned by only one expert amounts to three. However, they all are of relatively minor interest (see Appendix 2).

8 However, this may be rooted to some extent also in the circumstance that the first expert had not explicitly mentioned the UMP and thus its position is based on information given by the second expert. Since the higher-rated expert mentioned also the parliament but indicated fewer deviations for this actor, interpretation of the results found for the UMP is somewhat impeded.

11 Germany

The promoter of European integration?

Stephanie Daimer and Thomas König

Germany is the largest country in the EU with a population of more than 80 millions. In spite of some concerns about Germany's role after unification in 1990 (Bulmer and Paterson 1996, Katzenstein 1997), German EU policy is committed to closer economic and political integration. Both after-unification governments, the Christian–liberal Kohl government and the social democratic–green Schröder government, have promoted European integration and constitution building, even though unified Germany is still a net contributor and struggling with an average growth rate of 1.3 percent[1] and high unemployment.[2]

Compared to other (federal) member states, Germany's second chamber, the *Bundesrat*, is a powerful veto player in legislative policy making, including EU affairs (Bräuninger and König 1999). In some areas, the *Bundesrat* even represents German interests in the Council. This has raised criticism about the effectiveness of German policy making, in particular in the event of different party majorities in the *Bundestag* and *Bundesrat* (Scharpf 1988, König 2001, König *et al.* 2003). Under the Schröder government, the opposition not only held the majority in the *Bundesrat*, but it also won the majority of seats in the 2004 European elections.[3]

With respect to recent economic problems, a major current issue concerns Germany's net contributions to the EU budget and the application of the criteria of the Stability and Growth Pact, which Germany could not meet in recent years. Unsurprisingly, Germany – like other EU net payers – rejects further extension of the budgetary contributions to the EU's financial framework for 2007–13.[4]

Domestic structures in a comparative perspective

According to Lijphart's (1999: 248) comparative study, Germany is the prototype of a consensus democracy with strong federalism and the highest degree of decentralization. After unification Germany's multiparty parliamentary system experienced only minor challenges by the rise of the post-communist PDS, and governments continued to consist of a two-party minimum winning coalition in the *Bundestag*. The number of

Länder increased from 11 to 16 in a federal structure which establishes a high number of political veto players promoting policy stability (Tsebelis 2002: 136).

Like a constitutional amendment, the ratification of international treaties requires two-thirds majorities in both chambers, the *Bundestag* and *Bundesrat*. Compared to domestic legislative politics, however, this bicameral ratification constraint never caused problems because almost all political parties support the idea of European integration. Only the regional parties, the CSU (regional Christian party of Bavaria) and the PDS (former communist party), take a more critical view on this issue. Moreover, the constitutional proposal is perceived as to improve Germany's position in the EU, i.e., establishing a voting procedure which better reflects population size as well as it confers more powers to the national parliaments (see below).[5]

While public support for the constitutional proposal has decreased in the course of Eastern enlargement,[6] opposition parties were trying to initiate a discussion about an additional referendum on the constitution – a suggestion that has been strongly opposed by the government (*EUobserver*, 2 August 2004). Even though recent polls show a vast majority in favor of the constitution,[7] general support for EU membership has fallen 12 points within six months to 46 percent.[8] Nevertheless on 12 and 27 May 2005 respectively the *Bundestag* and the *Bundesrat* succeeded in ratifying the constitution.

Due to high portfolio autonomy of the ministries, German EU policy formation is characterized by strong ministerial coordination, especially in the case of EU secondary legislation. Issues and proposals related to COREPER 1 are coordinated under the lead of the ministry of finance and involve a large number of ministerial actors. Formerly, these have been the "four musketeers," namely the ministries of foreign affairs, economics, agriculture and finance. But nowadays this group is complemented by the ministries of the interior, justice and environment due to growing EU competencies (Bulmer *et al.* 2002, Maurer 2003b). In addition to strong ministerial coordination, the *Länder* also participate in this process. Since the Maastricht Treaty (1993), Article 23 of the Basic Law requires participation of the *Länder* in the Council when their competencies are at stake (see for more details Maurer 2003b).

Constitutional policy coordination

In preparation for the IGC, the government attempted to employ a more effective coordination process. The ministry of foreign affairs (MFA) was responsible for coordinating institutional issues and treaty revisions (primary legislation). In October 2002 Foreign Minister Joschka Fischer also became the government's delegate to the European Convention, and a newly established MFA task force attempted to improve communication

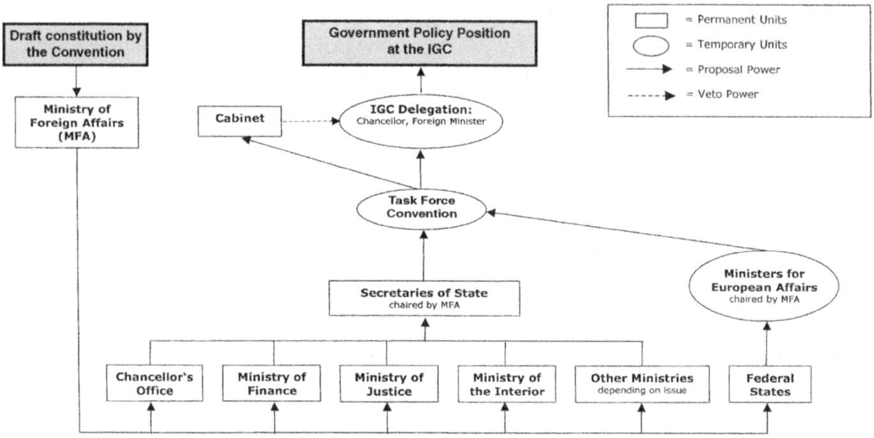

Figure 11.1 Germany: domestic policy coordination for the IGC 2003–4.

with the office of Secretary of State Hans-Martin Bury, Fischer's alternate in the Convention and chairman of the inter-ministerial committee of state secretaries and of the ministers for European affairs from the *Länder*. Officially, this coordination structure ended with the Convention's final session. At an informal level, however, the task force coordinated further discussions and strategies.

With respect to the chancellor's right to define the policy principles of the government, the chancellor's office also played an important role and was perhaps one of the most relevant actors in this policy formation process. The MFA task force and the EU division at the chancellor's office were permanently in touch, and Chancellor Schröder and Foreign Minister Fischer frequently exchanged their views and coordinated their strategies.

The government also attempted to include the *Länder*'s views in anticipation of the *Bundesrat*'s veto power in the ratification process. Although the *Länder* ministers and state secretaries with responsibility for EU affairs met almost every month, the two committees and the task force only prepared the decisions which were made by the foreign minister and the chancellor. With respect to the principle of joint decision making, the cabinet officially decided on the most important and contested issues.

To sum up, the German coordination process slightly differed from previous IGC preparations.[9] Although this coordination process included many actors, the chancellor and the MFA set the agenda and took the final decisions. This suggests that Chancellor Schröder and Foreign Minister Fischer prevailed over the portfolio principle, which is characteristic of regular German EU policy making. Another explanation suggests that most of these actors had similar views on the constitution. Whether the chancellor and the foreign minister dominated or were in accordance with the other actors might be answered by looking at the distribution of the positions of the actors involved.

Data and empirical analysis of forming positions on the constitution for Europe

The data on the positions of the actors involved were gathered in interviews with four experts identifying five relevant German domestic actors. All experts mentioned the two central actors, the MFA and the chancellery (PM). Furthermore, the *Länder*, the ministry of finance (MF) and the ministry of the interior (MI) were also indicated by some of the experts. Except for the ministry of justice, the experts identified the sample of actors of the formal coordination process.[10]

On closer inspection, a few institutional issues were of central importance for Germany, i.e., the "double" majority (50 percent of the states, 60 percent of the population) for qualified majority voting in the Council, the extension of QMV for tax and CFSP matters (exceptions: migration and asylum, labor rights, defense) as well as creating the office of a European Foreign Minister. The issue of a single president for the European Council was a German–French initiative launched already during the Convention (in January 2003). Several models were discussed before, in which the MFA favored a "two hats" solution, while the MF always preferred to maintain the status quo. MFA and PM additionally preferred to establish a legislative Council and launched this idea in the Convention. To reduce the size of the Commission was a vital issue for Germany, inasmuch it became vital for other states. The German position against the position to keep one commissioner per country was to fall back to the Nice solution with two German commissioners.

The *Länder* advocated two issues, a stronger control of the principle of subsidiarity (also a chamber of parliament shall have the right to bring a legal action to the European Court of Justice, which was more important for them than the early warning system; this right is now included in the draft constitution), and limited EU competencies in the field of services of general economic interest (Article III-6 of the draft constitution). While the government supported the *Länder* on these issues, it did not follow the *Länder* to call for a reference to Christianity in the preamble, as this was considered to be too partisan (Baden-Württemberg has a Christian Democrat government). According to the interview partner from the ministry of the state in Baden-Württemberg, only the Bavarian CSU (Christian Social Union) promoted an "anti-constitutional" position during the domestic coordination process.

Out of 65 issues, the German actors share a common position on 40 issues and disagree only on 25 issues. Across these 25 contested issues we find 52 positions of actors deviating from the national position (see Table 11.1). About half of this amount is determined by the *Länder*,

Table 11.1 Cohesiveness of actors' positions in the German coordination process

National position comparison	*Actor(s) (No. or type)*	*Observations (No.)*	*Deviations*									
			from national position		*on integration*				*related to*			
					toward less		*toward more*		*institutional issues*[a]		*policy fields*[a]	
			No.	*%*	*No.*	*%*	*No.*	*%*	*No.*	*%*	*No.*	*%*
All actors	5	325	52	16.0	41	12.6	11	3.4	26	12.1	26	23.6
Subset												
Lead unit	MFA	65	8	12.3	5	7.7	3	4.6	3	7.0	5	22.7

Deviations related to institutional issues
Right to withdraw from the Union; Presidency of the Council; Appointment of Commission president; ECJ jurisdiction; Legislative initiative for citizens; Voting rule (Council) for Area of Freedom, Security and Justice, for employment policy, for social policy, for social security rights, for foreign policy; Decision rule (EP) for social policy, for social security rights; Rights of EP in the adoption of the budget

Deviations related to policy fields
Religious reference in the preamble; Economic objectives: employment; Level of competence for agriculture, for the Area of Freedom, Security and Justice, for economic policy, for tax harmonization, for employment policy, for social policy, for health policy, for education policy, for research, technological development and space; External borders; Migration and asylum

Vital interests
Qualified majority threshold; Number of commissioners; Appointment of the Foreign Minister; Regulation of jurisdiction with respect to services of general economic interest; Council voting rule for Common Security and Defense policy, and for immigration policy

Notes

a Percentage shares refer to subsets of institutional (43) and policy (22) issues. *Lead Unit* Leading unit in domestic coordination: Prime Minister's Office (PM) or Ministry of Foreign Affairs (MFA).

including the division of competencies in the Area of Freedom, Security and Justice (AFSJ) as well as in agricultural, economic, employment, tax harmonization, health and education policies, and the voting rule on AFSJ, labor, foreign and social policies. In general, the *Länder* fear a continuous loss of their competencies due to further transfer to the EU level and more QMV decision making.

Inter-ministerial disputes between chancellery and MFA on the one side, and the ministry of finance (and in some cases also the ministry of the interior) on the other, relate to the issues of the presidency, budgetary procedure and decision rules in the field of social security policy. The budgetary procedure has been highly important for the MF, as it opposes to grant the EP a final say in the annual budgetary procedure. Another salient issue for the MF is a strengthening of the Euro group in the coordination of the monetary policy.

For some issues the national position does not correspond to the position of the two most important actors, MFA and PM. These are migration policies, the citizens' initiative, the religious reference in the preamble, the right of withdrawal and the specification of the objective of employment policy, for which the leading actors preferred to maintain the status quo, the management of external borders and the appointment of the Commission president, for which they favored to go for more integration than the draft proposes. The location of the national position separate from the most relevant domestic actors suggests that Germany employed a strategic national position with respect to the official German position to abstain from threatening the draft (Cuntz 2003). The German national position is only promoting the status quo in two cases (migration and asylum and labor rights should be voted on unanimously in the council), and differs from the draft in only a few cases, which are for example tax harmonization and foreign policy. Here, Germany wants to introduce QMV as a general voting rule in the Council.

Except for the issues mentioned above, there is almost complete coherence between the national position and the positions of the leading ministry, the MFA, as well as between the national position and the position of the second most important actor, the chancellery (PM). The PM's position matches the national position slightly better, as they both support to introduce a European space policy, which is not shared by the MFA.

Conclusion

In the EU constitution-building process Germany played an important role for promoting institutional reform, often introducing proposals jointly with the French delegation. The European Foreign Minister, the single president of the EU and the new voting system in the Council are examples of the German efforts to shape the future constitutional architecture. Due to economic stagnation the government tried to link the country's status as the biggest net payer in the EU with the constitutional bargains to influence the outcome of financial issues, such as the EU budget and the euro rules.

This position has been supported by German political elites, although policy formation usually involves a higher number of actors with intensive debates on the German position. For the IGC preparation most powers were assigned to the MFA (as the coordinating unit) and the chancellery, while few other relevant domestic actors were involved in this process. These are in particular the *Länder*, which are powerful veto players in the ratification process. However, only a few issues were contested among these actors suggesting consensus of the *Bundestag* and *Bundesrat* on the constitution, while a referendum would be more critical for the ratification of the constitutional proposal.

Notes

1 Average 1996–2003 of real GDP growth rates (at constant prices, 1995 = 100; Eurostat 2004).
2 9.3 percent in 2003 (EU-average at 8.0 percent; Eurostat 2004).
3 The distribution of votes and seats in the most recent elections for parliament and the 2004 elections for the European Parliament, including the EP bloc affiliation of the parties, can be downloaded from the projects' website at dosei.dhv-speyer.de.
4 A paper circulated by France, Germany, the UK, Sweden, Austria and the Netherlands wants the budget to be capped at 1.0 percent of the gross national income, while the Commission is calculating in its proposal with 1.27 percent (*EUobserver*, 18 March 2004).
5 Shortly before the vote in the *Bundesrat* on the constitution the federal states threatened again successfully the government and negotiated additional EU competencies, like their involvement in the choosing of judges for the European Court of Justice (*EUobserver*, 29 April 2005).
6 Thirty-eight percent of the Germans are in favor of enlargement, 42 percent are clearly against (only the French support rate is lower; Eurobarometer 2003b).
7 Eighty-three percent in favor of the constitution, 66 percent support for the government concession making in order to ensure the adoption of the constitution (Eurobarometer 2004a).
8 Additionally, 10 percent consider EU membership as a bad thing (Eurobarometer 2003b).
9 Compared to the 1996 IGC, there are some differences: The IGC task force was affiliated at the MFA European Union division and inter-ministerial coordination did not only take place at the state secretary level, but also at two lower levels (directorate heads and officials; see Thurner *et al.* 2002).
10 The interviews were conducted at the end of 2003 with officials from institutions involved in the IGC coordination process (a member of the foreign ministry's task force, higher ranked officials from the EU directorates in the chancellery as well as in the ministry of finance and an official from the EU affairs division in the ministry of state of Baden-Württemberg which was delegate and chief negotiator for the federal states in the Convention and the subsequent IGC).

The data gathered by the interviews with four experts show high coherence. For the NP as well as for those actors mentioned by all four experts the empirical coherence is about 61 percent, while it reaches a 79 percent for those actors mentioned by two experts only. Modifying the coherence for the number of experts interviewed we can compare the mean adapted coherence of the German case (0.90) with the overall coherence in the DOSEI data set, which is worse (0.85; see Appendix 2).

12 Greece

Overcoming negative stereotyping

George Pagoulatos and Spyros Blavoukos

Following EC accession in 1981, Greece's record during the first decade was one of consistent divergence from the EC policy standard and a general failure to assimilate the European Community into political thinking (Verney 1994, Pagoulatos 2004). This divergence reached its apogee in the late 1980s and beginning of the 1990s, with serious concern being aroused regarding Greece's dangerous oscillation between European integration and Balkan marginalization (Featherstone and Ifantis 1996). The macroeconomic adjustment and market-oriented policies inaugurated in 1990 by the center-right wing ND government were pursued with new vigor under the 1993 and especially the 1996 PASOK governments resulting to gradual economic stabilization (Tsoukalis 2000).

Adjustment and economic progress, supported by very substantial and continuous financial inflows under the second and third Community Support Frameworks, was highlighted by the successful EMU entry, a slow convergence to the EU-15 per capita GDP and an improved outlook of public finances. In political terms, economic progress helped Greece restore its lost credibility vis-à-vis the EU (Featherstone 2003). Membership in the EMU boosted Greek confidence and reinforced the country's intention to affirm a more constructive role in EU affairs, taking part in the vanguard of European integration (Pagoulatos 2002).

This new vigor and dynamism was manifested in the enthusiastic embracement of enhanced cooperation during the Nice IGC as opposed to previous IGCs where "variable geometry" schemes had been rejected or at best very reluctantly accepted (Ioakimidis 2001, Papadopoulos 2002). This attitude shift toward differentiated integration reflected the new role envisaged for Greece in the EU. The successful 2003 presidency "confirmed the completion of Greece's long course from the reluctant margins to the willing core of the European Union" (Blavoukos and Pagoulatos 2003: 163).

Domestic structures in a comparative perspective

The EU has had a crucial role in the political, economic and social transformation of the Greek polity (Ioakimidis 2000, Featherstone 1998). Membership in the EC/EU became the modern battleground of the old perennial confrontation between the two ever competing political cultures in Greece, reinforcing – schematically put – the "modernizing" camp against the "traditionalist" one (Diamandouros 1997, 1993, Fatouros 1993). Pressures for administrative and institutional isomorphism were internalized with varying results in the Greek polity, depending on the exposure of particular structures to the impact of Europeanization (Ioakimidis 1996).

The political system of Greece that emerged after the 1974 transition to democracy has been that of a parliamentary democracy with the executive power shared between the President of the Republic and the government. However the role of the President of the Republic was significantly curtailed after the 1986 constitutional amendments (and remained so in the latest 2001 reform) rendering the prime minister the actual center of the governmental and policy-making system. The Greek parliament (*Vouli ton Ellinon*) has 300 members, elected for a four year term by a system of reinforced proportional representation in 51 multi-seat constituencies and five single-seat constituencies.[1] Although there are specific provisions for calling referenda on major issues of national interest, this is not the case in practice, with the parliament approving constitutional reforms or major international and EU treaties. A majority of three-fifths is necessary for such ratification.

Given the prevalent role of political parties in the post-authoritarian Greek polity, the trajectory of Greece in the European integration process has been very much dependent upon the position adopted by the main political parties (Featherstone 1994). Given the constant support to the EC/EU project by ND and the equally constant rejection of the process by the Greek Communist Party (KKE), it was PASOK's gradual realignment that has most contributed to the emergence of almost a consensus in the Greek society and political stage as regards European integration and the role of Greece in the EU. Indicative of this Europeanist consensus are the similar positions espoused by the two ruling parties, PASOK and ND, in the European Convention, converging toward a more "federalist" transmutation of the European polity. Building on that cross-party consensus, the ratification of the European constitution by the parliament that took place in April 2005, could count on the positive vote of both ND and PASOK. Late efforts from PASOK and the coalition of the Left and Progress Party to trigger public debate for a referendum, a position also espoused by the Communist Party, failed to have any substantial impact. Both the left coalition and the Communist Party oppose the European constitution.

Constitutional policy coordination

The nation-centric, defensive and mainly budgetary oriented attitudes of the early years of membership could be also attributed to some extent to the domestic administrative and policy-making framework with its inherent pathological weaknesses (Passas and Dimitrakopoulos 2004, Makrydimitris and Passas 1994, Ioakimidis 1993). In this framework, "the role of institutions and bureaucratic structures as factors in defining the policy-making process appears limited or in some cases non-existent" (Ioakimidis 1999: 142). In the absence of institutionalized horizontal and vertical communication and coordination and due to the very centralized authority at the top political layers, strategic planning and decision making has been often entrusted to a multitude of political appointees (Sotiropoulos 1999, Spanou 1998, 1996).

Indicative of the Greek-styled dirigisme, the Greek policy-making system on EU affairs has also been characterized by a near monopoly position of the central government with intermediary bureaucratic layers operating as one-way transmission belts of government policies (Tsinisizelis 1996). In this system consultation with and input from civil society and socioeconomic interest groups have been very limited due to the feebleness of an engaging and pluralistic policy-making culture.[2] The leading role at the intra-governmental level has oscillated between the ministry of foreign affairs (MFA) and the ministry of coordination (after 1982, Ministry of National Economy), with the former finally prevailing after an internal political and bureaucratic battle on the basis of the weight of the political component in Greece–EU relations (Spanou 2000). In the absence of a systemic institutional framework of foreign policy-making (Stoforopoulos and Makridimitris 1996), the political leadership of the MFA – as opposed to collective institutionalized bodies – has been primarily responsible both for the articulation of policy and the development of the EU policy-making and policy-coordinating structures (Ioakimidis 1999).

The *ad hoc* nature of most institutional arrangements and the central role of the MFA in coordinating EU policy making were manifested yet another time during the European Convention and the subsequent IGC (see Figure 12.1). The Greek government's intention to engage in the vanguard of European integration and make a substantial contribution to it increased awareness of the debate on the future of Europe underlining its significance. At an organizational level, the significance attributed to the process can be testified by the setting up in the MFA of two *ad hoc* bodies, a Convention working group and a task force, to prepare the grounds for Greece's representation in the Convention. The working group operated within the framework of the MFA General Directorate for European Affairs and functioned as the filter mechanism bringing together inputs from the various departments of the general directorate

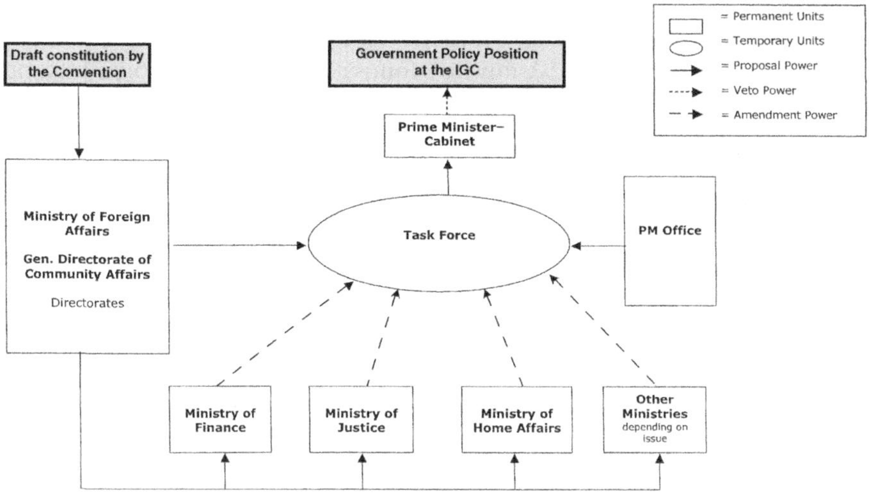

Figure 12.1 Greece: domestic policy coordination for the IGC 2003–4.

and other relevant ministries. The other relevant ministries were represented in this body by appointed political envoys of the ministers, who had continuous and direct access to their respective political "master." This format was deemed more appropriate especially in the final stage of the debate when flexibility and immediate response was required and the pre-existing regular channels of inter-ministerial communication (i.e., at general directors level, etc.) were deemed as rigid and time-consuming. The output of the working group was then transmitted to the Convention task force, which evaluated proposals and made the final recommendations to the government representatives in the Convention. The task force comprised high profile academics and senior diplomats. Three diplomats participated in both the working group and the task force, playing the role of "institutional hinges" between these two bodies. The then Minister of Foreign Affairs, George Papandreou, took part some times in the meetings of the task force.[3] It is worth noting that this rather elaborate structure took its final shape only after the beginning of the Greek presidency in January 2003. Given that the successful timely conclusion of the Convention was one of the priorities of the presidency, Foreign Minister Papandreou, undertook the post of government representative to demonstrate the presidency's commitment to the process (Blavoukos and Pagoulatos 2003).

As regards the IGC, one should distinguish between the formal/institutionalized policy-making structures and the informal ones. The *ad hoc* task force set up for the needs of the Convention was maintained, with representatives from the prime minister's office taking part as well. Existing channels of communication with the other ministries and government agencies were used to gather the other actors' inputs. However, the contribution of most ministries was considered of little value or relevance to the actual issues in discussion.[4] A novelty, compared to past EU policy-making practices, was the keen interest and direct involvement in the process of Prime Minister Simitis. Accordingly, that reinforced the role of the PM office in both the formal and informal policy-making structures and contributed to the even greater centralization of the process with less leeway for other actors beyond the PM office and the MFA to make substantial contributions. Given the nature of the challenges raised by the draft constitution and the great degree of membership overlap in the policy-consulting mechanisms in those two institutional actors, their views exhibited considerable convergence and different approaches never escalated to an open discord situation.

The IGC was debated thoroughly and exclusively in a cabinet meeting that took place after the launch of the IGC on 9 October 2003. Key ministers, whose portfolio was directly related to issues discussed in the IGC, had been consulted well in advance of the cabinet meeting, prior to the formulation and formal submission of the Greek positions to the Italian presidency. A much less substantial and focused debate on the IGC took place later in the parliament with the intention of raising political and public awareness on the ongoing discussions.

Data and empirical analysis of forming positions on the constitution for Europe

The data for Greece was collected through three interviews with experts, advisors and diplomats from the ministry of foreign affairs, who combined academic expertise and first hand knowledge of the policy-making process and the most relevant actors involved in it. One interview was based on the structured questionnaire developed for the needs of the project whereby the other two focused more on the position formation process in the old and new (following the change of government in the March 2004 elections) administration.[5]

The aim of Table 12.1 is to illustrate the degree of homogeneity among the different domestic actors involved in the position formation process. The table is displaying cases and issues where positions of actors deviated from the indicated national position. The table actually suggests for Greece an identical approach to the main issues on the agenda. Two factors can be credited for this consensus. The first is related to the country's firm political orientation and aspiration to participate in the group of countries leading the European integration process. This overall strategic choice, filtered through the preoccupation with particular national interests, prescribed most of the positions held by these actors. The second has more to do with the position formation process, which

Table 12.1 Cohesiveness of actors' positions in the Greek coordination process

National position comparison	*Actor(s) (No. or type)*	*Observations (No.)*	*Deviations*									
			from national position		*on integration*				*related to*			
					toward less		*toward more*		*institutional issues*[a]		*policy fields*[a]	
			No.	*%*	*No.*	*%*	*No.*	*%*	*No.*	*%*	*No.*	*%*
All actors	2	130	0	–	0	–	0	–	0	–	0	–
Subset												
Lead unit	MFA	65	0	–	0	–	0	–	0	–	0	–

Deviations related to institutional issues
Nil

Deviations related to policy fields
Nil

Vital interests
Qualified majority threshold; Number of commissioners

Notes
a Percentage shares refer to subsets of institutional (43) and policy (22) issues. *Lead Unit* Leading unit in domestic coordination: Prime Minister's Office (PM) or Ministry of Foreign Affairs (MFA).

was led by a small number of two (MFA and PM office) *continuously* interacting key actors. That process of constant interaction engendered convergence of positions of the few actors involved, conveying an image of nearly total homogeneity.

In general, the positions held by the Greek government in the IGC were consistent with the intention to enhance the pace of integration while securing national interests. There was widespread satisfaction with the draft outcome of the Convention and there were fears that negotiations should be kept to a minimum so as not to reopen Pandora's box (Yannis 2004). To some extent this satisfaction derived from the fact that the Greek government felt that part of the draft glaze was rubbing off on to the Greek presidency, which had successfully managed to see through the process on the agreed time schedule.

Content-wise, during the negotiations, Greece's most salient issues were those related to the institutional architecture of the EU. The Greek government had strong preferences in support of the status quo as regards the Commission's composition with one commissioner (with voting rights) per member state as well as the modality of selecting and approving the Commission college. As regards decision-making rules, support was expressed for the abolition of the complex and counterproductive Nice arrangements and the adoption of the double majority principle setting the threshold at 50 percent for both countries and population. There was broad agreement on the need to enhance the external representation of the EU by appointing an EU foreign minister equally accountable to both the Commission and the Council according to the draft constitution.

A significant readjustment of the Greek position took place with regard to the question of a permanent president of the European Council. During the Convention debate Greek government delegates had rejected such prospect arguing in favor of streamlining the existing rotating system with the introduction of team presidencies of one-year terms preferably shared among three member states. On the way toward the concluding stages of the Convention, the Greek side gradually came to terms with the dawning reality of the wide support – at least by large countries – to a permanent president post and even some of the benefits of such an institutional development. Hence, no objections were raised subsequently during the IGC. In this case, Greece seemed to shed off reservations expressed by the small and medium-size countries (with the exception of the Benelux countries). Being clear about the country's position in the integrationist camp, the Greek government made a conscious choice to side along this group and pragmatically adopt their views regarding the institutional configuration of the enlarged EU.

This broad embracing of further political integration was consistent with the Greek government's support for extending majority voting in almost all areas possible in order to make the policy-making system in its enlarged format more flexible and capable of delivering policy. This extension of majority voting would also include the CFSP, allowing however still for member states to invoke vital national interest in order to block a common action. In that case the issue in question would be referred to the European Council whereby decision would be taken by unanimity. Along the same lines, the Greek government called for an enlarged scope for enhanced cooperation schemes to cover all areas of EU activities including defense integration and the development of a common integrated management system for the EU external borders.

Finally, the change of government following the March 2004 elections resulted in fully embracing the inclusion of the religious reference to the preamble of the constitution in departure from the earlier expressed national position.

Conclusion

In sum, there is little doubt about the magnitude of the centripetal forces around the ministry of foreign affairs and the prime minister's office. Inputs from other governmental or societal actors were of marginal importance, with these two actors monopolizing to a large extent the policy-making process. The expressed interest of the prime minister led to a more active involvement of his office, without however any serious divergence of views. This was largely indicative of the more or less consensual politics surrounding the country's European vocation following its successful Europeanization.

It was this crystallized cross-party consensus (with the exception of the Communist Party) over Greece's positive stake in a "closer" and "deeper" EU that glued together different individual political strategies in a policy deliberation environment still characterized by limited institutionalization, residual bureaucratization, and a prevalence of personalized elements.

The views endorsed in the IGC reflected the manifest transformation of Greece over the 1990s and encapsulated the determination to be a constituent member of the new EU architecture. Generally speaking, despite the strong feelings on some issues primarily of institutional nature, there was little doubt that should it ever come to a "take it or leave it" situation about the draft, Greece would embrace it so as not to risk derailment of the integration process. Cross-party consensus, wider public endorsement of the integration process and the fact that the ratification of the constitution would go through the parliament, ensured that the ratification process in Greece, completed in April 2005, was unproblematic.

Notes

1 The distribution of votes and seats in the most recent elections for parliament and the 2004 elections for the European Parliament, including the EP bloc affiliation of the parties, can be downloaded from the projects' website at dosei.dhv-speyer.de.
2 Interview, political advisor to the minister of foreign affairs (February 2001).
3 Interview, member of the task force and liaison of the task force with the minister of foreign affairs (June 2003).
4 Interview, member of the task force during the Convention and the IGC and advisor to the minister of foreign affairs (4 November 2003).
5 Given that the structured questionnaire was completed by only one expert, there is no point commenting on the level of experts' coherence (see Appendix 2).

13 Hungary

United in support, divided by borders

Anna Gwiazda and Kenneth Benoit

United in support for the EU constitution, the Hungarians none the less remember the past dismemberment of their country, as a result of which a significant number of Hungarian minorities live in neighboring countries. Hence, it was not surprising that the Hungarian government's position at the IGC 2003–4 focused on the protection of minority rights, although institutional balance was also important. The only "exclusive" Hungarian proposal of the "protection of ethnic and national minorities" was supported by both the socialists and the opposition Fidesz–Hungarian Civic Party.

Hungary joined the European Union on 1 May 2004. EU membership had been a top priority of Hungarian foreign policy since 1990 (Vida 2002: 47). After having signed the association agreement with the EC in 1991, Hungary applied for EU membership in 1994 and began the EU accession negotiations in 1998. Hence, EU constitution building was overshadowed by the last stage of accession negotiations in 2002 and the EU accession referendum in 2003. The priority for the Hungarian government was to secure favorable terms of entry into the European Union followed by the positive outcome of its accession referendum. In fact, the information campaign for the referendum made almost no connection between Hungary's future membership and EU constitution building.

In Hungary support for European integration has always been high. Both the 2003 accession referendum and the 2004 parliamentary vote ratifying the EU constitution confirmed that both the public and major political parties support the European Union. The accession referendum, held on 12 April 2003, showed that 83.8 percent of voters favored Hungary's EU membership. In November 2004 the Hungarians' trust in the European Union was third highest (64 percent) among all the member and candidate states. Moreover, 62 percent of those surveyed supported the EU constitution, while only 9 percent opposed it (Eurobarometer 2004b). Similarly, all mainstream parties, although presenting different degrees of Euro-enthusiasm, favored both Hungary's EU membership as well as passage of the EU constitution. Unsurprisingly, in a parliamentary ratification, the EU constitution was overwhelmingly supported by the Hungarian legislature in December 2004.

Domestic structures in a comparative perspective

Hungary's political system is organized around its parliament, the *Országgyűlés*, Hungary's directly elected, single-chamber legislature. Comprising 386 elected representatives elected to fixed four-year terms, parliament selects the prime minister by a simple majority vote. The prime minister then selects his own ministers, which do not have to be chosen from the legislature. The constitution provides for a "constructive motion of no confidence" similar to the German provision, but such a motion has never been put forward. The Hungarian system also provides for a President of the Republic to act as a largely ceremonial head of state, elected by two-thirds of parliament but real executive power is vested in the prime minister and the government.

The Hungarian electoral system is one of the most complicated in use anywhere. The electoral system currently in use emerged from complex bargaining during the 1989 roundtable talks between the outgoing Communist Party and the opposition. The law establishes a mixed-member system of representation where 176 districts are elected using a two-round runoff format, and the rest of the seats are elected according to proportional representation with a minimum nationwide vote of 5 percent required to win seats in the proportional allocation.

At the beginning of EU constitution building Hungary was deep in the midst of an extremely divided electoral campaign for the elections of April 2002. Despite predictions that the coalition of the Fidesz–Civic Party and the Independent Smallholders' Party that had governed from 1998 to 2002 would win re-election, they were narrowly defeated by the electoral coalition of the Hungarian Socialist Party and the Alliance of Free Democrats which formed a coalition government headed by Prime Minister Péter Medgyessy.[1]

While politics on most issues is sharply divided between the left-of-center ruling coalition and the right-of-center Fidesz–Hungarian Civic Party, there is a general consensus among all major parties favoring European accession and the strengthening of EU institutions. There are nuances, however; the Fidesz–Civic Party represents "Euro-realism" (*Magyar Hírlap*, 27 January 2003) characterized by a degree of "hidden Euro-skepticism" (Hegedűs 2003). However, the only parties openly against European integration were extreme parties with no seats from the 2002 election and only a few percentage points of the vote share. On the far right, the Hungarian Truth and Justice Party (MIÉP), with 4.4 percent of the list vote in 2002, was openly against Hungary's increased participation in a stronger EU. On the far left, Euro-skeptic views were expressed by the Hungarian Workers' Party, the *Munkáspárt*.

Constitutional policy coordination

In Hungary the minister of foreign affairs is responsible for leading and coordinating relations with the European Union. The analysis of the institutional elements of the ministry of foreign affairs illustrates the structural dimension of its centrality to the coordination and management of EU business in the Hungarian executive (Ágh and Rózsád 2004: 29).

The MFA hosts and facilitates the State Secretariat for Integration and External Economic Relations (SSIEER). Established in 1996, the SSIEER ensures a coherent approach to the EU and horizontal coordination of all aspect of EU–Hungarian relations. The EU coordination department in the SSIEER hosts an inter-ministerial Committee for EU Integration and an European Integration Council. While the inter-ministerial committee assures the coordination between the ministries, the European Integration Council is a consultative forum for the social partners focusing on European issues (Vida 2002: 65). Moreover, Prime Minister Medgyessy re-established an integration cabinet under his leadership which comprises the ministries of foreign affairs, of finance, of economy and of agriculture (Ágh and Rózsád 2004: 30).

Similarly, EU constitution building was coordinated by the MFA and, in particular, the State Secretariat for Integration and External Economic Relations. The SSIEER hosted an inter-ministerial task force composed of the representatives of the relevant ministries and different departments of the MFA. The Hungarian position at the IGC was approved by the integration cabinet, and soon after, the government approved the general mandate which was later discussed in the Grand Committee on European Integration[2] in the parliament in October 2003. During the IGC the reporting was constant and the foreign minister and the prime

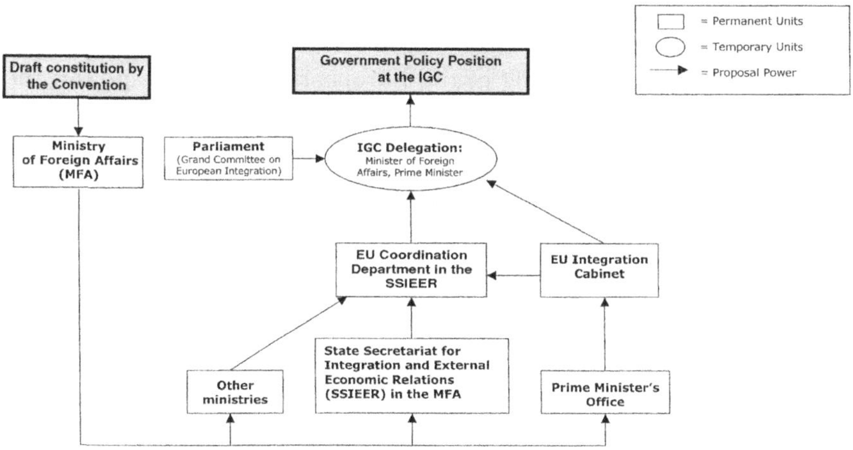

Figure 13.1 Hungary: domestic policy coordination for the IGC 2003–4.

minister, if needed, approved the adjustments to the Hungarian original position.

Data and empirical analysis of forming positions on the constitution for Europe

To investigate the positions of Hungarian actors on the EU constitution, we conducted two interviews with Hungarian experts in early 2004. One interviewee was an official from the State Secretariat for European Integration and External Economic Relations in the MFA while another interviewee was an outside government expert, an independent academic specializing in Hungary's EU relations. Both experts mentioned the MFA and the SSIEER as the most prominent in the formal coordination process.[3]

The vital issues for the Hungarian government at the IGC 2003–4, as presented by Foreign Minister László Kovács at the Grand Committee on European Integration in October 2003, included institutional balance and the protection of minority rights.

First, the institutional balance of the new European Union and the equality of all member states, regardless of their size and date of accession, should be preserved. The Hungarian representatives at the European Convention signed a joint initiative of 16 small and medium-size countries on institutional reform which emphasized the equality of member states and the preservation of the power equilibrium in the institutional triangle (European Parliament–Council–Commission). In general, the Hungarian government desired that the elements of the institutional reform should be considered in a package. The Hungarian position advocated keeping the rotating principle of the presidency. The Hungarian government favored a strong, independent Commission, extending its exclusive right of initiative and supported one commissioner per member state as envisaged in the Nice Treaty (Vida 2003). The Hungarian government accepted further strengthening of the European Parliament's power: the extension of majority voting in the Council, coupled with the co-decision procedure (Vida 2003). Moreover, it supported the European Parliament gaining extended rights in the adoption of the annual budget and the multi-annual financial framework.

Second, the rights of national and ethnic minorities should be protected and regarded as EU values. An SzDSz deputy justified the Hungarian position as follows: "the protection of the rights of minorities is an issue which is important for us, in the first instance, for domestic political reasons because there are significant Hungarian minorities which live in some neighboring countries" (Wekler 2003). Balázs, the Hungarian representative at the European Convention, added: "national minorities is a very special issue . . . after several divisions of former states, after the First World War, the Second World War, the collapse of the Soviet empire, nation and state are very different things in this part of the world" (*JEF Europe* 2003). The Hungarian government supported the protection of ethnic minorities because a significant number of Hungarian minorities live in neighboring countries as a result of previous dismemberment of Hungary, in particular the 1920 Treaty of Trianon.[4] This was an interesting postulate for the IGC, given the controversial Hungarian Status law[5] introduced in 2001 which granted special rights to ethnic Hungarians in neighboring countries. The opposition party also strongly supported the government's postulate. The Fidesz deputy put forward the idea of setting up a consultative committee for national and ethnic minorities representing the interests of the different minorities in the member states (Vida 2003: 53). For Mr Orbán, former Fidesz prime minister, the new essence of EU membership was "the spiritual association"[6] of all Hungarians inside and beyond the country's borders.

The two main postulates of the Hungarian position at the IGC had the support of all governmental actors mentioned by the experts as well as political parties. Our results confirm this view: the average governmental actor did not deviate from the national position (see Table 13.1). There were no deviating positions for policy related questions (0.0) as well as for institutional issues (0.0 percent). The domestic debate was thus characterized by no differences between the governmental actors.

However, the point of disagreement among the parliamentary parties was the Hungarian position on the inclusion of Christian values into the EU constitution. The official position of the Hungarian government was "not opposing, but not supporting." In fact, the Hungarian Socialist Party was not enthusiastic about a religious reference. However, the opposition, in particular Deputy Szájer (Fidesz) wanted the religious reference to be included in the preamble. In fact, during the EU constitution-building debate, the opposition criticized the government mainly on two issues: inadequate involvement of the opposition parties in the preparation and the lack of support regarding Christian values.

According to one of the interviewees, the Hungarian government also supported the advancement of a social market economy at the European level, although there was no discussion of exactly what this entailed. In the area of migration, the visa requirements for Hungarian minorities living abroad were considered to be problematic. Moreover, for the Hungarian government a progressive framing of a common defense policy was an option. The Hungarian position had two basic points: first, to allow enhanced cooperation only if half of the member states participate in it; and second, that the members of enhanced cooperation should support those who are unable to join in their efforts for joining later.

The vital issues mentioned above were salient for the Hungarian government. However, they could not be regarded as credible threats to block a possible agreement. In fact, after the IGC had commenced and after the compromise proposals of the Italian presidency of the EU

Table 13.1 Cohesiveness of actors' positions in the Hungarian coordination process

National position comparison	*Actor(s) (No. or type)*	*Observations (No.)*	*Deviations*									
			from national position		*on integration*				*related to*			
					toward less		*toward more*		*institutional issues*[a]		*policy fields*[a]	
			No.	*%*	*No.*	*%*	*No.*	*%*	*No.*	*%*	*No.*	*%*
All actors	5	325	0	–	0	–	0	–	0	–	0	–
Subset												
Lead unit	MFA	65	0	–	0	–	0	–	0	–	0	–

Deviations related to institutional issues
Nil

Deviations related to policy fields
Nil

Vital interests
Protection of ethnic and national minorities; Qualified majority threshold; Number of commissioners; Economic objectives; Enhanced cooperation; Regulation of jurisdiction with respect to external borders, immigration; Council voting rule for Common Security and Defense Policy

Notes
a Percentage shares refer to subsets of institutional (43) and policy (22) issues. *Lead Unit* Leading unit in domestic coordination: Prime Minister's Office (PM) or Ministry of Foreign Affairs (MFA).

Council of Ministers had been put forward (and later confirmed by the Irish presidency), the Hungarian position slightly evolved.

While the original Hungarian proposal, put forward at the European Convention and subsequently reiterated in the Hungarian position at the IGC, was to include in the preamble or among the fundamental rights the "protection of ethnic and national minorities," there was resistance from several countries, like Latvia, Belgium, Spain and France, to the proposal but the compromise formulation enabled them to reach agreement. The Hungarian government considered the compromise mentioning "rights of persons belonging to minorities" in Article I.2. to be acceptable. Consequently, the Hungarian government stressed that the final text of the EU constitution addressed the Hungarian concerns since the request of inclusion of the protection of minority rights as well as the "one country – one commissioner" principle until 2014 was accepted.

Moreover, with respect to enhanced cooperation in the area of foreign and security policy, although it was important for Hungary that the EU should develop its common defense policy, the government emphasized the danger of inefficient parallel structures and competition with NATO.

Furthermore, an important point of the Hungarian position was to maintain the equal rotation of member states for presidency of the Council. The proposal of the Italian presidency that three countries rotate during one year was acceptable for Hungary, and the government could support the permanent chairman of the Foreign Affairs Council.

On 20 December 2004 the Hungarian parliament voted overwhelmingly in favor of the EU constitution, with the 322–12 vote easily garnering the two-thirds majority of the 386 legislators required for passage. Of the 12 Hungarian deputies who voted against, seven were from the opposition Fidesz party and the rest were right-wing independent deputies. The Hungarian constitution permitted, but did not require, a binding and consultative referendum on the EU constitution. Such was the political support for the EU constitution that it was not deemed necessary. After the president had signed the EU constitution, Hungary's ratification process was formally completed.

The public debate in Hungary on EU constitution building was limited. In 2003 the communication strategy mainly focused on the EU accession referendum, while the debate on the future of Europe was marginal. The European Convention was discussed by a small group of experts with the debate being far from the public, although the so-called Friends of the Convention, the initiative of Péter Balázs, the Hungarian government's representative at the European Convention, represented an attempt to initiate debate. Nevertheless, the main debate focused on economic benefits of EU membership and favorable terms of EU accession, which was criticized mainly for a lack of vision of future Europe. As Csaba puts it:

> the real question is not what Hungary or any other accession country is likely to gain in terms of the net balance of official transfers, but instead, what model of the future EU is likely to be in the best interest of Hungary and other newcomers?
>
> (Csaba 2002: 5)

None the less, there was one issue in the future of Europe debate which gained the particular attention of the public: "the issue of protection of ethnic minorities dominated the news and policy analyses as if it had been the key issue regarding the historic European project" (Hegedűs 2004: 5). There were voices that the Hungarian priority had only relevance to domestic politics, so the Hungarian representatives at the IGC should have tried to talk "as little as possible" about this issue. "The Hungarian narrow-minded approach was not set in the context of the broader European debate on the future of the EU as in some other member states" (Hegedűs 2004: 5).

Conclusion

The parliamentary ratification of the EU constitution confirmed that there is a general consensus on the EU among all major political parties. Moreover, the Hungarians remain the third most pro-EU nation in the enlarged EU as the Eurobarometer survey showed in November 2004 (Eurobarometer 2004b). Although the degree of Euro-enthusiasm is varied, with the Fidesz–Hungarian Civic Party representing "Euro-realism" (*Magyar Hírlap*, 27 January 2003), two vital postulates for the IGC 2003–4 were supported.

The Hungarian vision of the EU focused on institutional balance and the protection of minority rights. The position of ministries coordinated by the State Secretariat for Integration and External Economic Relations in the MFA was united on the contested issues during the IGC. In addition, the only "exclusive" Hungarian proposal was also supported by the opposition Fidesz–Hungarian Civic Party. Certainly, for the Hungarians the past was important when designing the future EU institutional framework.

Acknowledgments

The authors would like to thank Dr Péter Györkös from the State Secretariat for Integration and External Economic Relations, Dr. István Hegedűs from the Hungarian Europe Society and an official from the ministry of foreign affairs for their support in conducting the research. Moreover, the authors want to thank the Delegation of the European Commission in Budapest and the Office for Foreign Relations in the Hungarian National Assembly.

Notes

1 Ferenc Gyurcsány replaced Péter Medgyessy as prime minister in August 2004, after Medgyessy had resigned due to a conflict with the coalition partner. The distribution of votes and seats in the most recent elections for parliament and the 2004 elections for the European Parliament, including the EP bloc affiliation of the parties, can be downloaded from the projects' website at dosei.dhv-speyer.de.

2 According to Agh and Rózsád (2004) the activities of the Hungarian parliament in European integration affairs are mainly carried out by parliamentary committees, especially by the Committee on European Integration Affairs and the Grand Committee on European Integration established in September 2002.

3 Modifying the coherence for the number of experts interviewed, we can compare the mean adapted coherence of the Hungarian case (0.98) with the overall coherence in the DOSEI data set, which is worse (0.85, see Appendix 2).

4 The Treaty of Trianon, signed in 1920, reduced the size and population of Hungary by about two-thirds, divesting it of virtually all areas that were not purely "Magyar." More than three million Hungarians were transferred to Romania, Yugoslavia and Czechoslovakia.

5 Under the 2001 Status Law ethnic Hungarians living in Romania, Slovakia, Ukraine, Serbia and Montenegro, Croatia and Slovenia were entitled to work in Hungary for a limited period, health treatment and education grants. Romania and Slovakia criticized the measure for being discriminatory and violating European standards. In June 2003 the Hungarian parliament amended the controversial law in an attempt to make it conform with EU guidelines, after the law had also been criticized by Brussels.

6 Cited in Hegedűs (2003).

14 Ireland

Pragmatism and the EU constitution

Anna Gwiazda

The EU constitution was agreed in June 2004 under the Irish presidency of the EU Council of Ministers. Certainly, the Irish pragmatic approach[1] facilitated the successful conclusion of the IGC 2003–4. Non-confrontational exploitation of opportunities as well as the negotiating skills and quiet diplomacy of *An Taoiseach* Bertie Ahern and his officials facilitated the final compromise (Institute of European Affairs 2004). This approach was not surprising given that the Irish politics and political culture are characterized by a pragmatic and non-ideological attitude. Similarly, "pragmatism, rather than any political or ideological commitment, frames the traditional picture of Irish attitudes toward European integration" (Tonra 2002: 201).

Ireland joined the European Communities in 1973 along with Denmark and the UK. Ireland's EC accession was a milestone in opening a poor European state to a global economy and reducing its economic dependence on the UK. A combination of domestic and international factors enabled Ireland to overcome its economic problems of the 1980s. The economy grew rapidly in the 1990s and Ireland came to be called Europe's "Celtic tiger." Per capita GDP in Ireland has increased from almost 60 percent of the EC average in 1973 to well over 100 percent today (Department of Foreign Affairs 2004).

EU constitution building attracted political attention in Ireland after the second Nice referendum in October 2002. Initially, it was overshadowed by the national argument on the Nice Treaty and the two referendum campaigns (Brown 2003: 1). Despite the widespread support for the EU (over three-quarters of the Irish regard Ireland's EU membership as "a good thing," Eurobarometer 2004b), the Nice referendum in June 2001 resulted in 54 percent of voters saying "no" on a turnout of 35 percent.[2] Following the negative result, the government wanted to reassure Ireland's EU partners that Ireland was committed to the EU and, consequently, held the referendum a second time. In October 2002, 63 percent favored the ratification of the Nice Treaty on the turnout of 49.5 percent.

Domestic structures in a comparative perspective

Ireland is a constitutional parliamentary democracy. The Irish system of government has been categorized as a variation of the Westminster model (Gallagher *et al.* 2006) which is characterized *inter alia* by the doctrines of cabinet responsibility and cabinet confidentiality.[3] One of the important differences from the Westminster model is the significance of the codified constitution in Irish politics and government (Coakley and Gallagher 2005). The 1937 constitution stipulates that the government exercises the executive power. In the Irish system the cabinet, headed by the *Taoiseach*,[4] is the center of political decision making. On legislative power, Article 15 of the Irish constitution stipulates that the parliament, which is known as the *Oireachtas*, consists of the president and two houses: a house of representatives called *Dáil Éireann*, which has 166 members and a senate called *Seanad Éireann*, which has 60 senators. Members of *Dáil Éireann*, called TDs,[5] are elected on the basis of STV proportional representation to serve five-year terms. The May 2002 parliamentary elections resulted in the re-election of the Fianna Fáil–Progressive Democrat government headed by *Taoiseach* Bertie Ahern (FF). Most of the major political parties, Fianna Fáil, Fine Gael, the Labor Party and the Progressive Democrats, have supported European integration, though Sinn Féin and the Greens are exceptions.[6]

Constitutional policy coordination

In Ireland the Department of Foreign Affairs (DFA) is responsible for coordination of day-to-day EU business while the macro sensitive dossiers are dealt with by the foreign affairs department and the *Taoiseach's* department (Laffan and O'Mahony 2003: 99, Department of the Taoiseach 2003). The DFA supervises developments in the EU from an institutional and political perspective while the Department of the *Taoiseach* (DT) is essential to the conduct of Ireland's EU policy because it serves as the secretariat of the *Taoiseach* (Laffan and O'Mahony 2003: 38). Moreover, other departments are involved in the management of EU business. Furthermore, the establishment of the EU Committee strengthened the Irish cabinet in the EU field.

Similarly, EU constitution building was coordinated by the department of foreign affairs. In particular, the European Union Division in the DFA, which manages Ireland's EU relations, was key to the coordination process (see Figure 14.1). The EU division cooperated with the political division, in the area of foreign and security policy and with the legal division on the Charter of Fundamental Rights. There were bilateral contacts between the DFA and other departments as well as interdepartmental activity. When the Irish government's position at the IGC was formed the consultation process was rather informal. The DFA took also the lead in the

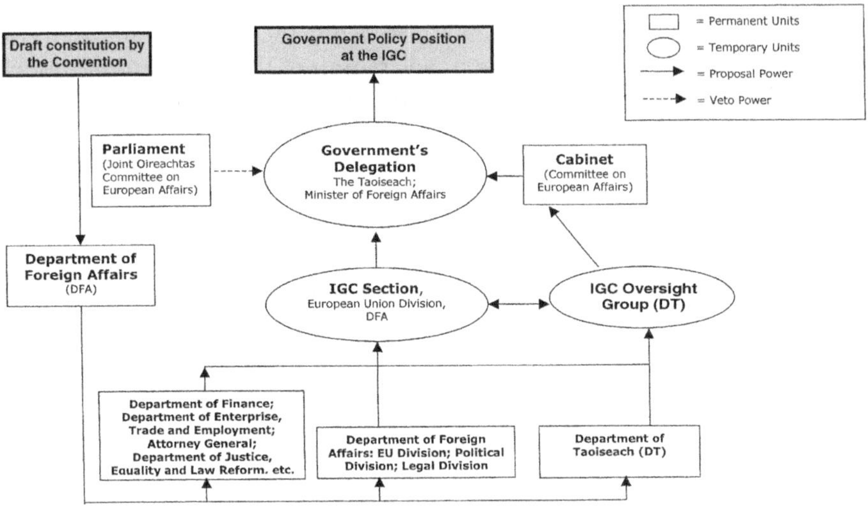

Figure 14.1 Ireland: domestic policy coordination for the IGC 2003–4.

coordination of the Irish presidency of the EU Council of Ministers during which there was extensive high-level political and official interdepartmental coordination and discussion of the IGC issues and the Irish government's position at the IGC 2003–4.

The EU and International Unit in the DT chaired and serviced the IGC Oversight Group, which was set up in October 2003 to monitor the IGC developments. Officials from the departments of foreign affairs, of finance, of enterprise, trade and employment and of justice, equality and law reform attended the sessions while the EU division in the DFA prepared briefing papers.

The Cabinet Committee on European Affairs chaired by the *Taoiseach* was the main formal forum for political coordination of the Irish government's position because key decisions were taken at cabinet level.

The Joint *Oireachtas* Committee on European Affairs consisting of the Select Committee of *Dáil Éireann* and the Select Committee of *Seanad Éireann* did not play a formal role in policy formulation. It had regular briefings from the minister of state for European affairs and the minister for foreign affairs. However, as one of the interviewees noticed there was no obvious policy input.

The role of the National Forum on Europe, established in October 2001 to keep the public informed about all EU issues, was limited in shaping the government's position on the IGC. However, it certainly has a role to play during the ratification process of the EU constitution.

Data and empirical analysis of forming positions on the constitution for Europe

For the study of domestic coordination process in Ireland, four experts were interviewed in November and December 2003 in Dublin. Two interviews were carried out with experts from within the governmental system: a senior official from the DT and a senior official from the DFA. Moreover, one interview was conducted with the Irish representative at the European Convention and the fourth interview was conducted with an academic specializing in Ireland's EU policy.

Of all the actors involved in the coordination process the experts mentioned the department of foreign affairs and the department of the *Taoiseach* as the most relevant, yet, other departments took part in the formation of the government's position at the IGC 2003–4.[7]

Overall, the Irish government welcomed the outcome of the European Convention, although there were some areas of concern such as defense, taxation and criminal law (Institute of European Affairs 2003: 2).

First and foremost, the Irish government advocated a balanced institutional framework in which the interests and fundamental equality of all member states were protected. The Irish government advocated strengthening and underpinning of each side of the institutional triangle – the Council, the Commission and the European Parliament. With respect to the European Commission, it should preserve its central role with the right to initiate legislation. The interviewees observed that the Irish government could live with the idea of having fewer commissioners than the number of member states, on condition that equality was secured. With respect to the six-monthly rotation of the presidency of the European Council, Foreign Minister Cowen considered possible changes to the running of Council presidencies (Cowen 2003). As regards a qualified majority voting threshold in the Council, the Irish government agreed in Nice to the Nice model. Yet, a preferable option was the Convention proposal. Consequently, the Irish government could assume a flexible approach to the contested institutional issues, such as the number of commissioners, the Council presidency modus, the Council voting rules, on condition equality of all member states was maintained. Any institutional arrangement could be possible as long as EU member states were equally represented. The Foreign Minister Cowen stated, "so long as basic principles are respected ... we will be open, imaginative and flexible" (Cowen 2003).

The Irish vital interest also included defense, taxation and criminal law. Roche emphasized in his contribution to the European Convention: "There should be a further extension of the co-decision procedure in the legislative field. Such a move would go hand in hand with QMV in the Council ... However, particular sensitivities of Member States may require different procedures" (Roche *et al.* 2003: 7). In fact, the Irish government insisted at the IGC on maintenance of unanimity in taxation. Moreover, the Irish government wanted to ensure that nothing in the EU constitution would threaten the national, common-law-based system in criminal law.

The Irish government expressed reservations about specific procedures in European security and defense policy. Foreign policy cooperation remained a controversial area because neutrality has always been a sensitive issue in Ireland. Roche recognized that while the Irish government "would not stand in the way of others, Ireland cannot participate in EU common defense policy without the prior consent of the people in a referendum" (Roche *et al.* 2003) Ireland's non-membership of NATO and a traditional policy of military neutrality made successive Irish governments cautious and constrained concerning the development of a security dimension to the EU's external action (Tonra 2001).

The main postulates of the Irish government's position at the IGC 2003–4 had the support of all government actors mentioned by the experts. Our results confirm this observation. There is a high consistency of positions (see Table 14.1): the average actor deviated on 0.5 percent of the issues from the national position. The average percentage of deviating positions mentioned for policy-related questions is higher (1.5) than for institutional issues (0.0 percent). There was some deviation in the area of the Stability and Growth Pact but as one of the interviewees noticed the reason might be the lack of the debate on this issue. Certainly, the government believed that the SGP should not be made more flexible and the rules should not be changed easily. In general, the domestic debate in Ireland was characterized by no difference between the actors on institutional issues. In fact, the priority of the institutional balance was understood in a broad sense and allowed flexibility in institutional arrangements as long as equality of all member states was preserved.

When Ireland took up the presidency of the EU Council of Ministers on 1 January 2004 it was to deal with a constitutional debate after the failure of the Italian presidency. At the spring European Council in March 2004 the Irish presidency announced relaunching of the IGC talks thus, "signaling a renewed sense of political resolve among EU leaders just two weeks after the terrorist bombings in Madrid" (Institute of European Affairs 2004). The strategy of the presidency reflected its willingness to consider every state's concerns and capitalize upon the progress made during the Italian presidency. This approach, supported by the stock of goodwill of all 25 EU member states, allowed successful steering through parliament of the EU constitution (ibid.).

The Irish presidency had an impact on Ireland's approach to the IGC: reaching a consensus became the top priority while Irish national interests were secondary and could not dominate the talks. One of the interviewees pointed out that the aim was to act as the presidency and not become caught up in the work of the department of finance (on tax issues) and

Table 14.1 Cohesiveness of actors' positions in the Irish coordination process

National position comparison	*Actor(s) (No. or type)*	*Observations (No.)*	*Deviations*									
			from national position		*on integration*				*related to*			
					toward less		*toward more*		*institutional issues*[a]		*policy fields*[a]	
			No.	*%*	*No.*	*%*	*No.*	*%*	*No.*	*%*	*No.*	*%*
All actors	3	195	1	0.5	0	–	1	0.5	0	–	1	1.5
Subset												
Lead unit	DFA	65	0	–	0	–	0	–	0	–	0	–

Deviations related to institutional issues
Nil

Deviations related to policy fields
Stability and Growth Pact

Vital interests
Status of Charter of Fundamental Rights; European Commission; Scope of jurisdiction of European Court of Justice; Regulation of jurisdiction with respect to defense; Council voting rule for taxes/tax harmonization, and for justice and home affairs (criminal law)

Notes

a Percentage shares refer to subsets of institutional (43) and policy (22) issues. *Lead Unit* Leading unit in domestic coordination: Prime Minister's Office (PM) or Ministry of Foreign Affairs (MFA).

the department of justice (on criminal matters). This approach was perceived as an obvious indication of Irish pragmatism.

Although Ireland, like other member states, did not achieve everything it sought, there was nothing in the final text of the constitution to which it was fundamentally opposed (Institute of European Affairs 2004). The final text guaranteed the maintenance of unanimity in the areas of taxation, social security, defense, and European public prosecutor. However, there was extension of QMV to certain procedural matters in the criminal law sphere and in immigration and asylum.

In June 2005 *Taoiseach* Bertie Ahern confirmed Ireland's plans to hold a referendum on the EU constitution. In fact, ratifications of previous significant steps of European integration in Ireland were based on referendums. Article 46 of the 1937 constitution stipulates that a proposal to amend the Irish constitution must be passed by both houses of the *Oireachtas* and then put to a referendum. Moreover, the supreme court judgment in the 1987 Crotty case was important for decisions to hold referendums on issues pertaining to the EU.[8]

The "yes" campaign for the ratification of the EU constitution was broad. The coalition government of Fianna Fáil and the Progressive Democrats as well as the opposition parties, Fine Gael and the Labour Party supported the EU constitution. Nevertheless, one political party which actively campaigned against the new constitution was Sinn Féin. Irish neutrality and fight against a "militarized Europe" were again significant parts of the anti-EU debate in Ireland. Moreover, in April 2005 the group, led by former Greens MEP Patricia McKenna, acting in a personal capacity and anti-EU "fringe" parties (such as the Workers' Party and the Communist Party of Ireland), launched a campaign against the EU constitution (*Irish Times*, 1 April 2005). Despite Ireland's traditional enthusiasm for the EU and the success of the Irish presidency, the Irish government could not take the "yes" vote in the referendum for granted. The Eurobarometer survey in November 2004 showed that 45 percent had never heard about the constitution (Eurobarometer 2004b). Moreover, only 28 percent of respondents were in favor of the EU constitution, while 67 percent replied "don't know." The lesson of the Irish referendums on the Nice Treaty is the need for the elites to inform and engage the Irish in the public debate.

Conclusion

The Irish government assumed a pragmatic approach during the IGC and its presidency of the EU Council of Ministers in the first half of 2004. After the breakdown of the Brussels summit in December 2003, one of the main priorities of the Irish presidency was to reach the final agreement on the EU constitution. The Irish strategy, supported by the goodwill of all 25 EU member states, allowed the successful passage of the EU constitution in June 2004.

During the IGC 2003–4 the core executive was crucial in determining the Irish strategy and formulating the preferences on the EU constitution, while the role of parliament was limited. The coordination focused in the department of foreign affairs and the department of the *Taoiseach*. The position of the key department was united. Any tensions among the departments were muted during the Irish presidency in order to facilitate the agreement on the EU constitution.

Acknowledgments

The author would like to thank Professor Brigid Laffan, University College Dublin, and two officials from the department of foreign affairs for their support in conducting the research. The author also wishes to thank Professor Michael Gallagher, Department of Political Science, Trinity College Dublin, for his comments on the final draft.

Notes

1 The author wants to acknowledge Professor Ben Tonra and Professor Michael Gallagher for their emphasis on the importance of pragmatism in Irish politics (Tonra 2002, Gallagher *et al.* 2006).
2 For the analysis of the "no" vote in the 2001 Nice referendum see Brown (2003: 1).
3 The Irish government is "collectively responsible" to the *Dáil*, i.e., all members of the cabinet are bound by all cabinet decisions. While "cabinet confidentiality" requires that all cabinet discussions remain confidential, as confirmed by the 1992 Supreme Court decision, yet, the position was changed slightly by a referendum on cabinet confidentiality in 1997 (Coakley and Gallagher 2005).
4 In Ireland the Prime Minister is called the *Taoiseach*.
5 TD, or *Teachta Dála*, is the Irish version of a Member of Parliament.
6 The distribution of votes and seats in the most recent elections for parliament and the 2004 elections for the European Parliament, including the EP bloc affiliation of the parties, can be downloaded from the projects' website at dosei.dhv-speyer.de.
7 Modifying the coherence for the number of experts interviewed we can compare the mean adapted coherence of the Irish case (0.95) with the overall coherence in the DOSEI data set, which is lower (0.85, see Appendix 2).
8 Crotty v. An Taoiseach and the other members of the Government of Ireland, Ireland and the Attorney General, Supreme Court, [1987] ILRM 4000, 9 April.

15 Italy

The presidency at work?

Tobias Schulz

As one of the founding members of the EU, Italy acted as a mediator, sometimes even as an initiator, in the process of European integration from the beginning until the end of the 1990s. This was not solely the program of the political elite but was strongly backed by public opinion (Hine 2004). However, the political elite has lost some of the Euro-enthusiasm it used to have in the early stages.

At the beginning of the European Convention, some observers feared that the Italian delegation would fail to form a common position (Fabbrini 2004). Although this clearly changed during the Convention and the IGC for most of the delegates (Fabbrini 2004), the profile of Prime Minister Berlusconi remained rather low (Fabbrini 2004). Ironically, Italy was foreseen as the next country to take over the presidency of the European Council and to host the concluding IGC. On the other hand, the "shadow of the IGC" probably helped the Italian actors to set back power struggles.

Euro-skepticism has become a quite important factor in the rhetoric of the ruling right-wing parties.[1] Because of the strong bi-polarity of the current party system, the junior partner UDC has no alternative but to build coalitions, although it is somewhat better disposed toward the EU than its partners in the government.

At the time of writing the constitutional treaty had already been ratified by the parliament, which is the only relevant actor in this last phase.[2]

From an economic point of view, however, the Italians might have good reason for a less pro-European attitude. Like most of the other big western European democracies, Italy experienced some growth weaknesses during the 1990s and now definitely joins Germany as the rear light. The unemployment rate is not only remarkably low (8.7 percent) but also varies greatly regionally. The agricultural sector in Italy is rather small and compared to France less influential. Similar to Germany (although to a much lesser extent), Italy is also a net contributor to the EU budget (Weise 2002) and struggling with the criteria of the Stability and Growth Pact.

Although Italy does have some partly autonomous regions, the country remains highly unitary. One important dividing line within the coalition is therefore the goal of the Northern League (LN) to decentralize the country.

Domestic structures in a comparative perspective

Italy clearly is a parliamentary system with a president who has nothing but ceremonial functions apart from small possibilities to set back legislation. After 1993, the party system completely changed: the formerly omnipotent Christian Democrats decayed and now remain a rather small party (UDC). Building on its voters, *Forza Italia* (FI) evolved, the party of the prime minister. Furthermore, the former fascists, the *Alleanza Nationale* (AN), were able to gain a rather strong standing in Italian politics. As a protest party, the *Lega Nord* (LN) conquered from the north but remained rather marginal. Those four parties form the government since 2001, and together they hold a comfortable majority over the somewhat divided left.[3]

The two chambers of the national assembly are symmetrical and congruent, which is classified as "medium-strength bicameralism" by Lijphart (1999). Since the overhaul of the electoral system in 1993, both chambers are elected according to a mixed system, with 75 percent of the seats based on single member districts.

Although the Italian party system has always been highly fragmented, its fragmentation even rose after the breakdown of the Soviet regimes in the east and the rise of the new center–region conflict: Before the 1990s the number of effective parties amounted to about four and a half but the new party system includes roughly six to seven effective parties (Armingeon *et al.* 2004). Some observers already find tendencies that point into the direction of a bi-polarization of the party system (Morlino 2001, Grassi 2003).

Thus, the Italian political system remains a special case even after the crisis of the 1990s.[4] The most distinctive feature that has remained so far is its "particracy" (Calise 1994), i.e., the dependence of the political process and its institutions on the parties. Italy has a weak government relative to parliament *and* a weak parliament relative to the parties. This has caused bad legislative performance, namely the production of a vast number of insignificant laws (so-called *leggine*) (Kreppel 1997) as well as the rise of "reiterated decrees,"[5] which reflects the tendency toward an ever growing number of parties participating in government coalitions (Kreppel 1997). Consequently, important and difficult decisions are partially resolved outside the parliament.[6]

The other distinctive characteristic of the Italian system is the instability of Italian governments.[7] The reason lies in the weakness of the prime minister, who has to assert his leadership through "persuasion, manipulation or negotiation" (Hine and Finocchi 1991). This requires either low-profile behind-the-scenes behavior or rhetoric strength. Former Prime Minister Berlusconi chose the latter option but it was also to his advantage that the new electoral system puts more weight on party leaders (Donovan 1995), and that many of the members of his government had already experienced the drawbacks of lacking coherence in his first cabinet (1994–6). Furthermore, Berlusconi was party leader and prime minister at the same time, which breaks an unwritten rule and hence strengthens his influence additionally.

Constitutional policy coordination

The administrative body that coordinated the national position (Figure 15.1), the General Directorate of European Integration, resides within the ministry of foreign affairs (*La Farnesina*). The *Farnesina* is the only place where such a task could be hosted. It has also been in charge of the Italian presidency of the European Council and the IGC in December 2003. It might be worth mentioning that the Foreign Minister, Frattini, seemed to be a relatively weak figure, at least at the beginning, being highly dependent on the prime minister and having certainly not the high profile of his predecessor Ruggiero. Besides the prime minister, Fini was at the forefront, since he is vice-premier, party leader (AN) as well as the delegate to the European Convention. With the nomination of Fini, the prime minister delegated the task but without giving up the influence of the prime minister's office. Additionally, a special ministry of "community politics" (DPCE) was set up and affiliated with the prime minister, headed by the minister without portfolio Rocco Buttiglione. Although this ministry is actually busy with supervising and coordinating the transfer of EU guidelines into national law, formally, Buttiglione was incorporated, and he certainly increased the influence of the prime minister's office further. However, as Hine (2004) puts it, although the prime minister's office had received more coordinating power with the administrative reform of 1999, it is unlikely

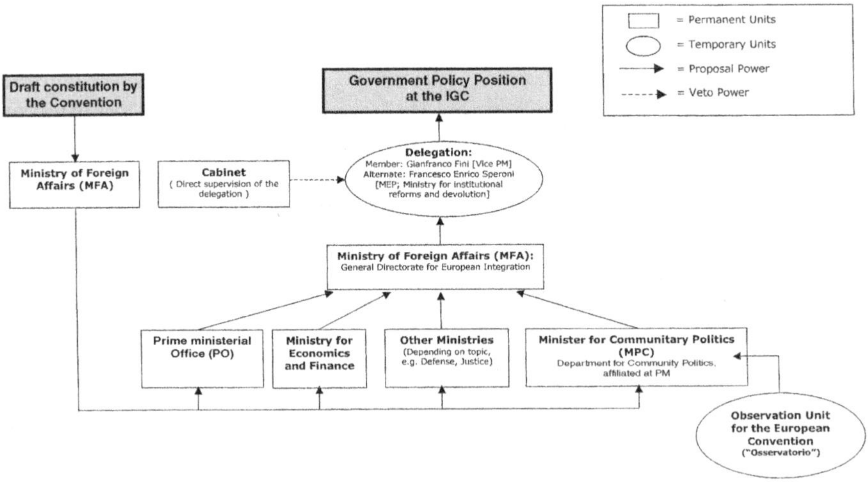

Figure 15.1 Italy: domestic policy coordination for the IGC 2003–4.

that this did affect the result and the potential for conflict between the foreign ministry and the prime minister's office remained marginal.

Obviously, all the (ruling) party leaders as well as the ministers with the most important portfolios were automatically included in the position formation process. President Ciampi has not had a very decisive role. However, he has arranged working meetings on the ministerial level at the Palazzo del Quirinale. One important such meeting took place in November 2002. Ciampi invited Prime Minister Berlusconi, Deputy Prime Minister Fini, Minister of Community Politics Buttiglione, Minister of Economic Affairs and Public Finance Tremonti, Minister of Defense Martino, Minister of Foreign Affairs Frattini and Secretary of the Prime Minister's Office Letta (*Corriere della Sera,* 30 November 2002).

At the beginning of the process, it was virtually impossible to perceive clear positions on the part of any of the prominent members of the government (Fabbrini 2004, Hine 2004). Nevertheless, the head of the powerful integrated super-ministry for public finance and the economy, Tremonti, was known to be very much determined to hinder progress in integration regarding tax and financial policies (Höhne 2003), and because of this strong position within the government his influence is obvious. Formally, Bossi has only indirect influence through the deputy delegate to the European Convention, Speroni, who is also a member of the LN (*Corriere della Sera,* 28 February 2003). Bossi's rather Euro-skeptical views were often far too extreme to be taken as serious proposals even by his coalition partners. According to our interviewees, he is suspected to have determined the Italian position concerning some (less important) questions.

By setting up an "observatory on the Convention," a temporary body that served as a platform for Italy's strong non-governmental organizations, the ministry of community politics (Buttiglione) promoted public debate. This body lacked any decision-making authority. Looking at its composition, however, reveals that important functionaries and counselors of the administration did follow and engage in the discussion. It is unlikely that this discussion had a direct influence on the position of the government, though.

Furthermore, no indication could be found that would substantiate the formal involvement of the parliament or the opposition in the position formation process of the government. Of course, the Vice-president of the European Convention, Amato, and the President of the Commission, Prodi, are both Italians and therefore they certainly did have some impact on the debate in their home countries and probably also on the Italian delegation during the Convention.

Data and empirical analysis of forming positions on the constitution for Europe

Two experts were interviewed in Italy between mid- and late November 2003. The first was a member of the government administration, namely the general directorate of European integration. The second was an academic working on European integration and the Convention.

Both interviewees mentioned the following key actors in the interviews: the prime minister, the deputy prime minister, the minister of foreign affairs, the minister of economic affairs and public finance and the minister of community politics.[8] The *Lega Nord* was explicitly mentioned only by one of the interview partners, the other one mentioned this party only tacitly. In addition, the minister of justice and the parliament were recognized as players with some influence only when prompted at the beginning.

Since decentralization (or "devolution") and Euro-skepticism had emerged as some of the main conflict lines during the last decades in Italy and since these issues are also burdening the government coalition quite heavily, it is only natural that these are also the most salient issues in the debate on the future of Europe. This is mirrored to some extent in the interventions of Fini: he proposed to restrict the free movement of persons and to prevent explicit mention of "federal" structures. Furthermore, he also spoke in favor of a common defense system and the importance of Christianity as the basis of European values (Quirico 2003, Hine 2004).

After all, it is difficult to determine a clear preference profile of Italy on the most important issues the Convention was dealing with. The main reason may be that Italy was already anticipating its special role as the country that had to host the next IGC. Therefore, most of the Italian positions are directed toward finding a compromise (Dassù *et al.* 2003).

Apart from that, one issue that obviously was somewhat important to the public discussion in Italy as well had been the reference to Christianity in the preamble. This discussion had been initiated by the Vatican (*La Stampa*, 31 May 2003). Other salient issues were debated in the media and in public merely because of the open disputes between the Italian government and the European Union, for example concerning the restriction of the European arrest warrant and the blocking of tax harmonization (Quirico 2003).

We are therefore able to present some additional information on the "vital" issues with our questionnaire: Our experts mentioned none of the fundamental institutional questions. Rather, they were indicating issues such as the delegation of competencies in certain areas, as for example the regulation of jurisdiction with respect to defense as well as the establishment of QMV in the areas of social policy, taxation and defense respectively.[9]

The main conclusion from these observations as well as the analysis of Hine (2004) and Fabbrini (2004) is that the Italian actors had been less divided than one would have expected. Our results confirm that a deviation from the national position can be detected in only four cases, which is not more than 0.8 percent (Table 15.1). Since for the questions

Table 15.1 Cohesiveness of actors' positions in the Italian coordination process

National position comparison	*Actor(s) (No. or type)*	*Observations (No.)*	*Deviations*									
			from national position		*on integration*				*related to*			
					toward less		*toward more*		*institutional issues*[a]		*policy fields*[a]	
			No.	*%*	*No.*	*%*	*No.*	*%*	*No.*	*%*	*No.*	*%*
All actors	8	520	4	0.8	4	0.8	0	–	3	0.9	1	0.6
Subset												
Lead unit	MFA	65	0	–	0	–	0	–	0	–	0	–

Deviations related to institutional issues
Subsidiarity (role of national parliaments); Right to withdraw from the Union; Voting rule (Council) for Area of Freedom, Security and Justice

Deviations related to policy fields
Charter of Fundamental Rights

Vital interests
Regulation of jurisdiction with respect to external policy; Council voting rules for taxes/tax harmonization, for Common Security and Defense Policy, for social security

Notes
a Percentage shares refer to subsets of institutional (43) and policy (22) issues. *Lead Unit* Leading unit in domestic coordination: Prime Minister's Office (PM) or Ministry of Foreign Affairs (MFA).

regarding the policy fields only one deviating answer can be found (0.6 percent), the three other deviations are related to institutional issues (0.9 percent).

The most problematic coalition partner, the Northern League, had caused three of those four deviations we were able to identify. These are issues for which the *Lega Nord* is known to have somewhat less integrationist views (the status of the charter of fundamental rights, the role of the national parliaments and the principle of subsidiarity as well as the right to withdraw from the EU). But all in all, these are rather limited differences.

We also have received some additional information about a deviation of the Italian minister of justice's position (who is a member of the *Lega Nord*): he obviously was reluctant to accept majority voting in the area of "freedom, security and justice."

If we compare the positions among the prime minister's office, the leading *Farnesina* and the position of the government as a whole, we have to conclude that we are not able to uncover such differences at all. This is maybe not surprising if one considers the low profile and the weak standing of Foreign Minister Frattini. We would probably have expected some differences between the prime minister's office and the MFA, but as Hine (2004) has pointed out, in the end that potential conflict turned out to be of minor impact.

Conclusion

No coalition breakdowns disturbed the rather long phases of the Convention and the IGC negotiations. Among the above-mentioned reasons for such enhanced stability, one possible reason might also have been that Italy was a key actor in the process, as it held the presidency of the European Council and hosted the first IGC, which had already been anticipated during the Convention stage.

However, all observers agree that the members of the Italian delegation made considerable progress during the Convention (Fabbrini 2004) in developing an original and – most notably – common position that did, however, not deviate as much from the traditional Italian position as the preceding rhetoric would have suggested (Hine 2004). Many governmental actors did not hold strong opinions on the issues discussed at the Convention and the subsequent IGCs. Although the office of the prime minister has gained in influence during the last few years and although the foreign minister was not a very strong figure, the *Farnesina* kept the traditional lead in the position formation process. Also, Deputy Prime Minister Fini received considerable freedom as the delegate of the government, which was a good opportunity for him to quietly dissociate himself from the obstructionist elements in the coalition. Of course, he did introduce some "reactionary" elements but since these suggestions were rejected by the Convention anyway, and since the opposition is even more in favor of the constitution as the government, ratification by parliament on 25 January 2005 (lower house) and 6 April 2005 (upper house) was no big deal, in the end.

Notes

1 Italy has long been regarded as a country that supports the federal vision of the EU. The immediate evidence seems to lie in the results of the famous referendum of June 1989 in which almost 80 percent expressed support for the idea of a European government being responsible to the European Parliament. The referendum, however, was only consultative and it is hypothesized that the strong support stemmed from the lacking trust of the Italians in their own institutions and parties (Rusconi 2003).

2 The procedure for the ratification of international treaties is particularly unspectacular in Italy: Article 75 explicitly precludes popular referendum from the ratification procedures and Article 80 foresees that the ratification of international treaties shall be authorized by law, which means that in the end it requires only simple majorities in both chambers if no constitutional amendment would be necessary. If a constitutional amendment is involved the parliamentarian procedure is somewhat more complicated but a referendum is still impossible. The lower house accepted the treaty on 25 January and the upper house on 6 April, both by a wide margin. Also the public still approved the constitution, as a Eurobarometer poll has indicated (Eurobarometer 2005).

3 The distribution of votes and seats in the most recent elections for parliament and the 2004 elections for the European Parliament, including the EP bloc affiliation of the parties, can be downloaded from the projects' website at dosei.dhv-speyer.de.

4 The complex nature of this political system is also confirmed if one looks at the veto-player index of Tsebelis (2002: 182): here, Italy ranks highest with an index of 4.7.

5 Legislators have taken the habit to pass decrees of time-limited validity which are reconfirmed before their validity will expire.

6 The tendency to partially exclude the democratic institutions from real decisions is also reflected in the informal rules. Sometimes important decisions are negotiated outside the legislature between the interest groups, the government and the parties. Such informal forms of "extra-governmental party bargaining" (Criscitiello 1993) have been established in the form of "majority summits."

7 Although Italian governments have been chronically unstable, they have nevertheless consisted of majority coalitions most of the time since the 1980s.

8 A comparison of the experts' answers reveals that overall their answers were reasonably coherent (0.88) and slightly above the mean of the questionnaire (0.85, see Appendix 2). Since neither interviewee uncovered many deviations from the national position anyway, the coherence index is about the same for all actors mentioned. Some minor players had been mentioned by only one expert, namely the higher-rated expert. Interestingly, some of them had been explicitly ruled out by the second expert.

16 Latvia and the EU constitution

A pragmatic "yes"

Stephanie Daimer

Public support for transferring national sovereignty to the European Union has never been large in Latvia, after it regained its independence from the Soviet Union only in 1991. EU support has never been above 50 percent in the last years, and in the country's first European elections in 2004 the nationalist Fatherland Party won four of the nine Latvian seats. NATO membership on the contrary has been welcomed by far more enthusiastically. However, there is broad pragmatic agreement about the economic necessity for integration in the EU, which is why a clear majority of 67 percent voted in favor of the country's EU membership in the accession referendum. A similar majority has expressed general support for the European constitution (European Forum 2004, Eurobarometer 2003c, 2004a). Nevertheless, the ratification of the constitution involved only the parliament (*Saeima*), which accepted it on 2 June 2005.[1] Similar to the ratification of the accession treaty, a large parliamentary majority could be expected given that the constitutional debate created no major conflicts between the parties and Euro-skeptic voices are now only weakly represented in the *Saeima*.[2]

Chronic instability marks the political situation of the independent Latvia, which is closely linked to severe economic problems caused by the transition process (Roberts 2003: 7). The cabinet of Prime Minister Aigars Kalvitis came into office in December 2004 and is no less than the third government since the 2002 general elections. After the failure of the preceding minority government, Prime Minister Kalvitis's conservative People's Party formed an oversized coalition with the conservative New Era, the Christian-Democratic First Party and the conservative-agrarian Greens and Farmers Union, holding 70 of 100 seats in the *Saeima*.[3]

The government's agenda shows that the pressing issues are economic and structural reforms, mentioning the health care system, a balanced budget, inflation, competitiveness and the privatization process. Although Latvia's economy has shown a very dynamic growth with an average (real) GDP growth rate of 6 percent in the last years, it is still the poorest EU country, where the per capita income lies at about 40 percent of the EU average.[4] Still, also corruption is a big issue, in particular high-level or "state capture" corruption, which shapes laws and regulations being dominated by business interests.[5] At the same time, Latvia has entered the Exchange Rate Mechanism (ERM 2), joining Lithuania, Estonia, Slovenia, Malta and Cyprus in the "waiting room" for the euro. Given that they meet the Maastricht criteria, which means for Latvia in particular efforts to reach the euro zone target for inflation, joining the single currency is possible after a minimum of two years in the ERM 2 and currently planned by the Latvian government for 2008 (*EUobserver*, 2 May 2005).

Latvia is strongly ethnically divided. About 30 percent of Latvia's 2.3 million inhabitants are of Russian origin, a fact that still presents a major integration problem. Due to international pressure, Latvia changed its naturalization law in 1998 and created a ministry of integration in 2002. Still, about half of the Russian population do not have Latvian nationality. Summed up with other minorities, about 20 percent of the population are excluded from political participation and economic rights (Schmidt 2004).

Domestic structures in a comparative perspective

Latvia has a parliamentary system, providing specific competencies for the unicameral parliament such as the election of judges and the president.[6] In a comparative perspective, the executive–legislative relationship turns out to be unbalanced, and measures of cabinet strength yield extreme low scores (Lijphart 1999, Roberts 2003).[7] Changes in the Latvian party system have often forced governments to form either minority or oversized coalitions in the parliament, both of which are formations that are likely to break.

The party system shows a comparatively great instability.[8] Party affiliation is not very stable, either among voters or among party elites. In every election since 1991 a party has won that had been founded less than one year before the poll. All governments so far have been supported by center–right coalitions. However, also the pattern of Western party system cleavages does not apply for the Latvian party system. A rough characterization of the parties on the classical left–right scale is possible, but what is crucial is more of an East–West cleavage; the attitude toward the heritage of the Soviet regime and the Russian part of the population. As Auers (2003) puts it "'Left' ideas in Latvia are associated with a pro-Russian citizenship and foreign policy as well as a psychological association with the former Soviet regime." As the independence of the Soviet regime and the integration into NATO and EU is central to a large majority, such leftist policy as described has a hard time.

To promote integration into the EU, a number of institutions have been established. Since 1995, the cabinet has met once a month with advisors as the European Integration Council (EIC) to coordinate the national strategy and to initiate the legislation necessary for the integration process. These decisions are implemented and monitored on a lower level by the inter-ministerial Council of Senior Officials (CSO). The EIC and CSO were supported by the European Integration Bureau (EIB), based in the state chancellery, which executed a number of coordinating tasks. In the beginning of 2004, the EIB was reorganized and became the European Affairs Bureau (EAB), more concerned with legwork for the prime minister, like the preparation of his participation in EU/EC meetings.[9] Unlike the preparatory phase of the EU accession, the accession negotiations themselves were coordinated and led by the ministry of foreign affairs (MFA). The EU department in the MFA has now in general the important task of defining Latvian positions on EU policy matters.

Constitutional policy coordination

The competencies to form the policy positions for the IGC 2003–4 have been clearly assigned to the MFA. This is even more straightforward than it was during the accession negotiations, when the MFA, although it had the lead, had to act in close cooperation also with the European integration bureau in the state chancellery. As the EIB, however, was under reconstruction during the IGC and its competencies were in parts redefined, it did not play a role in the whole IGC coordination process.

This means for the IGC coordination process that the MFA is the central and almost the only governmental actor (see Figure 16.1). The EU policy department in the MFA was the central unit, which drafted a position that consequently had to be approved by the cabinet. There has been no institutionalized inter-ministerial coordination below the cabinet level. The EU policy department contacted other ministerial units as far as they were concerned by the issues discussed. These actors made their (nonbinding) proposals to the MFA.

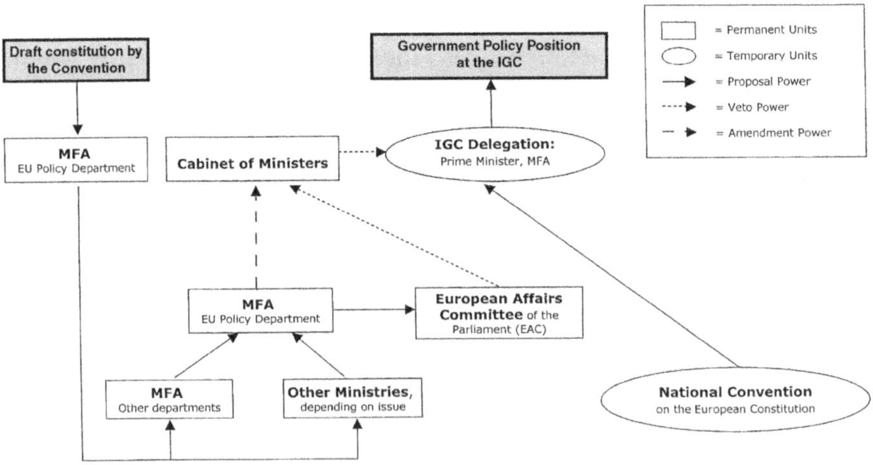

Figure 16.1 Latvia: domestic policy coordination for the IGC 2003–4.

The Latvian parliament, the *Saeima*, exercises all its involvement in EU matters through its European Affairs Committee (EAC). The EAC has the right to review and approve the national positions prior to their submission to European Union's institutions.[10] In the IGC coordination, it was kept informed and received the position draft by the MFA and reported its opinion and approval directly to the cabinet.[11]

As the inter-ministerial coordination was dominated by the foreign ministry, the MFA's briefing for the cabinet and the IGC delegation has had a decisive influence. The large cohesiveness of the actors' positions reached in the coordination process prevailed over the potential for conflicts in the delegation between the MFA and the state chancellery.

Data and empirical analysis of forming positions on the constitution for Europe

To gather policy positions on the IGC we interviewed five experts from inside and outside government: three MFA officials involved in the IGC coordination and two academics. The state chancellery (EIB) did not feel to be able to give an interview on the government's position. This is an interesting finding as such and it supports the findings on the policy-making structures, where the EIB turned out to be not important in the particular case of the IGC. All experts agreed on the MFA as being the most important actor, whereas only two and one experts respectively mentioned the European Affairs Committee of the *Saeima* and the National Convention.[12]

In the current institutional debate the most important issue for Latvia is in general to guarantee influence for small member states. The top priority in the negotiations was to struggle for a commissioner with full voting rights. Institutional issues of vital importance were further the distribution of EP seats as agreed to at the Nice summit and a simplified voting system in the Council. Latvia favored the European Commission proposal of two simple majorities, i.e., decision in the Council would require the assent of half of the member states, representing half of the EU population. With regard to the reform of the Council, it was important for the Latvian delegation not to create a separate legislative council. The reform of the EU presidency was not supported by Latvia either, although only during the Convention stage (when they called for keeping the rotation model). For the IGC they changed their position and will now accept the draft proposal for a single president, elected for a longer term. Finally, and very important, Latvia wants a clear definition of EU jurisdiction in defense policy and clarification of the relationship with the NATO. This includes also a very restrictive application of the instruments of enhanced and structured cooperation as well as to keep unanimity voting in the Council in the field of foreign policy as a general rule.

In a number of issues, Latvia does not agree with the draft constitution, but prefers alternatives that go further. Latvia would like to assign more competencies to the EU in economic policy, the "classical" field of European integration. They would also favor to strengthen the EP in economic and employment as well as monetary policies by introducing the co-decision procedure in these fields. Public health and tourism are two additional policy fields, where EU competencies should be strengthened according to the Latvian position.

On six issues the government prefers the status quo regulation, which is – most important – to leave the competencies of the EU in the fields of foreign and defense policies as they are. Regarding the budgetary procedure there was a strong claim made by the ministry of finance not to extend the rights of the European Parliament (EP), which was adopted as national position. They also opposed the idea of making the EP a co-equal legislator in the area of freedom, security and justice (AFSJ). Although the Latvian constitution contains a number of direct democratic elements, there was no strong support for the idea to grant also the European citizens a right of initiative. Finally, with respect to the Union's objectives, the Latvian government considered the current wording "high level of employment" as being a more adequate objective of EU policy than the "full employment" proposed by the draft.

With respect to the introduction of rules regulating the withdrawal from the EU, the preamble of the constitution, as well as migration and social policies, Latvian actors did not like the draft proposal (or the status quo regulation). It is considered to be important that a right to withdraw from the EU should be granted to the member states without constraints, i.e., it should be possible that a government can unilaterally declare to withdraw from the Union. The draft provides a right to request withdrawal, which has then to be negotiated among the member states. A restrictive position is also held on the issue of a religious reference in the preamble of the constitution. Here, at least a reference to a belief in God is favored by the government; however, there were also claims for an explicit mention of Christianity in Latvia. Migration and asylum policies are a very sensitive issue in Latvia, too. If at all, a common policy with respect to asylum is preferred by the government; for the remaining issues the EU should only have the right to set minimum standards. There is always a fear of "alienation" present in society after long periods of occupation in the national history that have left their marks like the Soviet settlement policy did. Finally, Latvia would like to see stricter decision rules for all issues of social policy and would prefer unanimity to QMV in the Council and no co-decision procedure.

The dominant role of the MFA in the formal organization process is empirically confirmed completely. All interviewees agreed that the national position and the MFA position were the same across all issues and that the MFA was the most important actor. Although they mentioned the parliament and the National Convention as additional actors these either had only the right to propose (national convention) or did not make use of their power, like the European Affairs Committee in the parliament, which agreed with the coordination work done by the MFA and did not recommend alternative positions to the cabinet. Thus, we find Latvia being a completely unitary actor in the IGC 2003–4 (see Table 16.1) without any deviating positions of actors across the 65 issues.

Conclusion

Neither executive weakness nor skepticism about the EU's foreign policy ambitions have severely challenged ratification of the EU constitution in Latvia. Due to the governmental change in autumn 2004, postponing the parliamentary vote became necessary, but on 2 June 2005 parliament ratified the constitutional treaty.

With respect to foreign and security policy, Latvia shares the position of its Baltic colleagues, who, after the collapse of the Soviet system, strove toward early and complete integration into Western international cooperation structures. Especially NATO membership was an important goal and the organization is still regarded as the most important agent for a common security policy. Thus, Latvia does not support the EU ambitions toward a unified foreign and defense policy. Additionally, it does not welcome a common migration policy, as the current situation for ethnic minorities is still a sensitive and controversial issue in domestic Latvian discussions as well as for its international partners.

For pragmatic reasons of expected economic and welfare benefits, Latvia favors more EU competencies in economic, employment and monetary policies and supports in principle the EU constitution. This baseline position is shared by the relevant domestic actors and makes a diversified coordination of positions obsolete. The policy coordination process on the IGC 2003–4 was clearly dominated by the foreign ministry, which drafted a position that was subsequently adopted by the delegation. Except for the nationalist Fatherland Party, which won the 2004 European elections, all party groups in the *Saeima* support the European integration process and were expected to approve the constitution. This overall cohesiveness already pointed to an unproblematic ratification in parliament, even more as a simple majority has been sufficient. Only if the adoption of the constitution required a constitutional amendment would a two-thirds majority be necessary for ratification.

Acknowledgment

The author would like to thank Tobias Meyer, University of Konstanz in Germany, for preparing, running and reporting the interviews with experts in Latvia.

Table 16.1 Cohesiveness of actors' positions in the Latvian coordination process

National position comparison	*Actor(s) (No. or type)*	*Observations (No.)*	*Deviations*									
			from national position		*on integration*				*related to*			
					toward less		*toward more*		*institutional issues*[a]		*policy fields*[a]	
			No.	*%*	*No.*	*%*	*No.*	*%*	*No.*	*%*	*No.*	*%*
All actors	3	195	0	–	0	–	0	–	0	–	0	–
Subset												
Lead unit	MFA	65	0	–	0	–	0	–	0	–	0	–

Deviations related to institutional issues
Nil

Deviations related to policy fields
Nil

Vital interests
Qualified majority threshold; Number of commissioners; Regulation of jurisdiction with respect to defense policy; Council voting rule for Common Security and Defense Policy; Number and distribution of seats in the EP; No legislative Council

Notes
a Percentage shares refer to subsets of institutional (43) and policy (22) issues. *Lead Unit* Leading unit in domestic coordination: Prime Minister's Office (PM) or Ministry of Foreign Affairs (MFA).

Notes

1 On the condition that an EU treaty reform "changes significantly" Latvia's EU membership, at least half of the *Saeima* members can request a (binding) referendum. The fact, that the EU constitution will fundamentally change the accession treaty has been denied by influential politicians, like President Vike-Freiberga.

2 Taggart and Szczerbiak (2004) find for an earlier period both high public and party-based Euro-skepticism, the latter expressed by the nationalist Fatherland and Freedom Party as well as by the Latvian Social Democratic Alliance (at that time with communist and nationalist leanings, meanwhile merged with the more moderate LSDSP).

3 The distribution of votes and seats in the most recent elections for parliament and the 2004 elections for the European Parliament, including the EP bloc affiliation of the parties, can be downloaded from the projects' website at dosei.dhv-speyer.de.

4 Average 1996–2003 of real GDP growth rates (at constant prices, 1995 = 100), Eurostat 2004.

5 Transparency International ranks Latvia lowest among all accession states (European Forum 2004).

6 The current president, Vaira Vike-Freiberga, was elected in 1999 as the first female head of state in an Eastern European country.

7 19.6 percent of time being governed by a minimum winning coalition or single party and with 0.83 years of average cabinet life, Latvia has the shortest cabinet tenure of all countries.

8 On the Effective Number of Parties (ENP) index, Latvia is almost at the very top with a score of 5.79 (Roberts 2003, see also Lijphart 1999).

9 EU information website of the Latvian government. Online. Available at: www.latvija-eiropa.gov.lv.

10 Saeima EU information center. Online. Available at: www.eiroinfo.lv/pages/SEUIC/index.jsp.

11 During the stage, when the European Convention worked upon the draft treaty, there was an additional actor. The Latvian National Convention on the European Constitution, which was established to enhance civil society participation in this process, reported on a non-binding basis to the government (and parliament) delegations to the Convention.

12 For the national position as well as for those actors mentioned by all five experts the coherence is about 58 percent, while it reaches 73 percent for the parliament which was mentioned by two experts only. Modifying the coherence for the number of experts interviewed we can compare the mean adapted coherence of the Latvian case (0.85), which is at the mean of the overall coherence in the DOSEI data set (0.85, see Appendix 2).

17 Lithuania

A priority for Europe

Stephanie Daimer

Lithuania became the first country in the EU to ratify the new constitution on 11 November 2004, passing it by 84 votes to four with three abstentions, while in principle a simple majority is sufficient to ratify international treaties. It was argued that a referendum was unnecessary given that one had been held on joining the EU in the first place in which 91 percent voted "yes." The small new EU member state has gone through a turbulent time for domestic politics. In April 2004, President Rolandas Paksas was forced to step down after an impeachment procedure for reasons of involvement in corruption and connections to the Russian mafia.[1] Despite the re-election of the popular Valdas Adamkus for president, corruption remains at the top of the daily news. During his campaign, offices of parties, all of them in support of Adamkus's candidature, were searched to check for illegal party financing. A national anti-corruption strategy has been adopted by the government in January 2002, the main problem, however, remains the lack of adequate enforcement of anti-corruption legislation (European Forum 2004). In the first European elections after enlargement Lithuanian voters, in line with the Europe-wide trend, punished the ruling parties. The newly founded Labor Party, whose populist campaign particularly addressed the "transition losers," repeated its success in the general elections held in October 2004, winning again almost 30 percent of the votes. The governing coalition of the Social democrats and New Union chose to bring the Labor Party along with the Peasants and New Democracy Union into government rather than forging an unstable "rainbow coalition" with right-wing parties.[2]

Major changes to the country's positions on European policies are not expected since Premier Algirdas Brazauskas remained in office and all leading politicians keep on underlining the importance of the European Union for Lithuania. However, Labor Party chairman Uspakich's spending plans may boost the budget deficit beyond the 3 percent EU limit and jeopardize Lithuania's chances of adopting the euro in 2007. Lithuania is the second-poorest EU nation behind neighboring Latvia and with purchasing power in 2003 at 46 percent of the EU average (Eurostat 2004) a new government may give priority to raising living standards over its euro ambitions. Chances for quick introduction of the euro, though, are high, since GDP growth rates are the highest in Europe[3] and Lithuania together with two other new EU member states – Estonia and Slovenia – has fixed the value of the currencies against the euro as the first step in adopting the single currency. High unemployment rates, especially in the big agricultural sector, are setbacks for the economic development.[4] The gap between rural and urban areas increased, farmers being amongst the most vulnerable in Lithuanian society. It is these groups that voted for the more populist voices in politics such as Rolandas Paksas and the recently founded Labor Party (European Forum 2004).

Domestic structures in a comparative perspective

Although centralized and unicameral like Estonia and Latvia, Lithuania is in some respects different from its Baltic neighbors. Among them, it has the largest (3.5 million) and most homogeneous population, with the Roman Catholic Church as the dominant religion.[5] Due to "premier-presidential" or "semi-presidential" structures (Rooper 2002) similar to those of the French system, the Lithuanian political system shows also some major differences. It is basically a parliamentary system, but has split executive powers between the government and a strong, directly elected president, whose domain is foreign policy. The premier is appointed by the president on the approval of the parliament, the *Seimas*. A "cohabitation," the situation when prime minister and president are from opposing political parties, has occurred so far only once in Lithuania. As a result, observers claimed a de facto strengthened role of the president (Tauber 2004). In contrast to France, no extreme executive dominance is visible on the cabinet duration index, which is used to estimate executive–legislative relations. With 1.31 years of average cabinet life, Lithuania currently fits the typical pattern of weak executives observed in the CEEC (Roberts 2003). Since the beginning of the 1990s, consolidation of the Lithuanian party system is observable, although major changes are still possible, as the success of the new Labor Party has shown. The ENP index[6] shows a declining trend and is currently at 3.84, which indicates a multiparty system that is more concentrated than in the other Baltic states (Roberts 2003).

Party-based Euro-skepticism is comparatively low in Lithuania and only represented in a "soft" version by two parties: the Center Union and the Peasants Party (Taggart and Szczerbiak 2004). Also, popular support for EU membership and the EU constitution is remarkably higher compared to other new member states and the EU average.[7] A major issue during the accession negotiations was the EU's claim to close the Chernobyl-like nuclear power plant Ignalina at the latest by 2009. This gave some grounds for anti-EU feelings, because Ignalina produces about 70 percent of Lithuania's electricity and the people feared dependence on foreign, especially Russian, power supplies (Valentinavicius 2003). As a compromise, additional EU subsidies will now support the transition to alternative energy sources or the opening of a new modern nuclear power plant. At the same time, Lithuanians are satisfied with the solution of the EU conflict with Russia over visa requirements for Kaliningrad. They are hoping that the strict regulation now in force will advance their goal to join the Schengen regime as soon as possible.

Constitutional policy coordination

In the field of foreign and EU policy, the president decides on the guidelines and acts in cooperation with the government. However, the presidential office lacks the resources to execute foreign policy on its own. Today, Lithuania's relations to the European Union are coordinated by a small number of actors under the lead of the European integration department of the foreign ministry. This used to be different for the accession negotiations that were coordinated by the European Committee under the Government (ECG), a unit, which is affiliated with the prime minister's office. Although the ECG's functions in the accession process were the main coordination and policy support for the negotiators, the delegation itself was led by the minister of foreign affairs (MFA). This structure seems to intend a competitive relationship between the ECG and the MFA.[8]

After the accession negotiations the lead in European policy was transferred to the MFA, which is also the central actor in the IGC coordination process. The units established for the accession process, in particular the ECG, were retained but underwent a reorganization, which actually did not affect the ECG's importance also for the IGC policy coordination. In principle, the duality of these two actors remained.

As Figure 17.1 shows the formal coordination process clearly intends a dominance of the MFA, which coordinated the whole process by collecting all actors' positions and by chairing the working group, which drafted a position paper for the cabinet as the final decision maker.

In fact, although the MFA was the leading actor in domestic coordination and took part in the IGC delegation, the principal IGC negotiator was the staff of the prime minister, i.e., the European Committee. This made the ECG the most important player besides the MFA, while other ministries, the president's office or the parliament could exercise proposal (and partially) amendment power by participating in the working group.

Data and empirical analysis of forming positions on the constitution for Europe

The set of relevant actors as laid out in the formal organization chart (Figure 17.1, opposite) was boiled down by two of the four interview

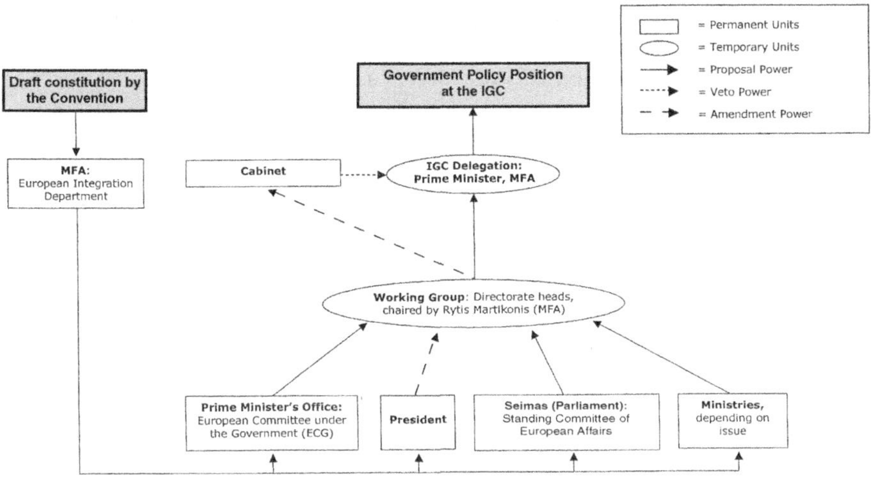

Figure 17.1 Lithuania: domestic policy coordination for the IGC 2003–4.

partners to two central actors: the MFA and the ECG. All interviewees mentioned issues, where the MFA and the ECG had taken different positions. The remaining two interviewees referred additionally to the parliament as a relevant domestic actor with diverging positions for a small number of issues. Finally, also the president was mentioned by one expert. To find empirically a set of four actors matches perfectly the above findings from the study of the formal coordination process. Although the coherence level of the interviews with the Lithuanian experts is comparatively good,[9] the different numbers of experts for each actor should be kept in mind for data interpretation.

Deriving actors' positions from different experts may cause in the case of Lithuania an overestimation of the conflict between the governmental and the non-governmental actors. Nevertheless, two patterns appear very clearly: First, the MFA was the dominant actor in this process and had the highest influence on the national position, and second, there have been domestic conflicts, where in some cases the European Committee (ECG) and in some the parliament took a different position.

EU and NATO memberships are a vital interest in Lithuania and seen as a means to reach economic stability, and safeguard independence by limiting the Russian influence. In the IGC negotiations Lithuania therefore carefully watched that further integration of defense policy would not undermine NATO. For the small country, essential issues have also been the qualified majority voting (QMV) threshold in the Council and the number of commissioners. With respect to the definition of the voting threshold in the Council, Lithuania supported in the IGC a double majority, but demanded a higher threshold than in the draft proposal, i.e., their preferred level was the assent of 60 percent of the member states representing 60 percent of the population. In the debates on the future composition of the European Commission, Lithuania claimed in cooperation with many small and medium-size states to keep one commissioner per country. Further, the distribution of the seats in the EP was of higher salience for the government. Finally, the Catholic country considered the religious reference in the preamble of the draft constitution to be unsatisfactory. All Lithuanian actors, and in particular the Lithuanian president, called for a specific reference to Christianity.

An often debated issue was the presidency of the European Council. During the Convention and at the beginning of the IGC, Lithuania favored keeping the rotation model or to accept a team presidency model. Toward the end of the IGC, the Lithuanian government was also ready to accept the solution to elect a single president as proposed by the draft.

A closer look at the domestic discussion in Lithuania reveals 21 of 65 issues without a unitary position across all actors (see Table 17.1). Most of the 38 deviations show a clear pattern: While the governmental actors promote the national position, the non-governmental actors, the parliament and the president do not share this position. This is the case for institutional issues primarily, like the election modes for the Council and Commission presidents and for the foreign minister, the right of legislative initiative, the jurisdiction of the European Court of Justice, enhanced cooperation, the extension of QMV in the Council and involvement of the EP for structural and cohesion, tax harmonization, economic and employment policies. In the question of the future role of national parliaments in monitoring the principle of subsidiarity, only the parliament is of a different opinion claiming more rights for national parliaments, while the other actors support the draft regulation of an "early warning system." However, the directions of the deviations show no clear pattern that would suggest bad prospects for ratification. As the domestic actors prefer almost equally often more and less integrationist solutions to the national position, they do not severely tie the hands of the IGC delegates. This may also explain why the ratification by parliament on 11 November 2004 gave rise to no problems.

On three very important issues, there was a conflict inside the government, between the MFA and the ECG. On the one hand, the ECG claimed to keep the status quo regulations for the EU presidency (rotation) and for the voting system in the Council (Nice Treaty model), and on the other hand it favored the draft proposal to grant the EP all rights in the budgetary procedure. With respect to all three issues, the IGC delegation adopted the MFA's position, i.e., they were ready to agree in principle with a long-term presidency and the introduction of a double majority for QMV, but were against the extension of EP rights. Overall, the national position was identical to the MFA's position, which shows clearly the MFA's decisive role in coordinating the policy formation process.

Table 17.1 Cohesiveness of actors' positions in the Lithuanian coordination process

National position comparison	*Actor(s) (No. or type)*	*Observations (No.)*	*Deviations*									
			from national position		*on integration*				*related to*			
					toward less		*toward more*		*institutional issues*[a]		*policy fields*[a]	
			No.	*%*	*No.*	*%*	*No.*	*%*	*No.*	*%*	*No.*	*%*
All actors	4	260	38	14.6	23	8.8	15	5.8	32	18.6	6	6.8
Subset												
Lead unit	MFA	65	0	–	0	–	0	–	0	–	0	–

Deviations related to institutional issues
Subsidiarity (role of national parliaments); Presidency of the Council; Election of the Council president; QMV threshold; Appointment of commissioners; Appointment of Foreign Minister (FM); Additional approval of the FM by the EP; ECJ jurisdiction; Legislative initiative for European Parliament, for Council, and for citizens; Enhanced cooperation; Voting rule (Council) for structural and cohesion politics, for tax harmonization; Decision rule (EP) for structural and cohesion politics, for economic policy, for employment policy; Rights of EP in the adoption of the budget

Deviations related to policy fields
Level of competence for structural and cohesion politics; Stability and Growth Pact; Migration and asylum

Vital interests
Religious reference in the preamble; Rotation of the presidency in the Council; Qualified majority threshold; Number of commissioners; Regulation of jurisdiction with respect to defense policy; Number and distribution of seats in the EP

Notes

a Percentage shares refer to subsets of institutional (43) and policy (22) issues. *Lead Unit* Leading unit in domestic coordination: Prime Minister's Office (PM) or Ministry of Foreign Affairs (MFA).

In a large majority of cases the national position of Lithuania supports the draft proposal of the European Convention. On only two sensitive economic and financial issues do the actors favor keeping the status quo: first, the specification of a "high level of employment" is preferred over "full employment" as an objective of EU policy and second, they reject an extension of the rights of the EP in the adoption of the budget (an opinion which is not shared by the ECG). The delegation further prefers unanimity in the council and not to have the EP as co-equal legislator for all issues of social policy, which would mean going behind current regulations. With respect to the Stability and Growth Pact (SGP), the promising EMU candidate Lithuania is one of the few countries welcoming to abandon the strict debt/GDP ratio criterion, i.e., to make the SGP more flexible.

Conclusion

Lithuania's commitment to European integration is durable and outstandingly high compared to other new EU member states. Despite recent turbulence for the presidential office and the government coalition parties, Lithuania's EU politics shows a clear position in favor of the EU constitutional process in principle and the regulations of the new constitution itself. Being close to the center of the IGC bargaining space is why Lithuania can be regarded as a winner in the IGC 2003–4 (König and Daimer 2005). This goes along with high public support for European integration and broad consensus among parties. Hence, despite parliamentary elections which took place at the same time, in October 2004, the country became the first to ratify the constitution only two weeks after the official signature by the European heads of state and governments. Although we find heterogeneous positions of the various actors on a large number of issues and especially contestation of some very important issues between the two central actors, the foreign ministry and the European Committee (based in the prime minister's office), the IGC delegation could easily accept the draft and the parliament could ratify this compromise.

Acknowledgment

The author would like to thank Tobias Meyer, University of Konstanz in Germany, for preparing, running and reporting the interviews with experts in Lithuania.

Notes

1 Surprisingly, the 2003 presidential elections were won by previous Prime Minister Rolandas Paksas despite high popularity rankings for the incumbent Valdas Adamkus. Paksas founded his own party in 2002, the Liberal Democratic Party. His presidential campaign had a populist undertone and succeeded in addressing xenophobic sentiments (Valentinavicius 2003).

2 The distribution of votes and seats in the most recent elections for parliament and the 2004 elections for the European Parliament, including the EP bloc affiliation of the parties, can be downloaded from the projects' website at dosei.dhv-speyer.de.
3 Average 1996–2003 of real GDP growth rates (at constant prices, 1995 = 100): 5.1 percent, Eurostat 2004.
4 In 2001, 17.1 percent of persons were employed in the agricultural sector (later figures not available). General unemployment rate in 2003: 12.7 percent (EU average: 8.0 percent). Eurostat 2004.
5 Over 80 percent of the population consider themselves Catholics.
6 Effective Number of Parties, cf. Lijphart (1999: 62 ff.).
7 Recent polls show that a very large majority of the Lithuanian population (81 percent) would prefer to have a European Constitution (EU-25 average: 78 percent; Eurobarometer 2004a).
8 Coordination of Lithuania's Integration into the European Union. Online. Available at: www.euro.lt/upl_images/20020309122555.doc (accessed 25 July 2004); Lithuanian delegation for accession negotiations. Online. Available at: www.euro.lt/upl_images/20020828090106.doc (accessed 25 July 2004).
9 The data are based on four interviews with experts from inside and outside government, all carried out in November 2003. For the national position as well as for those actors mentioned by all four experts the empirical coherence is about 58 percent, while it reaches a 73 percent for the parliament, which was mentioned by two experts only. Modifying the coherence for the number of experts interviewed, we can compare the mean adapted coherence of the Lithuanian case (0.84) with the overall coherence in the DOSEI data set, which is at about the same level (0.85, see Appendix 2).

18 Luxembourg, the Convention and the IGC

Consensus and concern for its economy

Christophe Crombez and Jan Lebbe

Luxembourg is a constitutional monarchy with a parliamentary system. It is a unitary state with a population of less than half a million. There are three official languages in Luxembourg: Luxembourgish, French and German. The legislature is unicameral. It consists of a chamber of deputies. The 60 members of the chamber are elected from four electoral districts. Elections to the chamber are held every five years. They coincide with the European elections. The last elections were thus held in June 2004.[1] Luxembourg uses the d'Hondt electoral system. There is also a Council of State with 21 appointed members. This institution plays an advisory role only in the legislative process.

Luxembourg is one of the founding members of the European Union, and there is a broad consensus among the principal political parties in favor of more European integration. The Luxembourg government decided in June 2003 to submit the EU constitution to a referendum, following Article 51 of the Luxembourg constitution. On 10 July 2005 Luxembourg voters voted in favor of the constitution. The referendum was preceded by a vote in the chamber of deputies on 28 June 2005, and will need to be followed by another such vote.

Luxembourg is a member of the Benelux and the Belgium–Luxembourg Economic Union. It is also part of the euro zone. Its economy is expected to grow by 3.2 percent in 2004. Its average GDP growth rate during the past ten years was 4.6 percent, well above the EU-15 average. Its GDP per capita at PPS is a staggering 86 percent above the EU-15 average, higher than in any other EU member state. Unemployment stands at 3.7 percent, well below the EU-15 average. Services account for more than 80 percent of its economy, whereas agriculture stands for 0.5 percent only. Luxembourg is a net contributor to the EU, to the amount of €125 per capita in 2003.

Domestic structures in a comparative perspective

The party political landscape in Luxembourg is similar to the Belgian landscape. The Christian democrats, socialists and liberals have traditionally been the principal political parties. Typically the Christian democrats form and lead the government in coalition with either the socialists or the liberals. There are also two smaller parties: a green party and a pensioners' party. All these five parties were represented at the Convention (if one considers the alternates). Like Belgium Luxembourg is historically a consociational state (Lijphart 1980). That is, society consists of a number of segments, often referred to as pillars, which tend to share power in the political institutions. The principal political parties are the political representatives of the pillars.

The approval of major policy initiatives requires agreement amongst the governing coalition parties. The current government consists of the Christian democrats and the socialists. It was formed after the June 2004 elections. It is led by the Christian democrat Prime Minister Jean-Claude Juncker. Juncker became prime minister in 1995, when his predecessor, Jacques Santer, assumed the Commission presidency. Prior to the 2004 elections Juncker governed in a coalition with the liberals, but he substituted the socialists for the liberals after the liberals' election defeat.

The Christian democrats (CSV) obtained more than 36 percent of the vote in 2004, a gain of 7 percent, thus strengthening their dominant position in the political landscape. The liberals (DP) got 16 percent, a loss of 5 percent, whereas the socialists (LSAP) retained their vote share of 23 percent. The greens received 11 percent and the pensioners' party (ADR) 10 percent.

As is the case in Belgium, the three major political parties in Luxembourg are strongly in favor of further EU integration. The Luxembourg economy depends largely on intra-EU trade and has thus benefited greatly from economic integration. Luxembourg coordinates its policies toward the EU with the other Benelux countries, but also has its specific concerns. It opposes tax harmonization, because its low taxes attract business. Specifically, its financial sector, which accounts for a quarter of its GDP, would suffer from tax harmonization. Foreign residents and cross-border labor account for nearly two-thirds of employment in Luxembourg. For this reason Luxembourg is also concerned about efforts to give the EU more powers in the areas of social and employment policy.

Constitutional policy coordination

The organization of the domestic debates in Luxembourg looks like a simplified version of the Belgian coordination process. However, in Luxembourg the prime minister's office led the debates in preparation for both the Convention and the IGC. Usually the foreign ministry takes the initiative in matters of foreign affairs in Luxembourg, but in the case of the Convention the prime minister's office took control and retained it at the IGC. It was assisted by the foreign ministry. The most important actors in the process were Prime Minister Jean-Claude Juncker, former Commission President Jacques Santer, who was the government representative at the Convention, and Foreign Minister Lydie Polfer.

Figure 18.1 shows that in Luxembourg the prime minister's office initiated the policy process. It received and gathered information about the relevant issues and passed it on to the relevant ministries. The different ministries then formulated their opinions on the matters and sent them to an "*ad hoc* group" consisting of the delegates, Prime Minister Juncker, Minister of Foreign Affairs Polfer, and a group of government officials and diplomats who assisted them. This was the main policy group in the process. It prepared the government positions that would subsequently be adopted by the delegation in coordination with the prime minister. As was the case in Belgium, a number of key institutional issues were decided at the Benelux level rather than the domestic level.

Game-theoretically the process can be simplified and modeled as follows: the prime minister formulates the proposals, the members of the delegation can amend them, and the approval of the prime minister and the coalition parties is required for adoption of a government position.

At the time of the Convention and IGC the Luxembourg government was formed by Christian democrats and liberals. The prime minister and the government representative at the Convention were both Christian democrats. The foreign minister was a liberal. In party-political terms we can say that the Christian democrats had agenda-setting and veto rights, and the liberals had amendment and veto rights.

Data and empirical analysis of forming positions on the constitution for Europe

The experts identified the following key actors in the coordination process: (1) Jean-Claude Juncker, Prime Minister and leader of the Christian democrats; (2) Jacques Santer, government representative at the

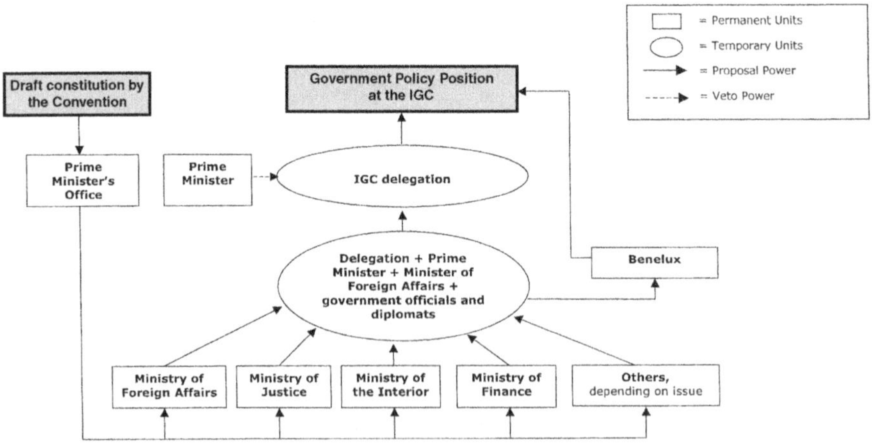

Figure 18.1 Luxembourg: domestic policy coordination for the IGC 2003–4.

Convention, former Prime Minister and former Commission President; and (3) Lydie Polfer, Deputy Prime Minister, Minister of Foreign Affairs and leader of the liberals. We interviewed two experts. Their adapted coherence was 0.6696, below the average for the entire project.

According to the experts there were few disagreements within the Luxembourg government and delegation. This is illustrated in Table 18.1. The table shows the extent of deviation between all actors and the national position, as well as specifically between the prime minister and the national position. In the table the percentages of policy disagreements, whether it be on further integration, institutional issues or policy issues, are all single-digit.

The Christian democrats had to significantly alter their proposals on three issues only. First, they wanted a religious reference in the preamble of the constitution. They had to settle for a reference to a secular inheritance. Second, they were willing to accept qualified majority rule and co-decision for tax harmonization. Third, they were also more willing to accept further integration in the area of migration policies. The foreign minister and the liberals opposed tax harmonization and were less willing to accept the integration of migration policies to protect the interests of the Luxembourg economy. In both cases the government adopted a position close to that of the liberals.

These outcomes are not surprising, given the policy process analyzed in the previous section. The Christian democrats had proposal rights. They were the agenda setter, but had to pay attention to the opinions of their liberal coalition parties, because the liberals had veto rights. On the religious reference in the preamble the Christian democrats had to give in to the liberals. On the issues of taxes and migration the liberals prevented the Christian democrats from giving in to demands by other member states for harmonization and further integration.

On the other major issues there was broad consensus among the coalition parties. They wanted the Charter of Fundamental Rights to be fully incorporated into the constitution and to be fully binding. They were also in favor of a "subsidiarity early warning system," but opposed to the right of withdrawal from the EU.

In general the delegation members were all in favor of more European integration. They wanted to provide for the possibility of enhanced co-operation in all areas. They were prepared to assign more powers to the EU in most areas, with the exception of agriculture, structural and cohesion policies, tax harmonization, health and the environment. Moreover, they favored qualified majority rule and co-decision in all areas, except for economic policy, social security rights and defense. They were also proponents of a common defense policy, with mutual defense commitments.

There was also consensus on institutional matters. The Luxembourg delegates wanted the president of the Council to be appointed by the

Table 18.1 Cohesiveness of actors' positions in the Luxembourg coordination process

National position comparison	*Actor(s) (No. or type)*	*Observations (No.)*	*Deviations*									
			from national position		*on integration*				*related to*			
					toward less		*toward more*		*institutional issues*[a]		*policy fields*[a]	
			No.	*%*	*No.*	*%*	*No.*	*%*	*No.*	*%*	*No.*	*%*
All actors	2	130	6	4.6	3	2.3	3	2.3	4	4.7	2	4.5
Subset												
Lead unit	PM	65	5	7.7	2	3.1	3	4.6	3	7.0	2	9.1

Deviations related to institutional issues
Presidency of the Council; Voting rule (Council) for tax harmonization; Decision rule (EP) for tax harmonization

Deviations related to policy fields
Religious reference in the preamble; Migration and asylum

Vital interests
Council voting rule for social security; Number and distribution of seats in the EP

Notes
a Percentage shares refer to subsets of institutional (43) and policy (22) issues. *Lead Unit* Leading unit in domestic coordination: Prime Minister's Office (PM) or Ministry of Foreign Affairs (MFA).

European Council only, by qualified majority. They were of the opinion that the Commission president ought to be proposed by the Council, acting by qualified majority, and approved by the Parliament. That is, they favored the Nice status quo on the appointment of the Commission president. They wanted the other commissioners to be chosen by the Commission president and approved by the Council and the Parliament. In their opinion the Union foreign minister had to be appointed by the Council, with the agreement of the Commission president, and be equally accountable to both the Council and the Commission. Moreover, the Luxembourg delegates wanted the Commission to retain its monopoly initiative on legislation.

As mentioned in Chapter 4 on Belgium the governments of Belgium, the Netherlands and Luxembourg adopted a Benelux position on three institutional issues: the Council presidency, the qualified majority rule and the composition of the Commission. Luxembourg was in favor of preserving the current system for the Council presidency, but altered its position after negotiations at the Benelux level. On the issue of the qualified majority threshold, however, it was able to convince the other countries to adopt its ideas. The position on the Commission composition was negotiated at the Benelux level.

Comparing the government positions of Belgium and Luxembourg we find a high degree of agreement on other issues as well. We mention four significant differences. (1) Belgium was in favor of a limited unilateral right of withdrawal from the Union, whereas Luxembourg was opposed. (2) Belgium wanted the creation of an EU border guard, whereas Luxembourg opposed it. (3) Belgium favored handing over more powers to the EU, more qualified majority voting and more co-decision in such areas as migration, tax harmonization, social and economic policy and health policy, than did Luxembourg. (4) Luxembourg chose to preserve the current system for the appointment of the Commission president, whereas Belgium wanted to give the Parliament the right of proposal and the Council veto rights only. Interestingly most of the issues on which Belgium and Luxembourg disagreed, were issues that were the source of debate within the Belgian and Luxembourg governments as well.

At the IGC the Luxembourg government defended the approval of the draft constitution. It was particularly concerned about tax harmonization and the further integration of social, economic and migration policies.

Conclusion

This analysis illustrates that in Luxembourg, as was the case in Belgium, policy toward the EU is consensus-oriented. There is widespread agreement amongst mainstream political parties on the issue of European integration and this consensus is reached in a political process that provides opportunities for all major parties to provide input.

Whereas usually the minister of foreign affairs sets foreign policy, in the case of the Convention and the IGC the prime minister took charge of the process. The Luxembourg government set up a committee consisting of the Convention delegates, the prime minister and foreign minister, and a number of government officials and diplomats to prepare for the Convention. As in Belgium coalition politics mandated that agreement amongst the coalition be required to determine the government position on the major issues. Thus agreement between the Christian democrats and liberals was required. As the Christian democratic prime minister controlled the process, the Christian democrats had agenda-setting powers, whereas the liberals had veto and amendment powers only.

The consensus position of the Luxembourg government and delegation was staunchly pro-European, as is Luxembourg foreign policy in general. Disagreements within the coalition government occurred mainly on three issues: the religious reference in the preamble, the legislative procedure and voting rule on the issue of tax harmonization, and immigration policy. These last two issues are of particular importance to Luxembourg, because it is heavily dependent on its financial sector, which accounts for a quarter of its GDP and would suffer from tax harmonization, and on immigrant and cross-border labor. On these issues the otherwise strongly pro-EU Luxembourg takes a more reluctantly integrationist position out of concern for its own economy.

On institutional issues, such as the composition of the Commission, the qualified majority rule and the Council presidency, the Luxembourg government cooperated with its Benelux partners to establish a consensus at the Benelux level and determine joint positions.

At the IGC Luxembourg favored the approval of the draft constitution. It was particularly concerned about tax harmonization and the integration of social, employment and migration policies.

Luxembourg scheduled a referendum on the constitution on 10 July 2005. Since the population of Luxembourg is very much pro-EU, ratification appeared highly likely. Hence, it was only partly surprising that the voters accepted the constitution by 56.5 percent "yes." The final ratification, however, has to be carried out by the parliament.

Note

1 The distribution of votes and seats in the most recent elections for parliament and the 2004 elections for the European Parliament, including the EP bloc affiliation of the parties, can be downloaded from the projects' website at http://dosei.dhv-speyer.de.

19 Malta

The importance of being unimportant

Spyros Blavoukos

The geographic location of Malta and the island's historical trajectory in the crossroads between Europe, Africa and the Middle East have left their marks on the Maltese polity identity (Mitchell 1998). In that respect two competing constructions of Maltese identity have emerged, one focusing on the "non-aligned Mediterranean identity" and the second emphasizing the European vocation of the Maltese state (Cini 2000). This problematic dichotomous self-identification process has led to ideological and political polarization as a result of which "identity politics" have largely prevailed in the domestic partisan constellation and power competition (Cini 2002, Lane 2000).

In the run-up to the April 2003 accession referendum, the debating space around EU membership was almost entirely (with the notable exceptions of the neutrality issue and the overall concern about the loss of sovereignty) taken up by the economic aspects of integration and the deriving costs and benefits for the Maltese economy (Xuereb 2004).[1] To meet these economic concerns, the Maltese government sought and managed to ensure special provisions, playing successfully the cards of domestic political divisiveness and the insignificant overall impact of the Maltese economy to the single market (Pace 2004b, 2002).

Domestic structures in a comparative perspective

Malta is a parliamentary democracy with a unicameral legislative body dominated by two parties attracting half of the electorate each and sharing between them all the seats in the house of representatives (*Il-Kamra tad-Deputati*). This political polarization results in a high degree of voters' mobilization and electoral participation (Hirczy 1995). The Maltese Labor Party (MLP) has pushed forward the "non-aligned Mediterranean identity" version whereas the Nationalist Party (PN) and – despite its marginal significance – the *Alternattiva Demokratika* (AD) have been associated with the more Europe-oriented version of the national identity (Cini 2000).

The ideological confrontation between the two main parties has been reflected in the relation of Malta with the EC/EU, which has been characterized by many twists and turns (Pace 2004a, 2001). The electoral victory of the MLP in October 1996 put on hold Malta's application (Pace 1997). The return to power of the PN after the 1998 elections (Calleya 1999) was followed by reactivation of the application and considerable effort to catch up with the front-runners.[2] The accession referendum of March 2003 and the general elections of April 2003 largely resolved this ambivalent Malta–EU relationship. High turnouts and marginal outcomes in both contests testified to the impressive degree of domestic political mobilization and polarization. Malta was the only acceding country with a major political party actively campaigning against EU membership (Cini 2003). The contested result of the referendum outcome turned the following elections to a kind of a second referendum of equally critical significance. The electoral victory of the incumbent PN and the adoption by the MLP of a more pragmatic approach on EU membership after the three consecutive defeats (1998 and 2003 elections and the referendum) suggest that Malta's membership seems to be most probably a settled issue. Hence, emphasis can be now laid not on the question of membership but on how the country will perform within the EU (Pace 2004b).

Holding a referendum for the constitution was excluded by the Maltese Prime Minister, Gonzi, in June 2004 and the ratification process was decided to go through the parliament by simple majority (Kurpas *et al.* 2005). Hence, given the parliamentary majority of the PN party, it was no surprise that the ratification went smoothly through parliament on 6 July 2005. However, the government had chosen to delay the ratification in order for the opposition party to complete its pragmatic shift on EU affairs in its 2005 party congress. Such a shift allowed a consensual vote on the constitution.

Constitutional policy coordination

Malta's small size and the limited availability of resources and human capital force a prioritization of goals and objectives in Maltese foreign policy (Pace 1999). In addition, strong adversarial politics has also contributed to the unnecessary dissipation of human resources with underutilization and marginalization of qualified personnel for political reasons (Pace 2003). Therefore political polarization has led to bureaucratic fractionalization with consequences in the administrative capacity of the state structures. These factors were implicitly taken into consideration by the Commission's 1993 opinion, which expressed concerns about the capacity of the Maltese state to cope administratively with EU membership (European Commission 1993: 14). Similar concerns existed regarding the sufficiency of internationally experienced diplomatic staff to cope with the obligations of membership (Cini 2000). In a nutshell, external and internal reasons can be accounted for the severe overstretching of Maltese administrative resources. The magnitude of the task of adapting to EU standards and accession negotiations together with domestic political polarization have placed severe strains on the Maltese administrative structures.

The focal point of the accession process was an *ad hoc* institutional scheme (MEUSAC), which was responsible for overseeing and coordinating overall domestic policy making.[3] The emergence of MEUSAC as a core player in the policy-making process during the accession negotiations introduced an unprecedented element of government consultation both intra-governmentally and within civil society (Pace 2003). The involvement of various societal, economic and political actors in the process canceled the MFA's monopoly although the EU directorate again clearly took the lead.

The unexpected side-effect of establishing this *ad hoc* scheme was the widespread feeling of success that surrounded this institutional novelty, which raised expectations of turning it into a permanent feature of EU affairs policy making in Malta, particularly in view of the European Convention and the IGC (Pace 2003). However, following the April 2003 elections there was a general deflation of interest and a period of inactivity after the very intensive period of the accession negotiations, referendum and the elections. Hence, MEUSAC's involvement in the IGC process came too late to provide any serious contribution coming out of its "winter sleep" only in autumn and having the first meeting on IGC-related issues very shortly prior to the official launch of the IGC.

In that respect, the official positions of the Maltese government have been exclusively the outcome of an intra-governmental policy-making process without any direct involvement this time by the civil society and

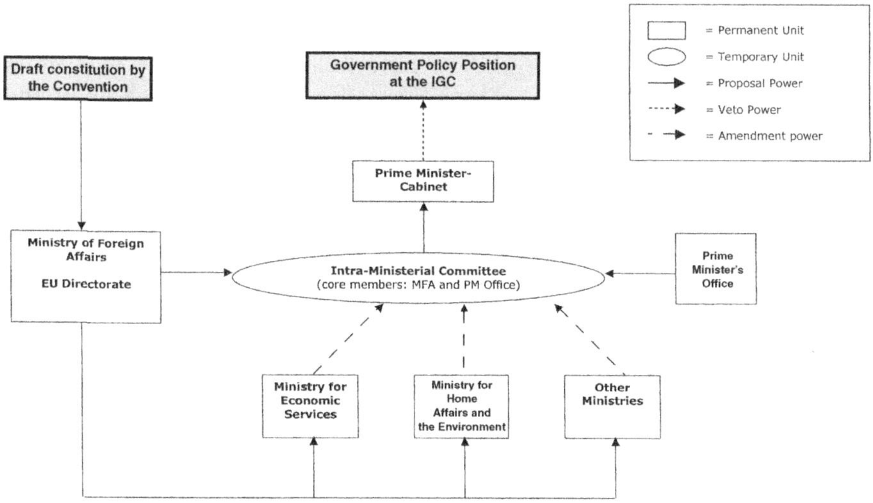

Figure 19.1 Malta: domestic policy coordination for the IGC 2003–4.

socioeconomic interest groups.[4] After the 2003 April election and the re-election to power of the incumbent PN party, and particularly from June onwards, the cabinet was split in two committees. The first dealt with internal policy-oriented EU affairs and the other with external EU affairs focusing mainly but not exclusively on CFSP and defense. It was actually in the context of the latter committee that the IGC and institutional/constitutional issues were discussed.[5] After the launch of the IGC, and more specifically from October 2003 onwards, another *ad hoc* intra-ministerial committee was set up to coordinate domestically and evaluate the ongoing IGC negotiations. Although membership in that committee was not clearly defined since it had a rather informal character, the main governmental bodies represented were the MFA and the prime minister's office whereas other ministries were asked to contribute their input on particular issues through the EU directorate whenever needed.[6]

The Maltese positions were debated *ex post* in a special meeting in the house of representatives with a high degree of convergence between the two political parties (*Malta Independent*, 6 November 2003). In this parliamentary debate the MLP exhibited its new pragmatic approach to European integration following the double defeat in the referendum and the elections, and the government reinstated its intergovernmentalist approach to integration, which it regarded as more capable of safeguarding a small country's interests in the process.

Data and empirical analysis of forming positions on the constitution for Europe

The data for this chapter were collected through three interviews with experts (two questionnaire-based and one rich-informative) from inside and outside the government, who have participated directly in the domestic policy formation process or have followed it closely. They comprised a member of the accession negotiating team and advisor of the minister of foreign affairs, the head of the Malta–EU information center and an academic specializing in EU–Malta relations. By interviewing people both from within and outside government we tried to minimize and control any governmental bias in the data-gathering procedure. In the Maltese case, the experts interviewed presented a high degree of coherence in their answers (about 88 percent which is above the average for the entire project of 85 percent) outlining the same principal domestic actors and largely agreeing on their inputs in the process.[7] This fact allows for the two following conclusions: (1) the actors involved in the domestic policy formation process were clearly demarcated and (2) their views on the great majority of issues on the agenda were straightforward and did not allow for misperceptions.

The positions of the key actors involved in the process have been identical, conveying an image of total homogeneity (see Table 19.1). The

Table 19.1 Cohesiveness of actors' positions in the Maltese coordination process

National position comparison	*Actor(s) (No. or type)*	*Observations (No.)*	*Deviations*									
			from national position		*on integration*				*related to*			
					toward less		*toward more*		*institutional issues*[a]		*policy fields*[a]	
			No.	*%*	*No.*	*%*	*No.*	*%*	*No.*	*%*	*No.*	*%*
All actors	2	130	0	–	0	–	0	–	0	–	0	–
Subset												
Lead unit	MFA	65	0	–	0	–	0	–	0	–	0	–

Deviations related to institutional issues
Nil

Deviations related to policy fields
Nil

Vital interests
Number of commissioners; Council voting rule for taxes/tax harmonization, for Common Security and Defense Policy, and for social security; Budgetary procedure; Number and distribution of seats in the EP

Notes
a Percentage shares refer to subsets of institutional (43) and policy (22) issues. *Lead Unit* Leading unit in domestic coordination: Prime Minister's Office (PM) or Ministry of Foreign Affairs (MFA).

identified absence of deviation between the position of the leading ministry and what became identified as the overall national position of the Maltese government during the negotiations can be understood in the light of the highly centralized position formation process. The number of key actors actually involved was limited down to two, namely the MFA and the PM's office, with continuous interaction between them and consensual ethos generating the amalgamation of any underlying differences.

Malta's positions on the draft European constitution and the main topics that were to be discussed in the framework of the IGC were expressed in a memorandum submitted to the Italian presidency on 8 September 2003 (Adami 2003). The two thorniest issues for the Maltese government were the minimum threshold in the EP representation and the preservation of one commissioner per member state. The proposed in the draft treaty minimum threshold of four MEPs found Malta totally opposed given the small size of the country. Six MEPs was regarded as the minimum number of representatives capable of adequately representing Maltese interests and political diversity. As far as the Commission composition is concerned, the Maltese government argued that although in principle it was disposed to consider all options that respected the principle of equality among member states, it was convinced that the best approach ensuring this equal representation was one commissioner per state with all commissioners enjoying equal status and voting rights. Malta would also prefer to see the Commission president nominated by the European Council acting by (super) qualified majority voting and approved by the EP.

Furthermore, in terms of voting arrangements, Malta preferred the Nice Treaty QMV provisions although they were considered discriminating against smaller member states. The Maltese government would ideally prefer to preserve the rotating system of the presidency or have it evolved in a system of "team presidency." If however the proposal for an elected president of the European Council was to go through, it would at least like to see some kind of guarantee to ensure an egalitarian system so that the incumbents of successive EU presidencies would come from a combination of member states along criteria of size, geographical location etc. The election of the EU president should be subject to qualified majority consisting of two-thirds of member states representing at least three-fifths of the Union's population. Finally, the exact system of presidency rotation in the Council formations required further clarification and elaboration.

The mandate and status of the proposed EU foreign minister should be also more clearly defined and any decisions in the field of defense should be adopted with respect to national constitutional requirements of the member states. The latter was a very sensitive issue for the Maltese government in the sense that the question of neutrality was in the front line of the domestic political confrontation. During the campaign for the membership referendum, the Labor Party argued that accession would render the country's neutrality status unsustainable. These concerns were entertained with a declaration attached to the treaty of accession (*Official Journal* L 236, 23 September 2003) whereby the Maltese government affirmed its commitment to the CFSP but stressed that any further move on defense integration would have to be taken by unanimity in the Council of Ministers and in accordance with the constitutional provisions of individual member states (Pace 2004b). This question resurfaced in November 2003 during the parliamentary debate on the IGC where the government re-emphasized that Maltese neutrality was not to be impinged by the relevant draft constitution provisions (*The Times* of Malta, 6 November 2003).

As regards other institutional amendments, the Maltese government would encourage a greater role for national parliaments in the EU policy-making process by enabling them to communicate to the EP or its committees recommendations on additional aspects of the Commission's legislative proposals. In terms of decision-making rules in particular policy areas, besides foreign policy and defense, unanimity should be preserved in taxation and the establishment of new categories of "own resources." Last but not least, in the preamble, Malta wholeheartedly supported the insertion of a reference to God and the Christian inheritance of Europe not as a discriminating feature against people of different faith but as an historical fact.

Conclusion

Timing is the critical parameter when it comes to analyzing the Maltese contribution to and interest in the European Convention and the IGC. The "Future of Europe" discussion coincided with two simultaneous and overwhelming processes that fully absorbed the resources and the interest of the Maltese polity. In the period following the Laeken European Council and the set up of the European Convention, Malta was preoccupied with speeding up and concluding accession negotiations on the one hand and the long and intensive referendum campaign on the other. Hence, throughout that period, the diplomatic and political focus was primarily on ensuring accession by negotiating successfully issues of special national sensitivity and "selling" the outcome to the Maltese public afterwards.[8] The two consecutive electoral contests kept the country on the campaign trail for more than two months, monopolizing media attention and overshadowing any other discussion topic. The unsurprisingly high turnout in the April elections masked to a large extent the growing public fatigue, which was evident in the closing stage of the pre-electoral campaigns with both camps giving signs of running out of steam (Cini 2003). Despite or perhaps even because of the continuous bombardment with EU-related information during the campaigns, the public developed a certain degree of apathy about the "Future of Europe."[9] In a nutshell, the inevitable saturation of the Maltese polity with EU affairs led to a rather low degree of interest in the final stages of the Convention and the IGC.

In organizational and administrative terms, the structure of policy making during the accession negotiations initiated an institutional novelty in the sense of full participation of the Maltese society. Owing its existence to a large extent to the domestic political polarization and ideological contestation about the role of the country in the EU, MEUSAC did none the less turn out to be a successful experiment in terms of societal involvement generating expectations for replication and formalization of its *ad hoc* nature. However, this did not materialize at least during the domestic preparations for the 2003 IGC, depriving any opportunities for the fostering of a favorable environment for an institutionalized structured dialogue between government and the public in the months following the April elections. Hence policy making during the IGC preparations was fully entrusted to and controlled by governmental structures, in particular the EU directorate in the MFA and the prime minister's office. The country's small size and the consequent small size of the domestic bureaucracy allowed more flexibility and informal structures. In turn, these informal structures created a cooperative and conducive environment for more intra-governmental consensual policy making.

This lack of internal crises was very much the result of the endorsement of the intergovernmentalist approach to European integration by both government and opposition. After years of intensive political struggles, the two parties alternating in power seems to have found a common platform as regards the country's relations with the EU. This platform included basically issues of adequate national institutional representation in the Commission and the EP and the need to keep the unanimity principle in sensitive areas like foreign policy, defense and taxation in view of the country's constitutional requirements and economic situation.

Notes

1 With the gross domestic product amounting to around 60 percent of the EU-15 average, quite a substantial budget deficit (up to 6 percent) and unemployment rate rising (but still under the EU-15 average) (but also with a reasonable debt level of around 67 percent of GDP and an inflation rate a little above the 2 percent) there were concerns expressed – especially from the opposition – about the country's economic future in the EU. Data taken from European Commission 2003c.

2 The distribution of votes and seats in the most recent elections for parliament and the 2004 elections for the European Parliament, including the EP bloc affiliation of the parties, can be downloaded from the projects' website at dosei.dhv-speyer.de.

3 Set in 1999 and chaired by the ministry of foreign affairs, the Malta–EU Steering and Action Committee (MEUSAC) brought together during the accession negotiations inputs from the various ministries and civil society, making the final policy recommendations to the cabinet committee on all aspects of the negotia-

tions. To a large extent this unexpected governmental call for broad participation in the process can be attributed to the domestic political polarization, which forced the government to take the EU membership bid outside the narrow government–opposition nexus (Pace 2003).

4 Interview, Dr Roderick Pace, Director of the European Documentation and Research Centre, University of Malta (26 November 2003).

5 Interview, advisor to the Maltese minister of foreign affairs on legal issues in the IGC and member of the accession negotiating team (26 November 2003).

6 Members included the head of prime minister's secretariat and chairman of EU secretariat, the heads of the MFA Secretariat and EU Directorate, the head of the EU–Malta Information Centre and one personal advisor of the minister of foreign affairs. Interview with advisor to the Maltese minister of foreign affairs (26 November 2003).

7 See Appendix 2 for more details on the measurement of coherence.

8 Interview, Mr Carmel Attard, head of the EU–Malta Information Centre.

9 Ibid.

20 The Netherlands

Domestic preference formation on the European constitution

Christine Arnold, Madeleine O. Hosli and Paul Pennings

During the early part of the deliberations of the Convention on the Future of Europe, Dutch politics were mostly occupied with domestic issues. One of the dominant issues in 2002 was the rise of Pim Fortuyn and his populist party (LPF) and his assassination. Another crucial issue was the Srebrenica disaster of 1995, which eventually led to the resignation of the government in 2002 and a new call for elections. Only as Dutch political life began to stabilize somewhat after the collapse of the government coalition with the LPF did the work of the Convention become more prominent. The two key preferences of the Dutch government throughout the Convention and the IGC were: the retention of unanimity in the multi-annual financial framework (Article I-54 of draft constitution) and the inclusion of coercive measures concerning the Stability and Growth Pact. These preferences can partly be explained by the neo-liberal stance of the Balkenende cabinet which underlines that the color and composition of a cabinet was crucial in the constitutional debate.

Domestic structures in a comparative perspective

As a constitutional monarchy, the Dutch national government comprises three main institutions: the monarch, the Council of Ministers, and the States General. The current Prime Minister is Jan Peter Balkenende (since 22 July 2002) who is also the head of government. The current government is a coalition of the center-right Christian democratic (CDA), conservative liberal (VVD) and left-of-center Democrats 66 (D66). The coalition parties hold 78 of the 150 seats in the second chamber of parliament (*Tweede Kamer*). The opposition includes the Labor Party (PvdA) with 42 seats and five other parties, each with less than 10 seats (Daalder 2003). At the heart of the government is the Council of Ministers (cabinet), which is headed by the prime minister.

The Dutch parliament (*Staten Generaal*) consists of two houses, the first chamber (*Eerste Kamer*) and the second chamber (*Tweede Kamer*). Of the two, the second chamber is by far the more important one. It alone has the right to initiate legislation and amend bills submitted by the council of ministers. The members of second chamber are directly elected for a four-year term on the basis of a nationwide system of proportional representation (the d'Hondt system of proportional representation). The last election of the second chamber was on 22 January 2003 (Daalder *et al.* 2003).[1]

The first chamber is composed of 75 members, who are elected indirectly for four-year terms.[2] The current first chamber was elected following provincial elections on 10 June 2003. In this election the parties received the following number of seats: CDA 23, PvdA 19, VVD 15, Green Party 5, Socialist Party 4, D66 3, and six for other parties.

The Dutch parliament was represented during the Convention by two delegates: Mr René van der Linden (CDA), who is a Member of the Dutch senate, and Mr Frans Timmermans (PvdA), who is a member of the *Tweede Kamer.* The representative of the Dutch government in the Convention during the short coalition government of Prime Minister Balkenende (CDA), including the Pim Fortuyn Party (LPF), was Mr Hans van Mierlo (D66). However, with the change of government in 2002 he was replaced by Mr Gijs de Vries (VVD) (*NRC Handelsblad,* 20 August 2002).

Lijphart provides a useful theoretical framework by which one can compare the institutional characteristics of different governments. According to Lijphart, all democracies essentially can be classified into one of two groups: they are either majoritarian or consensual. He finds that the Netherlands is an example of a consensual model of democracy (Lijphart 1999).

The economic system of the Netherlands achieves high income per head with a fairly even distribution of wealth as can be seen in the Gini coefficient of 32.6 for 1994, the latest year for which data are available (World Bank 2004). The economy is noted for moderate levels of unemployment and a sizable current account surplus. In 2003 the unemployment rate of 3.8 percent was far below the EU-wide rate of 8.1 percent and was among the lowest in Europe, bettered only by Luxembourg, which was at 3.7 percent (Eurostat 2003). The employment rate for the Netherlands was 73.5 percent, which was considerably above the EU-wide rate of 64.4 percent. At the heart of the Dutch economy are exports and imports of goods. The five most important export (and import) partners in 2002 were: Germany 25.1 percent (17.8 percent), Belgium 12.7 percent (9.7 percent), the UK 10.7 percent (6.9 percent) and France 10.2 percent (5.5 percent), indicating the economic relevance of the EU for the Dutch economy (OECD 2004).

As a founding member of the European Economic Community, the Netherlands has for long played an important part in promoting EU integration and in pioneering closer European ties (Dinan 1999: 61). Concerning public support for the draft constitution, a Eurobarometer survey found that 75 percent of the Dutch rather agree with the statement that the European Union must adopt a constitution, while 20 percent disagree and 5 percent don't know (Eurobarometer 2004a). The public support is very close to the EU average of 78 percent, 15 percent and 7 percent.

Constitutional policy coordination

The formal coordination process through which the Dutch government arrived at its national position regarding the European constitution was dominated by two domestic actors. Both the ministry of foreign affairs (MFA) and the prime minister's office were the key actors who determined the policy priorities and the negotiation strategy of the Dutch government. Both actors were, however, leveraging their respective influence at different stages of the policy coordination process. During the Convention and the early part of the IGC, the MFA played a central role both as the coordination unit, relaying preferences of diverse departments to the cabinet and the prime minister's office and as the first receiver of the outcomes of supranational deliberations. As can be seen in Figure 20.1, central to the formal policy coordination process through which the Dutch government was able to arrive at its national position on the constitutional draft proposal were the cabinet meetings.

The ministry of foreign affairs has special responsibility for the preparation of position papers which are deliberated, amended and, if need be, thoroughly modified by the cabinet. Central to this task is the Coordination Committee for European Integration and Association Issues (CoCo), a standing committee, which coordinates all policy proposals the Dutch government submits to the European Council of Ministers. Coco is chaired by the Secretary of State for European affairs Atzo Nicolaï, who

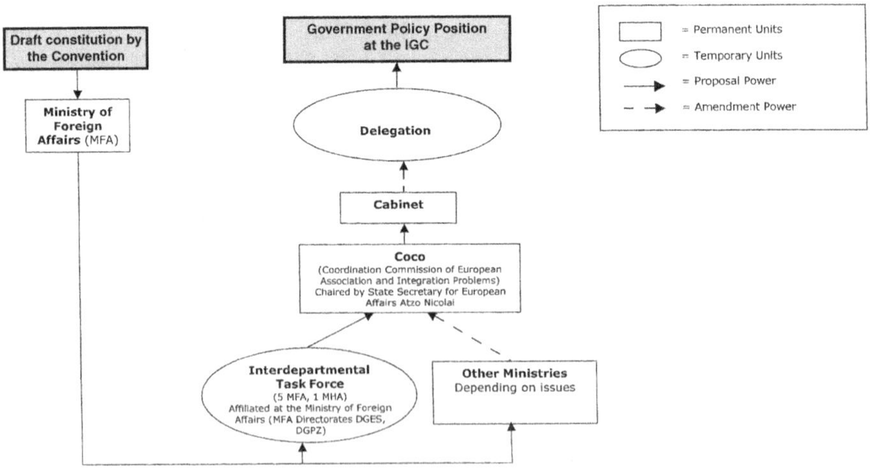

Figure 20.1 The Netherlands: domestic policy coordination for the IGC 2003–4.

"participates in cabinet meetings where the conclusions of the CoCo meetings are considered" (Soetendorp and Hanf 1998: 40).

During the Convention this coordination process was supported by an administrative unit with the title Interdepartmental Convention task force. This ad hoc organizational unit consisted of six lower-level civil servants and had the responsibility to prepare policy proposals, which it coordinated with Coco. The task force was headed by Mr Van der Plas who is head of the department of institutional affairs, which is located in the directorate-general for European cooperation in the MFA.

Given the fact that the formal responsibilities for interdepartmental policy coordination rests with the MFA, the prime minister plays only a rather modest role in the day-to-day process of defining the Dutch negotiation position during the Convention and the IGC. During the final negotiations of the IGC, however, the role of the prime minister had certainly become more pronounced. This increased prominence of the prime minister has been called "prime ministerialisation" of the Dutch government (Andeweg 1991: 125–6).

Data and empirical analysis of forming positions on the constitution for Europe

The Dutch national position was based on two principles: the equality of member states and the maintenance of inter-institutional balance (Pelkmans and Limonard 2003). The first principle guided the Dutch preferences concerning the inclusion of compelling, coercive agreements concerning the Stability and Growth Pact applicable to all member states that are guided by the rules of the Economic and Monetary Union. In the Ecofin Council of November 2003, Mr Zalm, however, was unable to foster agreement to impose a fine on those countries that were violating the agreed budget norms.[3] Additionally, the retention of unanimity in the multi-annual financial framework was considered to be of vital interest (Article I-54 of the draft constitution). Given the fact that the Netherlands is the largest net contributor to the EU (in terms of percentage of GDP), Mr Zalm and Mr Nicolaï insisted that other countries should not decide over the Dutch contribution, and therefore wanted to retain the veto power.

The principle of inter-institutional balance guided the Dutch preferences concerning the reform of the Commission and the Council of Ministers. In its negotiation position, the Netherlands continued its longstanding backing of a strong Commission. Viewing the Commission as an honest broker between member states, the Dutch government insisted that each member state should be able to appoint one commissioner. Furthermore, it favored a process of appointing commissioners who would allow member states to select several candidates and give the Commission president the final prerogative of selection. Additionally, it was supportive of a proposal that suggested that the Commission president should be elected by the European Parliament. In contrast, the Dutch government was opposed to a (semi-)permanent president of the European Council, as this would give the European Council more (undue) weight, especially in contrast to the Commission and thereby disturb the inter-institutional balance. The rotating presidency was much preferred. Nevertheless, a chosen president from amongst the leaders themselves who consequently cannot be more than part-time was still acceptable.

It should be noted that the influence of the national parties on the Dutch negotiation position was quite weak. Although the parties in parliament had several debates with Mr Balkenende about the government's positions in the IGC, their ultimate input was rather limited. This was apparent in the discussion on the issue of reference to religion in the preamble of the constitution. In June 2003, parliament adopted an opinion which urged the government to refrain from any religious reference in the preamble. Mr Balkenende, however, remained strongly in favor of the reference to a Christian heritage on behalf of the Dutch government at the IGC in October. Later, he was strongly reprimanded in a confrontation with the senate because of having ignored the wishes of parliament (*NRC Handelsblad*, 5 November 2003). But despite the strong language of the session in the senate, the coalition parties in government, that is the D66 and VVD, did not openly oppose the position of Balkenende. This underlines the fact that the cabinet, in conjunction with the ministry of foreign affairs, is the ultimate decision-making body on what position the Dutch government should be taking in the IGC.

Empirical data gathered during expert interviews confirm the policy priorities discussed above.[4] As can be seen in Table 20.1, interviewees identified the following issues as vital interests of the Dutch government: religious reference in the preamble, the presidency of the Council, the election of Commission president; appointment of commissioners and the budgetary procedure. This table also demonstrates that the preferences of the Dutch actors were tightly clustered around the national position with very few numbers of deviations. Out of a total of 195 observations, only in 0.5 percent of cases was there a deviation from the national position. Also it should be noted that the number of deviations are equally spread in the direction of less integration and more integration, and thus the disagreement with the national position does not appear to be indicative of pro- or anti-European attitude.

Conclusion

The analysis of the domestic policy coordination process in the Netherlands demonstrates that both the MFA and the prime minister's office were key actors who determined the policy priorities and the negotiation strategy of the Dutch government, and that they were leveraging their

Table 20.1 Cohesiveness of actors' positions in the Dutch coordination process

National position comparison	*Actor(s) (No. or type)*	*Observations (No.)*	*Deviations*									
			from national position		*on integration*				*related to*			
					toward less		*toward more*		*institutional issues*[a]		*policy fields*[a]	
			No.	*%*	*No.*	*%*	*No.*	*%*	*No.*	*%*	*No.*	*%*
All actors	3	195	1	0.5	1	0.5	0	–	1	0.8	0	–
Subset												
Lead unit	MFA	65	0	–	0	–	0	–	0	–	0	–

Deviations related to institutional issues
Presidency of the Council

Deviations related to policy fields
Nil

Vital interests
Religious reference in the preamble; Presidency of the Council; European Commission; Election of Commission president; Appointment of commissioners; Budgetary procedure

Notes
a Percentage shares refer to subsets of institutional (43) and policy (22) issues. *Lead Unit* Leading unit in domestic coordination: Prime Minister's Office (PM) or Ministry of Foreign Affairs (MFA).

respective influence at different stages of the policy coordination process. During the Convention and the early part of the IGC, the MFA played a central role both as the coordination unit, relaying preferences of diverse departments to the cabinet and the prime minister's office and as the first receiver of the outcomes of supranational deliberations. The prime minister's office played a central role in the final negotiations during the EU summits.

The Dutch national policy position was characterized by two key preferences: the retention of unanimity in the multi-annual financial framework (Article I-54 of draft constitution) and the inclusion of coercive measures concerning the Stability and Growth Pact. These preferences follow the restrictive monetarist policy orientation of this cabinet and its position as net contributor to the European Union.

A referendum on the European constitution in the Netherlands was held on 1 June 2005. The question Dutch citizens answered negatively was "Are you in favor or against approval by the Netherlands of the treaty establishing a constitution for Europe?" The outcome of this consultative referendum was far from certain. Since there has been growing Euro-skepticism in the Netherlands, the Dutch vote was expected to be rather narrow. In the end the voters rejected the constitution by a large majority of 61.7 percent. Despite the fact that the referendum is not legally binding, the outcome can nevertheless be expected to be decisive for the Dutch ratification of the constitution, given that a large number of parties in parliament (PvdA, Greens, D66 and CDA) have expressed their intention to follow the decision of the Dutch voters. Although these parties are in principle supportive of the constitution and together clearly hold a majority in parliament, the fate of the ratification of the constitution appears to have been decided by the Dutch citizens with the help of the French.

Notes

1 The distribution of votes and seats in the most recent elections for parliament and the 2004 elections for the European Parliament, including the EP bloc affiliation of the parties, can be downloaded from the projects' website at dosei.dhv-speyer.de.

2 These elections are indirect in the sense that voters elect the members of the 12 provincial councils, who in turn elect the members of the senate: Drenthe, Flevoland, Friesland, Gelderland, Groningen, Limburg, Noord-Brabant, Noord-Holland, Overijssel, Utrecht, Zeeland, Zuid-Holland.

3 During an "emergency debate" in parliament almost all parties supported the position taken by Mr Zalm and Mr Balkenende (*NRC*, 28 November 2003).

4 The four interviews were conducted between mid-November and mid-December 2003. Interviewees were selected from the prime minister's office, the ministry of foreign affairs, and parliament. Our results indicate that the coherence of the experts was very high. If one takes into account the numbers of experts interviewed and modifies the coherence accordingly, we get a mean adjusted coherence of 0.93, which is better than the overall coherence in the DOSEI data set which is 0.85 (see Appendix 2).

21 Poland

The struggle for Nice

Anna Gwiazda

The EU constitution, agreed at the European Council in June 2004, was not exactly what the Polish government had envisaged at the beginning of the IGC in October 2003. Polish leaders were to defend Polish vital interests and to respond to domestic pressures represented by a slogan "Nice or death."[1] In December 2003, the IGC had failed partly because Poland and Spain vetoed the agreement. Both states were not willing to give up the voting weight granted to them by the Nice Treaty. In March 2004 socialist Prime Minister Zapatero came to power in Spain and announced Spain's willingness to compromise. Having lost a coalition partner the Polish government was prepared for compromise. It wanted to play an important role in the EU, instead of being left on its own.

Poland joined the European Union on 1 May 2004 after more than a decade of intensive accession preparations. EU membership, a political and economic aspiration of successive Polish governments, became a reality. The "return to Europe" began shortly after the collapse of the communist regime in 1989 when Poland entered negotiations for an association agreement with the EC signed in December 1991. The Polish government applied for EU membership in 1994, and the accession negotiations lasted from March 1998 until December 2002.

In 2002 and the early 2003 EU constitution building was not a top priority of Poland's EU policy because of the closing accession negotiations and the EU accession referendum in June 2003. There was almost no connection between the preparations for the accession referendum and EU constitution building (Trzaskowski 2003). The accession referendum showed that 77 percent of voters favored Poland's EU membership. Following this positive outcome, Poland's EU debate focused on the EU constitution in autumn 2003 when the government's position at the IGC 2003–4 was presented, and the *Sejm* passed a resolution obliging the government to defend Polish vital interests.

Domestic structures in a comparative perspective

Poland is a constitutional parliamentary democracy. The democratic reforms – begun in 1989 after the collapse of the communist regime – focused on the transformation of the political system as well as the modernization of Poland's economy (Pyszna 2002: 7). The early years of democratic transition consisted mainly of the re-establishment of a multi-party democratic political system and its institutions. In 1990, the Mazowiecki government began a comprehensive reform program to replace the centralized command economy with a market-oriented system. In the 1990s the twin processes of systemic transformation and EU accession preparation required fundamental legal, economic and social change on an unprecedented scale (Mayhew and Tokarski 2000: 4).

The 1997 constitution stipulates that legislative power is vested in the *Sejm* and the Senat, executive power is exercised by the president and the Council of Ministers and judicial power is vested in courts and tribunals. The lower chamber of parliament, the *Sejm*, has 460 members, elected for four-year terms by proportional representation in multi-seat constituencies with a 5 percent threshold for individual parties and 8 percent for coalitions. The upper chamber of parliament, the *Senat*, has 100 members elected for four-year terms.

The Polish party system is the most complicated and the most dynamic in Eastern Europe (Benoit and Hayden 2004: 12). In the 1990s Poland had a two-bloc system, comprising parties aligned into rival groupings of the post-communist left and the post-Solidarity center-right (Herbut 2000: 100). However, with the election to parliament in 2001 of two anti-EU parties, the League of Polish Families and the Self-defense, a new, pro- versus anti-EU cleavage emerged. An additional characteristic of the Polish party system is a degree of defections and party switching (Benoit and Hayden 2004, Gwiazda 2005). Seven parties were represented in the *Sejm* after the 2001 parliamentary elections, while in June 2004 there were 16 political groups.[2]

After the September 2001 parliamentary elections the Democratic Left Alliance (SLD) formed a coalition government with the Polish Peasant Party (PSL) and the Labor Union (UP), with Leszek Miller (SLD) as Prime Minister. His government faced a long list of problems, including poor economic growth, high unemployment and poverty. In March 2003, PSL left the coalition while in March 2004 some 30 deputies quit the governing SLD to found a new party, Polish Social Democracy. Consequently, as expected Prime Minister Miller resigned in May 2004 and Marek Belka (SLD) became Prime Minister.

Constitutional policy coordination

In Poland management of EU business has been coordinated, depending on the agenda, by three departments: the ministry of foreign affairs

(MSZ), the Office of the Committee for European Integration (UKIE) and the chancellery of the prime minister (KPRM). While the KPRM mainly dealt with the accession negotiations, the MSZ and UKIE were key departments coordinating the European Convention and the IGC 2003–4. In fact, the Polish government's position on the IGC was prepared by the MSZ on the basis of comments sent by ministries.

Besides the ministry of foreign affairs, the Office of the Committee for European Integration played an important role in dealing with EU business and coordination of EU constitution building (see Figure 21.1). The UKIE is "a supreme governmental administration body competent for programming and coordination of policy relating to Poland's integration with the European Union."[3] The UKIE was headed for several years by the Secretary Danuta Hübner who also represented the Polish government at the European Convention, while the minister of foreign affairs along with the prime minister represented Poland at the IGC.

After the government's position on the IGC gained inter-ministerial approval, it was accepted by UKIE and by the cabinet. The government's position was then discussed in parliament. Deputies supported the *Sejm* resolution on the EU constitution so effectively there was no veto of parliament. President Kwaśniewski played a limited role in the debate, being informed but not participating in the formation of the government's position.

Data and empirical analysis of forming positions on the constitution for Europe

To investigate the positions of Polish actors on the EU constitution two interviews with Polish experts were conducted in Warsaw in January 2004.

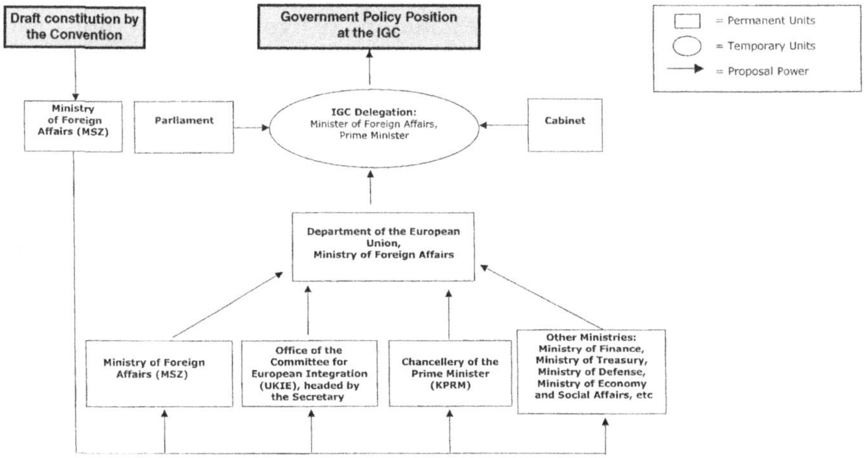

Figure 21.1 Poland: domestic policy coordination for the IGC 2003–4.

One expert was a government official working in the office of the Committee for European Integration while the other was an academic specializing in Poland's EU relations. Of all the actors involved in the coordination process the experts mentioned the MSZ and the UKIE as particularly relevant.[4] The role of the secretary of the UKIE was emphasized, as her attitude was more integrationist in comparison with the government's position.

Poland's approach to the IGC 2003–4 should be analyzed in two distinct phases: October–December 2003 and March–June 2004. The first period began with the IGC opening in Rome in October 2003 and finished with the breakdown of the Brussels summit in December 2003. The second period was marked by the parliamentary elections in Spain and the spring European Council in March 2004 and ended with the agreement on the EU constitution in June 2004.

Phase I: October–December 2003

Before the IGC commenced, the Polish government presented its position at the IGC. The Polish government's position was initially accepted at the inter-ministerial level, and then by the committee for the European integration on 5 September and the cabinet on 9 September. The Polish government "assesses positively the text of the EU constitution, as adopted by the European Convention, which is a good basis for the intergovernmental negotiations ... However, there are issues which need to be discussed further and revised" (Government of Poland 2003). Four vital issues were included in the government's position: a religious reference, security policy, the number of commissioners and the threshold for qualified majority voting in the Council.[5] They were the issues that the Polish government wanted to "discuss further" at the IGC 2003–4.

In 2003 the *Sejm* issued two resolutions obliging the government to defend the Nice system of weighted votes. The first resolution of the *Sejm* of 2 October 2003 asked the Polish delegation:

> to demand a reference to Christian values in the preamble of the EU constitution; to recognize NATO as a basis for European security; to support a principle one commissioner per each state and a team presidency of the Council; and the voting rules accepted in Nice in 2000. [In particular, the final postulate was emphasized:] In this subject matter [Nice voting rules] we [*Sejm* deputies] demand a firm position of the Polish government. A veto is possible if our reasons are not accepted at the IGC.
>
> (Sejm 2003a: 694; addenda in brackets by the author)

A majority of deputies supported the resolution with 279 votes in favor and 122 against (Sejm 2003b). The Democratic Left Alliance, the Labor

Union and the Civic Platform favored the resolution. Most of deputies from the Law and Justice Party and the Polish Peasant Party did not support the resolution. All deputies of the Self-defense Party and the League of Polish Families voted against the resolution. In December 2003 the *Sejm* reiterated its declaration with a particular emphasis on the Nice voting rules in another resolution presented just before the commencement of the European Council (Sejm 2003c: 901).

Certainly, all the issues mentioned in the resolutions were salient and could become a reason for the Polish government to block a possible agreement. The number of commissioners, the Council presidency modus but also security policy and the religious reference were crucial, however, the issue accorded the greatest importance was the Council voting rule. The main concern was that the formula proposed by the European Convention seriously weakened Poland's position in the Council decision making (see Chapter 1 in this volume).

According to the interviewees other issues included incorporating the charter of fundamental rights as a legally binding part of the constitution. The Polish government also supported the European Convention proposal to establish the post of the EU minister of foreign affairs, which was regarded by the government as an important achievement of the Convention. Furthermore, the government wanted to preserve the unanimity requirement in such areas as the harmonization of social standards and taxation.

Regarding the role of the European Parliament in the adoption of the budget, the MSZ position differed from that of the UKIE. For the office of the committee for European integration, the European Parliament should have extended rights in the annual budgetary process and the multiannual financial framework, while the MSZ advocated no change to the EP's rights in the budgetary procedure.

Our results confirm this view: the average actor deviated on 1.5 percent of the issues from the national position (see Table 21.1). There was good agreement on policy-related questions, while the average percentage of deviating positions mentioned for institutional issues is 2.3 percent. The domestic debate was characterized by a slight divergence of positions between the actors. However, they remained united on Polish vital issues.

At the European Council in December 2003 the Polish government responded to domestic pressures and firmly defended its position. "The Poles were justified in claiming that, having recently won a referendum on the terms of EU membership, it would be wrong (and politically risky) to give away the prize of near-equality of voting weights with France and Germany" (Dinan 2004: 40). Moreover, at the negotiation table Poland had a coalition partner because Spanish Prime Minister Aznar also supported the Nice Treaty.

Table 21.1 Cohesiveness of actors' positions in the Polish coordination process

National position comparison	*Actor(s) (No. or type)*	*Observations (No.)*	*Deviations*									
			from national position		*on integration*				*related to*			
					toward less		*toward more*		*institutional issues*[a]		*policy fields*[a]	
			No.	*%*	*No.*	*%*	*No.*	*%*	*No.*	*%*	*No.*	*%*
All actors	2	130	2	1.5	2	1.5	0	–	2	2.3	0	–
Subset												
Lead unit	MFA	65	1	1.5	1	1.5	0	–	1	2.3	0	–

Deviations related to institutional issues
Rights of EP in the adoption of the budget

Deviations related to policy fields
Nil

Vital interests
Qualified majority threshold; Presidency of the Council; Number of commissioners; Regulation of jurisdiction with respect to Common Security and Defense Policy; Religious reference in the preamble

Notes
a Percentage shares refer to subsets of institutional (43) and policy (22) issues. *Lead Unit* Leading unit in domestic coordination: Prime Minister's Office (PM) or Ministry of Foreign Affairs (MFA).

Phase II: March–June 2004

March 2004 was a turning point in EU constitution building. In March 2004, shortly after the surprise March election outcome in Spain, new socialist Prime Minister Zapatero assumed a more conciliatory position toward the EU and announced his intention to support other members' preference for the decision-making rules of the Council of Ministers of the EU. Poland lost a strategic partner. In March 2004 the Irish presidency announced relaunching of the IGC talks thus, "signaling a renewed sense of political resolve amongst EU leaders just two weeks after the terrorist bombings in Madrid" (Institute of European Affairs 2004).

Following the change in the European political scene, the Polish prime minister immediately signaled that Poland should avoid being left on its own as regards the EU constitution (*Gazeta Wyborcza*, 7 May 2004). Poland assumed a more compromising attitude but at the same time it tried to accommodate some of its concerns. In May 2004 it was announced that the "Nice or death" slogan was out of date and Poland signaled its agreement to the double majority rule. However, the condition was that its "vital interests were not endangered" (*Gazeta Wyborcza*, 7 May 2004). The Polish government wanted to distance itself from the "Nice or death" rhetoric but having spent considerable political capital in defense of the Nice Treaty, it also tried to include a "rendez-vous" clause in order to save face when reaching a compromise. Consequently, Poland pushed the debates on additional provisions until the last moments of negotiations, with the result that it managed to secure extra provisions to a double majority.[6]

After the IGC agreement was reached, Prime Minister Belka was pleased with the outcome of the negotiations (Belka 2004). However, the government could not expect a positive reaction at home from the major opposition parties.

Initially, Poland was supposed to hold a referendum in autumn 2005. However, after the French and Dutch "no" votes, President Kwaśniewski announced that the October 2005 referendum was not realistic. In July 2005 the *Sejm* voted to postpone a decision on whether to ratify the EU constitution by referendum or parliament. If the referendum is held, a minimum turnout of 50 percent is needed in order to make it valid. If turnout is low, ratification will then proceed through the parliamentary procedure which would require a two-thirds majority in favor in both parliamentary chambers. As regards the public opinion, while in April 2005, 56 percent of the Poles declared the support for the EU constitution (CBOS 2005a), after the French and Dutch referendums the support significantly decreased to 43 percent (while 24 percent were against the EU constitution, CBOS 2005b).

Polish political parties are divided over the issue of the EU constitution. Center-left parties – the Democratic Left Alliance and the Polish Social

Democracy as well as the Labor Union – are in favor of the EU constitution. In contrast, the main conservative opposition party – the Civic Platform (PO) tends to be against ratification. Although the Civic Platform supports European integration and in the 2004 European Parliament elections its slogan was "European Union – the best choice for Poland," it has assumed a lukewarm attitude to the EU constitution. Its parliamentary group leader's rallying cry "Nice or death" meant a struggle, by all means, for the Nice voting rules at the IGC. Similarly, the Polish Peasant Party (PSL) emphasizes that the EU constitution should be agreed on the Polish terms because Nice provisions are advantageous for Poland (Sejm 2004). Other important opposition parties such as the Law and Justice Party, the League of Polish Families and the Self-defense Party are openly against the EU constitution. The anti-ratification campaigners claim that institutionally Poland will lose influence if the EU constitution is implemented. The new voting arrangements in the Council are interpreted as leading to a decreased capability of Poland to incorporate its very specific concerns into EU politics. Moreover, the lack of a religious reference in the preamble is an argument to vote against the EU constitution especially for the supporters for the League of Polish Families.

Conclusion

In the first phase of the IGC 2003–4 (October–December 2003) the Polish government negotiated rather fiercely with the aim to defend Poland's vital interests, as supported by two *Sejm* resolutions. In the second phase of the IGC (March–June 2004) the position of the Polish government evolved. After the final agreement had been reached, the governing SLD was pleased to announce that Poland managed to secure additional provisions to a Convention double majority system. However, the opposition parties criticized the new voting arrangements in the Council as well as the lack of a religious reference in the preamble.

During the IGC 2003–4 Poland showed determination to achieve its goals by struggling until the end for the favorable outcome, yet it also demonstrated its ability to cooperate and compromise. Certainly, by rejecting a stance of "no compromise," it demonstrated that it wanted to be a constructive member of the European Union.

Notes

1 The slogan: "Nice or death" (Nicea albo śmierć), expressed by Deputy Rokita (PO) during the *Sejm* debate in September 2003, represented the domestic demand for a bitter struggle for the Nice voting rules at the IGC.

2 The distribution of votes and seats in the elections for parliament and the 2004 elections for the European Parliament, including the EP bloc affiliation of the parties, can be downloaded from the projects' website at dosei.dhv-speyer.de.

3 Law of 8 August 1996 on the Office for European Integration, *Official Journal* 1996, No. 106: 494.
4 Modifying the coherence for the number of experts interviewed we can compare the mean adapted coherence of the Polish case (0.81) with the overall coherence in the DOSEI data set, which is slightly better (0.85, see Appendix 2).
5 Additional postulates included: a team presidency of the Council, an efficient institutional design and no General and Legislative Council (Government of Poland 2003).
6 The European Council agreed to define qualified majority as 55 percent of the member states (but at least 15) representing at least 65 percent of the EU's population from 1 November 2009. A blocking minority can be formed by at least four member states. However, Council members representing at least three-quarters of a blocking minority (either at the level of member states or at the level of population) can demand that the Council should discuss the issue further.

22 Portugal

Quest for a new role

Spyros Blavoukos and George Pagoulatos

The breakdown of the authoritarian regime in 1974 and the end of the Portuguese empire with colonies in Africa and Asia led to a more general identity crisis as well as a redirection of the country's foreign policy (Magone 2000a, Faria 1999). Portugal's early expressed intention to join the European Community was motivated (like in Spain and Greece) by the political objective of underwriting democratic stability along with ending the country's prolonged isolation (Medeiros Ferreira 1993, Seixas da Costa 2000, Royo and Manuel 2003). Following formal accession in 1986, the Portuguese polity engaged in considerable economic, socio-political and administrative transformation (Magone 2000b).

In a nutshell, Portugal's EU trajectory reveals an important rupture in the mid-1990s as regards the perception of the country's European vocation. The first period is characterized by a more defensive, nation-centric approach focusing on domestic socioeconomic development in its national dimension (de Vasconcelos 2000) and endorsing intergovernmentalism (de Meirelles 1992). In the process, domestic political realignments, growing maturity in EU–Portugal relations, and the EMU contributed to a different conceptualization of national interest through the lens of an active involvement in European integration (de Vasconcelos 2000).[1]

The EMU process in particular was of particular importance to the Portuguese attitude as regards European integration. The economic and political connotations of EMU did not pass unnoticed generating a strenuous reform effort to meet the Maastricht criteria and become a constituent member of the integrationist "hard core" (Braga de Macedo 2003, Torres 2000, Corkill 1999, Marques-Mendes 1993). A potential failure to participate threatened Portugal with marginalization and exclusion from the decision-making vanguard, which would lead the future pace of integration (Torres and Fraga 2004). Following successful accession to the EMU, the Portuguese economy entered a period of intensive monitoring after breaching the rules of the Stability and Growth Pact in 2001. The imposed budgetary restrains, though precipitating an economic downturn, restored the country to the – at that time still ineffectually challenged – SGP orthodoxy.

Domestic structures in a comparative perspective

A case of "third wave democratization" (Huntington 1991), the consolidation of the democratic regime in Portugal occurred through a series of partial settlements initiated by a military coup and accompanied by processes involving both substantial mass mobilizations and an army disengaging gradually from political affairs (Gunther *et al.* 1995). The authoritarian-corporatist Salazar regime was replaced with a semi-presidential system, which favored two parallel centers of power. This conscious choice of political system aimed to avoid both the dangers of an excessively strong executive – reminiscent of the previous period – and the weaknesses of parliamentary instability (Elgie 1999, Sartori 1997, etc.). The *Assembleia da República* (Assembly of the Republic) has 230 members, elected for a four-year term by proportional representation in multi-seat constituencies.[2]

In terms of domestic party competition, the main parties, the Communist Party (PCP) being the sole exception, have embraced European integration to various degrees and also adjusted rapidly their operation and political discourse to the new environment (Lobo 2003, Salgado de Matos 1993). The two main political parties (PSD and PS), which control about two-thirds of the vote, have avoided the politicization of the integration cleavage and have been ardent supporters of integration. The Communist Party did acknowledge at some point some of the inherent benefits from accession adjusting but not abandoning its critical rhetoric. Another change in the domestic political stage occurred prior to the Maastricht Treaty with regards to the small CDS-PP on the right of the political spectrum, which following a declining political course adopted a more critical stance on European integration. However, after joining government in the previous elections, it has also adopted a more pragmatic approach (Salgado de Matos 1993, Lobo 2003).

Although the EU constitution could be ratified by the parliament by simple majority (Kurpas *et al.* 2005), both the outgoing and the incoming (after the early 2005 elections) governments decided to hold a referendum, initially planned to have taken place in spring 2005 had it not been for the unexpected political developments. Although both main parties are in principle in favor of the constitution, the outcome of the referendum became entangled in domestic politics, with a prior constitutional amendment required to allow for increased specificity in the referendum question wording. The PSD leader has threatened to block the required national constitutional revision if the government goes ahead with an abortion referendum in June 2005. Currently, the referendum is simply postponed.

Constitutional policy coordination

The Portuguese administrative and policy-making framework on EU affairs developed its longstanding features following accession in 1986.

Governmental stability and continuity, the 1992 presidency and the successive IGCs carried an impact on the organizational format of policy making, rendering EU policy coordination more salient within the Portuguese administrative structure (Magone 2000b, de Vasconcelos and Antunes 1996). In general Portugal has adopted flexible administrative and coordinating structures able to adjust to the dynamic nature of the integration process. The center is located in the State Secretariat for European Affairs (SSEA) in the ministry of foreign affairs, which is responsible for the inter-ministerial meetings at various levels of the administrative hierarchy supported by the administrative unit of the General Directorate for Community Affairs (DGAC). The latter is the focal point in the everyday running of Portugal–EU relations assuming the tasks of inter-ministerial information gathering and dissemination as well as communication with the Portuguese Permanent Representation. The senior body in the Portuguese EU policy coordination process is the inter-ministerial Committee for Community Affairs (CIAC) providing general strategic guidance and arbitration in inter-ministerial conflicts of interest. It involves representatives from all other ministries directly involved in EU affairs and aims at resolving policy formulation problems (Magone 2000b). In addition to these permanent structures, the preparation of major dossiers such as treaty revisions, enlargement or the negotiation of the financial perspectives are sometimes entrusted to *ad hoc* coordinating structures, under the broad supervision of the CIAC (de Vallera 2000).

The convergence of views on EU affairs among the main Portuguese political parties – with the exception of the Communist Party – gives the parliament a secondary role in monitoring and controlling government action in EU affairs (de Vasconcelos and Antunes 1996). Interest groups do not directly approach the administrative unit responsible for the coordination of EU policy but have developed their own networks with the respective ministries that take their requests to CIAC (Magone 2000b).

This institutional structure was used in the two previous IGCs (Thurner *et al.* 2002). The preparation of the Portuguese representation for the European Convention and the subsequent IGC largely conveys the same image with two notable points (see Figure 22.1). No special formal structures were set up either for the Convention or the IGC and the CIAC played again the main coordinating role with the EU directorate in the MFA being the center of the governmental policy-making hub responsible for communication with other departments and ministries. The first point that should be made is related to the distinctive nature of the two stages of the European Convention. During the initial period of work of the Convention, the government representatives felt a greater degree of freedom to express more personal views under the broad guidance offered by the prime minister. There was no concrete mandate but rather a general outline of the Portuguese views about the future institutional organization of the EU. In this early stage the Convention was seen more as a forum for

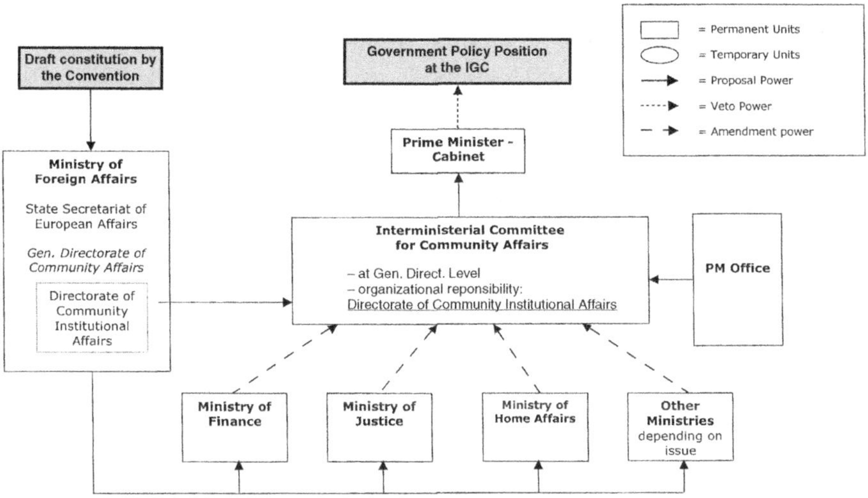

Figure 22.1 Portugal: domestic policy coordination for the IGC 2003–4.

the exchange of ideas about the future of Europe with less emphasis on the need to come up with a coherent blueprint for the following IGC. However, as the concluding months approached, and an increasing number of foreign ministers became involved in the process as government representatives, the leeway was dramatically reduced and it was felt that expressed positions became more rigid.[3]

The second point worth mentioning is the active engagement of the prime minister's office in the preparation of the Portuguese positions in the IGC. This was due to the personal interest of the prime minister himself deriving from his past service as minister of foreign affairs and his strong personal interest in European affairs.[4] However this strong interference of the PM's office in the process did not lead to any serious intragovernmental struggle for supremacy. This was mainly due to the almost consensual approach to the issues discussed in the IGC, which resulted in the absence of any serious disagreements between the prime minister's office and the diplomatic community in the MFA.[5] The central role of the prime minister and his office became more apparent after the change of guard in the ministry of foreign affairs a week before the October 2003 European Council in Brussels.[6]

The positions of the Portuguese government were almost exclusively formulated within the formal institutional framework described above with minimal inputs from other sources. The sophisticated political and institutional nature of the topics deterred civil society, interest groups and the public in general, with the small exception of the Roman Catholic Church on the question of the religious inheritance of Europe. Apart from the nature of the issues discussed, the detachment of interest groups – in particular trade unions – from the Convention/IGC debate can be also attributed to the very limited tradition of their involvement in domestic policy making in EU affairs (Torres and Fraga 2004).[7] Given the broad domestic political consensus – again with the exception of the Communist Party – the distinctive input of political parties was also marginal. The influence of the junior coalition partner CDS-PP Party, which in the 1990s had carried an anti-EU rhetoric, can be seen in the support for an increased role for national parliaments in monitoring the competence allocation in the EU, and in the inclusion of the reference to Christianity in the preamble of the constitution despite the reaction of the opposition.[8]

Data and empirical analysis of forming positions on the constitution for Europe

We have contacted five experts in Portugal to collect the relevant information on the domestic actors involved in the position formation process and their input in it. We approached experts both from inside and outside the government. Two of the interviewees were high-ranking diplomats directly involved in the process and the remaining three were members of the academia, civil society and highly appraised journalists. The experts interviewed presented a remarkable level of coherence (above 90 percent) both as regards the identification of the key actors involved and their actual positions. This high percentage indicates that the position formation process was quite straightforward and the views of the main actors identified were clear and easily discernible.

The position formation in Portugal conveys a picture of complete homogeneity among the views of the leading ministry, the other actors involved in the process and what became identified as the national position of the Portuguese government in the negotiations (see Table 22.1). The core issues on the agenda of the IGC were subject to consensual treatment deriving from the country's political orientation and intention to take part in the integrationist vanguard without sacrificing its national interests.

Hence, one can argue about a mixture of a pro-integration stance, a degree of pragmatism and an attempt to ensure national representation in the institutional bodies of the EU. Despite initial ambivalence not to say rejection of the Convention method by the main Portuguese political parties, the process was broadly embraced in the end (Torres and Fraga 2004). Portugal was satisfied to a large extent with the Convention's draft constitution, with the notable exception of the establishment of the post of the president of the European Council, and hence preferred the preservation of the balance struck in the Convention context.

Institutional issues, in particular the Commission composition and the

Table 22.1 Cohesiveness of actors' positions in the Portuguese coordination process

National position comparison	*Actor(s) (No. or type)*	*Observations (No.)*	*Deviations*									
			from national position		*on integration*				*related to*			
					toward less		*toward more*		*institutional issues*[a]		*policy fields*[a]	
			No.	*%*	*No.*	*%*	*No.*	*%*	*No.*	*%*	*No.*	*%*
All actors	2	130	0	–	0	–	0	–	0	–	0	–
Subset												
Lead unit	MFA	65	0	–	0	–	0	–	0	–	0	–

Deviations related to institutional issues
Nil

Deviations related to policy fields
Nil

Vital interests
Religious reference in the preamble; Qualified majority threshold; Number of commissioners; Number and distribution of seats in the EP; Legal meaning of constitution (supremacy toward national constitution

Notes
a Percentage shares refer to subsets of institutional (43) and policy (22) issues. *Lead Unit* Leading unit in domestic coordination: Prime Minister's Office (PM) or Ministry of Foreign Affairs (MFA).

establishment of an elected president for the European Council, were the most contentious for Portugal in the IGC negotiations, along with rejecting a list of competencies of the Union. The Portuguese government supported the preservation of the rotating format of the presidency accepting as a fallback position also the possibility of a team presidency under the condition of prior clarification of its membership and operating rules. This support was based not only on the greater visibility it offered to individual member states but also on the very positive experience of the two past Portuguese presidencies, which raised the country's profile and provided an opportunity to portray its integrationist credentials. Throughout the negotiations, the Portuguese delegation made substantial efforts to reduce the powers of the single president and in general undermine the credibility and feasibility of this prospective institutional development.

Furthermore, there was a strong preference to one commissioner per member state with the application of "one commissioner – one vote" principle. Ensuring national representation in the Commission college was considered a prerequisite for endorsing further competence allocation and power transfer to the Commission. The appointment of an EU minister of foreign affairs was met sympathetically as a step that would promote Europe's international standing but further clarification of the official tasks and exact status of the post were requested. Extended jurisdiction for the European Court of Justice in all areas except defense and foreign policy was also well taken whereas there was some skepticism toward an increased role for the European Parliament. This distrust to the EP owes a lot to the limited capacity of the country to influence decisions in it and to the domestic political culture, which credits the executive at the expense of the legislative bodies of governance. Hence, Portugal preferred a stronger Commission to a stronger EP.

As regards decision-making rules, the favored option was the simple majority of states and population, consenting during the negotiations to increasing the required percentage of the population to appease smaller member states. In concordance with the country's ambition to take part in the core of the European integration process, enhanced cooperation schemes were embraced in all fields possible, to pave the way for more rapid integration. Along the same lines extension of qualified majority voting was endorsed in principle in most areas with the exception of EU structural policies and with some reservations in the fields of economic policy and the area of freedom, security and justice. In general, Portugal was comfortable with the transfer of more competence to the EU level in most policies including security and defense, and justice and home affairs as long as national representation in the Commission was guaranteed.

Conclusion

The above discussion of the institutional structures and mode of policy making during the Convention and the IGC 2003–4 conveys the image of a very centralized system the heart of which was situated in the ministry of foreign affairs with informal networks and communications occurring during the negotiations to add flexibility and velocity of responsiveness to the arising challenges. A departure from previous important negotiations was the direct and intensive involvement of the prime minister's office in the process. However the addition of a new potent and potentially competitive actor in the process did not lead to any major power crisis nor did it undermine the cohesiveness of the positions or the unitary nature of the policy-making process. That was largely due to the consensual approach to the main issues discussed in the IGC, issues associated with the scope and pace of European integration, and hence met with broad agreement in the Portuguese polity. Other actors like the junior coalition partner were able to affect positions in some cases whereas the involvement of civil society was very marginal with the Roman Catholic Church being the exception that confirms this general rule.

The most salient issues for Portugal in the IGC were the abolition of the rotating presidency and the Commission composition. In general, Portugal endorsed enhanced cooperation, more competence allocation to the Commission (but not so much to the EP) and further use of QMV. In that respect the IGC 2003–4 was another opportunity for the Portuguese government to identify itself with the integrationist camp.

Should the constitution referendum become disentangled from domestic politics and contestation, the prospects of ratification would be very good given the endorsement of the EU constitution by the main political parties and the public.

Notes

1 The 1996 and 2000 IGCs and the 2000 Portuguese presidency have highlighted continuity and change in Portugal's view of the EU. Continuity can be seen in the form of safeguarding national representation in the institutional bodies of the EU. It is also evident in the mostly reactive nature of the Portuguese engagement in European integration (Torres and Fraga 2004). Change was manifested in embracing ambitious schemes of differentiated integration and incorporating national objectives into EU policies. Expressed support to clauses of enhanced cooperation in Nice and the "Lisbon agenda" set forward during the Portuguese presidency testify to this evolution (Guerra Martins 2002).

2 The distribution of votes and seats in the most recent elections for parliament and the 2004 elections for the European Parliament, including the EP bloc affiliation of the parties, can be downloaded from the projects' website at dosei.dhv-speyer.de.

3 Interview, Deputy Director General of European Affairs and alternate member for the Portuguese government in the European Convention (3 December 2003).

4 Interview, Professor Álvaro de Vasconcelos, Director of the Institute for Strategic and International Studies, Lisbon (2 December 2003).
5 Interview, Deputy Director General of European Affairs. In any case the prime minister's office is staffed with diplomats from the ministry of foreign affairs, which guarantees a large degree of convergence of views, and does not act as a separate policy unit but rather in close contact with the MFA.
6 Interview, Dr Francisco Sarsfield Cabral, News Director in the Rádio Renascença LDA (2 December 2003).
7 Interview, Professor Álvaro de Vasconcelos.
8 Ibid.

23 Slovakia

Avoiding conflict to secure stability

Tobias Schulz and Martina Chabreckova

Before 1998 it looked like Slovakia would not be able to keep pace with the other Eastern European countries because of lacking reforms. The reason for this lay in the undemocratic developments during the 1994 to 1998 term of Prime Minister Mečiar and his party, the HZDS (Movement for a Democratic Slovakia). The appointment of the government in 1998 marked thus a turning point in the history of the young democracy of Slovakia. The new Prime Minister Dzurinda together with his party, the SDKÚ (Slovak Democratic and Christian Union), was able to push through economic and institutional reforms that are without equal and hence paved the way into the European Union.

In 1997 the EU did not include the country into the circle of the states that were considered for enlargement (European Commission 1997). Slovakia finally managed to overhaul the constitution in 2001 (Učeň 2002) and to join the first wave of Central and Eastern European countries that gained membership in spring 2004. After the negotiation of accession conditions in December 2002, over 92 percent of voters agreed to this step in the accession referendum in May 2003, although the necessary turnout quorum of 50 percent was met only just closely.

The SDKÚ, still the second strongest party behind the openly Euroskeptic HZDS, remained the driving force toward the goal of the country's integration into the EU and NATO. The new ANO (Alliance of the New Citizen) is very similarly oriented. The SMK-MKP (Party of Hungarian Coalition), and the KDH (Christian Democratic Movement) on the other hand, are known to be somewhat less ambitious in this direction. The latter party occasionally tried to capitalize on these differences (Gyáfášoá 2003).

All Slovak parties are generally rated higher in terms of Euro-enthusiasm than those in many of the other new members (Taggart and Szczerbiak 2004: 16). There will be no referendum on the constitutional treaty[1] and ratification by parliament went smoothly on 11 May 2005.

Economically, the strong commitment has paid off: the Slovak Republic's growth lay ahead of that of the Czech Republic's and now lies well above 4 percent. The GDP-share of the agricultural sector is already below

3.5 percent. On the other hand, unemployment is still the main obstacle because, apart from the regions near the capital, economic structures are very weak in the periphery and hence Slovakia has one of the highest unemployment rates of about 16–17 percent. Slovakia also managed to target the issue of compliance with the EMU criteria rather early and now is regarded, together with other smaller new members, as Latvia for example, to be able to enter the Exchange Rate Mechanism 2 (ERM-2) in 2005. Lithuania, Estonia and Slovenia have already taken this step.

Domestic structures in a comparative perspective

Slovakia is a parliamentary democracy, although it has a directly elected president. This president, however, is holding very limited powers, actually only the possibility to dissolve the assembly under certain circumstances. In addition, he might send back legislation to the assembly. There, however, a simple majority can easily overrule the decision.

All parties except the Party of the Hungarian minority (SMK-MKP) and the KDH are "new" parties that resulted from shifts during the first legislature of Dzurindas government: The ANO was newly founded in 2001 and the SDKÚ emerged in 2000 from the KDH after the exit of Prime Minister Dzurinda.

The government consists of a four-party coalition (ANO, SDKÚ, KDH and SMK-MKP) that narrowly secured a majority during the time of the Convention and the IGC 2003–4. The SDKÚ is the largest with a share of seats in the lower house of about 35 percent.[2] However, because of the resignation of three ANO members from their party and because of the refusal of the seven members of the Free Forum (SF) – that had split from the SDKÚ in December 2003 – to join the government, the government majority has virtually disappeared, although former Defense Minister and SF leader Ivan Simko declared that he will not overthrow the government (Učeň 2003; *Neue Zürcher Zeitung*, 2 October 2003; *Frankfurter Allgemeine Zeitung*, 16 January 2004).

The Slovakian parliament is unicameral, with 150 members that are elected according to a highly proportional electoral system. Formally, the dominance of the assembly stands on firm grounds. Not only can it provoke a vote of confidence and vote down the government or even a single member of government, it is also authorized to impeach the president, to call for a popular recall of the president, to call for referendums and even to establish governmental departments.

However, the power of government very much depends on the political context and party discipline in particular (Malová 2001). Whereas in 1998 4.7 effective parties had been counted, this figure rose to about six in 2002 (Armingeon and Careja 2004), which underlines the low stability of the party system (Morlino 2001).

Beside party stability and coherence, there are additional reasons for the instability of the political system (Morlino 2001: 94). First, the assembly has to approve individual ministers with a qualified majority. This results in a situation similar to that in Italy, where the parties have much influence on the choice of ministers. Second, in the beginning of the republic, informal rules had been established that have not fostered stability (Bárány *et al.* 2001).

Despite these pitfalls, majority governments have always been possible to form in the Slovak Republic, although the margin became very narrow for Dzurinda in 1998 (Blondel and Müller-Rommel 2001: 223). The government of Dzurinda had been reaffirmed in the 2002 elections but the path to stability is still not assured. The problem nowadays is that the main political conflicts have to be settled within the government. Although the fear of the political return of former Prime Minister Mečiar still unites the governing parties, party discipline is in decline again.

Also similar to the Czech Republic, Slovakia has undergone a reform of its system of federalism. This had led to the establishment of eight regional districts and 79 sub-districts and to a general expansion of the administration. However, this was not necessarily accompanied by a strengthening of self-administration and autonomy, which is still an ongoing process (Kipke 2004: 296). Therefore, Slovakia remains a centralized system in which the regions do not really participate in national politics.

Constitutional policy coordination

In the case of the Slovak Republic, the administrative body that stood in the center of the position formation process was the Department of Internal Affairs and Institutions of the European Union affiliated to the division for European affairs of the foreign ministry (Figure 23.1). Its head, State Secretary Ivan Korčoc was also the delegate to the European Convention. His deputy, Juraj Migaš is the head of the mission of the Slovak Republic to the European Communities in Brussels.

One would therefore assume that in Slovakia also, the process was organized in a conventional way, with the ministry of foreign affairs being responsible for the formulation of the position. However, following an initiative of former State Secretary Jan Figel in December 2000, the ministry of foreign affairs itself initiated a National Convention,[3] i.e., a temporary organization that aimed at providing a platform for interested persons and organizations outside the government to discuss the proposals of the EU Convention. The National Convention was composed of actors from citizens' action groups (NGO's), the churches, think tanks and all parties (Bilčík 2003).

The National Convention had its constituent assembly in May 2001 and met twice a year. Contrary to the Czech National Forum, its influence on the Slovakian position was considerable. From August 2002 on, it had

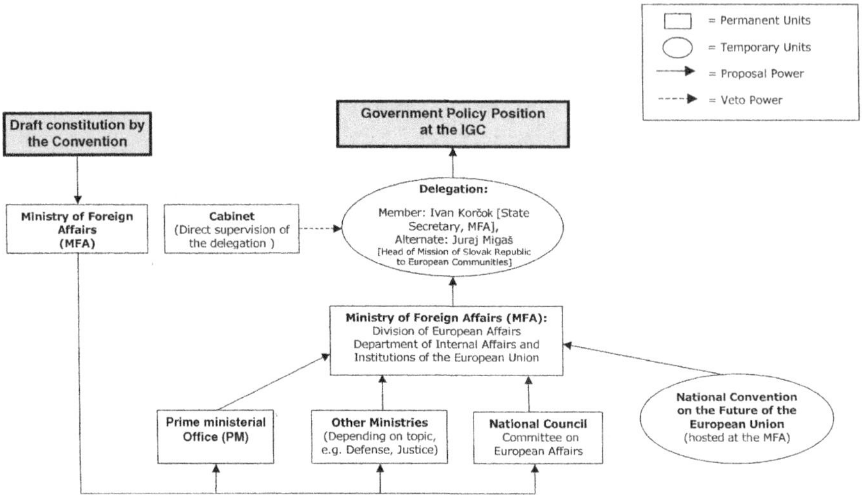

Figure 23.1 Slovakia: domestic policy coordination for the IGC 2003–4.

been the explicit task of the National Convention to formulate a position on the EU draft constitution. Of course, the foreign ministry still was in charge of the coordination and the formulation of the final texts, however, the input from the National Convention cannot be ignored. In April 2003 the National Convention approved a final document that had been drafted by the foreign ministry (*Tlacova Agentura Slovenskej Republiky* and *BBC Monitoring European*, 1 April 2003). This document then was discussed in the government. Moreover, the National Council was involved in a similar manner. Apart from the regular consultations that occurred between the government and two commissions of the parliament that had been entrusted with the task,[4] the National Council also had been consulted at about the same time – on 26 February 2003 – and it acknowledged and supported a report of the government on the European Convention (Bilčík 2003). The final position of the Slovak government was then again presented to and discussed in the National Council as well as the National Convention in September before being adopted by the cabinet (*Tlacova Agentura Slovenskej Republiky*, 14 September 2003a and 17 September 2003). As we believe that the National Convention, which met repeatedly,[5] had a relatively strong standing in the process, we have integrated this player in Figure 23.1. However, our interviewees did not consider it as an equal partner in the whole process. In a strict sense, the National Convention was not meant as a forum to produce input for the governmental position.

The impression still prevails that the position formation process had been somewhat more open than in other countries. This might have been the case mainly because of the fragility of the governmental coalition, the relatively strong standing of the parliament and lacking party discipline. Obviously, the integration of the four parties in government had been fostered through this process whereas the opposition parties had somewhat confusing positions (*Tlacova Agentura Slovenskej Republiky*, 14 September 2003b)[6] and did not manage to influence the governmental position perceivably.[7]

Data and empirical analysis of forming positions on the constitution for Europe

Two experts had been interviewed in Slovakia. The interviews were conducted between mid- to late November 2003. The first is a member of the government administration, namely the Department of Internal Affairs and Institutions of the European Union. The second is an academic and member of a think tank, working on European integration and the convention.

Both interviewees unanimously mentioned the same key actors in the interviews: the ministry of foreign affairs, the parliament and the National Convention.[8]

Slovakia joined the group of 15 smaller countries criticizing the draft constitution (*Slovenska Tlacova Agentura*, 14 October 2003). Also, together with the other Visegrád countries (Poland, Czech Republic and Hungary) it expressed concerns relating to the mentioning of Christianity in the preamble, its preference for the structures of the Nice Treaty and against enhanced cooperation (*Neue Zürcher Zeitung*, 1 October 2003). It is therefore not surprising that the main topic of the Slovak discussion had been the reform of the decision-making process in the European Union. Slovakia expressed five priorities for the final discussion in Brussels: the "one state, one commissioner" principle, the mentioning of "God" in the preamble, the unanimity rule for decisions over the application of majority voting in certain policy areas, the preservation of the majority voting rule of the Nice Treaty and of the rotating presidency (Foreign Ministry of Slovakia 2003). Other important concerns were the external representative with double responsibility and the principle of co-equal decision of the European Parliament. Still, Slovakia spoke in favor of retaining veto power in some areas such as social policy, taxes and the CFSP. Enhanced cooperation would only be acceptable during the implementation phase of the CFSP (Bilčík 2003).

From our questionnaire, we were able to infer some additional information on the "vital" issues given by our experts, which allowed us to weight the issues given above. Both mentioned the qualified majority threshold in the council as well as the number of commissioners. One of them also referred to the reference to Christianity in the preamble. These are exactly the three first issues given in the list above.

Consensus on these issues is generally high in Slovakia and hence it is difficult to make out any deviations from the national position for any of the actors identified by our interviewees (Table 23.1). In only 2.7 percent of the questions there had been some disagreement, although this affects the policy questions equally strongly (2.3 percent) as the institutional issues (2.9 percent).

Most of the information we had been able to collect with regard to deviating positions is also obvious from other sources. Particularly the position of the most skeptic coalition partner, the KDH, must be mentioned. In our interviews, all deviations had been assigned to this coalition party, although this might partly also be caused by the fact that the KDH was the only actor that our second rated expert had mentioned in addition to those mentioned by the first expert. Still, this party had actually tried to take somewhat contrasting positions within the government coalition. Four of its deviations are less integrationist: the Charter of Fundamental Rights, the organization of the presidency of the European Council, the scope of jurisdiction of the European Court of Justice and majority voting regarding structural funds. On the other hand, it also had more integrationist positions regarding the preamble (reference to God), majority voting related to common foreign policy and the alternation of the rights of the European Parliaments regarding the budget.

Consequently, we are not able to find any differences between the leading ministry and the national position. This is not very surprising given the strong lead of the foreign ministry and the low degree of conflict within the coalition, with the KDH being the only party visibly taking different stances in a small number of issues.

Conclusion

After some troublesome years under the problematic government of Mečiar, Slovakia had become the model child of eastern enlargement and European integration. Hence, in a country where even the communists are more or less in favor of the constitutional treaty, ratification was unproblematic. The position formation process, although at every point in time firmly in the hands of the foreign ministry, was relatively open and even included the parliament during the convention stage. One reason for this probably was the narrow majority of the government coalition during the period of the European Convention and the subsequent IGC. Obviously, the government felt no need to call a referendum. Ratification by a popular referendum would have bore some risks: Shortly before the final IGC, the presidential elections in April 2004 resulted in a defeat of the government's favorite candidate.

Table 23.1 Cohesiveness of actors' positions in the Slovak coordination process

National position comparison	*Actor(s) (No. or type)*	*Observations (No.)*	*Deviations*									
			from national position		*on integration*				*related to*			
					toward less		*toward more*		*institutional issues*[a]		*policy fields*[a]	
			No.	*%*	*No.*	*%*	*No.*	*%*	*No.*	*%*	*No.*	*%*
All actors	4	260	7	2.7	4	1.5	3	1.2	5	2.9	2	2.3
Subset												
Lead unit	MFA	65	0	–	0	–	0	–	0	–	0	–

Deviations related to institutional issues
Presidency of the Council; ECJ jurisdiction; Voting rule (Council) for structural and cohesion politics, for foreign policy; Rights of EP in the adoption of the budget

Deviations related to policy fields
Charter of Fundamental Rights; Religious reference in the preamble

Vital interests
Religious reference in the preamble; Qualified majority threshold; Number of commissioners

Notes
a Percentage shares refer to subsets of institutional (43) and policy (22) issues. *Lead Unit* Leading unit in domestic coordination: Prime Minister's Office (PM) or Ministry of Foreign Affairs (MFA).

Acknowledgment

We would like to express our gratitude to Barbara Gähwiler, who was one of the interviewers.

Notes

1 Ratification of international treaties requires a simple majority of votes of the assembly if no transfer of sovereignty is involved. Otherwise a three-fifths majority is required (Article 84 of the constitution). Also, a binding referendum is required on "a constitutional law on entering into a state alliance with other states or on withdrawing from that" or on "other important issue of public interest" and it could be triggered either by 350,000 signatures of entitled voters or by the parliament. Both would oblige the president to call such a referendum (Article 95). However, there have been important debates – involving the constitutional court – about the applicability of referendums and also whether they really should be envisaged to alter the constitution directly (Bárány *et al.* 2001: 173).

2 The distribution of votes and seats in the most recent elections for parliament and the 2004 elections for the European Parliament, including the EP bloc affiliation of the parties, can be downloaded from the projects' website at dosei.dhv-speyer.de.

3 Information on the meetings and the members of the National Convention. Online. Available at: www.konvent.sk/en/index.php.

4 Committee for External Relations and Committee for European Integration

5 Till October 2003, the Convention held nine meetings altogether.

6 Former Prime Minister Mečiar even seemed to speak against the interests of his own country in claiming that the position of the government would offend the big states like France and Germany (*Tlacova Agentura Slovenskej Republiky*, 14 September 2003).

7 Although they had been part of the National Convention, the opposition parties did not really engage in the process. This is illustrated by their failure to participate in a survey at the end of the sixth meeting (February 2003) that was meant to help eliciting and clarifying the positions of the members of the National Convention (Bilčík 2003).

8 The mean coherence of the answers between the actors (0.91) lies well above the questionnaire average (0.85) and it is the same across all actors mentioned, except the KDH, which was only mentioned by the second rated expert. The disagreement between the actors is mainly caused by a high number of missing values for the second expert. In the end, the experts had very much the same opinion on a quite narrow base of issues.

24 Slovenia

Consensus, integration and the protection of identity

Giacomo Benedetto

Slovenia is one of the smallest member states with a population of two million. Having declared independence from Yugoslavia in 1991, it established itself as a unitary parliamentary republic. The constitution guarantees special rights and protection to the indigenous Italian and Hungarian minorities.[1] The directly elected president has largely ceremonial powers, while executive formation occurs as a result of legislative elections. The prime minister is nominated by the president and approved by an absolute majority of parliamentarians.[2] If this fails, the National Assembly can elect an alternative candidate as prime minister, despite the preferences of the president. Apart from resignation, death, or losing a vote of confidence on its own initiative, the government can only be removed by a vote of constructive no confidence,[3] whereby a new prime minister is simultaneously elected by an absolute majority of parliamentarians. This is comparable to the German Basic Law.

Slovenia has the highest GDP per capita of the eight new member states from Central and Eastern Europe. Slovenia's status as a net recipient is therefore likely to be temporary and may influence its approach to budgetary questions. The country is also a front runner among the new states for adoption of the euro in 2007. Its currency has been stable against the Deutschmark and euro since independence, while public debt and inflation are within the Maastricht criteria. Natural long-term allies of the Slovenian government within the EU are likely to be the smaller, net contributors in northern Europe.

Domestic structures in a comparative perspective

The second chamber of the Slovenian legislature, the National Council, is largely consultative and designed to represent institutionalized civil society: employers; employees; professions; and local interests. To pass legislation, a simple majority is sufficient in the National Assembly, although if rejected by the National Council, an absolute majority is required.[4] The requirement of absolute majorities to pass legislation under these circumstances or to elect a prime minister necessitates the formation of oversize coalitions, in preference to any attempt to form minority administrations. Constitutional revision[5] is subject to a vote of at least 60 of the 90 members of the National Assembly. The party system in Slovenia is dominated by the Liberal Democrats (LDS), which emerged in 1992 from the Communist Party and the broad coalition that had achieved Slovenian independence. Apart from a brief period of right-wing government between May and November 2000, the LDS has retained office consistently in conjunction with smaller coalition partners until October 2004.[6] Euro-skepticism is weak in Slovenia, although there is a significant nationalist constituency. Since 1991, Slovenia has been committed to joining the EU and is one of the most pro-integrationist of the new member states. Because of its size, interdependence with its neighbors and history of domination by them, the post-1991 administration has sought to combine liberal nationalism with pragmatic pro-Europeanism (Bucar and Brinar 2005). This consensus shared by the main parties of government and opposition was strong during the period of the Convention on the Future of Europe, since Alojz Peterle, the leader of the opposition Christian Democratic New Slovenia (NSi) and the first post-independence prime minister of Slovenia, was a member of the Praesidium. However, the main party of opposition the Slovenian Democrats (SDS) displayed stronger and more right-wing nationalism until its victory in October 2004. The small Slovenian National Party has a more strident tone but is at the margins of the party system (Krasovec and Kustec-Lipicer 2005).

The European Parliament elections of June 2004 were subject to a second-order effect (Reif 1997, Reif and Schmidt 1980), with a low turnout at just 28.3 percent. The significant shift occurred in the loss of the Liberals, falling to 21.9 percent, and the rise of Peterle's NSi to 23.6 percent, partly on account of his visibility on European issues (Brinar 2005), although in the national elections of October its support fell back to 9 percent. The result was affected by a domestic second-order issue pursued by the opposition, namely a referendum to prevent long-term residents in Slovenia from other parts of former Yugoslavia from gaining Slovenian citizenship. This led to the defection to the opposition of one of the governing parties, the Slovenian People's Party, whose support remained stable on 8.4 percent. The performance of the ruling LDS was disappointing, leading to its defeat in October. However, this affected neither the positions of the Slovenian government in the final stages of the IGC nor parliamentary ratification by the new majority. On 1 February 2005 the Slovenian National Assembly ratified the EU constitution by 79 votes, easily exceeding the requirements for constitutional amendment, with four deputies of the right-wing Slovenian National Party opposed.

Constitutional policy coordination

The government of Slovenia was at first represented at the Convention by Matjaz Nahtigal, the head of the government legal service. When the Prime Minister Janez Drnovsek was elected as President of Slovenia at the end of 2002, the new Prime Minister, Anton Rop, appointed the minister of foreign affairs as the new representative. During the earlier stages of the Convention, a consultative Forum on the Future of Europe was established, consisting of social partners and other parts of civil society, such as the universities or agricultural interests, and not least the highly influential chambers of commerce. Social partners and civil society play an important role in Slovenian public life.

An inter-institutional task force formulated the positions of the Slovenian government on the Convention and IGC, having consulted the Forum on the Future of Europe and received the views of different ministries in Ljubljana. The two representatives of the Slovenian parliament, their substitutes, and the government's representatives all participated in the work of the task force. Although a member of the opposition, Peterle's role as accession state observer on the Praesidium placed him in an influential position, so the Slovenian government was anxious to include him in policy formulation during the period of the Convention.

The most significant institutional actor within the Slovenian executive was the EU Section in the ministry of foreign affairs, responsible directly to Dimitrij Rupel, the Foreign Minister. This office has coordinated the Slovenian position throughout the IGC (see Figure 24.1). The inter-institutional task

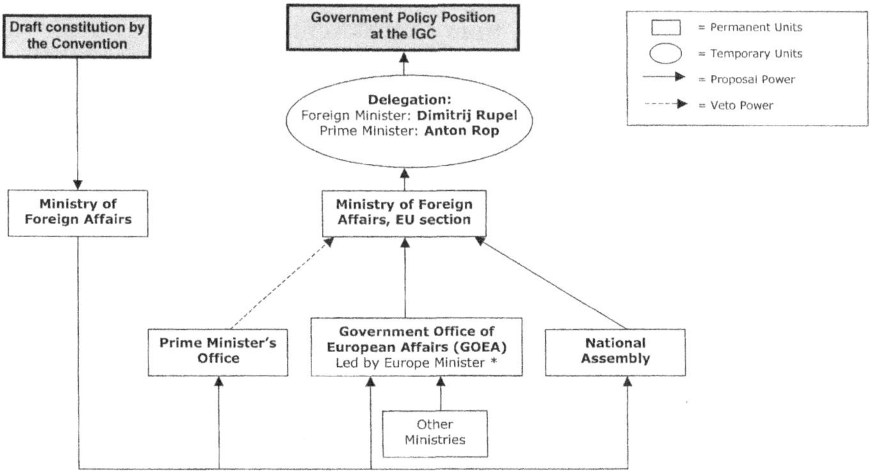

Figure 24.1 Slovenia: domestic policy coordination for the IGC 2003–4.

Note

* Responsible for negotiating Slovenian membership of the EU and concerned with policy issues.

force also received input directly from the prime minister's office, and the Government Office of European Affairs. Its competence was limited to coordinating the accession negotiations and was staffed by personnel delegated from other ministries. It therefore specialized in all matters concerned with the EU other than institutional affairs.

The result of the discussions at the Convention and on the Praesidium would filter their way to the inter-institutional task force. The Forum on the Future of Europe was allowed to suggest proposals on such topics as social and economic policies. When the Slovenians wished to contribute to policy development at the Convention, the task force would coordinate, working with the EU Section at the foreign ministry, the prime minister's office, the relevant ministry for the policy sector concerned, and the Convention members from Slovenia.

Data and empirical analysis of forming positions on the constitution for Europe

Three government officials, an advisor at the National Assembly, and one academic expert[7] provided information on the policy formulation processes during the Convention and IGC. Among those contacted, there was consensus that the key institutional actors in forming the position of the Slovenian government with regard to the Convention and IGC were: the foreign ministry; the Government Office of European Affairs subordinate to the prime minister; and the parliament. The latter was listed because of the presence of Peterle on the Praesidium. One actor also listed Chambers of Commerce as particularly influential.[8]

The non-negotiable issues from the Slovenian perspective were the subject of a wide consensus by the main institutional and political actors. These comprised:

1 One commissioner per member state.
2 A minimum of five MEPs per state (Slovenia has seven).
3 Preservation of Slovenian as an official language of the Union.

Slovenia, as a small country, was opposed to the permanent presidency of the European Council, but was prepared to accept it. On the question of the presidencies of Council formations, the Slovenians were persuaded to abandon a previous commitment to equal rotation, in favor of fair division between states in *team* presidencies. The weighting of Council votes was not a contentious issue for the Slovenes, who had calculated that under whichever of the proposed systems, their country would have approximately 1 percent of the votes. During the earlier period of the Convention, the Slovenian delegation had supported the proposal to elect the European Commission via an electoral college of national parliamentarians. All actors in Slovenia, whether during or following the Convention, were opposed to suggestions that the European Parliament should elect the Commission, since the Parliament represents population without taking into consideration an adequate weighting for states. Those working close to EU issues and who understand EU institutions were of the unofficial opinion that there is a case for reducing the number of commissioners, but for political reasons it was not realistic to defend this standpoint. Of these the only one not guaranteed in the Convention's draft constitution, or in the new Treaty of Rome after 2014, is the size of the Commission.

Apart from the identity-related areas of *vital interests*, there was widespread support for integrationist positions, particularly on burden sharing in the Area of Freedom, Security and Justice. Slovenia has a population of 2 million but a 1,000 km border with Croatia, for which Slovenian officials are open about their need of assistance in policing.

The government has opposed ceding further budgetary powers to the European Parliament, differing in this case with the National Assembly. In the knowledge that it has no hope of controlling the EU budget, the Slovenian legislature is happy to delegate this power to its European counterpart. The academic respondent was of the view that on many issues key actors in government had limited understanding of institutional issues: for example through favoring the extension of QMV and co-decision in certain fields, at the same time as opposing further integration in those areas.

The respondent from the ministry of foreign affairs would not reveal positions on the Area of Freedom, Security and Justice, nor on CFSP (the ministry's sectoral policy area), and refused to comment on the level of competence with regard to social policy, or on whether social policy should be decided by QMV and co-decision. So far as the foreign ministry was concerned, tax had also become a *vital interest* as well as the above mentioned identity issues. This indicated that the Slovenian government was rethinking its positions on social policy, consistent with its neo-liberal economic policies. The changing approach to tax and social policy revealed some proximity to the British position and may be linked to the influence of chambers of commerce. In terms of competence levels, one actor proposed reducing EU powers in the field of agriculture and explained that during one stage of the Convention, Slovenians supported a review every five years at which the Council would re-approve levels of competence. The others did not share the reticence on social policy of the foreign ministry respondent, although there was consensus in opposing the extension of QMV to tax, CFSP, and ESDP.

All actors that were contacted supported enhanced cooperation in all areas, subject to the support of at least half of the member states (rather than one-third as proposed by the constitution). The perspective of the Government Office of European Affairs was slightly different from that of the foreign ministry (Table 24.1). This office had negotiated accession and was specialized in EU public policy. It strongly supported burden

Table 24.1 Cohesiveness of actors' positions in the Slovenian coordination process

National position comparison	*Actor(s) (No. or type)*	*Observations (No.)*	*Deviations*									
			from national position		*on integration*				*related to*			
					toward less		*toward more*		*institutional issues*[a]		*policy fields*[a]	
			No.	*%*	*No.*	*%*	*No.*	*%*	*No.*	*%*	*No.*	*%*
All actors	6	390	64	16.4	14	3.6	50	12.8	29	11.2	35	26.5
Subset												
Lead unit	MFA	65	14	21.5	4	6.2	10	15.4	6	14.0	8	36.4

Deviations related to institutional issues
Right to withdraw from the Union; Presidency of the Council; QMV threshold; Number of commissioners; Appointment of Commission president; Appointment of commissioners; External representation of the EU (Foreign Minister); Appointment of Foreign Minister; Legislative initiative for Council, for citizens; Voting rule (Council) for tax harmonization, for monetary policy, for employment policy, for social policy, for foreign policy, for defense policy; Decision rule (EP) for social policy, for foreign policy, for defense policy; Rights of EP in the adoption of the budget

Deviations related to policy fields
Charter of Fundamental Rights; Religious reference in the preamble; Economic objectives: kind of market economy, employment, and competitiveness; Level of competence for agriculture, for structural and cohesion politics, for the Area of Freedom, Security and Justice, for economic policy, for tax harmonization, for employment policy, for social policy, for environment policy, for education policy; Stability and Growth Pact; Migration and asylum

Vital interests
Presidency in the Council; Number of commissioners; Enhanced cooperation; Council voting rule for taxes/tax harmonization, for immigration policy; Number and distribution of seats in the EP; Language (Slovenian)

Notes
a Percentage shares refer to subsets of institutional (43) and policy (22) issues. *Lead Unit* Leading unit in domestic coordination: Prime Minister's Office (PM) or Ministry of Foreign Affairs (MFA).

sharing on the issue of borders, increased competence in the Area of Freedom, Security and Justice, CFSP, economic policy, and research and development, although opposed to extending QMV to CFSP. Besides the identity-related issues, the Government Office lists the importance of equality between states in the rotation or team presidency systems on the Council and burden sharing on borders as *vital interests*.

The respondent from the National Assembly revealed that the institution's influence was overestimated because of the presence of expert deputies from Slovenia on the Convention. Being divided between secularists and more traditional Catholic conservatives, the Assembly had not been able to take a view on the issue of religion or secularism in the constitution preamble. The government opposed including references to religion. On other questions, the Assembly believes that a strong, representative Commission and a strong European Parliament better protected its interests. Additional *vital interests* for the Assembly were: a weak Council presidency and a clarification of the roles of the European Council president and foreign minister.

There was a deviation of 16 percent in the perception of the national position of the Slovenian government from other institutional actors, rising to 21 percent in relation to the government position vis-à-vis the foreign ministry. Most of these deviations were geared toward more rather than less integration, by 13 percent to 4 percent with regard to all institutional actors, and by 15 percent to 6 percent with regard to the foreign ministry. The least deviation applying to perceptions of interviewees by subject area concerned institutional questions, at 11 percent with regard to all institutional actors and 14 percent for the foreign ministry, compared with the official government position. The deviations for policy fields and vital interests for all actors was 27 percent and for the leading ministry was 36 percent. It should be noted that respondents only contradicted each other if they were no longer working on the issues concerned, which may have evolved in the meantime.

Conclusion

During the IGC, the EU section of the foreign ministry coordinated policy. It accepted input from the Government Office for European Affairs, which filtered the views of other ministries, and from the National Assembly. It worked closely with the prime minister's office, in preparation for the full meetings of the IGC on which both Anton Rop and Dimitrij Rupel participated.

While supporting burden sharing in the management of external borders, extended EU competence in several other policy areas, the eventual adoption of the ordinary legislative procedure of co-decision and QMV, and the reweighting of Council votes, Slovenia retained a short list of non-negotiable *vital interests*. These are connected to questions of identity for a small country and concern the composition of the European Commission, a minimum of five MEPs per state, and the conservation of Slovenian as an official language. The government, like the majority of governments, also opposed any move toward QMV over tax, CFSP and ESDP. The only *vital interest* protected by neither the draft constitution nor the eventual new treaty was the composition of the Commission. It seems likely the government was persuaded to accept the final result, subject to delayed implementation in 2014 and the principle of equal rotation thereafter. Slovenia's preferences for the existing procedure for appointing the Commission and an equal distribution of Council presidencies were reflected in both the draft constitution and the eventual treaty. The Slovenian parliament ratified the treaty on 1 February 2005.

Notes

1 Constitution of the Republic of Slovenia, Article 64.
2 Article 111.
3 Article 126.
4 Article 91.
5 Article 168.
6 The distribution of votes and seats in the most recent elections for parliament and the 2004 elections for the European Parliament, including the EP bloc affiliation of the parties, can be downloaded from the projects' website at dosei.dhv-speyer.de.
7 Five interviewees were contacted: one from the EU section of the foreign ministry; one from the Government Office for European Affairs; one who had worked on the Slovenian government's delegation to the Convention; a National Assembly official who advised Alojz Peterle; and an academic expert in EU politics who advised the Forum on the Future of Europe during the Convention.
8 The adapted coherence of the perceptions held by the interviewees of each of the institutional actors was high at 0.98 for the Government Office of European Affairs and for the official position of the Slovenian government, falling to 0.92 for the National Assembly, but overall above the average of the DOSEI project (0.85, see Appendix 2).

25 Spain

Preference formation and European constitution building

Raj S. Chari and Alfonso Egea-de Haro

In general, both the public and parties alike have shown strong signs of pro-Europeanism since Spain became a EU member in 1986. This pro-Europeanist attitude was recently manifest during the referendum on the constitutional treaty in February 2005. The referendum results underline two facts. First, there was general support toward the European integration process as reflected in the 76.73 percent of voters that backed the European constitution. Second, there was a low level of participation (42.3 percent) coupled with a lack of knowledge of the actual details of the constitutional text.[1] These facts point to a passive acceptance rather than an active assessment in the citizens' support toward the EU. At the core of this perception lays the understanding of the EU as a "modernization" force in contrast to the inward-looking and international isolationism of the former authoritarian regime (Jauregui 2002). Moreover, this support is also fostered by the positive attitude of Spanish political parties toward the EU.

However, the general support toward the EU does not necessarily mean that all parties have a similar European identity or a similar project for the EU. In this sense, some political parties campaigned for the "no" vote during the European constitution referendum by highlighting shortcomings of concern to their electoral base, such as a lack of social dimension and no recognition of regions' interests at the European level.[2]

During its membership, one of the main concerns for Spaniards was to catch up with the most economically developed European countries. The Spanish record in economic terms has been impressive in part due to the European funds received (i.e., cohesion fund and structural economic aid). During the mid-1990s the economy grew by nearly a fifth, even reaching the fastest rate of the euro zone in 1999 (*Economist*, 9 March 2000). In addition, the Spanish economy started to perform better: inflation fell throughout the 1990s and early 2000s, while the unemployment rate was reduced from 23 percent in 1995 to 11 percent in 2004.

Domestic structures in a comparative perspective

The Spanish political system responds to the unbalanced bicameral system model.[3] Hence, the lower chamber (Congress of Deputies), and the upper chamber (Senate) participate in the legislative process by proposing bills and making amendments, although the former decides in case the two chambers disagree. In addition to this, the senate does not play the role of some upper chambers representing territorial power in federalist systems. On the contrary, the relationship between the central government and the regional ones follow a more informal scheme and is instead based on the interaction between ruling parties at the two levels of governance.[4]

Different scholars have made different attempts to theoretically characterize policy making in contemporary Spain. One main body of literature (Perez Diaz 1993) points to the corporatist tradition in Spain, most acute throughout the transition to democracy. Clearly guided by the larger corporatist literature, as seen in Schmitter and Lehmbruch's (1979) work, it is contended that specific interests – particularly capital and labor – who enjoy a monopoly of representation, had fixed positions along with the state in the formulation of economic and social policies. Transcending the corporatist model, a second school points to the importance of economic elites in formulating public policy. Another model, as discussed by Rhodes (1997), Peterson (1995) and more recently Chari (2004a), is the "policy network" approach. This paradigm depicts a policy-making process characterized by a limited number of players that operate in a largely insulated fashion, and present a consensus between actors.

Less attention, however, has been paid to how Spain has developed its positions in foreign policy. This may be due to the fact that foreign policy and the EU in particular have been usually excluded from being a main issue in electoral party competition. Nevertheless, the PP (Popular Party) government that ruled between 1996 and 2004 slightly swayed away from Spain's traditional pro-Europeanism when it decided to involve Spain in the US-led Iraq War outside a EU Common Foreign and Security Policy framework, and opposed the EU draft constitution. In the run up to the March election, then, throughout the early part of 2004 the opposition Socialists developed an alternative by criticizing the PP's foreign policy position and proposing a more Europeanist approach toward international relations.

Despite the strong economic performance under the PP government, such as a GDP growth rate above the EU average coupled with the reduction of unemployment by 9 percent over eight years, the aftermath of the terrorist attack in Madrid on 11 March raised other additional concerns among voters (Chari 2004b). As a result, the PSOE (Socialist Party) defeated the PP government and was in a position to develop different policies, particularly that regarding Spain's position in Europe. The outcome of the general Spanish election of 14 March 2004 subsequently had a deep impact on EU constitutional negotiations.

Constitutional policy coordination

This section comparatively explores the general characteristics of the domestic policy-making process by considering the potential impact of the shift in government due to the last general election. Figure 25.1 depicts the various actors that were involved in the formation of the Spanish position, considering the differences under both administrations. From the outset, the chart depicts that there were some slight differences (highlighted in gray in the PSOE administration): the ministry of the economy had a slightly limited role under the PSOE because the Irish presidency was less focused on economic issues; unlike Aznar (PP), Zapatero (PSOE) did not altogether ignore the parliament committee because of his desire to increase institutional ties; and members of the delegation not unsurprisingly changed with the Socialist administration. Despite these small differences, complemented with the larger ones pertaining to the two parties' views regarding overall foreign policy objectives as highlighted in the March election, one may nevertheless argue that the overall coordination process presented similar features under both administrations.

Concretely, the Spanish domestic coordination process presented a high level of *centralization*: in both cases the Convention went through the International Relations and Security Office of the prime minister's office (PMO) to the Spanish representatives in the European Convention.

The ministry of foreign affairs would then play a key role in establishing the "Coordination Committee" (task force: henceforth referred to as CC). CC, whose actions were coordinated by the General sub-directorate of European Affairs (under the ministry of foreign affairs), consisted of representatives of all ministries. The CC, which is clearly one of the most significant parts of the coordination process of both administrations, had as a key objective to deliberate and discuss the governmental position on all aspects of the Convention. It is significant to note, however, that even though some of the representatives of the different ministries in the CC may have changed from one administration to the other, the high-level civil servants belonging to the General sub-directorate of European Affairs remained the same for both administrations. This points to a high level of *stability* in the process over time despite there being a change in (political) administration. The PMO would also be involved in policy making in the CC because, as one expert interviewer attested, there were also *informal* contacts throughout the process with the General sub-directorate of European Affairs.

The other two committees that were established during the process (namely, the "Regional Committee," consisting of representatives of the *Comunidades Autónomas*, and the "Parliamentary Committee" on European Affairs, consisting of house deputies, were simply informed of decisions taken in the CC.

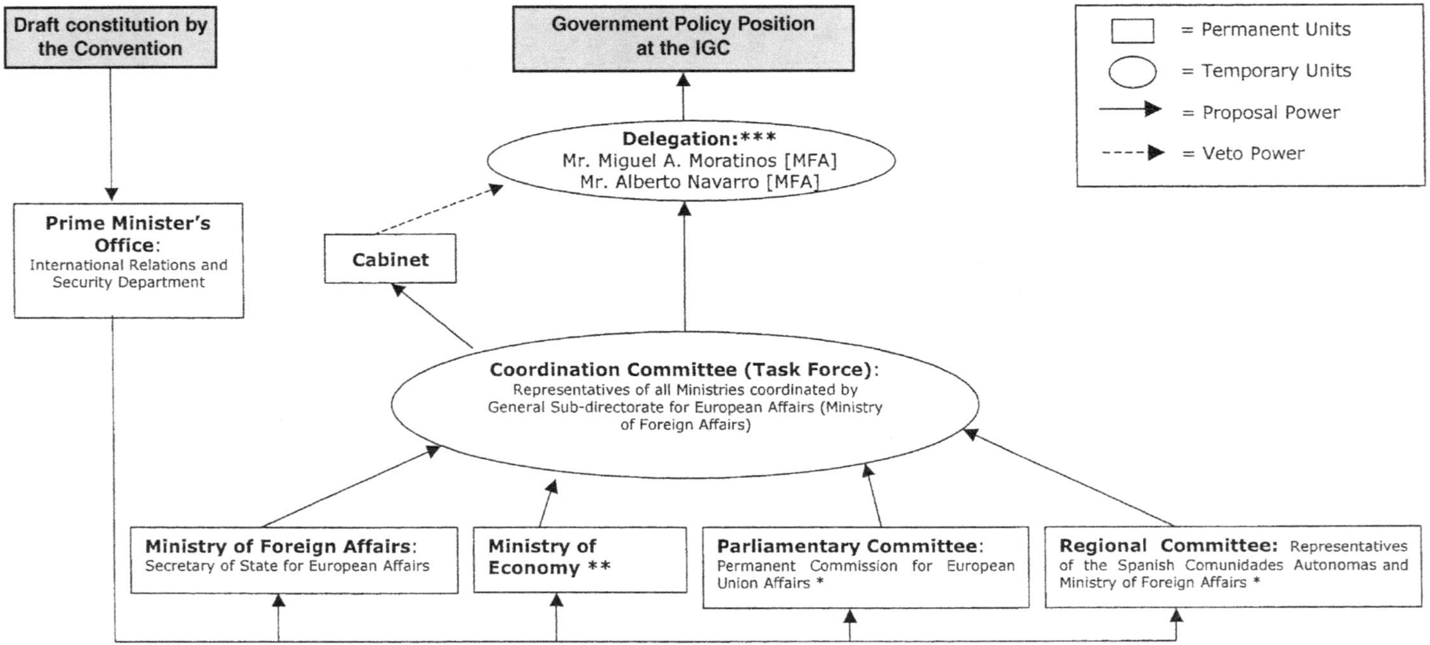

Figure 25.1 Spain: domestic policy coordination for the IGC 2003–4.

Notes

* Although this kind of relationship is maintained on a non-binding basis, the current cabinet has fostered the salience of this institution. ** The role of the Ministry of the Economy, though important, lost some salience owing to the fact that the Irish presidency was more focused on other issues than economic ones (such as Justice and Home Affairs). *** Mr Moratinos, as the current Minister of Foreign Affairs, replaced former Minister de Palacio. Mr Dastis (former General Secretary for European Affairs) was replaced by Mr Navarro, who is current Secretary of State for European Affairs. (Notice that according to the Spanish organigram of the Public Administration, Secretary of State is a top position, just behind the Minister, whereas Secretary General occupies the following position in rank after Secretary of State.)

Given the evidence, one may argue that there are two main characteristics of the coordination process when the Spanish position on the draft constitution was formed. First, the process was strongly centralized around three principal actors: the ministry of foreign affairs, the PMO, and the cabinet. The first played a key role in terms of coordinating the position, the PMO informed, guided, supervised or supported the actions of foreign affairs at various stages of the process whereas the cabinet adopted the final decision (i.e., veto power). Second, despite the changes in government, there was stability in the process, which would lead to a type of coherence in terms of the process under both administrations.

Data and empirical analysis of forming positions on the constitution for Europe

Relying on the expert surveys conducted both before and after the Spanish general elections of 14 March, this section analyses experts responses regarding the policy-making process under the PP and PSOE cabinet.[5] The total number of deviations between the national position and the main political actors in the decision-making process was a 24.6 percent under PSOE government from which the bulk of the deviations (15 percent) referred to a preference toward more integration which underlines a more pro-Europeanist perspective of the PSOE (see Table 25.1). With regard to the type of issues, the highest frequency of deviations is concentrated in relation to institutional issues. When turning to the deviations between the national position and the leading actor (MFA), the deviation percentage is 27.7. These percentages contrast with the less number of deviations found in the case of the PP government. This higher level of deviations is due to the addition in the second wave of interviews of political actors outside the core of the policy making such as a member of parliament.

However, the level of coherence between institutional actors increases dramatically as far as vital interests are concerned. All actors interviewed underlined the QMV at the Council of Ministers as the main concern for the Spanish position.

In relation to this, and despite the Socialists' criticisms of PP's views of Spain's role in Europe as discussed earlier – where the PSOE rebuked the PP for its apparent anti-Europeanist approach manifest in its desires to maintain the Nice voting system in the Council – this posture was somewhat maintained with the new PSOE government. The slight difference between both parties was seen when the PSOE avoided using the term "blocking minority" and preferred, instead, discourse of "influence capacity."

In order to gain more detailed insights into the Spanish position regarding the qualified majority threshold (QMT), it is important to estimate the blocking minority power for each national delegation under

Table 25.1 Cohesiveness of actors' positions in the Spanish coordination process

National position comparison	*Actor(s) (No. or type)*	*Observations (No.)*	*Deviations*									
			from national position		*on integration*				*related to*			
					toward less		*toward more*		*institutional issues*[a]		*policy fields*[a]	
			No.	*%*	*No.*	*%*	*No.*	*%*	*No.*	*%*	*No.*	*%*
All actors	4	260	64	24.6	25	9.6	39	15.0	43	25.0	21	23.9
Subset												
Lead unit	PM	65	18	27.7	12	18.5	6	9.2	13	30.2	5	22.7

Deviations related to institutional issues
Subsidiarity (role of national parliaments); Right to withdraw from the Union; Election of the Council president; QMV threshold; Appointment of commission president; Appointment of commissioners; External representation of the EU (Foreign Minister); Additional approval of the Foreign Minister by the EP; ECJ Jurisdiction; Legislative initiative for European Parliament; Voting rule (Council) for tax harmonization, for monetary policy, for economic policy, for employment policy, for social policy, for social security rights, for foreign policy, and for defense policy; Decision rule (EP) for tax harmonization, for monetary policy, for economic policy, for employment policy, for social policy, for social security rights, for foreign policy, for defense policy; Rights of EP in the adoption of the budget

Deviations related to policy fields
Charter of Fundamental Rights; Level of competence for agriculture, for structural and cohesion politics, for tax harmonization, for employment policy, for health policy, for environment policy, for education policy, for research, technological development and space; Stability and Growth Pact; Defense; Migration and asylum

Vital interests
Status of Charter of Fundamental Rights; ECOFIN authority; Qualified majority threshold; Number and distribution of seats in the EP; Language (recognition of Spain's sub-national languages)

Notes
a Percentage shares refer to subsets of institutional (43) and policy (22) issues. *Lead Unit* Leading unit in domestic coordination: Prime Minister's Office (PM) or Ministry of Foreign Affairs (MFA).

the Nice and constitution rule.[6] In this line, the "weighted vote," which provided Spain privileged position was removed as a criterion in order to build a majority under the constitutional treaty (Chari *et al.* 2004). Hence, the Spanish reluctance to the new rules is better understood when considering its loss in power to block Council decisions: although Spain loses political power in the Council of Ministers as the bulk of member states except the big four (namely, France, Germany, United Kingdom and Italy), Spanish government rejection is based largely on this specific aspect of political power (blocking minority power).

The final agreement arrived at in June 2004 established a QMT of at least 55 percent of the members of the Council comprising at least 65 percent of the population of the Union. This represents a net loss in the blocking capacity of the Spanish state even higher than under the constitution draft (from 8.86 to 8.65 in terms of the probability of forming a blocking minority[7]). The acceptance of this by the PSOE could represent one of two things: either the resignation of the Spanish position to defend a high "capacity of influence" due to new foreign policy objectives, or the unsuccessful attempt of defending the relative power in Nice that was negotiated by the PP who sought to increase the strength of Spain in the EU.

In order to understand which of these two options is most likely to have taken place, one may first consider the proposals made by the new PSOE Minister of Foreign Affairs (Mr Moratinos). His proposal was to establish a QMT of 66.6 percent, which implies that a successful blocking minority would comprise at least 33.5 percent of the Union's population. In fact, this proposal is not significantly different when considering the relative power of the countries to form majorities. However, the formula dramatically changed the capacity to form blocking minorities. For example, a coalition between Spain and two other big states (for instance, Italy and UK) would represent 34.73 percent of the EU-25 population. This would mean that a coalition as such would be able to block legislation in case of the 66.6 percent QMT, but not in the other cases (60 percent QMT – Constitution – would imply a 40 percent for blocking, a 62 percent QMT – Nice – would imply a 39 percent, and a 65 percent QMT – Final agreement – would imply a 36 percent). Consequently, the initial position defended by the PSOE does not seem substantially different from that of the PP: it remained focused on maintaining an important blocking minority power.

From this perspective, the final agreement suggests an unsuccessful attempt was made by the Spanish government to defend this blocking power. However, an additional provision establishing that the blocking coalition needs the consent of at least four states does help guarantee Spain some of its influence. Under this provision it is no longer possible that three big states could form a blocking coalition even though they may represent the blocking population requirement. In other words, the blocking power is balanced with a membership criterion that represents an equal distribution between member states.

Conclusion

This chapter has examined how Spain formed its national position toward the draft constitutional proposal. It was suggested that the Spanish case is unique, if not complicated, because there was a change of government between the IGC failure in Rome 2003 and the eventual agreement in Brussels in June 2004. As such, developments under both the Popular Party and the Spanish Socialists were examined. By considering the role of various actors in the process and by analyzing responses to the DOSEI group's elite surveys, two main findings were arrived at.

The first, with regard to policy-making coordination, is that there are two main characteristics of the coordination process when the Spanish position on the draft constitution was formed. First, the process under both administrations was centralized around three principal actors: the ministry of foreign affairs, the prime minister's office and the cabinet. Second, despite the change in government, there was stability in the process. This coherence between administrations was maintained because high-level civil servants involved in the coordination of the PP's position were also involved under the PSOE.

The second main finding, with regard to the empirical evidence, was that – somewhat surprisingly – there was not particularly much difference between some of the positions taken by both the PP and the PSOE administrations. In particular, and despite generally being more pro-European than its conservative counterpart, it was argued that the Spanish Socialists were equally concerned as the PP about losing "blocking minority" power under the draft constitution. This was reflected in Foreign Affairs Minister Moratinos's proposal shortly after the Socialist victory. As a result, the PSOE did secure some power vis-à-vis the larger states by guaranteeing the minimum presence of at least four states when blocking a proposal.

Notes

1 According to the Center of Sociological Research (CIS), 89 percent of respondents did not report any knowledge of the constitution text.

2 The radical left (IU) and some regionalist political parties (ERC, BNG, EA, CHA, NA-BAI) rejected the European model as established in the constitution. The domestic political system (i.e., the Spanish *Estado de las Autonomías* and its multinational nature) affects the representation of national and European identities (Egea-de Haro and Ruiz-Jimenez 2005). Therefore, the recognition of regional identities at the European level is also raised by regional political parties as a condition to support the integration process.

3 The distribution of votes and seats in the most recent elections for parliament and the 2004 elections for the European Parliament, including the EP bloc affiliation of the parties, can be downloaded from the projects' website at dosei.dhv-speyer.de.

4 The PP occupies a position characterized by the defense of the status quo as established in the Spanish constitution of 1978, whereas the PSOE is more prone to further territorial decentralization.

5 The data gathered correspond to the period of November 2003 (first wave) and May 2004 (second wave). The experts interviewed (two in the first wave and three in the second wave) are representative of high-level officials in the ministry of foreign affairs, prime minister's office and parliament. In both waves, the expert coherence was at about 66 percent. Modifying the coherence for the number of experts interviewed we can compare the mean adapted coherence of the first wave (0.76) and of the second wave (0.83) with the overall coherence in the DOSEI data set, which is slightly better (0.85, see Appendix 2).

6 It is important to note that the chances of building a blocking minority depend on the criteria required to create a majority: in other words, considering that the Nice Treaty established three criteria to form a majority to pass legislation (based on population, vote, and membership), there were three opportunities for member states to block such legislation.

7 Estimation based on Bräuninger and König's (2001) computer program IOP.

26 Sweden's "third way" toward the EU constitution

Promoting social policies and safeguarding neutrality

Hartmut Lenz and Han Dorussen[1]

During the autumn of 2003, newspaper headlines in Sweden focused on the murder of Anna Lindh, the country's popular pro-Europe Minister of Foreign Affairs, and the vote against membership in the European Monetary Union. Discussion about the EU constitution failed to generate similar interest, but nevertheless many people remain critical about Sweden's participation. Swedish involvement in the European Union (EU) has always been controversial. Sweden joined the EU in January 1995, after a majority of 52.3 percent supported EU membership in a referendum. The narrow support exemplified the country's historically ambivalent relationship with Europe. Uncertainty about Sweden's place in Europe remains to this day. The continuing debate involves not only the conflicting interests of urban areas and rural residents, but also the divergent emphasis that citizens place on Swedish neutrality.

No referendum is scheduled for the EU constitution. Instead parliament was scheduled to vote on the issue in December 2005 on the basis of a proposition presented in September 2005, but this procedure was postponed after France and the Netherlands rejected the constitution. The general expectation is that parliament will ratify the constitution. Some groups are campaigning for a referendum in Sweden, but the government is reluctant to call for one, undoubtedly stung by the outcome of the euro referendum and the results of recent referendums in Europe.

The Swedish economy is among the most dynamic in Europe. Modern infrastructure combines with a highly skilled labor force (e.g. the engineering sector accounts for 50 percent of industrial output). The country's population (8.9 million) enjoys a high standard of living with extensive welfare benefits. The GDP composition by sector shows that 69 percent of national revenue comes from the service industry, with 29 percent from other industries and 2 percent from agriculture. The average economic growth between 1996 and 2003 was 2.6 percent, but in 2003 it did not exceed 1.6 percent. Yet the inflation rate remains well below the EU average and does not currently exceed 2.3 percent. Additionally, Sweden has an unemployment rate of 5.6 percent, again substantially below the European average of 8 percent (CIA World Fact Book, Eurostat 2004).

Domestic structures in a comparative perspective

Sweden is a constitutional monarchy, having introduced its formal constitution in 1975. The country has a unicameral parliament, the *Riksdag*, whose 349 members are elected by popular vote to serve four-year terms. The general election in September 2002 produced a minority-ruled government led by the Social Democrats under Prime Minister Göran Persson.[2] The Left and Green parties support the government under specific stipulations agreed upon with the Social Democrats. On the issue of EU integration, the Social Democrats, Liberal Party, Moderate Party, Christian Democratic Party, and Center Party generally favor integration, whereas the Left Party, the Greens, and the June List (*Junilistan*) oppose it. However, all Swedish political parties contain factions that oppose integration (Aylott 2002, Ferrara and Weishaupt 2004).

Regardless, pro-European parties command a sizable majority – a maximum of 302 out of 349 votes – in parliament. Parliamentary ratification requires most probably a three-fourths majority, which is likely to be obtained. The Prime Minister Persson as well as four pro-constitution opposition leaders oppose calling a referendum. The support of one-third of parliament is needed to call a referendum but only the Greens (6.4 percent) and Left Party (2.4 percent) are in favor.

The integration of Sweden into the EU suffered several serious setbacks during 2003 and 2004. In September 2003, the Swedish public rejected the adoption of the euro (instead of the *krona*), even after an extensive pro-euro campaign jointly launched by the Social Democrats and their opposition.[3] In the June 2004 election for the European Parliament, a new Euro-skeptic party, the *Junilistan*, emerged as a political power. The party attained 14.4 percent of the popular vote and sent three delegates to the European Parliament. The ruling Social Democrats obtained 24.7 percent of the votes, but lost one of its six seats. The unexpected success of the *Junilistan* might be the result of low voter turnout; only 37.8 percent of qualified voters participated. However, the rise of the *Junilistan* might also signify a rising Swedish ambivalence toward integration with Europe (Mattila 2003).

In some ways, Sweden's EU membership would seem an inevitable consequence of the strongly export-reliant domestic economy. In spite of its neutral status, Sweden has long associated with Western Europe, both economically and politically. Sweden was a member of the Common Market before it joined the EU. Since then, the political and economic elite of Sweden has consistently supported EU membership (Widfeldt 1996), but integration remains much less popular among ordinary citizens. Euro-skepticism persists, and the EU is widely perceived as a huge bureaucracy that will provide few benefits (Johansson 2003, Eurobarometer 2003a, b).

Since joining the EU, Swedish governments have highlighted Swedish-specific issues and have left a distinct imprint on the common EU agenda

(Thorhallson 2000). The generally weak support for the EU among the Swedish public has made the active and strong defense of Swedish interests in intergovernmental negotiations even more important.

Although Swedish EU policy aims to build consensus, political priorities are very much dominated by the Social Democratic Party. The Social Democrats have pushed for the development of a Swedish-style active labor market policy in the EU. Accordingly, employment had top priority in the negotiations of the Amsterdam treaty, as well as at the IGC 2003–4 (Thurner *et al.* 2002). The government has also acted as enthusiastic and unequivocal supporter of EU enlargement, providing special advocacy for the Baltic States.

Constitutional policy coordination

The decision-formation processes of the Scandinavian members of the EU show many similarities. Combined with relatively similar attitudes toward policy positions, there are obvious reasons to put Sweden, Denmark and Finland all into the "Nordic model." There is some support for this generalization; these countries have more or less the same structures for domestic coordination (Petersen and Sjursen 1999). Furthermore, when Sweden became member of the EU in 1995, the country's government included many aspects of the Danish model. Figure 26.1 summarizes the policy formation process in Sweden.

The policy position presented by the Swedish delegation at the IGC 2003–4 was a position formulated in the prime minister's office, combined with the suggestions of the Advisory Committee on EU Affairs. Final responsibility for the IGC negotiations was in the hands of the delegation sent to the actual negotiation meetings. In the preparation of policy

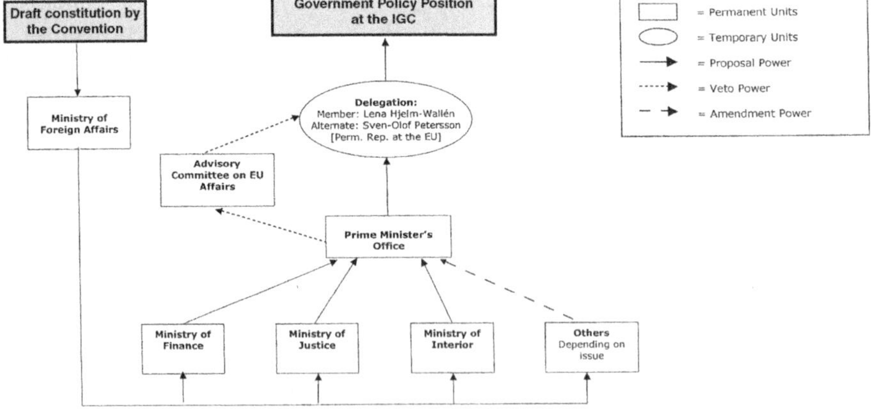

Figure 26.1 Sweden: domestic policy coordination for the IGC 2003–4.

position the ministry of foreign affairs and relevant ministries play key roles. The eventual proposed policy position is discussed at the prime minister's office, where experts from the ministry of foreign affairs, relevant ministry officials, and the head negotiator discuss the proposal. The Advisory Committee on EU Affairs, a parliamentary standing body, is also included at this stage of discussion. This committee requires updates on all decisions made by the ministry and retains the general role of an advisory and supervisory body.

When setting up the Advisory Committee on EU Affairs, Sweden copied the Danish model by placing the EU affairs committee in a very similar role. However, although parliament remains an important agent in both countries with respect to EU issues, the Advisory Committee on EU Affairs holds a less prominent role in Sweden than its Danish equivalent. The committee primarily acts as a forum for consultation with the Swedish government. The committee keeps parliament informed and confers over Sweden's position on basic matters. Yet, at least formally, the powers of the committee are limited, since it does not provide mandates. The committee can neither make binding decisions about Sweden's position during negotiations, nor can it submit issues under deliberation to the chamber for plenary debate. The somewhat weaker role of Swedish parliament provides other branches of government with considerable freedom (Miles 1997).

Nevertheless, the committee holds a tangible influence because government officials take the group's recommendations into serious consideration. Governmental ministers or their advisors often attend EU affairs committee meetings, and the Swedish government regularly consulted the committee during the IGC 2003–4.

The government provides the primary source of issue-specific information for the committee. Even though relations between these two branches are amiable, the committee occasionally seeks outside information, especially from the cabinet of the Swedish commissioners. Other sources of information include various databases and documentation from other parliamentary units dealing with European affairs, notably those of other Nordic member states. By expressing a healthy dose of skepticism toward the government, the committee is able to keep its independence.

Data and empirical analysis of forming positions on the constitution for Europe

For the study of the domestic coordination process, three expert interviews have been held in Stockholm during November and December 2003, just before the IGC 2003–4. The selection of experts was based on their position within the domestic decision-making process. The experts worked closely with the government, but were from different institutional backgrounds. The consistency of the answers given by the experts was high; this applied to the answers on the national position as well as the positions of parliament.[4]

Concerning the EU constitution, Sweden has had a very open national policy formation process. In the Swedish parliament, such issues receive extensive attention, and the government has set up numerous open consultation sessions. Indeed, the policy positions of important institutions are largely in agreement, and the Swedish national position is very consistent.

Table 26.1 gives an overview of the deviations of domestic actors from the national position on key issues. Confirming the high agreement with and consistency of policy positions in Sweden, the average actor deviated on 16 percent of the issues from the national position. The levels of deviation toward more integration (7 percent) and toward less integration (9 percent) are nearly balanced. Fluctuations involving institutional issues are relatively low (9 percent), whereas shifts concerning political issues are considerably higher (30 percent). The ideal policy position of the leading unit (prime minister's office) is identical to the national position.

Sweden's neutral status was the only true vital issue for the Swedish government. The country has not participated in any war for almost two centuries. Armed neutrality was preserved in both World Wars. Since the original draft constitution seriously challenged the Swedish policy against military alliances, this became a key issue during Swedish negotiations at the IGC. The Swedish government adopted a pragmatic attitude toward existing alliances and joint operations, but rejected proposals for a common defense policy, along lines of collective security, in the EU.

At the IGC 2003–4, in addition to employment, Sweden emphasized other "social" issues, such as equal opportunities for men and women, consumer protection, the environment, as well as governmental openness and transparency. Further issues of significance include tax harmonization, migration, and asylum policy, where Sweden urged the EU to take on a more liberal mentality. Sweden reluctantly accepted the flexibility clause, which implies that some member states can proceed with further cooperation and integration without the agreement of all EU partners. From Sweden's perspective, as one of the smaller EU members, the notion of flexibility favors the larger member states, which could eventually form an EU "hard core." The Swedish government is also concerned with changing the composition of the Commission and qualified majority voting (QMV) in some areas. Despite these concerns, the government is very much in favor of the constitution.

One of the issues under contention is the reorganization of the rotation of the presidency of the European Council. The government preferred a fixed-term president, while the parliament preferred retaining the rotation system or even allowing group presidency. A second issue was the QMV threshold in the Council of Ministers. The government favored the solution delineated in the Nice Treaty, while parliament wanted a simple majority of member states and three-fifths of the population. Later on, parliament

Table 26.1 Cohesiveness of actors' positions in the Swedish coordination process

National position comparison	*Actor(s) (No. or type)*	*Observations (No.)*	*Deviations*									
			from national position		*on integration*				*related to*			
					toward less		*toward more*		*institutional issues*[a]		*policy fields*[a]	
			No.	*%*	*No.*	*%*	*No.*	*%*	*No.*	*%*	*No.*	*%*
All actors	3	195	32	16.4	18	9.2	14	7.2	12	9.3	20	30.3
Subset												
Lead unit	PM	65	0	–	0	–	0	–	0	–	0	–

Deviations related to institutional issues
QMV threshold; External representation of the EU (Foreign Minister); ECJ jurisdiction; Voting rule (Council) for tax harmonization, for foreign policy; Decision rule (EP) for Area of Freedom, Security and Justice

Deviations related to policy fields
Charter of Fundamental Rights; Level of competence for agriculture, for structural and cohesion politics, for the Area of Freedom, Security and Justice, for employment policy, for social policy, for environment policy, for education policy; External borders; Migration and asylum

Vital interests
Regulation of jurisdiction with respect to external policy (Sweden's neutrality) and with respect to the environment; Council voting rule for taxes/tax harmonization

Notes
a Percentage shares refer to subsets of institutional (43) and policy (22) issues. *Lead Unit* Leading unit in domestic coordination: Prime Minister's Office (PM) or Ministry of Foreign Affairs (MFA).

assented to the government's position. A third point of contention involved the management of external borders. Here, the government called for a common integrated management system for external borders without direct EU supervision, while the parliament proposed the opposite.

Conclusion

This chapter focused on the formation of a national consensus concerning the EU constitution in Sweden. Apart from the government, another key political agent is parliament, and in particular the Advisory Committee on EU Affairs. Yet, the expert surveys have clearly shown that the interests of the different agents exhibit little variation. It is important to stress that the unitary Swedish polity is highly centralized compared to most other EU countries, especially the federal or semi-federal states. In the formation of Swedish policy on the EU constitution, the degree of centralization is equally important.

Formally, the policy formation process in Sweden, like that in Finland, has been modeled on the Danish example. However, the so-called "Nordic model" is not identical in all three contexts. In Sweden, the Advisory Committee on EU Affairs only has a supervisory position, with no formal decision-making power.

In Sweden, the government and a clear majority in parliament are pro-Europe, and they provide broad support for the EU constitution. The Swedish government does not have to rely on a referendum to ratify the constitution, and the opposition against the constitution is unable to "force" a referendum. Parliamentary ratification of the EU constitution was initially scheduled for December 2005, but put on hold after France and the Netherlands rejected the constitution.

The Swedish government generally has maintained clear control on the policy formation process. This may explain the lack of strong disagreement about policy positions on the EU constitution, but the ensuing consensus – and high probability of ratification – still remains somewhat surprising, since the Swedish population is highly Euro-skeptic and the policy formation process was very open. Possibly, the open and heterogeneous domestic policy formation process actually resulted in a homogeneous policy position. It is, however, also possible that the EU constitution has so far failed to generate sufficient public interest to mobilize the strong anti-EU sentiments in the general population.

Notes

1 Equal authorship.

2 The distribution of votes and seats in the most recent elections for parliament and the 2004 elections for the European Parliament, including the EP bloc affiliation of the parties, can be downloaded from the projects' website at dosei.dhv-speyer.de.

3 The murder of the Minister of Foreign Affairs, Anna Lindh, halted the campaign a few days before the referendum. The impact of the murder on the outcome of the referendum is very unclear. Although clearly a shocking event in Swedish politics, the murder turned out not to be politically motivated.

4 The coherence of the three experts on the national position is 64 percent and on the policy position of parliament 63 percent. Modifying the coherence for the numbers of experts interviewed, the mean adapted coherence of the Swedish case (0.85) is identical to the overall coherence in the DOSEI data set (see Appendix 2).

27 The United Kingdom

Position taking and the protection of red lines

Giacomo Benedetto

Great Britain is the only member of the EU which does not have a written constitution. As a political system, Britain is characterized by one-party dominance of the executive, which in turn dominates the legislature. Although alternation is rare, having occurred three times since Britain joined the EU in 1973, the party of government always has an eye on the median voter since vast numbers of seats can be lost or gained at elections with comparatively few popular votes shifting, on account of the electoral system. British governments are unlikely to take risks with issues such as European integration that do not immediately appeal to the median voter. Following the re-election of the Labour government in 2005[1] and the "no" votes in France and the Netherlands the forecast referendum to ratify the constitution in Great Britain was abandoned. Holding the referendum would, in any event, have been divisive for both the Labour and Conservative parties.

The British economy is primarily service-oriented and avoided recession during the global downturn following 2000. Great Britain is a net contributor to the EU budget. The government has resisted attempts in the past to increase the EU budget ceiling and own resources, sought a cut in the financial perspectives to 1 percent of GDP, refusing to compromise on the budget rebate that over-compensates Britain with regard to the other large net contributors.

Domestic structures in a comparative perspective

Government legislation is usually passed by the British parliament without challenge, on account of strict party discipline enforced on parliamentarians of the majority party, and a weak committee system. The second chamber is not elected and has powers only of consultation and delay.

Just before the EP election of June 2004, the decision of Tony Blair to call a referendum on the ratification of the EU constitution did not prevent the decline of the Labour Party to 22 percent and rise of the UK Independence Party to 16 percent. Nevertheless, it probably strengthened the hand of Blair in protecting "non-negotiable" policy areas during the closing stages of the IGC 2003–4. It was also intended to remove the issue from national electoral politics, while putting the Euro-skeptics on the defensive. The wishes of the British government to anchor itself both to the EU and the United States is unquestioned. To this end it has unwillingly supported the constitution and the creation of the machinery for advancing intergovernmental aspects of enhanced cooperation in police and judicial cooperation, and in CFSP, consistent with the long-term ambivalence of British governments toward European integration (Hix 2003).

It has used its historic reluctance and perceived Euro-skepticism of domestic public opinion as bargaining chips to resist changes to unanimity for own resources and the financial perspectives, tax harmonization, and CFSP and ESDP. This approach is familiar, having been used at Nice (red lines), Maastricht (EMU and social chapter), and Corfu (1994 veto of Jean-Luc Dehaene as President of the Commission and near veto of the 1995 enlargement). Bipolar competition at national elections between Labour and the Euro-skeptic Conservatives has made the government mindful of the Euro-skepticism present in public opinion. The UK Independence Party is a right-wing "new populist" (Taggart 1995, 1998) party, exhibiting a discourse similar to the FPÖ in Austria or Pim Fortuyn in the Netherlands. Its performance in the 2004 EP elections has further constrained the room for maneuver on the EU for both Labour and the Conservatives.

The absence of a pro-integration campaign by the Labour government and the prevalence of Euro-skepticism within much of the British media cast doubt on the success of a referendum early in 2006 in ratifying the constitution, well before the success of the "no" votes in France and the Netherlands. Although the government was re-elected with a sufficient parliamentary majority in 2005, its loss of votes was substantial and it had a lead of only 3 percent above the Euro-skeptic Conservatives. The referendum was scheduled to occur one year after the 2005 elections, when a mid-term second-order effect might reward the Conservatives, under the new leadership of David Cameron. The likelihood of ratification was further compounded by divisions in the Labour Party itself, such that a likely leader of the "no" campaign would have been Gisela Stuart, who was a member of the Praesidium and has since spoken against the constitution.

Constitutional policy coordination

As the domestic coordination chart shows (Figure 27.1), the key institutional actors have been the Future of Europe Section at the Foreign Office and the EU Secretariat in the cabinet office. Within the ambit of EU affairs, the Foreign Office is the sectoral ministry for CFSP and EU institutional questions. The Future of Europe Section worked closely with

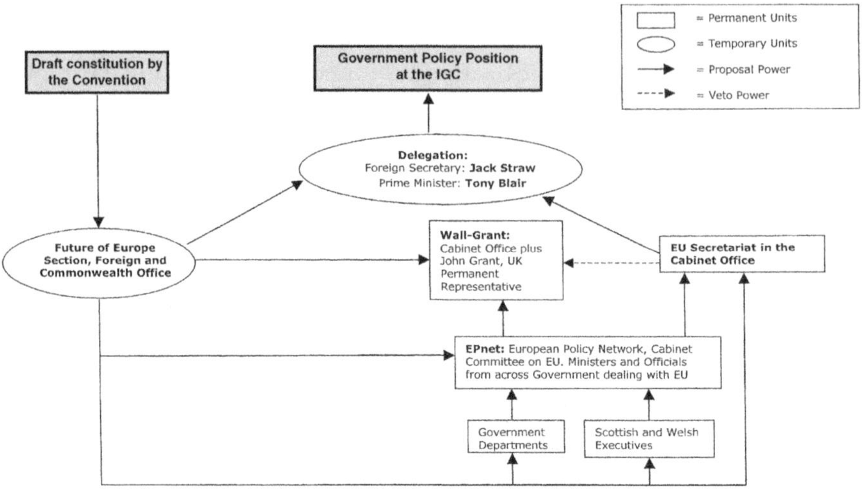

Figure 27.1 United Kingdom: domestic policy coordination for the IGC 2003–4.

Stephen Wall, the head of the EU Secretariat in the cabinet office, responsible directly to the prime minister, and Peter Hain, the British government representative at the Convention. Many of the staff of the EU Secretariat are drawn from the Foreign Office, rather than being in conflict with it. In terms of monitoring the developments at the Convention and IGC, it is the Foreign Office that takes responsibility, but inevitably the office of the prime minister, via the EU Secretariat, that makes decisions. Key questions were resolved at the weekly and permanent meeting between Stephen Wall and the UK Permanent Representative to the EU, John Grant, known as Wall–Grant, which prepared the agendas for the prime minister and foreign secretary before meetings of the IGC, carrying out the same tasks for Hain and Baroness Scotland, the government's substitute representative, during the Convention.

Officials from the Future of Europe Section accompanied Hain and Scotland to the Convention. The section filtered contentious issues onto EPnet (European Policy Network), following their discussion at the Convention. EPnet is a permanent cabinet committee based in Downing Street, composed of ministers and officials across all departments that deal with the EU. It receives input from Stephen Wall and the EU Secretariat in the cabinet office. For example, the Home Office would raise concerns about the Area of Freedom, Security and Justice at EPnet, which would find themselves into the contributions made by Hain or Scotland to the Convention via this mechanism. Once the Convention had been concluded, the Future of Europe Section continued to manage the IGC negotiations, working closely with Downing Street. Throughout the

Convention and IGC, competence appears to be shared by the Foreign Office, in the institutional sense, and Downing Street in a more directly political sense. It is significant that neither Hain nor Scotland were Foreign Office ministers.

Data and empirical analysis of forming positions on the constitution for Europe

Three officials and one politician were interviewed during the period of the IGC.[2] There was not complete consensus as to the identity of the most influential institutional actors in forming government policy. While those at the Foreign Office listed their own ministry as the most influential actor, followed by Downing Street, the Treasury, the Confederation of British Industry, and the Department of Trade and Industry. The interviewees from parliament listed Downing Street, the Foreign Office, and parliament as influential, although the MP described the Foreign Office as a "bit player," compared to the Treasury, which has been Gordon Brown's institutional mechanism for influencing events in Europe beyond the purely budgetary and economic. The adapted expert coherence with regard to the national position and Foreign Office was highest at 0.87, falling to 0.86 for the Treasury, 0.79 for Parliament and to 0.74 for Downing Street. This reflects a consensus that the Foreign Office and Treasury have consistent, though diverse, priorities, while the opinions of Downing Street are somewhat more opaque and those of the Westminster Parliament are more diffuse.[3]

Compared to other governments, the key institutional actors were unusually united during the Convention and IGC. One of the only divisions cited by a source at the Foreign Office was the Department of Trade and Industry and the Confederation of British Industry favoring the adoption of competitiveness rather than full employment as an EU objective. Since the publication of the British government's report on the draft constitution in September 2004, policy was to support the draft subject to the conservation of unanimity in Council concerning the "red line" areas. The source did not reveal any divergence from this.

The government was one of the strongest supporters of the permanent presidency of the European Council, although the British parliament would always have preferred a team presidency for the Council consisting of several governments. On the subject of the threshold for QMV, the British government supported the Convention proposal, but was happy to accept the Nice formula. The British did not wish to depart from the existing mechanism for appointing the European Commission and opposed the creation of a joint presidency for the Commission and Council.

The vital interests that would have caused the British government to block approval of the constitution if not respected were Council unanimity on tax, CFSP, ESDP, and social security and the non-applicability in domestic law of the Charter of Fundamental Rights. Although strongly voiced, British views on the budgetary procedure and the permanent presidency of the Council were not vital interests.

In a similar vein to Council votes, Britain supported reducing the number of voting commissioners, as foreseen by the draft constitution, but would accept an outcome in which each state retains a full commissioner. Once the IGC had been resuscitated in 2004, the British position on reforming the system of votes in the Council and composition of the Commission had reverted to the compromise tabled by the Irish presidency that was eventually accepted. Westminster never took a position on other institutional questions: the Council voting system; composition of the Commission; appointment of the President of the Commission, members of the Commission, or EU Foreign Minister. However, Westminster was unwilling to allow the EP increased institutional powers in the belief that its own powers would be undermined.

On the subject of the EU Foreign Minister, the British were more favorable than public discourse would suggest. Publicly they have opposed the fact that s/he would be referred to as a "minister." The British believe that the Foreign Minister should be responsible primarily to the Council, rather than as a commissioner. The British wish to protect the Commission's monopoly of legislative initiative, with some exceptions: citizens' initiatives could lead to legislative initiation; the Commission should lose its exclusive right of initiative on the EU annual budget;[4] and legislative initiative in the Area of Freedom, Security and Justice, and in Common Foreign and Security Policy should reside with Council. The sources in the British parliament who had scrutinized events during the Convention and IGC had the impression that in this policy area, only minimum standards should be adopted. Despite the impression given by public discourse, the British government is in favor of a common European border guard so long as Britain is able to guard its own frontier, whether external or with other EU states.

The significant evolution for the British since the conclusion of the Convention was the question of budgetary powers. During the spring of 2003, Peter Hain had tabled a radical amendment to the Convention, to move the proposed new budgetary procedure away from co-decision or a revised version of the procedure for non-compulsory expenditure.[5] In the event of Council and the EP disagreeing, a co-decision-type conciliation committee would be convened. If this failed to reach an agreement, the annual budget would be deemed automatically adopted, but with the lower amounts for each heading as voted by either Council or the EP going forward. However, the previous year's total expenditure for that heading would prevail if it were higher. The Hain proposal also removed the EP's right of veto over the budget. In the light of the attempt by the treasury and finance ministries of the other large net contributors to cut the EU's multi-annual budget to 1 percent of GDP, this proposal is very odd since it makes cutting the budget more difficult, the default position being the previous year's spending, unless both Council and EP can agree to cut by the same amount. The exact wording of the Hain proposal was re-presented to the IGC by ECOFIN in October 2003, and formed the basis of the British position on the budgetary procedure once the Irish presidency had reconvened the IGC in 2004. However, this was not a vital interest and the final outcome of the IGC settled on a variant of the co-decision procedure for deciding the annual budget, thus providing the EP and Council with a mutual veto. This outcome was preferable to the British when compared to the draft constitution, which permitted the EP to overrule Council by a three-fifths majority. The Treasury's attempt to "sabotage" the powers of the EP may have been a negotiating position to protect other "red line" areas, as well as a realistic attempt to amend the provisions of the original draft. Throughout this period, Westminster remained indifferent as to the powers of the EP over the budget. The British were also in favor, along with certain pro-integration states like the Netherlands, of deleting the Convention proposal that the multi-annual budget or financial perspectives should be decided by QMV rather than unanimity.

In line with the draft constitution, the British supported enhanced cooperation, limited to areas where unanimity exists. In terms of competencies, the British supported limited extension of EU competence in the Area of Freedom, Security, and Justice, as well as in Environment and Research and Development, while "renationalizing" powers in Agriculture and Structural and Cohesion policies. The latter was a particular preference of Gordon Brown and the Treasury.

The parliamentary sources viewed Westminster as influential in the debate on subsidiarity, in which Gisela Stuart had successfully proposed the introduction of the early warning system, whereby one-third of national parliaments would be able to request that the Commission reconsider legislative proposals. On this question, the British parliament would have preferred to gain a definitive right of veto, at the same time as gaining, alongside citizens' initiatives, the right of legislative initiative at EU level. Westminster also supported the right to unilateral secession for member states, rather than the slower option of negotiated withdrawal.

The government, supported by the Foreign Office, Treasury, and Westminster wished to avoid mention of religion in the preamble of the constitution, differing from the personal preference of Tony Blair to include reference to God.

Among those interviewed, deviations in the perception of the national position compared to the positions of other institutional actors occurred on 14.5 percent of occasions, of which two-thirds (nearly 10 percent) were oriented toward less integration than the official position (Table 27.1). Perceptions of Downing Street differed from the official national positions on 28 percent of occasions, of which 15 percent were oriented toward

Table 27.1 Cohesiveness of actors' positions in the British coordination process

National position comparison	*Actor(s) (No. or type)*	*Observations (No.)*	*Deviations*									
			from national position		*on integration*				*related to*			
					toward less		*toward more*		*institutional issues*[a]		*policy fields*[a]	
			No.	*%*	*No.*	*%*	*No.*	*%*	*No.*	*%*	*No.*	*%*
All actors	7	455	66	14.5	44	9.7	22	4.8	26	8.6	40	26
Subset												
Lead unit	PM	65	18	27.7	10	15.4	8	12.3	9	20.9	9	40.9

Deviations related to institutional issues
Subsidiarity (role of national parliaments); Right to withdraw from the Union; Presidency of the Council; Election of the Council president; Additional approval of the Foreign Minister by the EP; Legislative initiative for European Parliament, for Council, for national parliaments, and for citizens; Voting rule (Council) for structural and cohesion politics, for Area of Freedom, Security and Justice, for employment policy, for social policy; Decision rule (EP) for agriculture, for structural and cohesion politics

Deviations related to policy fields
Charter of Fundamental Rights; Religious reference in the preamble; Economic objectives: kind of market economy, employment; Level of competence for agriculture, for structural and cohesion politics, for the Area of Freedom, Security and Justice, for foreign policy, for health policy, for environment policy, for research, technological development and space; Defense; External borders; Migration and asylum

Vital interests
Council voting rule for taxes/tax harmonization, for Common Security and Defense Policy, and for social security

Notes
a Percentage shares refer to subsets of institutional (43) and policy (22) issues. *Lead Unit* Leading unit in domestic coordination: Prime Minister's Office (PM) or Ministry of Foreign Affairs (MFA).

more integration. Deviations in relation to perceptions of institutional questions were recorded in 9 percent of occasions, rising to 21 percent in terms of perceptions toward Downing Street, as the most important "ministry." Concerning policy fields, these deviations rose to 26 percent with respect to all institutional actors and to 41 percent with respect to Downing Street. Consensus as to which questions constituted vital interests was more complete, with a deviation of perceptions at 11 percent with respect to all institutional actors and at 12 percent for Downing Street.

Conclusion

Following the conclusion of the Convention in July 2003, the British government declared satisfaction with the document. Once it became clear that a consensus among the member state governments did not exist and that the Italian presidency of the Council would have to conduct broad negotiations, the British also declared a series of objections: on the one side, the "red lines;" on the other, issues such as the budget, where they raised objections.

The red lines consisted of retaining unanimity for deciding on the revenue of the EU, social security, tax harmonization, the creation of a public prosecutor, CFSP, ESDP, and the non-applicability in domestic law of the Charter of Fundamental Rights. Although these had been challenged during the Convention, the final draft constitution guaranteed these points. The British clarified that these issues should not be challenged during the IGC, on threat of veto. Negotiable areas where Britain would have preferred another outcome included the budget and the creation of a European public prosecutor, although this has to be decided by unanimity.

Although supportive of the bulk of the text of the draft constitution, statements made as the failed Brussels Council of December 2003 approached suggested that the British were prepared to logroll. While the red lines were reiterated, it was made known that the British could settle with the Nice Treaty formula for voting at Council and with the concept that each member state should retain a European commissioner. The British preferences for the status quo in the appointment procedure for the European Commission and for the creation of a permanent Council presidency were met by both the draft constitution and the eventual treaty.

The final result of the constitution, as agreed in June 2004 is satisfactory for the British. Any division between institutional actors within the British government was insignificant, although Downing Street, whether in the form of the office of the prime minister or the EU Secretariat in the cabinet office, appears dominant.

The decision for indefinite postponement of the referendum to ratify the constitution contains the division inside both the Labour and

Conservative parties. It also saves the British government from a likely second-order defeat of calamitous proportions. The status quo of the Treaty of Nice protects many of the British preferences for intergovernmentalism and unanimity concerning social security, tax, the multi-annual budget and CFSP.

Notes

1 The distribution of votes and seats in the most recent elections for Parliament and the 2004 elections for the European Parliament, including the EP bloc affiliation of the parties, can be downloaded from the projects' website at dosei.dhv-speyer.de.

2 From the Foreign Office: two officials. From the British parliament: one member and one official. However, one of the officials from the Foreign Office did not complete the questionnaire, so the analysis is reliant on three experts.

3 The mean adapted coherence of the British case (0.84) corresponds to the average for the entire project (0.85, see Appendix 2).

4 Peter Hain: Amendment to Draft Article I-55, Convention for the Future of Europe, undated.

5 Peter Hain: Amendment to Draft Article III-310, Convention for the Future of Europe, undated.

28 The Commission, the Convention and the IGC

Consensus and concern for its role

Christophe Crombez and Jan Lebbe

The Commission is often referred to as the EU executive.[1] The other two principal institutions involved in the EU legislative process, the Parliament and the Council, are then considered as two chambers of a legislature. This description is not completely accurate, however, because the Commission has powers national executives do not tend to have, whereas it lacks other powers they usually do have.

One of the most striking characteristics of the EU legislative process is that the Commission has monopoly proposal rights. No legislative initiative can be undertaken, if the Commission does not formulate a policy proposal. No legislation can be approved without an initiative by the executive. This is most unusual in contemporary democracies. The legislature itself, the Council and the Parliament cannot take initiatives, they can merely suggest that the Commission do so. Unlike other executives, however, the Commission is not solely responsible for the implementation of legislation, but rather it often merely oversees the implementation of EU legislation by the member states, which bear the responsibility of incorporating EU legislation into national law. The Commission is also responsible for ensuring that the EU treaties and legislation are respected. It is supposed to protect the general interests of the EU and is the EU's external representative. The Commission is not a signatory to the EU treaties. Ratification of the constitution by the Commission is thus not required.

Politics in the Commission

The Commission is appointed by the Council and the Parliament for a five-year term, following European Parliament elections. The appointment of a new Commission occurs in two stages: first the Council nominates a Commission president by qualified majority, next the proposed president and the Council, again by qualified majority, nominate the other commissioners. In both stages approval by the Parliament is required. The Parliament can censure the Commission during the term by a two-thirds majority of the votes and a majority of its members.

The number of commissioners has increased with each enlargement of the EU. So far the smaller member states each had one commissioner, whereas the larger member states had two. Thus the Prodi Commission consisted of 20 members. The Nice Treaty limited the number of commissioners to one per member state, and provided for a further reduction when the number of member states reaches 27. As a result the Barroso Commission consists of 25 commissioners.

The commissioners are to be independent. They are not supposed to protect the interest of their own member states, nor are they allowed to take instructions from their member states' governments. None the less, the commissioners' policy preferences tend to reflect the preferences of their member states' governments, because these governments play a dominant role in their appointment. The Parliament and the Commission president have had little influence on the choice of commissioners thus far.

The Prodi Commission was appointed in 1999 when the left was in charge in 11 of the 15 member states. As a result a majority of the commissioners hailed from the left. At its appointment in 1999 the Prodi Commission consisted of ten socialists, seven Christian democrats and conservatives, two liberals, and one green. In the Barroso Commission, by contrast, the right has a majority. The Barroso Commission will consist of 12 Christian democrats and conservatives, seven socialists, and six liberals.

The Commission President allocates policy portfolios among the commissioners. The most important portfolios include competition, trade, external relations and agriculture. The Commission acts as a college, however, which means that all major decisions are taken by the Commission as a whole at its weekly meetings. Below the commissioners the Commission administration is divided into a number of Directorates General.

Legislative proposals are prepared by the Directorates General that are in charge of the related policy domains. For this purpose the Directorates General use an elaborate network of committees that include representatives of member states, and industry and other interests. Proposals are then forwarded to the cabinets of the responsible commissioners. Next they are considered in the meetings of the heads of cabinet, until they finally reach the college of commissioners.

Recent Commissions, such as the Santer and Prodi Commissions, have often been perceived as ineffective. Their performance is then unfavorably compared to the successful tenure of the Delors Commissions, which were in charge from 1985 till 1995, and played an important role in the conclusion of the Single European Act and the Maastricht Treaty, and the single market and monetary union they established. Consistent with this observation several studies have shown that the reforms of the legislative process have reduced the Commission's powers to the advantage of the Parliament.[2] Moreover, the combined reforms of the legislative and Commission appointment processes raise the prospect that status quo-minded member states become isolated in these processes and find themselves in an opposition role, as pointed out by Crombez and Hix (2004). Member states may have appointed weak Commissions in the past ten years to avoid such situations.

Constitutional policy coordination

To prepare for the Convention and IGC the Commission formed a "Task Force for the Future of the Union and Institutional Matters." This task force was led by Paolo Ponzano and Pieter Van Nuffel, two Commission officials. The former also served as Commissioner Vitorino's alternative at the Convention. The task force consisted of around ten members. It was the principal body that prepared the Commission position on the issues discussed at the Convention and IGC. Its role in the policy coordination process can be compared to the role that the network of committees plays within the Directorates General for the preparation of proposals in the legislative process.

The policy documents prepared by the task force then followed either of two routes, as shown in Figure 28.1. Proposed policy positions on minor issues were sent directly to Commission president, Romano Prodi, and Michel Barnier and Antonio Vitorino, the Commission representatives at the Convention. They then determined the Commission positions on the issues and defended them at the Convention and IGC. The Commission was not formally involved at the IGC. None the less it could formulate policy suggestions.

On most issues, however, the entire Commission got involved. As mentioned above the Commission is a collegiate body that makes decisions and sets policies at its weekly meetings. This was also the case as far as the Commission preparations for the Convention and IGC were concerned.

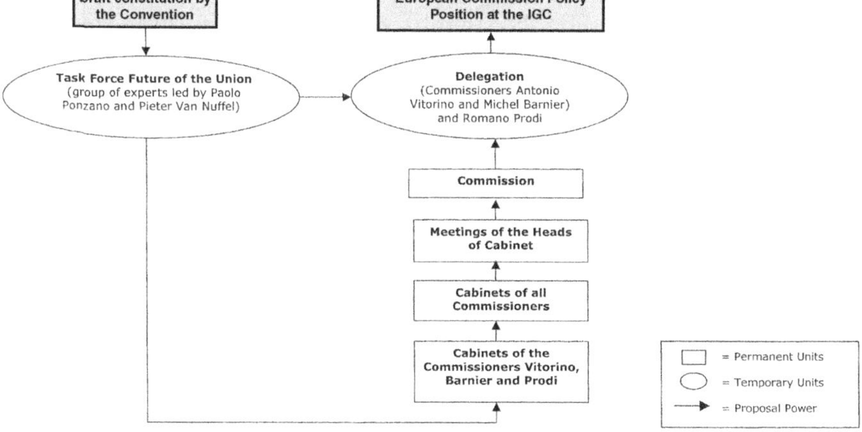

Figure 28.1 European Commission: Policy coordination for the IGC 2003–4.

The task force thus sent its proposals to the cabinets of the three aforementioned commissioners. The three commissioners could then retain the task force's proposals or formulate their own proposals for a Commission position. Next, they forwarded their proposals to the cabinets of the other commissioners. The policies were then discussed at the regular meetings of the heads of cabinet and subsequently at the weekly meetings of the Commission. This approach is similar to the approach taken by the Commission on other policy issues.

The Commission president and the two Commission representatives at the Convention were the main actors within the Commission. The policy initiative lay with them. They needed to agree for a proposal to be defended at the Convention and IGC. Interestingly the three principal actors belonged to the three main political groups in the EU: the Christian democrats/conservatives (Barnier), the socialists (Vitorino) and the liberals (Prodi). It seems that the Commission was well organized at the task force level, but that the actions of the three commissioners were not always well coordinated. This may have hampered the effectiveness of the Commission.

The other commissioners could amend or block proposals at the Commission meetings, if they obtained the support of a majority of the commissioners. In practice the other commissioners played only a minor role though, and agreement between the three principal commissioners was thus the key to determine the Commission position. For all practical purposes the three principal commissioners thus had proposal, amendment and veto rights, whereas the other commissioners had formal amendment and veto rights as a college.

Data and empirical analysis of forming positions on the constitution for Europe

The experts identified the following three commissioners as the key actors in the coordination process, consistent with our remarks above: (1) Romano Prodi, Commission president; (2) Michel Barnier, Commissioner for Regional Policy and Institutional Affairs, and Commission representative at the Convention; and (3) Antonio Vitorino, Commissioner for Justice and Home Affairs and Commission representative at the Convention.[3]

Public policy disagreements among the three principal commissioners involved in the process, Prodi, Vitorino and Barnier, were minimal. This is illustrated in Table 28.1. In the table the percentages of policy disagreements, whether it be on further integration, institutional issues, policy issues or issues of vital interest are all in the single digits. The three key commissioners failed to agree on just one policy issue: the religious reference in the preamble. Commission President Prodi favored such a reference, whereas the other two commissioners were more reluctant. In the end the Commission did not take any position on this issue.

Table 28.1 Cohesiveness of actors' positions in the Commission's coordination process

Official Commission position	*Actor(s) (No. or type)*	*Observations (No.)*	*Deviations*									
			from national position		*on integration*				*related to*			
					toward less		*toward more*		*institutional issues*[a]		*policy fields*[a]	
			No.	*%*	*No.*	*%*	*No.*	*%*	*No.*	*%*	*No.*	*%*
Commission delegates	3	195	1	0.5	1	0.5	0	–	0	–	1	1.5

Deviations related to institutional issues
Nil

Deviations related to policy fields
Religious reference in the preamble

Vital interests
European commission; Number of commissioners; More QMV areas in general

Note
a Percentage shares refer to subsets of institutional (43) and policy (22) issues.

Two issues led to considerable debate within the Commission: the composition of the Commission and the status of the EU Foreign Minister. First, regarding its composition, the Commission disagreed with the Convention, which proposed a two-tier Commission. It argued that such a system would create a system of first and second-class commissioners, that it would destroy the institution's collegial nature, and would result in a loss of legitimacy and effectiveness for the EU as a whole. The three principal commissioners proposed as an alternative that each member state would have a commissioner, and that decision making would be devolved to subsets of commissioners in charge of specific areas. The full college would then decide on issues of strategic and political importance only.

Second, regarding the status of the EU Foreign Minister, the Commission was of the opinion that he/she should be accountable to the Council and the Commission and that the approval of both these institutions should be required for his/her appointment. There was agreement within the Commission that the Commission should be the only institution with a right of initiative, that the president should be proposed by the Parliament and approved by the Council, acting by qualified majority, and that the president should choose the commissioners, who would then be subject to approval by the Council and the Parliament.

In general the Commission was in favor of the draft constitution. It was particularly keen on extending qualified majority voting, and was concerned about preserving the "community method" of decision making and thus its role in the EU. In that context it appreciated that the Convention confirmed its monopoly of legislative initiative in the (former) first pillar (the EC) and strengthened its right of initiative in the (former) third pillar (justice and home affairs). The issue of the number of commissioners mentioned above was also considered as vital by the Commission. In the end the IGC did revert to the "one commissioner per member state" principle, as the Commission wanted.

Furthermore, the Commission valued the Convention proposal that the president have a bigger say in the nomination and dismissal of the other commissioners and thus see his powers were extended. He would be able to choose the other commissioners out of a list of three candidates, presented by the member states, and would no longer need the approval of the other commissioners to dismiss a commissioner. At the IGC the former extension of the president's powers was not preserved, whereas the second was.

Conclusion

This analysis illustrates that in the Commission policy toward EU integration and constitutional issues is consensus-oriented, as is the case in Belgium and Luxembourg, as well as for policy in general in the Commission. There was widespread agreement amongst the commissioners on the issues discussed at the Convention and IGC, and this consensus was reached in a political process that provided opportunities for all commissioners to provide input.

In practice Commission President Prodi and the two Commission representatives at the Convention, Michel Barnier and Antonio Vitorino, played the most important roles in the preparation of the Commission positions for the Convention. The other commissioners played a minor role only. The three commissioners determined the Commission positions, which were then discussed, and usually approved, by the entire body. Agreement among the three commissioners was the key to establishing the Commission position. The three commissioners hailed from the main three political parties in the EU, the Christian democrats and conservatives, the socialists and the liberals, and thus represented the party ideological diversity within the Commission.

To prepare for the Convention the Commission set up a "Task Force for the Future of the Union and Institutional Matters." This task force played the role the Commission's network of committees usually plays to prepare its proposals in the legislative process. The task force discussed the relevant issues and forwarded proposals for Commission positions to the three commissioners. The three commissioners would then agree on a Commission position, and this position would usually be approved by the entire body. The task force seems to have been well organized, but the coordination among the commissioners may have been somewhat ineffective.

The consensus position of the Commission was staunchly pro-integration, as it usually is. Public disagreements within the Commission occurred only on the issue of the religious reference in the preamble. In the end the Commission did not take a position on that issue.

At the IGC the Commission favored the approval of the draft constitution with the exception of the proposed rules for the composition of the Commission. The Commission did not accept the proposed system of a two-tier Commission. It wanted to preserve the "one commissioner per member state" principle. The extension of qualified majority voting and the maintenance of its exclusive right of legislative initiative represented two other vital issues for the Commission.

Notes

1 See Edwards and Spence (1994), Dinan (1999) and Nugent (2003a) for more information about the Commission.
2 See, for example, Crombez (1997).
3 We interviewed two experts. Their adapted coherence was 0.67, below the average for the entire project (0.85, see Appendix 21).

29 The European Parliament

Consensus and coordination for enhanced powers

Giacomo Benedetto

The institutional powers of the European Parliament

The European Parliament is a supranational institution. A separation of powers and decentralized federalism characterize the political system of the European Union. In fields of community competence, legislative power is shared between the EP and the Council of Ministers, and the Commission exercises executive power. Unlike in most national systems, the executive does not depend on a parliamentary majority, the Parliament exercises its powers independently from executive control by the Commission, and the procedures for selecting both the Parliament and Commission are separate.

The Parliament has always been a protagonist in the integration process. At each reform of the EU treaties these powers have increased. Between 1970 and 1975, Parliament gained influential powers over the EU budget. Once directly elected, following 1979, it engaged in a concerted campaign to gain more power, supported by a broad coalition of all the major parties represented in Parliament. Although Parliament has no formal power over approval or veto of new EU treaties, its informal influence has been significant, most recently during the Convention on the Future of Europe. Parliament is required to express an *opinion* on treaty change, which has never been negative. Since doing so would cause a ratification crisis, it may be best to think of the EP having a *de facto* veto on EU treaty change. In 1987 the Single European Act allowed Parliament the right to set the agenda by proposing legislative amendments to the Council. Subject to the support of the Commission and at least one government, these were easier for the Council to accept by qualified majority than to reject by unanimity (Tsebelis 1994, Tsebelis and Garrett 2000). The subsequent treaties further enhanced Parliament's powers of legislation and appointment. Despite this, there were still many areas of policy, where the powers of Parliament remained consultative.

Political developments since 1999

The Parliament of 1999 to 2004 was one of unprecedented constitutional activity. Just after its election in June 1999, the European Council of Cologne established a Convention to draft a Charter of Fundamental Rights for the EU. This consisted of MEPs, members of national parliaments, representatives of national governments, and a European commissioner. The Charter produced by this Convention coincided with the end of the 2000 IGC at Nice. Parliament's Constitutional Affairs Committee (AFCO) had produced the EP's official opinions on the IGC and the final treaty, as well as to the deliberations of the Charter's Convention. In December 2001, the European Council scheduled a new IGC for 2004 and established a Convention to make proposals for the new post-enlargement EU. The Convention for the Future of Europe was based on that of the Charter. Its MEP members were drawn overwhelmingly from AFCO, which produced reports in the period leading to the new IGC of 2003–4. The EP supported a rapid conclusion of this IGC before the elections of June 2004, for fear that the momentum of the EP in securing many of its objectives for the draft constitution might be at risk with the expected arrival of new and less experienced MEPs.

The Parliament elected in June 2004 was less easy to predict given the arrival of 162 MEPs (22 percent) from the new member states, the EP's domination by domestic opposition parties, but with an oversized majority for the pro-system and pro-constitution groups: European People's Party (EPP), Socialists (PES), Liberals and Democrats (ALDE), and Greens. Collectively, they held 82 percent of seats in both the Parliaments of 1999 and 2004.[1] The heterogeneity of the Parliament's Euro-skeptics and limited numbers reduce any chance of carrying over electoral success in a few member states into achievements within the Parliament (Benedetto 2006). The chances of the EP entering a positive *opinion* on the outcome of the new treaty were therefore unaffected.

The preparation of Parliament's *opinion* on the constitution was tightly controlled by AFCO and those had been influential throughout the period of the Convention and IGC. The co-rapporteurs were the coordinators of both the EPP and PES groups on the committee, Inigo Mendez de Vigo, who had also been a member of the Convention's Praesidium and one of Parliament's representatives to the IGC, and Richard Corbett. While acknowledging disappointment at the constitution failing to go further, Parliament's opinion called for rapid ratification by the member states. It was approved by 500 votes to 137, including most members of the four largest groups, as well as the nationalist UEN. The constitution was opposed by the British Conservatives, Ulster Unionist, Czech Civic Democrats and Polish Peasants' Party from the EPP, by two MEPs from the Finnish Center Party from the ALDE, by the regionalists from Scotland, Wales and Catalonia, as well as the Swedish and Flemish Greens from the

Green Group, by the Danish Freedom Party and Polish Law and Justice Party from the UEN Group, and by the extreme right and the Democratic Unionists from Northern Ireland among the non-attached. The Slovak HZDS and one member of the German PDS (its representative on the Convention) voted in favor of the constitution. Abstentions were recorded by Polish Civic Platform and the Slovak Christian Democrats (KDH) from the EPP, by nine French Socialists and the Maltese Labour Party from the PES, by two Italian Communists from the Left Group (GUE), by one English Green, and by Polish Self Defense and Hans-Peter Martin from among the non-attached (see Table 29.1).

Constitutional policy coordination

The EP is not a unitary actor. It encompasses a more diverse range of views than any one government and was represented by 32 full and alternate members on the Convention from across the ideological spectrum. The Parliament also had two seats on the Praesidium. AFCO, which had a partly overlapping membership with the Delegation to the Convention, monitored developments. Parliament's two Praesidium members: Klaus Hänsch (PES) and Iñigo Mendez de Vigo (EPP) appeared frequently before AFCO. Other key actors were parliamentary officials on the Convention task force and, within that, the delegation secretariat. Many were seconded from AFCO and other committee secretariats, while the task force included relevant officials from the secretariats of the political groups.

Discussion at the Convention and AFCO fed into the work of the Convention delegation secretariat. The votes of the Parliament's plenary, prepared by AFCO, were official Parliament policy and contributed to the work of the Convention and the Praesidium.

The political groups also had a direct link to the Convention via their individual Convention delegates. The Parliament delegation held meetings but never adopted an actual position. The 32 members and alternates signed motions as individual members of the Convention. This was inten-

Table 29.1 Parliamentary vote of approval for the EU constitution, 12 January 2005

Group	*Total*	*Yes*	*No*	*Abstain*	*Absent from vote*
EPP	268	192	34	19	23
PES	200	171	1	12	16
ALDE	88	81	2	0	5
G/EFA	42	33	7	1	1
GUE	41	1	34	2	4
IND/DEM	37	0	34	0	3
UEN	27	18	8	0	1
Non-attached	29	4	17	6	2
Total	732	500	137	40	55

tional, because initiatives signed at the Convention in the name of *Parliament's delegation* would have alienated other institutional actors.

Following the conclusion of the Convention, Parliament's two members of the Praesidium served as the EP representatives at the full meetings of the General Affairs Council. The officials of Parliament's IGC secretariat (previously the Convention delegation secretariat) attended all meetings. At the end of November 2003, Elmar Brok replaced Mendez de Vigo as representative from the EPP Group. The President of Parliament, Patrick Cox, also attended IGC meetings of the full European Council.

The Gil-Robles/Tsatsos report of September 2003 on the conclusion of the Convention was official Parliament policy mandating Hänsch, Mendez de Vigo and Brok for the IGC. The representatives also appeared before an informal group consisting of a representative from each political group, usually the group coordinators on AFCO, called the *Groupe de Suivi*. This allowed the smaller groups not represented directly at the IGC to keep nominal tabs on the processes. The IGC task force and secretariat continued to interact with the political groups at other levels, as well as with sectoral committees of the Parliament. Of these, the most relevant was the Budgets Committee following the attempt by the Council of Finance Ministers (ECOFIN) to amend the Convention's proposals regarding the budgetary procedure (Figure 29.1).

Data and empirical analysis of forming positions on the constitution for Europe

Six key individuals were contacted in order to ascertain policy formation.[2] The key institutional actors in the European Parliament were AFCO and

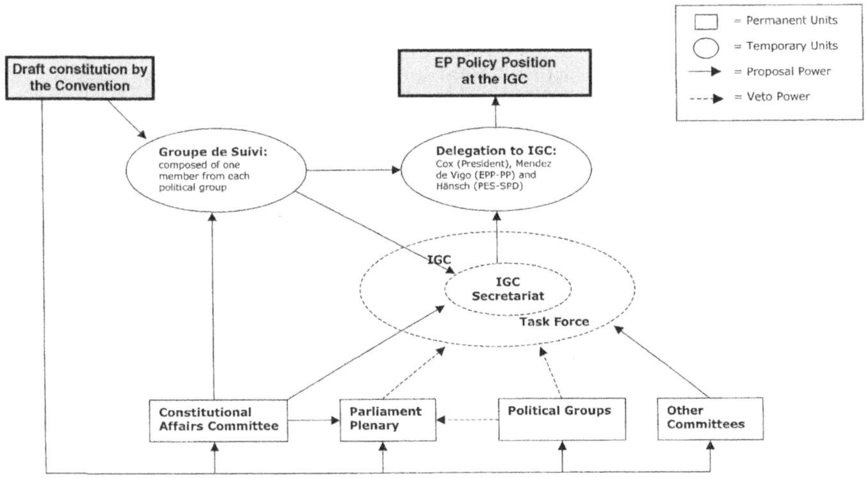

Figure 29.1 European Parliament: domestic policy coordination for the IGC 2003–4.

the three largest groups: the EPP, PES and ELDR, since renamed ALDE. The respondents believed that the groups were more influential than AFCO. One preferred to cite specific individuals as having the influence to shape the constitutional approach of Parliament: the party group coordinators from the three largest groups on AFCO; the AFCO chairman, Giorgio Napolitano; Jo Leinen; Dimitris Tsatsos; Elmar Brok, one of Parliament's repeat representatives to IGCs; Alain Lamassoure; Jean-Louis Bourlanges; and Monica Frassoni from the Green Group. These individuals had experience and have worked closely together on AFCO, and then try to build support within their party families for Parliament to have a unified and convincing position on constitutional questions.

The success of consensus building on IGCs between parliamentary parties that normally compete with each other was recognized by all respondents. Bilateral meetings between the IGC representatives and the main coordinators from AFCO were frequent.

Adapted coherence of the various institutional actors in Parliament revealed high levels of coherence in perceptions of the official positions both of Parliament and AFCO, at above 0.99.[3]

Compared to national governments, the European Parliament has substantial expertise and power through knowledge, even if in the formal sense it has no power to veto treaty changes. Although it tries to construct a united front on constitutional issues, it is generally more divided than any of the other institutional actors in the IGC, which are all national governments, apart from the Commission. As a way out of the impasse on continued use of voting weights or use of the double majority in Council, some of Parliament's experts urged the Italian presidency to support a new "Ioannina compromise." This would allow the new system of voting in the Council to come into force, giving the right for *losing* member states to request that votes be held under the previous weighting system on an ad hoc basis. The Irish presidency retabled this proposal, but eventually the governments of Poland and Spain accepted a higher threshold for QMV at 55 percent of states and 65 percent rather than 60 percent of population. Poland and Spain have also been compensated with an allocation of more MEPs, raising the future membership of the EP to 750, breaching the upper membership limits set at 700 by the Treaty of Amsterdam and at 732 by the Treaty of Nice.

Concerning institutional reforms to the Commission and Council, Parliament was divided. Although there was a majority in favor of a joint presidency for both Council and Commission, there was no agreement over its ideal procedure for appointment or for relative voting weights on the Council. Significant portions of the EPP Group continued to propose that Parliament should gain the power to elect the Commission, although the Socialist Group has argued against this since it would enable a blocking minority in the Council to block the democratic choice of Parliament.

Division on whether there should be fewer members of the European Commission than member states and on the voting weights of the states on the Council is pronounced in the European Parliament, and depends on the member state of MEPs rather than their political group. The governments were unwilling to agree with the proposal to create a joint presidency of the Council and Commission, so the major groups in Parliament accepted a permanent presidency of the European Council, hoping to be able to minimize its powers.

The *vital interests* for the Parliament were that:

1 Parliament's budgetary powers must be protected and enhanced.
2 Co-decision must accompany QMV in all legislative areas.
3 The Charter of Fundamental Rights must be included.

The most drawn-out vital interest of Parliament was the ECOFIN "budget ambush" of October 2003. This had originally been proposed by Peter Hain, on behalf of the British government during the Convention. In December, before the Council in Brussels, the Italian Council presidency proposed a compromise on the budget to concede an "unusable" power of veto to the Council. This appeared to be a substantial concession by the Parliament, but in reality the chance of the Council being able to agree to veto definitively a budget amended by Parliament would be slight. However, not all of the key actors in Parliament were prepared to accept this compromise. So far as the parliamentary respondents from across the parties were concerned, this case was evidence that governments and national officials, with little institutional memory, had no idea about what they were doing. Under the Hain proposal, if ECOFIN and Parliament disagreed on the amounts of any expenditure heading, of the two amounts voted by ECOFIN and Parliament, whichever of the two were lower would automatically be deemed adopted, unless the previous year's spending for that heading were higher. The result would be that ECOFIN and Parliament could mutually sabotage each other's spending priorities, while making it difficult to cut spending.

The Groups reluctantly accepted the *yellow card* system of subsidiarity checks by national parliaments against the Commission. Minor divisions occurred on the principles underlying the social and economic objectives of the Union. The EPP accepted the compromise on the social market as an objective, with the Liberals (more right-wing on certain aspects of social policy than the EPP) holding out for a commitment to the free single market only. The Liberals oppose tax harmonization, but consistent with a more federal position, support the use of QMV and co-decision in this area, the principle being that the EU should not legislate on taxation but should have the power to do so. The Liberals reluctantly accepted the right of citizens' initiatives requiring the consideration of the Commission, although consistent with their secular traditions, raised concerns about Catholic initiatives against abortion and similar questions on the liberty versus authority dimension.

There were some divisions on ESDP, with the Socialists supporting the outcome of mutual defense commitments, while the Liberals and much of the EPP would have preferred a European armed force. The Socialist view was that Europe is not yet ready for harmonization in this area. However, the EPP adopted a more skeptical approach than the other groups in opposing full harmonization of immigration and asylum policy, and the establishment of rights for third-country nationals.

References to religion in the preamble of the constitution were the subject of division in the European Parliament as in other parliaments. The Socialists and Liberals wanted no reference to religion, to the displeasure of Christian Democrats.

Some division existed not on the right of withdrawal from the EU but on the correct approach to this in the constitution. The right of secession exists in international law, so some actors in the EP, of varying parties, believed it unnecessary in the constitution. Others thought it useful as a way to reassure public opinion that might otherwise turn toward Euroskepticism.

All of the major groups, as well as AFCO, have favored leaving the level of competencies for all policy areas as they are, although the Socialists would have preferred more in economic, employment and social policies. Parliament wished to see QMV and co-decision or assent in all areas except defense.

In addition to the vital interests of Parliament as a whole, areas that would have incited a negative vote by Socialist MEPs against the constitution were a result that would "emasculate" the Commission or the bulk of the text of the draft constitution. For the Socialists, advancing social policy or at the very least preventing the EU from being an "entirely free market exercise" is a *vital interest*, while for both Socialists and Liberals, the inclusion of God in the preamble would have resulted in a negative *opinion*.

Among those interviewed, the perceptions of key institutional actors within the Parliament (the groups, AFCO, and delegations to the Convention and IGC) deviated from those of the Parliament's position as a whole in 20 percent of instances. Most of this deviation was oriented toward more integration (12 percent) rather than toward less integration (8 percent). When analyzed according to thematic area, the deviation between perceptions of parliamentary actors and Parliament as a whole was higher with regard to policy areas (33 percent) than to institutional questions (13 percent). This indicates a greater degree of consensus on institutional matters than on policy issues. It is consistent with the findings that MEPs were divided on the emphasis of social and economic policy in the constitution.

Table 29.2 Cohesiveness of actors' positions in the Parliament's coordination process

Official EP position	*Actor(s) (No. or type)*	*Observations (No.)*	*Deviations*									
			from national position		*on integration*				*related to*			
					toward less		*toward more*		*institutional issues*[a]		*policy fields*[a]	
			No.	*%*	*No.*	*%*	*No.*	*%*	*No.*	*%*	*No.*	*%*
EP groups	7	455	91	20.0	38	8.4	53	11.6	40	13.3	51	33.1

Deviations related to institutional issues
Right to withdraw from the Union; Presidency of the Council; QMV threshold; Number of commissioners; Appointment of commissioners; External representation of the EU (Foreign Minister); Additional approval of the Foreign Minister by the EP; Legislative initiative for citizens; Voting rule (Council) for tax harmonization, for social security rights, for defense policy; Decision rule (EP) for tax harmonization, for social security rights, for foreign policy, for defense policy

Deviations related to policy fields
Religious reference in the preamble; Economic objectives: kind of market economy, employment, and competitiveness; Level of competence for structural and cohesion politics, for the Area of Freedom, Security and Justice, for foreign policy, for employment policy, for social policy, for health policy, for environment policy, for research, technological development and space; Stability and Growth Pact; Defense; External borders; Migration and asylum

Vital interests
Status of Charter of Fundamental Rights; Economic objectives (only the PES); No emasculation of European Commission; Number of commissioners; Election of Commission president; Appointment of the Foreign Minister; Co-decision should accompany QMV in all areas; Budgetary procedure

Note
a Percentage shares refer to subsets of institutional (43) and policy (22) issues.

Conclusion

Each of Parliament's three main *vital interests* was secured with the creation of the ordinary legislative procedure to cover all areas of legislation in the community sphere. Notable exceptions applied to taxation, social security, and aspects of cultural policy designed to protect the European audiovisual sector from deregulation. These were nevertheless subject to co-decision, although with the Council deciding unanimously. Parliament had to accept co-decision for the budget, which amounted to a diminution of its powers compared to those in the draft constitution which allowed Parliament to overrule the Council. The Charter of Fundamental Rights is reproduced as Part II of the constitution.

The areas on which Parliament was divided reflected the divisions in national parliaments between left and right, demonstrating that the EP is not a unitary actor. These included the nature of the social and economic objectives of the Union, the extent to which social policy or powers of taxation should be enhanced, the case for harmonization in areas such as defense or immigration, and whether God or religion should be cited in the preamble. Institutional questions such as whether each member state should have a commissioner, or the reform of the Council voting system caused division between nationalities rather than party families. While MEPs divided on the question of the appointment procedure for the Commission, Parliament was unsuccessful in securing a joint presidency of both Commission and Council. This is reflected in the data finding the most coherent group was perceived to be the Liberals, bridging the ideological gap between the other groups, while a greater deviation was located on policy than on institutional issues.

Although Parliament gained in terms of legislative powers, the compromise on reforming the voting system of the Council was reached by increasing the number of MEPs to a level that Parliament opposes for the sake of its own ability to function efficiently. However, this is a small loss compared to its gains in most other areas. The extension of co-decision and QMV in legislation and of the assent procedure to CFSP is a very significant increase in power for the Parliament, approved by a majority of MEPs that was predictably "oversized."

Notes

1 The state of groups in the European Parliament 1999 and 2004 can be downloaded from the projects' website at dosei.dhv-speyer.de.

2 Four MEPs each drawn from the groups of the EPP, PES, ELDR (renamed ALDE in July 2004), and Greens/EFA, one official was advisor to a political group, while a further interviewee worked for the secretariat of the Parliament on the delegation to the Convention. Interviews completed in January 2004.

3 These were followed by the coherence in the perceptions of the Liberal Group (0.98), Socialists (0.96) and EPP (0.95), indicating that the Liberals were also perceived as the group with the most pronounced views on constitutional

questions. Parliament's delegation to the IGC, cited as a relevant actor by only two of the six respondents, was subjected to the lowest coherence at 0.74. This reflects the delicate negotiating position to which the IGC delegation was subject. Modifying the coherence for the numbers of experts interviewed, the mean adapted coherence of the EP case (0.89) is higher than the overall coherence in the DOSEI data set (0.85, see Appendix 2).

Conclusion

Simon Hug and Thomas König

Undeniably, the process leading up to the IGC concluded one of the most complex negotiation processes of an international treaty. Compared to previous treaty negotiations in the EU (e.g., Laursen and Vanhoonacker 1994, Moravcsik 1998, Laursen 2002, Thurner *et al.* 2002) the preparatory stages differed and involved a much broader set of actors. This "new method" should not only set the agenda for institutional reform, but also increase transparency and legitimacy of the constitutional framework. After the European Convention and in preparation of the IGC negotiations, many national governments attempted to associate domestic groups in the national preference formation process. In Robert Dahl's (1971: 7) terms, such processes raise questions about the extent of popular inclusion and the extent of public contestation, providing the public opportunities to voice ideas and concerns about elements of the constitution and opening debates about the final document. The previous chapters have provided in-depth analyses of this process of inclusion and the debates within all 25 member states plus Commission and European Parliament.

The outcome of the rather involved process was a lengthy document consolidating the preceding treaties, but also comprising several fundamental changes. Obviously, constitutions that "allow everyone to introduce substantive demands, constitutions that ratify compromises by enshrining substantive commitments are often impossible to implement" (Przeworski 1991: 35). As discussed in the preceding chapters, it was also many of these changes, which raised considerable opposition. The change in the formula to be employed for qualified majority voting in the Council is a considerable reform with a compromise outcome. Similarly, the creation of a stronger Council president with a longer term in office, together with a EU Foreign Minister are important negotiated innovations. Apart from these and many other more institutional elements, the constitution also settles several policies differently, by retrenching its powers in some areas while expanding in others. Thus, the constitutional document finally reflects the feasibility of institutional reform in an enlarged EU with 25 countries, from which ten became members of the EU during the constitution-building process.

Once the constitutional draft was delivered at the 2003 Thessaloniki summit, the action moved to the 25 domestic arenas. The preceding chapters have demonstrated the way in which preferences of the national governments have been formed. In this chapter we will compare the different preference formation processes and link them with the characteristics of the domestic political systems. In a first step we will compare the formal preference formation processes and attempt to asses whether we can detect systematic similarities and differences. Given that some of these elements might depend on the ways in which domestic political systems are organized, we will assess this link. In a second step our focus will be on the vital issues that have characterized the national positions during the negotiations. Vital issues usually refer to very salient issues, and in the context of the EU they recall the times before the Luxembourg compromise (1966) when France blocked EU decision making because the Commission proposed the application of qualified majority voting for "vital" agricultural issues. On the one hand we wish to assess whether similar vital issues were raised by particular groups of countries, and on the other we will also attempt to determine whether particular groups of countries have been more successful to have their vital issues addressed. Finally, the wealth of data reported in the preceding chapters also allows us to assess how coherent the national positions were in a comparative perspective. Again, we would suspect that the way in which divergences concerning the national positions emerged is affected by the national domestic context. While the number of actors involved indicates the extent of inclusion, coherence is a major indicator for public contestation.

Formal preference formation processes

The individual country chapters highlighted the diverse manner in which domestic preferences on the constitution were formed, once the European Convention delivered its draft. Nevertheless, some commonalities appear across the 25 countries. While the receiving actor differs among the member states, almost in all countries the ministry of foreign affairs and, to a lesser extent, the prime minister's office had the most important influence in this phase. This is an amazing concentration which contrasts "regular" EU decision making, in which the portfolio ministries play the major role channeling the domestic interests. Table 30.1 reports for each country the leading ministry in the preference formation process. Quite clearly it appears that in most countries the ministry of foreign affairs played this role. Only in eight countries, in three of which the role was shared, did the prime minister or the president play the central role. Interesting to note in this context is that all countries with a comparatively speaking strong presidency (e.g., Austria, Finland, France, Portugal) (e.g., Martinez Martinez 1999) concentrated the preference formation process at least in part more closely at the top of the executive.

Table 30.1 Leading ministries

Ministry	*Countries*	*n*
Prime minister	AU BE (EE) FI FR (President) (IE) LU (PT)	8
Ministry of Foreign Affairs	CY CZ DK (EE) GE GR HU (IE) IT LV LI MA NL PL (PT) SK SL ES SW UK	20

While Table 30.1 suggests a rather top-heavy process, this did not imply that other ministries or domestic actors failed to have a significant impact. In almost all member states the other ministries were consulted and able to make proposals on the issues relating to their portfolio. Divergences of views at the governmental level were then often attempted to be resolved in task forces, committees and working groups. This indicates the two-sided strategy to present a coherent national position at the IGC negotiations without excluding too many domestic interests.

Given the goal to open up the discussion of the constitutional text with the European Convention, it cannot surprise that this also led to the inclusion of actors outside of government in the preference formation process. The close consultations with institutions of the respective parliaments can almost be considered as a "Nordic model." In Denmark the European Affairs Committee was closely associated, as were the corresponding parliamentary committees in Finland and Sweden. To a lesser degree the European Affairs Committee (EAC) in Latvia played a similar role. Other countries were less inclusive in their cooperation with parliament, even though parliamentary delegates participated in the deliberations of the European Convention and would have to ratify the constitutional document after the IGC negotiations.

Another consequence of the European Convention was that actors associated in this event kept in part their influence in the domestic preference formation stage. Hence, the former Belgian Prime Minister Jean-Luc Dehaene and the former Commission president Jacques Santer from Luxembourg as delegates for their respective countries continued to influence the preference formation at the domestic level. In a similar vein the important impact of the governments of the *Länder* in Germany can be considered under this angle. Even further in this opening up of the preference formation process went Slovakia, where a National Convention associated civil society. However, in most countries we find a rather bureaucratic model of preference formation, which does not necessarily mean that this model neglects other domestic interests.

The formal preference formation occurred in a more predictable way in the European Commission and Parliament. In the Commission most of the relevant processes involved the Commission president, Romano Prodi, and the two commissioners present in the European Convention, namely Vitorino and Barnier. In the European Parliament the concerned committees were mostly implicated together with the largest party groups.[1]

Compared to the European Convention, where parliamentary and governmental delegates were represented, most of the domestic formal preference formation processes were coordinated within the executive, mostly under the responsibility of the foreign office and sometimes in the hands of the prime minister's office. The formal process focused on inter-ministerial coordination but some countries offered access to the public, in particular the Nordic countries. This suggests that countries were more interested in the preparation for the IGC negotiations rather than starting a national debate on constitutional issues. Unsurprisingly, the preparation processes of the constitutional document hardly received public attention in the 25 countries.

Vital issues and domestic political institutions

While the comparative analysis of the formal preference formation process showed at the same time important similarities and considerable differences, the same also applies to the vital issues raised in this process. The term "vital" has a long tradition in the history of the EU, signaling a national threat against Europeanization in order to avoid violation of member state sovereignty. As the preceding chapters highlighted, in many countries particular issues addressed in the constitution raised important concerns. The most frequently mentioned issues concerned the hotly debated changes already alluded to before, namely the composition of the Commission, the voting rules in the Council and the competencies of the new EU foreign minister.

Tables 30.2 and 30.3 give a more solid foundation for this contention by listing the issues vital for the various national actors. It shows that the issue appearing as vital for most member states concerned the number of commissioners, which is about changing the distribution of commissioners due to the enlarged EU. For more than half of all member states this issue proved to be of vital importance. Not surprising is the fact that all countries considering this to be a vital issue are smaller member states and comprises as a block all the newly admitted members fearing a restricted access to the Commission. Quite clearly this issue pitted the large member states against the smaller ones. This also transpires from the fact that with the exception of Germany, Greece and Poland, all the countries for which this issue was vital were also signatories of the paper addressed to the Convention by 16 smaller countries (CONV 646/03) and taking position, among others, for keeping one commissioner per country. This conflict on commissioners' nomination raises some skepticism on the argument of a supranational Commission; it rather indicates that the countries see the Commission as an information and influence pool, to which they want to safeguard their national access.

Table 30.2 Vital issues shared across member states

Vital issue	*Countries*	*n*
Number of commissioners	SK EP PT MT CO SI CY PL LV LT EL FI DK EE CZ DE HU	17
Qualified majority threshold	HU SK FR DE PT ES 2 CZ ES PL LV EL LT EE	13
Regulation of jurisdiction with respect to external policy	FR FI CZ SE PL LT LV AT IT IE	10
EP number and distribution of seats	CY SI PT LU MT LV LT ES 2	8
Legislative procedure/Council voting rule: Taxes	EE MT IE SE SI IT UK	7
Legislative procedure/Council voting rule: Common security and defense policy	DE IT LV FI UK HU MT	7
Religious reference in the preamble	PT NL LT FR PL SK	6
European Commission	AT CO NL EP IE	5
Budgetary procedure	MT UK FR NL EP	5
Presidency in the European Council	SI NL FI PL FR	5
Economic objectives	HU EP AT	4
Legislative procedure/Council voting rule: Immigration	DK IE SI DE	4
Legislative procedure/Council voting rule: Social security	IT UK MT LU	4
Appointment of the Union Minister of Foreign Affairs	EP DE FR	3
Status of Charter of Fundamental Rights	ES 2 IE EP	3
Application of legislative procedures and council voting rules	EP BE CO	3
Enhanced cooperation	HU SI BE	3
Appointment of commissioners	IE NL	2
Role of national parliaments in monitoring the principle of subsidiary	DK HU	2
Rotation of presidency in the European Council	LT AT	2
Scope of jurisdiction of European Court of Justice	HU IE	2
Special provisions (Danish and Finnish accession treaties)	DK FI	2
Election of Commission president	EP NL	2
Language	ES 2 SI	2

Table 30.3 Vital issues singled out by one member state

Vital issue	*Country*	*n*
Legal meaning of constitution (supremacy toward national constitution)	PT	1
Legislative Council	LV	1
Legislative procedure/Council voting rule: Culture	FR	1
Legislative procedure/Council voting rule: CAP	FR	1
Reform Euratom	AT	1
Regulation of jurisdiction with respect to external borders, immigration	HU	1
Regulation of jurisdiction with respect to services of general economic interest	DE	1
Regulation of jurisdiction with respect to environment	SE	1
Regulation of jurisdiction with respect to taxation harmonization	EE	1
ECOFIN	ES 2	1

The conflict line regarding the second most often cited vital issue, namely the voting threshold for qualified majority rule, was a bit more complicated. Tsebelis's analysis (in this volume) clearly demonstrates the reasons for the importance of this issue, and the countries citing this issue as vital confirm his analysis. We find on the one hand the two countries having raised this issue most dramatically, namely Spain and Poland, and on the other two larger countries, namely France and Germany. Apart from these big players we also find mostly smaller countries from Eastern Europe, together with Portugal, raising this issue. A major reason for this configuration is the overrepresentation of the two "almost" large countries Spain and Poland, which feared to become less powerful in case of using a more population sized voting rule, while the unified Germany would profit from this rule.

Next follows the issue regarding foreign policy, which was a vital issue for ten countries. The remaining issues listed in Table 30.2 were only cited by a single-digit number of countries. Many of these issues relate to institutions, like the Commission, and the appointment of the EU Foreign Minister, but also policy issues like taxation, economic objectives, etc. Table 30.3 lists the vital issues which were mentioned only in one member country. Again we find a few institutional issues relating to the decision-making rules for particular policy areas, and a set of policies.

The analysis of the vital issues clearly supports the predictions of the theoretical analysis and the findings on the European Convention's conflict structure. Most importantly, the access to the Commission, defined in the nomination procedure, has been the most contested issue among member states, and particularly smaller countries were against the Convention's proposal to reduce the number of commissioners. Qualified majority voting was the second most contested issues, followed by the regulation of jurisdiction with respect to external policy. Except for Poland

and Spain, compensation was possible between the two hottest issues by guaranteeing overall access to the Commission and introducing the new voting rule.

The vital issues that were mentioned only in one member country rather indicate the possibility of exemptions in terms of transition periods or special provisions. It should be easier for a single country to receive concessions on a particular issue when all other countries consider this issue as less salient. However, the large list of vital issues suggests that the European Convention could not settle all conflicts among member states. The draft text made a number of suggestions which raised concerns in the member states.

Divisions and domestic political institutions

Having identified the most vital issues and assessed the differences regarding them among the member countries, we can now turn to the question of how divided the national domestic actors were in their respective preference formation process. This will give an indication on the extent of public contestation. Dividedness also expresses the amount of conflict in the preference formation process, and may thus be used as an indicator for negotiation success and ratification problems. Under certain conditions, credible dividedness is a good argument for asking for concessions but it also runs the risk of ratification failure because domestic interests are split.

In the country chapters the authors find some considerable differences in terms of cohesion of the consulted actors in the preference formation process. While these analyses already highlight the large diversity, in this concluding chapter we wish to assess two things in a systematic comparative fashion. First of all we wish to determine how the differences among domestic actors relate to the overall bargaining process. More precisely, it might be that in a particular country domestic actors hardly agreed with each other, but at the same time defended positions which made them agree on the benefits of the constitution compared to the status quo. Conversely a very unified set of domestic actors may have led to a situation where only a subset of actors saw clear advantages in the draft constitution. To disentangle these various possibilities we need to summarize the information contained in the responses to our expert survey and attempt to place all actors in a common policy space.

Second, we also wish to determine to what degree the level of cohesion among domestic actors relates to institutional, economic, and political factors. Quite clearly we would expect the cohesion of the domestic actors to be influenced by the general characteristics of the political system in which the preference formation process took place. To assess these influences we propose a systematic analysis based on information provided in the country chapters.

To carry out the first task, we start with deriving a common political space, where all actors at the domestic level can be placed in relationship to the status quo, the draft treaty and the IGC outcome.[2] To do so, we employ the maximum set of questions from our expert survey (see Appendix 1 for the list of questions used) and attempt to derive a simple political space. Given that all variables derived from the answers to the questions are ordinal in nature, traditional factor analysis is inappropriate. Hence we employ a factor analysis for ordinal variables developed in the context of Bayesian statistics (Quinn 2004).[3] Given that we do not have any priors concerning the structure of the political space, we base our derivation of the political space on the means of the posterior densities.[4]

Figure 30.1 depicts for each country separately the location of the status quo, the draft treaty and the IGC outcome as well as the positions of all national actors relative to these three institutional points in two dimensions. Each subfigure uses exactly the same axes, thus the relative positions of the domestic actors compared to the various draft texts can be directly compared. We find that the two dimensions derived relate to two sets of issues dealt with in the EU constitutional treaty. The first dimension relates strongly to some policy issues like taxation, structural and cohesion policies, but also to the institutional issues of the number of commissioners and their nomination procedure. The second dimension reflects mostly the way in which the European Parliament should be involved in particular policy areas. More precisely, whether the EP should be more strongly associated in decision making on social security and defense issues is strongly related to this second dimension.

While the substantive interpretations of the 25 policy spaces are interesting, our main focus concerns the way in which domestic actors cluster in these spaces and where they are located relative to the status quo, the IGC outcome and the draft treaty. A first important point is obviously to assess the coherence of the domestic actors. In most of the subfigures in Figure 30.1 we find all domestic actors tightly clustered around a single point, most likely the national position. For some countries we find, however, some domestic actors with quite distinct positions, which point to a high level of public contestation. With the exception of France, Germany and Spain, we see that these countries are all recent accession countries. Thus in the Czech Republic the Civic Democratic Party (ODS) defended a position much closer to the status quo than all other domestic actors. Similarly but on the other side, in Lithuania the ministry of foreign affairs, the national position, as well as the position of the "European Committee under the Government of the Republic of Lithuania" were much closer to the draft treaty than those of the president and the parliament. Finally, in Slovenia the parliament has a very distinct position much removed from those of the other domestic actors.

In the three older member countries the situation is in part different. In France the UMP party defended a position almost identical to the draft

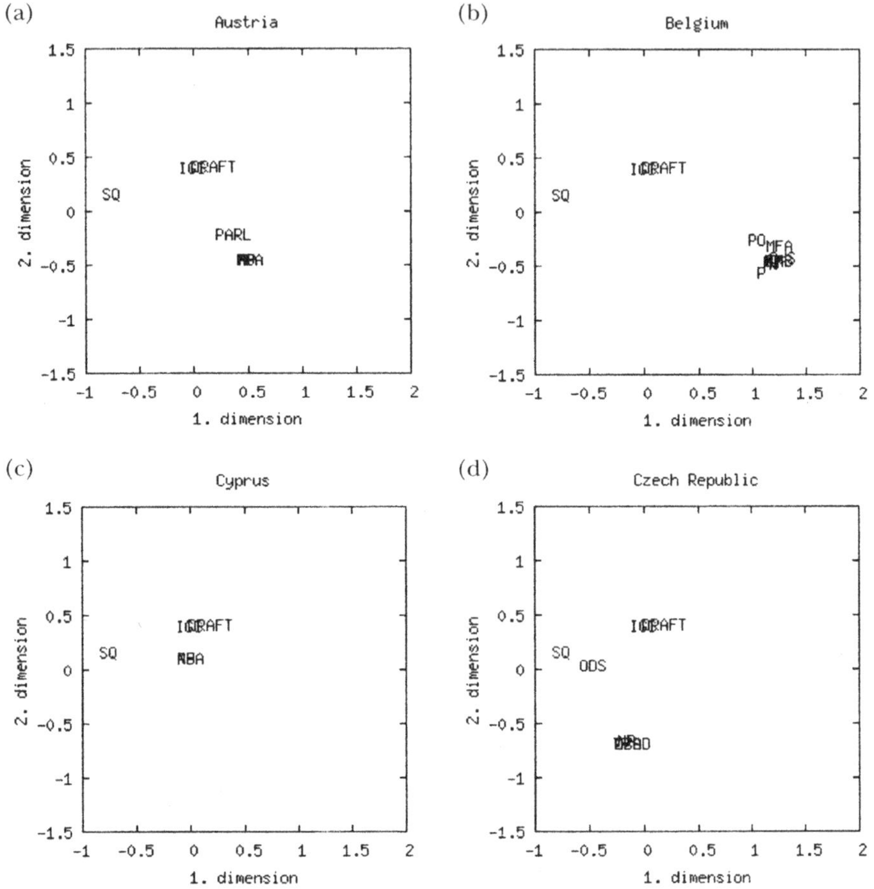

Figure 30.1 Cohesion and preferences of domestic actors.

Notes

AFCO Constitutional Affairs Committee, *CBI* Confederation of British Industry, *CC* Chamber of Commerce, *DTI* Department of Trade and Industry, *Draft* Convention draft, *EMB* Permanent representation, *EUCHP* EU big committee of the Parliament, *EUM* Minister of EU Coordination, *FED* Federal states (*Bundesländer*), *GOEA* Government Office of European Affairs, *IGC* IGC outcome, *ME* Ministry of Economic Affairs, *MEU* Minister of European Affairs (Noelle Lenoir), *MF* Ministry of Finance, *MFA* Ministry of Foreign Affairs, *MI* Ministry of the Interior, Home Office, *MJ* Minister of Justice, *MR* Minister of Research, *NCONV* National Convention, *NP* Government, *P* Party, *PARL* Parliament, *PO* Prime Minister's Office, *PRES* President, *SQ* Status quo.

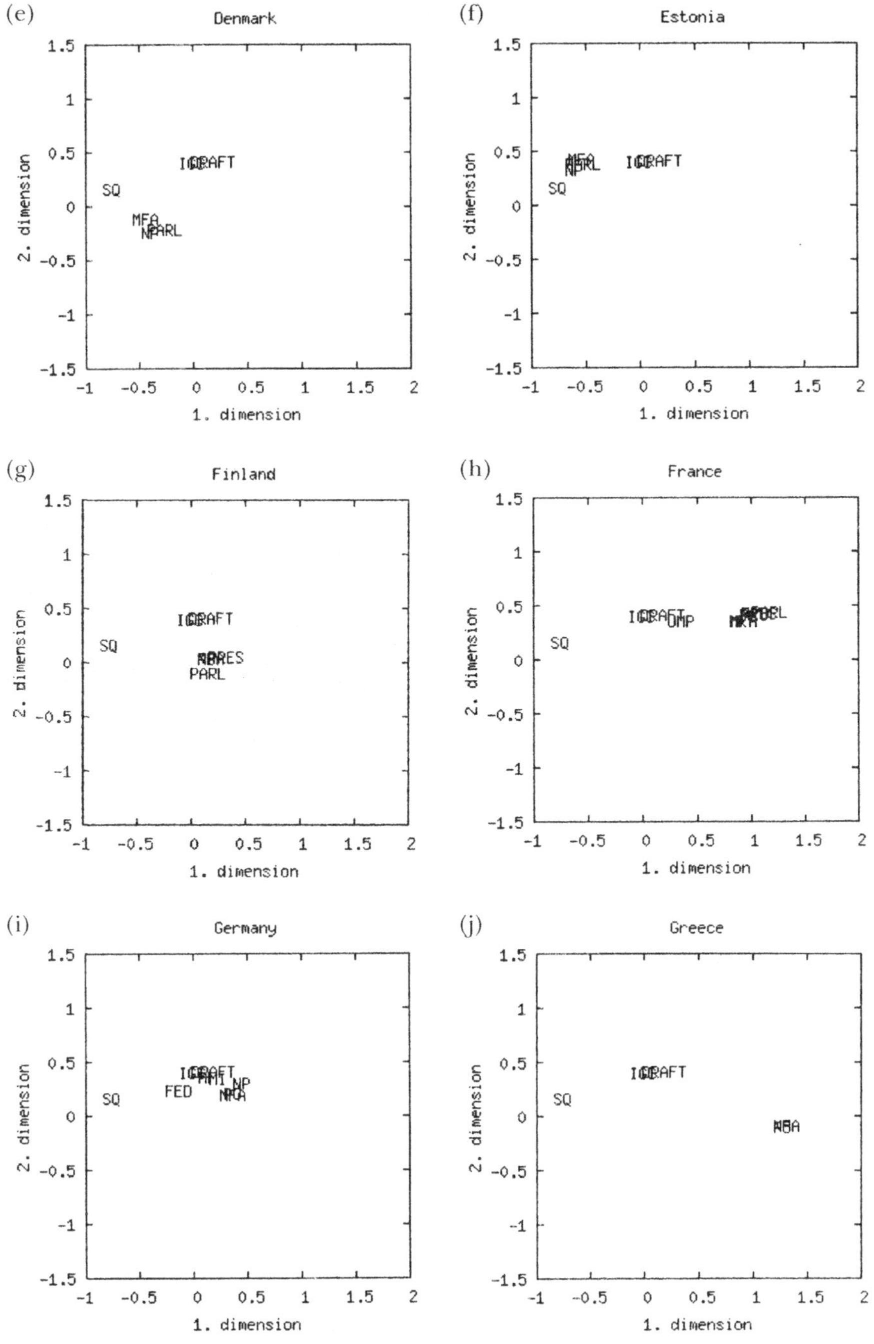

Figure 30.1 contd.

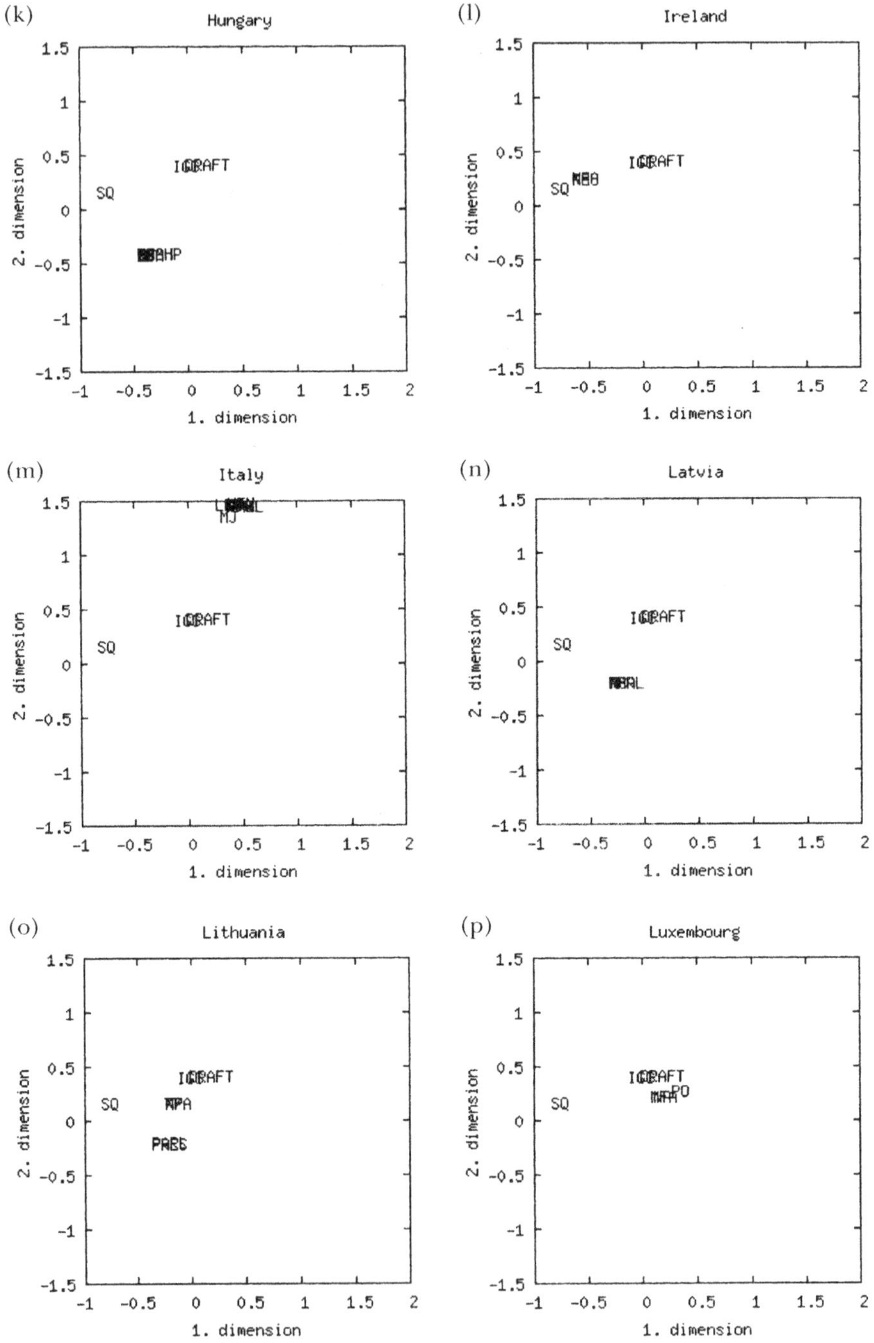

Figure 30.1 contd.

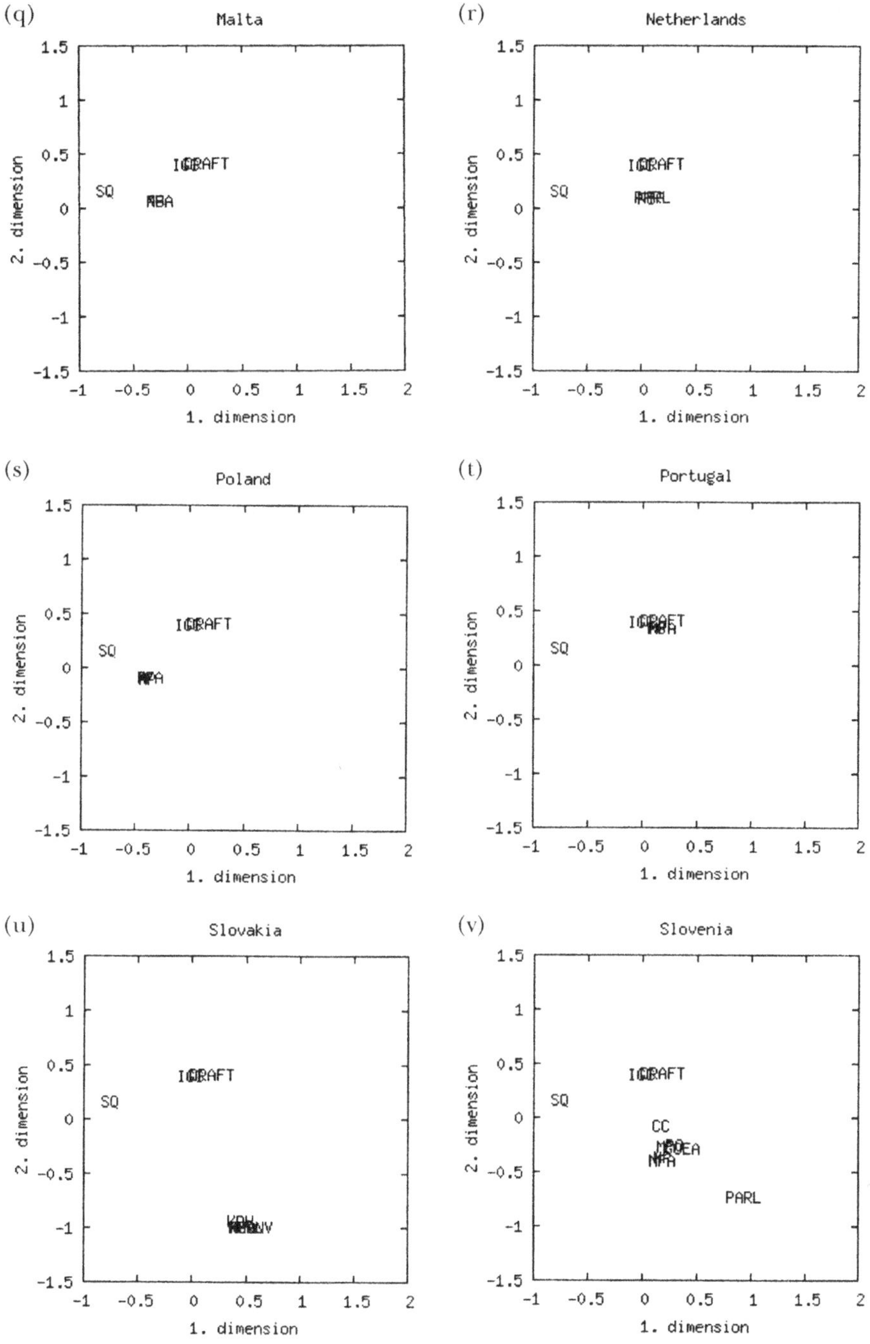

Figure 30.1 contd.

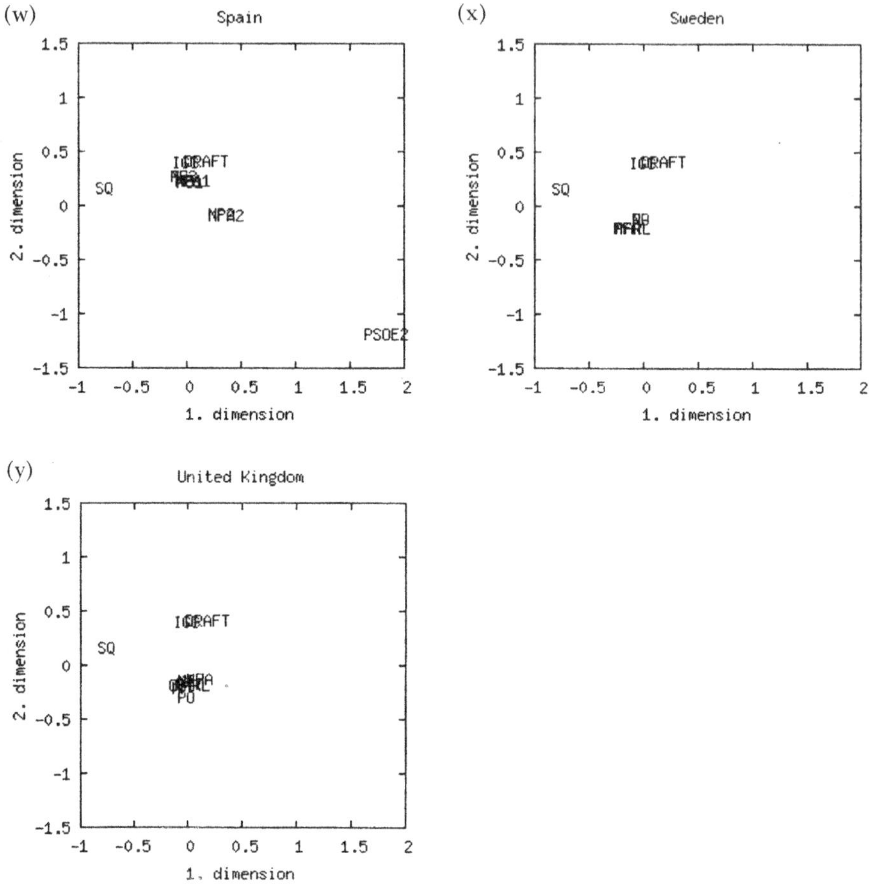

Figure 30.1 contd.

treaty, but all remaining domestic actors were at some distance. In Spain again a party with a very distinct position, namely the PSOE's position under the new government. Interestingly all remaining domestic actors in Spain under both the Aznar and Zapatero governments are located quite close to the draft treaty, with the exception of the minister of foreign affairs and the national position under the Zapatero government. Finally, for Germany, on the hand, the federal states favor a position much closer to the status quo than any other domestic actor, followed at some distance by the ministry of finance. The remaining domestic actors are closely clustered around the national position which is very close to the location of the draft treaty.

While this relative assessment of the coherence of the national positions provides an interesting comparative perspective, another one focuses on the relative positions of the domestic actors. This focus provides insight into the problems of EU constitution building in each country. Here we find three distinct patterns in the 25 subfigures (Table 30.4).

The first set of configurations is characterized by the fact that almost all domestic actors are located roughly on a line connecting the status quo and the draft treaty (row 1 in Table 30.4). The clearest illustration for this configuration is Ireland, where all domestic actors are located somewhere between the locations of the status quo and the draft. In this configuration it is obviously of prime importance whether particular domestic actors are located closer to the status quo than the draft treaty, which would suggest that they would prefer rejecting the constitution. Such examples appear most clearly in Estonia and Ireland. Both countries have immediately postponed their ratification processes after the negative referenda in France and the Netherlands in spring 2005.

The second configuration is characterized by the fact that all domestic actors are located at some distance above this connecting line. The prime examples are the Czech Republic and Latvia. In both of these countries the domestic actors appear to have defended positions quite different from the draft constitution. Again the question arises whether some domestic actors found themselves closer to the status quo than the draft treaty. In Poland all domestic actors are closer to the status quo than the draft treaty, while the picture is more diverse for Slovakia, Slovenia and the United Kingdom. Slovakia and Slovenia have already ratified the constitutional document, while it remains even unclear whether and when Poland and the United Kingdom will hold a referendum on the text.

Finally the third configuration has all domestic actors located roughly on the line linking the status quo and the draft treaty but beyond the location of the draft. This suggests that all domestic actors, though perhaps internally divided, prefer strongly the draft to the status quo. The clearest example for this configuration is France. But a whole set of other older members of the EU are in exactly the same configuration, suggesting that this is particularly an "old Europe" configuration. Until today, nine countries stopped their ratification processes, two "old" experienced negative referenda, while seventeen ratified the constitutional text.

Although these pictures provide insights into each country, these different patterns raise the question whether institutional, political and

Table 30.4 Configurations of domestic actors

Configuration	*Countries*	*n*
1	CY EE IE MA	4
2	CZ DK HU LV LI NL PL SV SL SW UK	11
3	AU BE FI FR DE EL IT LU PT ES	10

economic factors may explain the degree of cohesion in the domestic arena. The main difficulty for systematic analyses of these effects stems from our research design. For reliability purpose, we attempted to interview at least two experts in each member country, and the interviewers were asked to supplement the number of interviews, if there were many differences between experts on the assessment of the positions adopted by the various national actors. Consequently, we have a rather intricate relationship between the number of deviations among actors at the domestic level and the number of interviews. On the one hand the number of interviews is by design likely to be higher if domestic actors were of diverging opinion, but at the same time a more important number of expert interviews is likely to identify additional differences in opinion among domestic actors. While obviously econometric fixes exist for such problems of endogeneity, the very limited number of cases, namely 25, make using these fixes almost impossible. For this reason, we propose using as our starting point a simple model where the share of deviating positions between the national position and any other domestic actor is explained by the number of experts consulted.

In addition to this endogeneity problem, the distribution of the dependent variable, since it is a percentage, is bounded both from below and from above. In practice, it is mostly the bound at 0 which causes problems, since the distribution is heavily left-skewed with several countries having 0 percent deviations. Such 0 deviations clearly signal a very low level of domestic conflict, but it might be argued that even in these countries some minimal amount of conflict existed. If we can assume this, then we can employ a simple tobit model, where observations with 0 deviations are assumed to be left-censored. Thus, for all analyses reported below, we report both the estimated coefficients from a simple OLS and those of a tobit model.

As discussed above our starting model includes as single independent variable the number of experts interviewed in a given country. Columns 2 and 3 in Table 30.5 report the respective results for the OLS and tobit model. Not surprisingly we find a positive effect of the number of experts interviewed on the percentage of deviations from the national positions. According to the simple OLS model we would predict for each additional expert interviewed an increase in the percentage of deviating positions by roughly 2 percent. The tobit model, assuming that there is an underlying latent dimension of conflict, suggests an even bigger effect.

As the discussion in the individual country chapters suggests, institutions, economic and political factors may explain the amount of divergence in opinions regarding the draft treaty. Hence, a first hypothesis we wish to test is whether the institutional context affects the amount of divergence. For this we employ three different measures, namely on the one hand the presence or absence of a federal system, the presence of bicameralism, and a compound measure developed by Henisz (2002) called political constraints. The results of the various models we estimated with these three variables measuring institutions are rather disappointing. While we observe a negative effect both for federalism and bicameralism on the percentage of deviating opinions among domestic actors, these are substantively rather small given the dichotomous nature of these variables. Interesting to note is that the effect of political constraints is positive and rather large, even though the scale of this variable is rather small. In addition, we can estimate the true effect only with considerable imprecision.

Hence, our conclusion must be that institutions hardly affected the divergences of opinions among domestic actors. Interestingly enough results in analyses not reported here, also show that economic variables, like inflation, unemployment and growth rates hardly affect the preference formation process. Columns 11 and 12 of Table 30.5 suggest, however, another political factor which appears to be quite crucial. Using aggregated results from opinion surveys we find that the percentage of respondents finding the EU a good thing, heavily depresses the amount of divergence among domestic actors. This result holds up if we control for the difference between new and old member states and also when introducing the other independent variables used in Table 30.5.

These results raise the issue why public opinion seems to have affected more strongly the divisions in the preference formation process than institutional features and economic factors. Is the constitution a symbolic proposal which attracts public contestation but hardly affects political and economic cleavages? Concerning the absence of effects of the latter on the divisiveness of the domestic preference formation process the explanation can be largely found in the content of the proposed EU constitution. Consequently, the proposed text, by largely consolidating the preexisting treaties and proposing innovations mostly in the realm of institutions, could hardly lead to domestic conflicts as a function of the prevailing economic conditions.

While the lacking effects of domestic conditions are likely to find their explanation in the content of the EU constitution, the absence of effects by institutions is very likely related to the process leading up to the document adopted at the IGC in 2004. The setup of the Convention already allowed different views to be expressed from each member state and already represented institutional variety. More precisely, countries with bicameralism and more important political constraints had the opportunity to send to the European Convention apart from a government representative two delegates from the national parliament. Most governments chose in that case to send a delegate each from governmental and opposition parties. Similarly, with respect to the regional representation in federal countries, delegates from the Committee of Regions were likely to express their views in the European Convention. Thus it seems that the Convention method by associating particular stakeholders in the constitution-building process related to the domestic institutions allowed to

Table 30.5 Explaining deviating positions among domestic actors

	ols b (*s.e.*)	*tobit b* (*s.e.*)	*ols b* (*s.e.*)	*tobit b* (*s.e.*)	*ols b* (*s.e.*)	*tobit b* (*s.e.*)	*ols b* (*s.e.*)	*tobit b* (*s.e.*)	*ols b* (*s.e.*)	*tobit b* (*s.e.*)	*ols b* (*s.e.*)	*tobit b* (*s.e.*)
No. of experts	2.22	3.24	2.32	3.38	2.44	3.36	2.08	3.02	2.27	3.02	1.50	2.37
	(1.18)	(1.57)	(1.22)	(1.58)	(1.25)	(1.60)	(1.24)	(1.60)	(1.32)	(1.63)	(1.15)	(1.45)
Federalism	–	–	−1.98	−2.55	−0.89	−2.76	–	–	−1.87	−5.25	–	–
	–	–	(3.71)	(4.68)	(4.19)	(5.15)	–	–	(4.76)	(5.79)	–	–
Bicameralism	–	–	–	–	−1.86	0.39	–	–	−1.32	1.87	–	–
	–	–	–	–	(3.10)	(3.80)	–	–	(3.37)	(4.14)	–	–
Political constraints (2002)	–	–	–	–	–	–	6.90	11.58	8.31	20.58	–	–
	–	–	–	–	–	–	(15.37)	(18.94)	(17.92)	(21.87)	–	–
Public opinion	–	–	–	–	–	–	–	–	–	–	−30.69	−31.49
(share EU good)	–	–	–	–	–	–	–	–	–	–	(13.23)	(15.91)
New member country	–	–	–	–	–	–	–	–	–	–	−1.95	−2.66
	–	–	–	–	–	–	–	–	–	–	(2.68)	(3.30)
Constant	−0.17	−4.66	−0.15	−4.66	0.24	−4.78	−3.08	−9.62	−3.38	−14.06	24.65	21.64
	(3.61)	(4.95)	(3.66)	(4.91)	(3.77)	(5.07)	(7.46)	(9.58)	(8.70)	(11.30)	(11.31)	(13.65)
Se	–	8.10	–	8.04	–	8.06	–	8.05	–	8.00	–	7.26
	–	(1.42)	–	(1.41)	–	(1.43)	–	(1.41)	–	(1.41)	–	(1.28)
See	43.74	–	45.14	–	46.50	–	45.31	–	48.30	–	38.13	
Llik	–	−68.96	–	−68.81	–	−68.80	–	−68.77	–	−68.35	–	−67.19
N	25	25	25	25	25	25	25	25	25	25	25	25

reduce divisions inside government, once the Convention submitted their proposals to the member state governments.

This explanation for the lacking effects of domestic institutions on the preference formation process suggests, however, a rather plausible explanation for why public opinion has such a strong effect on whether a government was divided in the preference formation process. First of all, this suggests that the Convention method, despite being touted as a much more democratic process than an IGC, has hardly allowed for direct influences of public opinion. Since ten member countries announced more or less in parallel to the preference formation processes discussed in this book referendums on the proposed EU constitution (e.g., Hug and Schulz 2005), it appears that only in this late stage of the process did governmental actors become aware of public opinion. Given the struggles in particular countries whether or not to hold a referendum (e.g., in France, Belgium, Czech Republic, Poland), it should hardly surprise that these struggles are related to divisions in governments. Thus, this effect of public opinion seems to indicate that the Convention method was hardly able to address divisions due to domestic citizen-level concerns, and that concern for these issues led to divisions in the governmental preference formation process rather late in the day, most likely also linked to the announcement of the ten referendums on the EU constitution. This may explain why an unprecedented number of ten referendums were announced, although the Convention was established to increase transparency and legitimacy of the constitution-building process.

Conclusion

The IGC in Brussels of June 2004 concluded one of the most involved processes of negotiation and preference formation the member countries of the European Union had ever experienced. Even though a large part of the EU constitution simply consolidates the pre-existing treaties, several innovations appeared in the new text. Many of these innovations figured prominently among the vital issues that the domestic actors saw in the new treaty. While a whole host of different issues were flagged as vital by some countries, especially the institutional innovations clearly created the potential for a stumbling block in the negotiations.

The theoretical and empirical analysis of the European Convention revealed that the new method helped to set the reform agenda but it could neither settle the conflicts among member states nor increase legitimacy of the new treaty on the constitution. This points to the importance of the domestic preference formation processes in the 25 countries and their inclusive nature in forming national positions. The preference formation process in most EU member countries was led by the prime minister's office and the ministry for foreign affairs. Despite this leadership at the senior level of the respective cabinets, we found quite some differences of opinion in government in the various countries. The comparative examination showed three distinct patterns of countries, two of them raising concerns of the success of the constitution-building process. Interestingly enough the degree of cohesion in opinions was unrelated to any economic and institutional differences we studied in this chapter. We found, however, that a public opinion clearly supporting the EU integration process depresses considerably the amount of divergent opinion.

We were also able to show that the divergences in opinion among the governmental actors did not have detrimental effects on the various national positions. Clearly, there were differences that did not matter, for instance the divergent view points in the Belgian government, whose actors all clearly favored the EU constitution. On the other hand, in some other countries like Denmark, the divergent views may have been more significant. In countries like this, we find that some domestic actors seem to have preferred the current set of treaties to the draft proposal. In these countries it will be interesting to assess whether the ratification process will show similar divisions or not. This analysis showed that the concern for some vital issues led to divisions in the governmental preference formation process rather late in the day, most likely also linked to the announcement of the ten referendums on the EU constitution. Whether the constitution will survive, whether the remaining countries will continue to ratify the treaty, and how France and the Netherlands will then react on this process remains an open question. However, our analyses surprisingly indicate that a constitutional solution would be possible, as long as the actors consider the Nice Treaty as the reference for the status quo.

Acknowledgments

We gratefully appreciate the research assistance by Stephanie Daimer and Annika Raudonat, as well as the financial support by the European Commission, the Swiss Bundesamt für Bildung und Wissenschaft (grant No. BBW 02.0313) and the Grundlagenforschungsfonds of the University of St Gallen (grant No. G12161103).

Notes

1 Given the focus on national domestic institutions in what follows, we will refrain from discussing the European Parliament and Commission in the sections that follow.

2 Hug and Schulz (2005) discuss the approach chosen here in more detail.

3 Martin and Quinn (2004) provide an implementation in *R*.

4 Jackman (2004) argues that the mean of the posterior distribution can be interpreted as the maximum-likelihood estimate under the assumption of uninformative priors.

Appendix 1

Questions employed and results of factor analysis

Question		λ_1 *(s.e.)*	Λ_3 *(s.e.)*	λ_3 *(s.e.)*
Q1	Charter of Fundamental Rights	1.644	−0.112	0.085
		(0.192)	(0.316)	(0.385)
Q2	Subsidiarity	1.794	0.021	0.146
		(0.216)	(0.384)	(0.349)
Q3	Religious reference	0.240	−0.054	0.120
		(0.121)	(0.300)	(0.325)
Q4	Right to withdraw from the Union	0.503	−0.125	−0.021
		(0.126)	(0.303)	(0.305)
Q5a	Market economy	2.278	−0.203	−0.032
		(0.296)	(0.480)	(0.480)
Q5b	Employment	1.658	−0.066	0.203
		(0.191)	(0.465)	(0.485)
Q5c	Competitiveness	1.969	−0.403	−0.126
		(0.347)	(1.015)	(0.955)
Q6	Presidency of the European Council	0.800	−0.142	0.172
		(0.144)	(0.456)	(0.548)
Q7	Election of the Council president	−0.756	0.208	0.148
		(0.151)	(0.629)	(0.534)
Q8	QMV	0.788	−0.185	0.146
		(0.148)	(0.469)	(0.581)
Q9	Number of commissioners	−0.167	−0.378	−0.073
		(0.163)	(0.866)	(0.847)
Q10	Appointment of Commission president	−0.887	0.040	0.098
		(0.138)	(0.301)	(0.260)
Q11	Appointment of commissioners	0.111	−0.346	0.116
		(0.160)	(0.751)	(0.883)
Q12	External representation	2.211	−0.095	0.064
		(0.284)	(0.251)	(0.306)
Q13a	Appointment of Foreign Minister	1.488	−0.084	0.117
		(0.185)	(0.335)	(0.380)
Q13b	Additional approval by the EP	−0.525	0.241	0.032
		(0.143)	(0.557)	(0.551)

continued

Question		λ_1 *(s.e.)*	Λ_3 *(s.e.)*	λ_3 *(s.e.)*
Q14	ECJ jurisdiction	1.040	0.085	0.182
		(0.152)	(0.507)	(0.415)
Q15.2	European Parliament	−1.700	0.362	0.257
		(0.271)	(1.091)	(0.922)
Q15.3	Council	−1.248	0.062	−0.060
		(0.152)	(0.266)	(0.294)
Q15.4	National parliaments	−2.590	0.155	−0.021
		(0.415)	(0.561)	(0.593)
Q15.5	Citizens	−0.374	−0.128	−0.001
		(0.128)	(0.318)	(0.331)
Q16	Enhanced cooperations	3.702	−0.852	0.082
		(0.516)	(1.790)	(2.010)
Q17.1	Agriculture	1.243	−0.011	0.089
		(0.146)	(0.232)	(0.235)
Q17.2	Structural and cohesion policies	1.888	0.002	0.092
		(0.210)	(0.261)	(0.242)
Q17.3	Area of freedom, security and justice	2.295	−0.298	0.058
		(0.286)	(0.667)	(0.760)
Q17.4	Foreign policy	0.457	−0.348	0.098
		(0.169)	(0.745)	(0.873)
Q17.5	Economic policy	2.710	−0.149	0.265
		(0.379)	(0.632)	(0.722)
Q17.6	Tax harmonization	2.782	−0.159	0.298
		(0.378)	(0.710)	(0.797)
Q17.7	Employment policy	2.842	0.047	0.264
		(0.409)	(0.659)	(0.573)
Q17.8	Social policy	2.298	−0.187	0.268
		(0.283)	(0.669)	(0.797)
Q17.9	Health	2.561	−0.234	0.081
		(0.363)	(0.512)	(0.611)
Q17.10	Environment	−0.838	0.038	0.247
		(0.155)	(0.620)	(0.536)
Q17.11	Education	2.553	0.002	0.167
		(0.376)	(0.406)	(0.385)
Q17.12	Research, technological development	0.220	−0.273	0.064
	and space	(0.144)	(0.582)	(0.677)
Q18a.2	Structural and cohesion policies	1.337	−0.129	0.005
		(0.168)	(0.348)	(0.368)
Q18a.3	Area of freedom, security and justice	0.500	−0.213	0.039
		(0.136)	(0.486)	(0.545)
Q18a.4	Internal market	2.319	−0.157	0.219
		(0.368)	(0.667)	(0.781)
Q18a.5	Tax harmonization	−0.197	−0.653	0.156
		(0.234)	(1.388)	(1.620)
Q18a.6	Monetary policy (for the euro states)	1.079	−0.203	0.308
		(0.202)	(0.786)	(0.921)
Q18a.7	Economic policy	1.042	−0.160	0.320
		(0.196)	(0.766)	(0.867)
Q18a.8	Employment policy	1.515	−0.169	0.256
		(0.239)	(0.678)	(0.796)

Question		λ_1 *(s.e.)*	Λ_3 *(s.e.)*	λ_3 *(s.e.)*
Q18a.9	Social policy	0.662	−0.366	0.056
		(0.175)	(0.775)	(0.869)
Q18a.10	Social security rights	0.019	−0.474	0.507
		(0.240)	(1.366)	(1.708)
Q18a.11	Common foreign policy	−0.055	−0.422	0.123
		(0.178)	(0.906)	(1.075)
Q18a.12	Defense policy	−1.667	−0.843	0.332
		(0.372)	(1.768)	(2.164)
Q18b.1	Agriculture	0.843	0.262	0.171
		(0.161)	(0.754)	(0.637)
Q18b.2	Structural and cohesion policies	1.360	0.122	0.244
		(0.187)	(0.707)	(0.587)
Q18b.3	Area of freedom, security and justice	0.530	−0.034	0.245
		(0.144)	(0.575)	(0.562)
Q18b.4	Internal market	2.167	0.240	0.652
		(0.409)	(1.728)	(1.449)
Q18b.5	Tax harmonization	−0.136	−0.400	0.847
		(0.302)	(1.964)	(2.230)
Q18b.6	Monetary policy (for the Euro states)	0.317	0.263	0.705
		(0.254)	(1.858)	(1.523)
Q18b.7	Economic policy	0.191	0.791	1.104
		(0.413)	(3.375)	(2.658)
Q18b.8	Employment policy	0.978	0.120	0.719
		(0.279)	(1.747)	(1.533)
Q18b.9	Social policy	0.718	0.006	0.394
		(0.185)	(0.920)	(0.864)
Q18b.10	Social security rights	−0.274	0.211	0.632
		(0.230)	(1.621)	(1.359)
Q18b.11	Common foreign policy	−2.734	0.125	0.818
		(0.552)	(1.942)	(1.692)
Q18b.12	Defense policy	−2.737	0.130	0.799
		(0.544)	(1.936)	(1.701)
Q19	Budgetary rights of the EP	0.350	−0.051	0.083
		(0.119)	(0.234)	(0.268)
Q20	Stability and Growth Pact I	−0.137	0.057	−0.034
		(0.115)	(0.178)	(0.207)
Q21	Stability and Growth Pact II	0.522	−0.118	0.011
		(0.126)	(0.288)	(0.311)
Q22	Defense	1.247	−0.803	0.129
		(0.303)	(1.664)	(1.894)
Q23	External borders	1.322	−0.158	0.020
		(0.162)	(0.351)	(0.381)
Q24	Migration and asylum	0.863	−0.518	−0.083
		(0.208)	(1.158)	(1.166)

Appendix 2

The measure of adapted coherence for the evaluation of experts

With respect to the comparability of the expert coherence across countries and actors we face the following problem. The number of experts differs between actors (and countries). A different number of experts naturally results in a different ex-ante probability of complete coherence, since if we only interviewed one expert we have an ex-ante probability of complete coherence equal to 1. Therefore the measure of adapted coherence (AC) is based on the following calculation. First we calculated the theoretical probability for all experts to agree with the most competent expert (TC) as a function of possible answers (c) to question i, the number of questions (n) and the number of experts (e):

$$TC = \frac{\sum_{i=1}^{n} (1/c_i)^{(e_i - 1)}}{n}$$

In case we are interested in the coherence at the level of entire countries n is the number of questions times the number of actors. Second, we adjusted the empirical coherence EC which reveals the percentage of times the experts made identical statements divided by 100 ($EC \in \{0;1\}$) using the theoretical probability for coherence: $AC = EC^{(TC/EC)}$.

Bibliography

Agapiou-Josephides, K. (2004) "Old and New Patterns of Domestic Politics in the European Perspective: the Debate in the Republic of Cyprus," *South European Society and Politics*, 9 (1): 152–72.

—— (2003) "The Political System of Cyprus at the Threshold of the European Union: Patterns of Continuity, Change, and Adaptation," in G.P. Xuereb (ed.) *Euro-Med Integration and the "Ring of Friends": The Mediterranean's European Challenge*, Vol. IV, University of Malta: European Documentation and Research Center.

Ágh, A. and Rózsád, Á. (2004) "Managing Europe from Home: The Europeanisation of Hungarian Core Executive," paper presented at the Final Plenary Conference: "The Challenge of EU Enlargement: Managing EU Business and Policy Implementation," Institute of European Affairs, Dublin, Ireland, September.

Agresti, T. and Finlay, B. (1997) *Statistical Methods for the Social Sciences*, Upper Saddle River: Prentice Hall.

Andeweg, R.B. (1991) "The Dutch Prime Minister: Not Just Chairman, Not Yet Chief?" *West European Politics*, 14: 116–32.

Archer, C. and Nugent, N. (2002) Special Issue on Small States and the European Union, *Current Politics and Economics of Europe*, 11 (1).

Armingeon, K. and Careja, R. (2004) "Comparative Data Set for 28 Post-Communist Countries, 1989–2004," Institute of Political Science: University of Berne. Online. Available at: www.ipw.unibe.ch/mitarbeiter/ru_armingeon/CPD_Set_en.asp (accessed July 2004).

Armingeon, K., Leimgruber, P., Beyeler, M. and Menegale, S. (2004) "Comparative Political Data Set 1960–2002," Institute of Political Science: University of Berne. Online. Available at: www.ipw.unibe.ch/mitarbeiter/ru_armingeon/CPD_Set_en.asp (accessed July 2004).

Auers, D. (2003) "Latvia's 2002 Elections – Dawn of a New Era?" *East European Constitutional Review*, 11 (4)–12 (1): 106–10.

Auffermann, B. (2003) "Das politische System Finnlands," in W. Ismayr (ed.) *Die politischen System Westeuropas*, Opladen: Leske + Budrich.

Aylott, N. (2002) "Let's discuss this later: Party responses to Euro-division in Scandinavia," *Party Politics*, 8 (4): 441–61.

Bárány, E., Brhlíková, R. and Colotka, P. (2001) "Slovakia," in A. Auer and A. Bützer (eds) *Direct Democracy: The Eastern and Central European Experience*, Aldershot: Ashgate.

Benedetto, G. (forthcoming 2006) "Explaining the Failure of Euroscepticism in the

European Parliament," in A. Szczerbiak and P. Taggart (eds) *Opposing Europe: The Comparative Party Politics of Euroscepticism*, Oxford: Oxford University Press.

Benoit, K. and Hayden, J. (2004) "Institutional Change and Persistence: The Evolution of Poland's Electoral System, 1989–2001," *Journal of Politics*, 66 (2): 396–427.

Bilčík, V. (2003) "National report Slovakia," in C. Franck and D. Pyszna-Nigge (eds) Positions of 10 Central and Eastern European countries on EU institutional reforms. Analytical survey in the framework of the CEEC-debate project. Louvain-la-Neuve/Brussels: Université catholique de Louvain. Online. Available at: www.euro.ucl.ac.be.

Blavoukos, S. and Pagoulatos, G. (2003) "A Medium Country's Middle-of-the-Road Success: The 2003 Greek Presidency of the European Union," *South European Society and Politics*, 8 (3): 147–64.

Blondel, J. and Müller-Rommel, F. (eds) (2001) *Cabinets in Eastern Europe*, Basingstoke and New York: Palgrave Macmillan.

Braga de Macedo, J. (2003) "Portugal's European Integration: The Good Student with a Bad Fiscal Constitution," *South European Society and Politics*, 8 (1–2): 169–94.

Bräuninger, T. and König, T. (1999) "The Checks and Balances of Party Federalism," *European Journal of Political Research*, 36 (2): 207–34.

Brewin, C. (2000) *The EU and Cyprus*, London: Eothen.

Brinar, I. (2005) "Slovenia," in J. Lodge (ed.) *The 2004 Elections to the European Parliament*, Basingstoke: Palgrave Macmillan.

Brown, T. (2003) "The Future of Europe Convention: into the last months," 8th meeting of EPIN on the Future of Europe Debate, Institute of European Affairs, 15 March. Online. Available at: www.epin.org/pdf/debate_ireland2.pdf (accessed 10 February 2005).

Bucar, B. and Brinar, I. (2005) "Slovenia – Political Transformation and European Integration," in A. Skuhra (ed.) *The Eastern Enlargement of the European Union, Efforts and Obstacles on the Way to Membership*, Vienna: Studien Verlag.

Bulmer, S. and Paterson, W.E. (1996) "Germany in the European Union: Gentle Giant or Emergent Leader?" *International Affairs*, 1: 10 ff.

Bulmer, S., Maurer, A. and Paterson, W.E. (2002) "Das Entscheidungs- und Koordinationssystem deutscher Europapolitik. Hindernis für eine neue Politik?" in H. Schneider *et al.* (eds) *Eine Neue Deutsche Europapolitik? Rahmenbedingungen, Problemfelder, Optionen*, Bonn: Europa Union Verlag.

Calise, M. (1994) "The Italian Particracy: Beyond President and Parliament," *Political Science Quarterly*, 109: 441–60 (Special Issue).

Calleya, S.C. (1999) "Early Elections in Malta," *Mediterranean Politics*, 4 (1): 113–18.

Cameron, D.R. (1992) "The 1992 Initiative: Causes and Consequences," in A. Sbragia (ed.) *Euro-politics*, Washington DC: Brookings.

Carrubba, C. (1997) "Net Financial Transfer in the European Union: Who gets What and Why?" *Journal of Politics*, 59 (2): 469–96.

Chari, R.S. (2004a) "State Aids in the Airline Sector: A Comparative Analysis of Iberia and Aer Lingus," Dublin: Policy Institute.

—— (2004b) "The 2004 Spanish Election: Terrorism as a Catalyst for Change?" *West European Politics*, 27 (5): 954–63.

——, Egea-de Haro, A., Benoit, K. and Laver, M. (2004) "Spain and EU Constitution building?" Working paper 2004/17. Real Instituto Elcano.

Christiansen, T. (2002) "The Role of Supranational Actors in EU Treaty Reform," *Journal of European Public Policy*, 9: 33–53.

Christou, G. (2003) "European Union Enlargement and the Solution of the 'Cyprus issue': Creating a Climate for Change," *Agora without Frontiers*, 8 (4): 383–403.

Cini, M. (2003) "Malta Votes Twice for Europe: The Accession Referendum and General Election, March/April 2003," *South European Society and Politics*, 8 (3): 132–46.

—— (2002) "A Divided Nation: Polarization and the Two-party System in Malta," *South European Society and Politics*, 7 (1): 6–23.

—— (2000) "The Europeanization of Malta: Adaptation, Identity and Party Politics," *South European Society and Politics*, 5 (2): 261–76.

Closa, C. (2005) "Why Convening Referendums? Explaining Decisions in EU Constitutional Politics," paper prepared for the ECPR Joint Sessions of Workshops, Granada, 14–18 April.

Coakley, J. and Gallagher, M. (eds) (2005) *Politics in the Republic of Ireland*, 4th edn, London: Routledge.

Corkill, D. (1999) *The Development of the Portuguese Economy: A Case of Europeanization*, London: Routledge.

Criscitiello, A. (1993) "Majority Summits: Decision-making inside the Cabinet and out: Italy, 1970–1990," *West European Politics*, 16: 581–94.

Crombez, C. (1997) "The Codecision Procedure in the European Union," *Legislative Studies Quarterly*, 22: 97–119.

—— (1996) "Legislative Procedure in the European Community," *British Journal of Political Science*, 26: 199–228.

—— and Hix, S. (2004) "Government–Opposition in the EU: Implications of EU Treaty Reforms for Commission Preferences and EU Policies," unpublished manuscript.

——, Steunenberg, B. and Corbett, R. (2000) "Understanding the EU Legislative Process," *European Union Politics*, 1: 363–81.

Csaba, L. (2002) "The Future of the EU: a Post-Laeken Perspective," Transformation, Integration and Globalisation Economic Research Working Paper, Warsaw, 21 July. Online. Available at: www.tiger.edu.pl (accessed 17 October 2004).

Cuntz, E. (2003) "Ein ausgewogener Gesamtkompromiss. Die Ergebnisse des Konvents aus Sicht der Bundesregierung," *Integration*, 26 (4): 351–6.

Daalder, H. *et al.* (2003) *Compendium voor politiek en samenleving in Nederland*, Dordrecht: Kluwer.

Dahl, R.A. (1971) *Polyarchy. Participation and Opposition*, New Haven: Yale University Press.

Dassù, M., Grassi, V. and Verola, N. (2003) "The European Convention: Unresolved Questions and Choices for Italy," paper prepared for the International Conference Aspen European Dialogue, Rome, 28 February–1 March.

Dauderstädt, M. (2004) "Transformation und Integration der Wirtschaft der postkommunistischen Beitrittsländer," *Aus Politik und Zeitgeschichte*, 5: 15–24.

Demetriou, M. (1998) "On the Long Road to Europe and the Short Path to War: Issue Linkage Politics and the Arms Build-up on Cyprus," *Mediterranean Politics*, 3 (3): 38–51.

Diamandouros, P.N. (1997) "Greek Politics and Society in the 1990s," in G.T.

Allison and K. Nicolaidis (eds) *The Greek Paradox: Promise vs. Performance*, Cambridge MA: MIT Press.

—— (1993) "Politics and Culture in Greece, 1974–91: An Interpretation," in R. Clogg (ed.) *Greece, 1981–89: The Populist Decade*, Basingstoke: Macmillan.

Dinan, D. (2004) "Governance and Institutions: The Convention and the Intergovernmental Conference," *Journal of Common Market Studies*, 42: 27–42.

—— (2002) "Institutions and Governance, 2001–02: Debating the EU's Future," *Journal of Common Market Studies*, 40 (1) (Supplement): 29–44.

—— (2000) "France," in Dinan (ed.) *Encyclopedia of the European Union*, London: Macmillan.

—— (1999) *Ever closer Union: An Introduction to European Integration*, Basingstoke: Macmillan.

Donovan, M. (1995) "The politics of electoral reform in Italy," *International Political Science Review*, 16: 47–64.

Earnshaw, D. and Judge, D. (1996) "From co-operation to co-decision: The European Parliament's path to legislative power," in J.J. Richardson (ed.) *European Union: Power and Policy-making*, London: Routledge.

Edwards, G. and Spence, D. (eds) (1994) *The European Commission*, London: Catermill Publishing.

Egea-de Haro, A. and Ruiz-Jimenez, M.A. (2005) "Spanish Political Elites: Ideological Preferences over the European Union," in M.A. Ruiz-Jimenez and J.I. Torreblanca Payá, *Una España Europea: elite y ciudadanos españoles entre la nación y Europa*, unpublished manuscript.

Ehin, P. (2003a) "Country-by-Country Update: Estonia," *East European Constitutional Review*, 12: 20–3.

—— (2003b) "Estonian Euroskepticism: A Reflection of Domestic Politics?" *East European Constitutional Review*, 11: 96–100.

—— and Veebel, V. (2003) "Answers to the UCL/TEPSA Questionnaire – Estonia," unpublished.

Elgie, R. (1999) "The Politics of Semi-presidentialism," in R. Elgie (ed.) *Semi-presidentialism in Europe*, Oxford: Oxford University Press.

Evriviades, M. and Bourantonis, D. (1994) "Peacekeeping and Peacemaking: Some Lessons from Cyprus," *International Peacekeeping*, 1 (4): 394–412.

Fabbrini, Sergio (2004) "When a pigmy acts as a giant: the role of the Italian representatives in the Brussels constitutional convention," *Modern Italy*, 9: 233–45.

Falkner, G. (2000) "How Pervasive are Euro-politics? Effects of EU Membership on a New Member State," *Journal of Common Market Studies*, 38: 223–50.

Faria, F. (1999) "The Making of Portugal's Mediterranean Policy," in S. Stavridis, T. Couloumbis, T. Veremis and N. Waites (eds) *The Foreign Policies of the EU's Mediterranean and Applicant Countries in the 1990s*, London: Macmillan.

Fatouros, A.A. (1993) "Political and Institutional Facets of Greece's Integration in the European Community," in H.G. Psomiades and S. Thomadakis (eds) *Greece, the New Europe and the Changing International Order*, New York: Pella Publishing.

Featherstone, K. (2003) "Greece and EMU: Between External Empowerment and Domestic Vulnerability," *Journal of Common Market Studies*, 41 (5): 923–40.

—— (2000) "Cyprus and the Onset of Europeanization: Strategic Usage, Structural Transformation and Institutional Adaptation," *South European Society and Politics*, 5 (2): 141–62.

—— (1998) "'Europeanization' and the Centre–Periphery: The Case of Greece in the 1990s," *South European Society and Politics*, 3 (1): 23–39.

—— (1994) "Political Parties," in P. Kazakos and P.C. Ioakimidis (eds) *Greece and EC Membership Evaluated*, London: Pinter and New York: St Martin's Press.

—— and Ifantis, K. (eds) (1996) *Greece in a Changing Europe: between European integration and Balkan disintegration?* Manchester: Manchester University Press.

Feldstein, M. (1997) "EMU and International Conflict," *Foreign Affairs*, 76 (6): 60–73.

Ferrara, F. and Weishaupt, T. (2004) "'Get Your act together.' Party Performance in European Parliament Elections," *European Union Politics*, 5: 283–306.

Gabel, M. (2000) "European Integration, voters and national politics," *West European Politics*, 23: 52–72.

Gallagher, M., Laver, M. and Mair, P. (2006) *Representative Government in Modern Europe*, 4th edn, London: McGraw-Hill.

Garrett, G. (1992) "International Cooperation and Institutional Choice: The European Community's Internal Market," *International Organization*, 56: 533–69.

—— and Tsebelis, G. (1996) "An Institutional Critique of Intergovernmentalism," *International Organization*, 50: 269–99.

Grassi, M. (2003) "Bipolarismus des Parteiensystems?" in B. Rill (ed.) *Italien im Aufbruch – eine Zwischenbilanz*, Munich: Hanns Seidel Stiftung.

Gray, M. and Stubb, A. (2001) "The Treaty of Nice – Negotiating a Poisoned Chalice?" *Journal of Common Market Studies*, 39 (1) (Supplement): 5–23.

Guerra Martins, A.M. (2002) "Portugal and the Treaty of Nice: the Fight against the 'Big Ones'," paper presented in the Conference on the Treaty of Nice, Centre for European Studies, University of Southern Denmark, Odense, 6–7 September.

Gunther, R., Puhle, H.J. and Diamandouros, P.N. (1995) "Introduction," in R. Gunther, H.J. Puhle and P.N. Diamandouros (eds) *The Politics of Democratic Consolidation: Southern Europe in Comparative Perspective*, Baltimore: Johns Hopkins University Press.

Gwiazda, A. (2005) "Europeanisation and Polish Competition Policy," unpublished PhD thesis, Trinity College, University of Dublin.

Gyáfášoá, O. (2003) "Slovakia heads for the EU: what was accomplished and what lies ahead" (Az Európai Tanulmányok (Európa 2002) Ročník IV), Bratislava: Institute of Public Affairs.

Hainsworth, P., O'Brien, C. and Mitchell, P. (2004) "Defending the Nation: The Politics of Euroscepticism on the French Right," *European Studies*, 20: 37–58.

Hanley, S. (2002a) "The Political Context of EU Accession in the Czech Republic," Briefing Paper, London: Royal Institute of International Affairs.

—— (2002b) "Europe and the Czech Parliamentary Elections of June," Election Briefing No. 5, London: Department of Politics, American Studies and History, Brunel University.

Hegedűs, I. (2004) "Political stereotypes in the Hungarian public culture and the mass media about the European Union," paper presented at the International Conference of Young Scholars "Communication in the Global World," Ljubljana, Slovenia, 12–14 November.

—— (2003) "After the Accession Talks, Facing the Referendum: Hungary and its Media Joining the European Union," paper presented at the workshop on Governance, Media and Enlargement, Robert Schuman Centre for Advanced Studies, Florence, Italy, 28 February–1 March.

Henisz, W.J. (2002) "The Institutional Environment for Infrastructure Investment," *Industrial and Corporate Change*, 11 (2): 355–89.

—— (2000) "The Institutional Environment for Multinational Investment," *Journal of Law, Economics and Organization*, 16: 334–64.

Herbut, R. (2000) "Parties and the Polish party system: The process of structuring the political space," in K. Cordell (ed.) *Poland and the European Union*, London and New York: Routledge.

Hine, D. (2004) "Explaining Italian Preferences at the Constitutional Convention," *Comparative European Politics*, 2: 302–19.

—— and Finocchi, R. (1991) "The Italian prime minister," *West European Politics*, 14: 79–96.

Hirczy, W. (1995) "Explaining Near Universal Turnout: the Case of Malta," *European Journal of Political Research*, 15 (2): 255–72.

Hix, S. (2003) "Britain, the EU and the Euro," in P. Dunleavy *et al.* (eds) *Developments in British Politics*, Basingstoke: Palgrave.

—— (2002) "Constitutional agenda-setting through Discretion in Rule Interpretation: Why the European Parliament won at Amsterdam," *British Journal of Political Science*, 32: 259–80.

Höhne, R. (2003) "Regieren in Italien. Wie durchsetzungsfähig ist die Regierung Berlusconi?" in B. Rill (ed.) *Italien im Aufbruch – eine Zwischenbilanz*, Munich: Hanns Seidel Stiftung.

Hosli, M. (1996) "Coalitions and Power: Effects of Qualified Majority Voting in the Council of the European Union," *Journal of Common Market Studies*, 34: 255–73.

Hug, S. and König, T. (2002) "In View of Ratification: Governmental Preferences and Domestic Constraints at the Amsterdam Intergovernmental Conference," *International Organization*, 56: 447–76.

Hug, S. and Schulz, T. (2005) "Using Mass Survey Data to Infer Political Positions," *European Union Politics*, 6 (3): 339–52.

Humphreys, M. and Garry, J. (2000) "Thinking about salience." Online. Available at: www.columbia.edu/~mh2245/papers1/salience.pdf (accessed 12 March 2004).

Huntington, S.P. (1991) *The Third Wave: Democratization in the Late Twentieth Century*, Norman: University of Oklahoma Press.

Iida, K. (1996) "Involuntary Defection in Two-level Games," *Public Choice*, 89 (2): 283–303.

Institute of European Affairs (2004) "Irish Presidency Issue No. 7," June, Dublin. Online. Available at: www.iiea.com (accessed 15 September 2004).

Institute of European Affairs (2003) "Convention Watch," No. 4, June, Dublin, Online. Available at: www.iiea.com.

Ioakimidis, P.C. (2001) *The Treaty of Nice and the Future of Europe*, Athens: Themelio (in Greek).

—— (2000) "The Europeanization of Greece: an Overall Assessment," *South European Society and Politics*, Special Issue on Europeanization and the Southern Periphery, 5 (2): 72–94.

—— (1999) "The Model of Foreign Policy-making in Greece: Personalities versus Institutions," in S. Stavridis, T. Couloumbis, T. Veremis and N. Waites (eds) *The Foreign Policies of the EU's Mediterranean and Applicant Countries in the 1990s*, London: Macmillan.

—— (1996) "Contradictions in the Europeanisation Process," in K. Featherstone and K. Ifantis (eds) *Greece in a Changing Europe: between European integration and Balkan disintegration?* Manchester: Manchester University Press.

—— (1993) "The Greek Administration and the Making of European Policy," in L. Tsoukalis (ed.) *Greece in the European Community: the Challenge of Adaptation*, Athens: Papazissis (in Greek).

Ismayr, W. (2004) "Die politischen Systeme der EU Beitrittsländer im Vergleich," *Aus Politik und Zeitgeschichte*, 5: 5–14.

Jabko, N. (2004) "The Importance of Being Nice: An Institutionalist Analysis of French Preferences on the Future of Europe," *Comparative European Politics*, 2: 282–301.

Jackman, S. (2004) "Bayesian Analysis for Political Research," *Annual Review of Political Science*, 7: 483–505.

Jauregui, P. (2002) "Spain: 'Europe' as a Symbol of Modern Democracy and Renewed International Prestige." Online. Available at: www.iue.it/RSCAS/Research/EURONAT/200204Spreport.pdf.

Johansson, K.M. (2003) "Sweden: another awkward partner?" in W. Wessels, A. Maurer and J. Mittag (eds) *Fifteen into One: The European Union and its Member States*, Manchester: Manchester University Press.

Joseph, S.J. (1997) *Cyprus: Ethnic Conflict and International Politics*, Basingstoke: Macmillan.

—— (1996) "Cyprus at the Threshold of the European Union," *Mediterranean Quarterly*, 7 (2): 112–22.

Katsourides, Y. (2003) "Europeanization and Political Parties in Accession Countries: the Political Countries of Cyprus," paper at EpsNet 2003 Plenary Conference, Paris, 13–14 June. Online. Available at: www.epsnet.org/publications/2003Proceedings/default.htm (accessed 25 March 2004).

Katzenstein, P.J. (ed.) (1997) *Tamed Power. Germany in Europe*, Ithaca: Cornell University Press.

Kipke, R. (2004) "Das politische System der Slowakei," in W. Ismayr (ed.) *Die politischen Systeme Osteuropas*, 2nd edn, Opladen: Leske + Budrich.

König, T. (forthcoming 2005) "The Dynamics of the Two-level Process of Constitution building," in M. Mokre (ed.) *The European Constitution* (working title), Vienna.

—— (2002) "Verfassungspolitik und Verfassungsdynamik," talk at the workshop "Expectations from a European Constitution" at the Heidelberger Akademie der Wissenschaften (in German), Karlsruhe, 21 October.

—— (2001) "Bicameralism and Party Politics in Germany: an Empirical Social Choice Analysis," *Political Studies*, 49: 411–37.

—— and Bräuninger, T. (2004) "Accession and Reform of the European Union. A Game Theoretical Analysis of Eastern Enlargement and Constitutional Reform," *European Union Politics*, 5 (4): 419–39.

—— and Bräuninger, T. (1999) "Finland auf dem Weg zum Mehrheitssystem? Eine vergleichende Analyse der politischen Willensbildung vor und nach den finnischen Verfassungsreformen der 90er Jahre," *Politische Viertelsjahresschrift*, 31: 40–64.

—— and Daimer, S. (2005) "Absolute and relative gains in European constitution building – and Why?" paper presented at the ECPR Joint Sessions of Workshops, Granada, 14–18 April.

—— and Finke, D. (2005) "Analyzing Delegates' Discretion in the Negotiations over a Constitution for Europe," paper prepared for presentation at the ECPR General Conference, Budapest, 8–11 September.

—— and Hug, S. (2000) "Ratifying Maastricht," *European Union Politics*, 1: 93–124.

——, Finke, D. and Daimer, S. (2005) "Ignoring the Non-ignorables: Missingness and Missing Positions," *European Union Politics*, 6 (3): 269–90.

——, Blume, T. and Luig, B. (2003) "Policy Change without Government Change? German Gridlock after the 2002 Elections," *German Politics*, 2: 86–146.

Kopecký, P. (2004) "An Awkward Newcomer? EU Enlargement and Eurocepticism in the Czech Republic," *European Studies*, 20: 247–68.

—— (2001) "Czech Republic: From the burden of the old federal constitution to the constitutional horse trading among political parties," in J. Zielonka (ed.) *Democratic consolidation in Eastern Europe*, Vol. 1, *Institutional Engineering*, New York: Oxford University Press.

Král, D. (2003a) "Czech non-paper on the institutional structure discussed by the convention on the future of Europe" (Comment, 10 February), Prague: EUROPEUM Institute for European Policy.

—— (2003b) "Questions over the future shape of Czech EU policies – a Czech cohabitation?" (Comment, May), Prague: EUROPEUM Institute for European Policy.

Krasovec, A. and Kustec-Lipicer, S. (2005) "Europe and the Parliamentary Elections in Slovenia, October 2004," EPERN Election Briefing 18. Online. Available at: www.sussex.ac.uk/sei/documents/epern_eb_18_slovenia.pdf.

Kreppel, A. (1997) "The impact of parties in government on legislative output in Italy," *European Journal of Political Research*, 31: 327–50.

Krotohvil, P. (2003) "National report Czech Republic," in C. Franck and D. Pyszna-Nigge (eds) Positions of 10 Central and Eastern European countries on EU institutional reforms. Analytical survey in the framework of the CEEC debate project. Louvain-la-Neuve and Brussels: Université catholique de Louvain. Online. Available at: www.euro.ucl.ac.be.

Kurpas, S., Incerti, M. and Schönlau, J. (2005) "What Prospects for the European Constitutional Treaty? Monitoring the Ratification Debates," European Policy Institutes Network (EPIN), Working Paper No. 12, January.

Kydland, F.E. and Prescott, E.C. (1977) "Rules rather than Discretion: The Inconsistency of Optimal Plans," *Journal of Political Economy*, 85: 473–91.

Laasko, M. and Taagepera, R. (1979) "Effective Number of Parties: A Measure with Application to West Europe," *Comparative Political Studies*, 12 (1): 3–27.

Laffan, B. and O'Mahony, J. (2003) "Managing Europe from home: The Europeanisation of the Irish Core Executive. Report on the Irish case study," Dublin European University, National University of Ireland. Online. Available at: www.oeue.net/papers/phaseicoreexecutivecasestudyi.pdf (accessed 15 September 2004).

Lagerspetz, M. and Mayer, K. (2004) "Das Politische System Estlands," in W. Ismayr (ed.) *Die politischen Systeme Osteuropas*, 2nd edn, Opladen: Leske + Budrich.

Lane, J.C. (2000) "A Survey of Elections in Malta, 1921–1998," in C. Vella *et al.* (eds) *The Maltese Islands on the Move*, Valletta: Central Office of Statistics Malta.

Laursen, F. (2003) "Denmark: in pursuit of influence and legitimacy," in W. Wessels, A. Maurer and J. Mittag (eds) *Fifteen into One: The European Union and its Member States*, Manchester: Manchester University Press.

—— (ed.) (2002) *The Amsterdam Treaty*, Odense: Odense University Press.

—— and Vanhoonacker, S. (eds) (1994) *Ratification of the Maastricht Treaty: Issues, Debate and Future Implications*, Dordrecht: Nijhoff.

Laver, M. (2001) "Position and salience in the policies of political actors," in M. Laver (ed.) *Estimating the Policy Positions of Political Actors*, London: Routledge.

Linek, L. (2003) "Czech Republic," *European Journal of Political Research*, 42: 916–30 (Political Data Yearbook 2001).

Lijphart, A. (1999) *Patterns of Democracy: Government Forms and Performance in Thirty-six Countries*, New Haven: Yale University Press.

—— (1980) *Democracy in Plural Societies: A Comparative Exploration*, New Haven: Yale University Press.

Lobo, C.M. (2003) "Portuguese Attitudes towards EU Membership: Social and Political Perspectives," *South European Society and Politics*, 8 (1–2): 97–118.

Luif, P. (2003) "Austria: Burdens of History," in J.A.K. Hay (ed.) *Small States in World Politics: Explaining Foreign Policy Behaviour*, Boulder: Lynne Rienner Publishers.

—— (1998) "Austria: Adaptation through Anticipation," in K. Hanf and B. Soetendorp (ed.) *Adaptation to European Integration: Small States and the European Union*, London and New York: Longman.

Magone, J.M. (2000a) "Portugal," in I. Manners and R.G. Whitman (eds) *The Foreign Policies of European Union Member States*, Manchester: Manchester University Press.

—— (2000b) "Portugal," in H. Kassim, G. Peters and V. Wright (eds) *The National Coordination of EU Policy: The Domestic Level*, Oxford: Oxford University Press.

Makrydimitris, A. and Passas, A. (1994) *The Greek Administration and the Coordination of the European Policy*, Athens: Sakkoulas (in Greek).

Malová, D. (2001) "Slovakia: From the ambiguous constitution to the dominance of informal rules," in J. Zielonka (ed.) *Democratic consolidation in Eastern Europe*, Vol. 1, *Institutional Engineering*, New York: Oxford University Press.

Marques-Mendes, A.J. (1993) "The Development of the Portuguese Economy in the Context of the EC," in J. da Silva Lopes (ed.) *Portugal and EC Membership Evaluated*, London: Pinter.

Martinez Martinez, R. (1999) "Semi-presidentialism: A Comparative Study," paper prepared for presentation at the ECPR Joint Sessions of Workshops, Mannheim.

Mattila, M. (2004) "Contested decisions: Empirical analysis of voting in the European Union Council of Ministers," *European Journal of Political Research*, 43: 29–50.

—— (2003) "Why Bother? Determinants of Turnout in the European Elections," *Electoral Studies*, 22 (3): 449–68.

—— (1997) "From Qualified Majority to Simple Majority: The Effects of the 1992 Change in the Finnish Constitution," *Comparative Politics*, 20: 331–45.

Maurer, A. (2003a) "Schließt sich der Kreis? Der Konvent, nationale Vorbehalte und die Regierungskonferenz. Teil I," SWP Working Paper. Online. Available at: www.swp-berlin.org/pdf/brennpunkte/eukonvregkonfanalyse01.pdf (accessed 7 June 2003).

—— (2003b) "Germany: fragmented structures in a complex system," in W. Wessels, A. Maurer and J. Mittag (eds) *Fifteen into One: The European Union and its Member States*, Manchester: Manchester University Press.

Mayhew, A. and Tokarski, S. (2000) "Impact assessment and European Integration Policy," Brighton: Working Paper No. 38, Sussex European Institute.

Medeiros Ferreira, J. (1993) "Political Costs and Benefits for Portugal arising from Membership of the European Community," in J. da Silva Lopes (ed.) *Portugal and EC Membership Evaluated*, London: Pinter.

de Meirelles, F.X.G.M. (1992) "Portugal," in F. Laursen and S. Vanhoonacker (eds) *The Intergovernmental Conference on Political Union*, Maastricht: EIPA.

Mikkel, E. (2003) "Election Briefing No. 11: Europe and the Estonian Parliamentary (Riigikogu) Elections of March 2nd 2003," unpublished.

Miles, L. (1997). "Sweden and the Intergovernmental Conference: Testing the Membership Diamonds," *Cooperation and Conflict*, 4: 339–66.

Milner, S. (2004). "For an Alternative Europe: Euroscepticism and the French Left since the Maastricht Treaty," *European Studies*, 20: 59–81.

Mitchell, J.P. (1998) "An Island in between: Malta, Identity and Anthropology," *South European Society and Politics*, 3 (1): 142–9.

Moravcsik, A. (1998) *The Choice for Europe: Social Purpose and State Power from Messina to Maastricht*, Ithaca: Cornell University Press.

—— (1993) "Preferences and Power in the European Community: A Liberal Intergovernmentalist Approach," *Journal of Common Market Studies*, 31: 473–523.

Morlino, L. (2001) "Constitutional design and problems of implementation in Southern and Eastern Europe," in J. Zielonka (ed.) *Democratic consolidation in Eastern Europe*, Vol. 1, *Institutional Engineering*, New York: Oxford University Press.

Müller, W.C. (2000) "Austria," in H. Kassim, G.B. Peters and V. Wright (eds) *The National Coordination of EU policy: The Domestic Level*, Oxford: Oxford University Press.

Neuhold, C. (2002) "Austria: Trailing behind, Raising the Flag," in F. Laursen (ed.) *The Amsterdam Treaty: National Preferences, Interstate Bargaining and Outcome*, Odense: Odense University Press.

Nouisianen, J. (2003) "Finnlands Regierungssystem." Online. Available at: www.om.fi (accessed 12 October 2004).

Nugent, N. (2003a) *The Government and Politics of the European Union*, Durham NC: Duke University Press.

—— (2003b) "Cyprus and the European Union: the Significance of Being Small," Occasional Paper 1, Centre for Small States Studies, Institute of International Relations, University of Iceland.

Pace, R. (2004a) *The EU's Mediterranean Enlargement: Cyprus and Malta*, London: Frank Cass.

—— (2004b) "Malta's EU Membership: Chapter 1 Concluded, Chapter 2 Just Started," *Mediterranean Politics*, 9 (1): 114–21.

—— (2003) "Malta and EU Membership: Adaptation, Change and Modernization," *Agora without Frontiers*, 8 (4): 365–82.

—— (2002) "A Small State and the European Union: Malta's Accession Experience," *South European Society and Politics*, 7 (1): 24–42.

—— (2001) *Microstate Security in the Global System: EU–Malta Relations*, Malta: Midsea Books.

—— (1999) "Malta's Foreign Policy in the 1990s," in S. Stavridis, T. Couloumbis, T. Veremis and N. Waites (eds) *The Foreign Policies of the EU's Mediterranean and Applicant Countries in the 1990s*, London: Macmillan.

—— (1997) "The European Union's Next Mediterranean Enlargement: Challenges and Uncertainties," Jean Monnet Working Papers in Comparative and International Politics No. 06/97, University of Catania.

Pagoulatos, G. (2004) "Believing in National Exceptionalism: Ideas and Economic Divergence in Southern Europe," *West European Politics*, 27 (1): 45–70.

—— (2002) "Greece, the European Union and the 2003 Presidency," Notre Europe, Groupement d'Etudes et de Recherches, Research and European Issues No. 21, December. Online. Available at: www.notre-europe.asso.fr/.

Pahre, R. (2001) "Divided Government and International Cooperation in Austria–Hungary, Sweden–Norway, and the European Union," *European Union Politics*, 2 (2): 132–62.

Papadopoulos, C.A. (2002) "Greece: the Difficult Road from Orthodoxy to Neo-orthodoxy," in F. Laursen (ed.) *The Amsterdam Treaty: National Preference Formation, Interstate Bargaining and Outcome*, Odense: Odense University Press.

Passas, A. and Dimitrakopoulos, D. (eds) (2004) *Greece in the European Union*, London: Routledge.

Peirce, W. (1991) "Unanimous Decisions in a Redistributive Context: The Council of Ministers of the European Communities," in R. Vaubel and T. Willett (eds) *The Political Economy of International Organizations*, Boulder: Westview.

Pelkmans, J. and Limonard, B. (2003) "EPIN Briefing note: The Netherlands and the Future of European Convention," The Hague: WRR. Online. Available at: www.epin.org/pdf/debate_netherlands.pdf (accessed 1 August 2004).

Perez Diaz, V. (1993) *The Return to Civil Society*, London: Harvard University Press.

Peterson, J. (1995) "Policy Networks and European Union Policy Making: A Reply to Kassim," *West European Politics*, 2: 389–407.

—— and Sjursen, H. (1999) *Decision Making in the European Union*, Basingstoke: Macmillan.

Pollak, J. and Slominski, P. (2003) "Influencing EU Politics? The Case of the Austrian Parliament," *Journal of Common Market Studies*, 41: 707–29.

Przeworski, A. (1991) *Democracy and the Market*, Cambridge: Cambridge University Press.

Putnam, R.D. (1988) "Diplomacy and domestic politics: The logic of two-level games," *International Organization*, 42: 427–60.

Pyszna, D. (2002) "The Management of Accession to the European Union: EU-related Decision and Policy-making in Poland," in D. Pyszna and K. Vida (eds) The management of accession to the European Union in Poland and Hungary, Working Paper No. 128, Budapest: Institute of World Economics.

Quinn, K.M. (2004) "Bayesian Factor Analysis for Mixed Ordinal and Continuous Responses," *Political Analysis*, 12 (4): 338–53.

Quirico, R. di. (2003) "Italy, Europe and the European Presidency of 2003," Research and European Issues No. 27, Paris: Notre Europe.

Reif, K. (1997) "European elections as member state second-order elections revisited," *European Journal of Political Research*, 31 (1–2): 115–24.

—— and Schmidt, H. (1980) "Nine second-order national elections: A Conceptual Framework for the Understanding of European Election Results," *European Journal of Political Research*, 8 (1): 3–44.

Rhodes, R.A.W. (1997) *Understanding Governance: Policy Networks, Governance, Reflexivity and Accountability*, Buckingham: Open University Press.

Roberts, A. (2003) "What Type of Democracy is Emerging in Eastern Europe?" paper presented at the Annual Conference of the Midwest Political Science Association, Chicago, 3–5 April.

Rodden, J. (2002) "Strength in Numbers? Representation and Redistribution in the European Union," *European Union Politics*, 3 (2): 151–75.

Rooper, S.D. (2002) "Are all Semipresidential Regimes the Same? A Comparison of Premier–Presidential Regimes," *Comparative Politics*, 34 (3): 253–72.

Royo, S. and Manuel, P.C. (2003) "Some Lessons from the Fifteenth Anniversary of the Accession of Portugal and Spain to the European Union," *South European Society and Politics*, 8 (1–2): 1–30.

Rusconi, G.E. (2003) "Italien und Europa von 1945 bis heute," in B. Rill (ed.) *Italien im Aufbruch – eine Zwischenbilanz*, Munich: Hanns Seidel Stiftung.

Salgado de Matos, L. (1993) "The Portuguese Political System and the EC: an Interaction Model," in J. da Silva Lopes (ed.) *Portugal and EC Membership Evaluated*, London: Pinter.

Sartori, G. (1997) *Comparative Constitutional Engineering: an Inquiry into Structures, Incentives and Outcomes*, New York: NYU Press.

Sbragia, A.M. (ed.) (1992) *Euro-politics:* Washington DC: Brookings.

Schain, M.A. (2004) "Politics in France," in G.A. Almond, G.B.J. Powell, K. Strøm and R.J. Dalton (eds) *Comparative politics: A world view*, 8th edn, New York: Longman.

Scharpf, F.W. (1988) "The Joint-Decision Trap: Lessons From German Federalism and European Integration," *Public Administration*, 66: 239–78.

Schelling, T.C. (1960) *The Strategy of Conflict*, Cambridge MA: Harvard University Press.

Schmidt, T. (2004) "Das politische System Lettlands," in W. Ismayr (ed.) *Die politischen Systeme Osteuropas*, 2nd edn, Opladen: Leske + Budrich.

Schmitter, P. and Lembruch, G. (1979) *Trends towards Corporatist Intermediation*, London: Sage.

Schneider, G. and Cederman, L.E. (1994) "The Change of Tide in Political Cooperation: A Limited Information Model of European Integration," *International Organization*, 48: 633–62.

Seixas da Costa, F. (2000) "A European Vocation," in A. de Vasconcelos (ed.) *Portugal: A European Story*, Cascais: Principia.

Signorino, C. and Ritter, J. (1999) "Tau-b or not Tau-b: Measuring the Similarity of foreign policy positions," *International Studies Quarterly*, 43: 115–44.

Siune, K and Svensson, P. (1993) "The Danes and the Maastricht Treaty: The Danish EC Referendum on June 1992," *Electoral Studies*, 12: 99–111.

Soetendorp, B. and Hanf, K. (1998) "The Netherlands: Growing Doubts of a Loyal Member," in K. Hanf and B. Soetendorp (eds) *Adaptation to European Integration. Small States and the European Union*, London and New York: Longman.

Sotiropoulos, D. (1999) "A Description of the Greek Higher Civil Service," in E.C. Page and V. Wright (eds) *Bureaucratic Elites in Western European States: A Comparative Analysis of Top Officials*, Oxford: Oxford University Press.

Spanou, C. (2000) "Greece: A Truncated Pyramid?" in H. Kassim, B.G. Peters and V. Wright (eds) *The National Coordination of EU Policy: the Domestic Level*, Oxford: Oxford University Press.

—— (1998) "European Integration in Administrative Terms: a Framework for Analysis and the Greek Case," *Journal of European Public Policy*, 5 (3): 467–84.

—— (1996) "Penelope's Suitors: Administrative Modernisation and Party Competition in Greece," *West European Politics*, 19 (1): 97–124.

Stavridis, S. (1999) "Double Standards, Ethics and Democratic Principles in

Foreign Policy: the European Union and the Cyprus Problem," *Mediterranean Politics*, 4 (1): 95–112.

Stoforopoulos, T.C. and Makridimitris, A.P.S. (1996) "The Greek Foreign Policy System: the Institutional Dimension: formation and monitoring, coordination and cohesion, policy analysis and implementation," Research Papers No. 38, Athens: Hellenic Centre for European Studies – EKEM.

Taggart, P. (1998) "A touchstone of dissent: Euroscepticism in contemporary Western European party systems," *European Journal of Political Research*, 33: 363–88.

—— (1995) "New Populist Parties in Western Europe," *West European Politics*, 18 (1): 34–51.

—— and Szczerbiak, A. (2004) "Contemporary Euroscepticism in the party systems of the European Union candidate states of Central and Eastern Europe," *European Journal of Political Research*, 43: 1–27.

—— and Szczerbiak, A. (2002) "The Party Politics of Euroscepticism in EU Member and Candidate States," SEI Working Paper No 51. Online. Available at: www.sussex.ac.uk/sei/documents/wp51.pdf.

Tauber, J. (2004) "Das politische System Litauens," in W. Ismayr (ed.) *Die politischen Systeme Osteuropas*, 2nd edn, Opladen: Leske + Budrich.

Thorhallson, B. (2000) *The role of Small States in the European Union*, Aldershot: Ashgate.

Thurner, P.W., Pappi, F.U. and Stoiber, M. (2002) "EU Intergovernmental Conferences. A quantitative Analytical Reconstruction and Data Handbook of Domestic Preference Formation, Transnational Networks, and Dynamics of Compromise during the Amsterdam Treaty Negotiations," Working Paper No. 60, University of Mannheim.

Tiilikainen, T. (2003) "Finland: smooth adaption to European values and institutions," in W. Wessels, A. Maurer and J. Mittag (eds) *Fifteen into One: The European Union and its Member States*, Manchester: Manchester University Press.

Tonra, B. (2002) "Ireland: The Politics of Pragmatism?" in F. Laursen (ed.) *The Amsterdam Treaty: National Preference Formation, Interstate Bargaining and Outcome*, Odense: Odense University Press.

—— (2001) *Europeanisation of National Foreign Policy: Dutch, Danish and Irish Foreign Policies in CFSP*, Aldershot: Ashgate.

Toots, A. and Vetik, R. (2004) "Estland vor dem EU Beitritt," *Aus Politik und Zeitgeschichte*, 5: 35–40.

Torres, F. (2000) "Lessons from Portugal's Long Transition to Economic and Monetary Union," in A. de Vasconcelos (ed.) *Portugal: A European Story*, Cascais: Principia.

—— and Fraga, A. (2004) "What 'Europe'? Portugal's Reactive Adaptation to European Institutional Changes," *South European Society and Politics*, 9 (1): 97–120.

Trzaskowski, R. (2003) "National Report Poland," in C. Franck and D. Pyszna-Nigge (eds) Positions of 10 Central and Eastern European countries on EU institutional reforms. Analytical survey in the framework of the CEEC debate project. Louvain-la-Neuve and Brussels: Université catholique de Louvain. Online. Available at: www.euro.ucl.ac.be.

Tsardanidis, C. and Nicolau, Y. (1999) "Cyprus Foreign and Security Policy: Options and Challenges," in S. Stavridis, T. Couloumbis, T. Veremis and N. Waites (eds) *The Foreign Policies of the EU's Mediterranean and Applicant Countries in the 1990s*, London: Macmillan.

Tsebelis, G. (2002) *Veto Players: How Political Institutions Work*, New York: Russell Sage Foundation and Princeton: Princeton University Press.

—— (1994) "The power of the European Parliament as a conditional agenda setter," *American Political Science Review*, 88 (1): 128–42.

—— and Garrett, G. (2001) "The Institutional Determinants of Supranationalism in the EU," *International Organization*, 55 (2): 357–90.

—— and Garrett, G. (2000) "Legislative Politics in the European Union," *European Union Politics*, 1: 9–36.

—— and Yataganas, X.A. (2002) "Veto players and Decision-making in the EU after Nice: Legislative Gridlock and Bureaucratic/Judicial Discretion," *Journal of Common Market Studies*, 40 (2): 283–307.

Tsinisizelis, M. (1996) "Greece," in D. Rometsch and W. Wessels (eds) *The European Union and Member States: Towards Institutional Fusion?* Manchester: Manchester University Press.

Tsoukalis, L. (2000) "Greece in the EU: Domestic Reform Coalitions, External Constraints and High Politics," in A. Mitsos and E. Mossialos (eds) *Contemporary Greece and Europe*, Aldershot: Ashgate.

Učeň, P. (2003) "Slovakia," *European Journal of Political Research*, 42: 1065–77 (Political Data Yearbook 2002).

—— (2002) "Slovakia," *European Journal of Political Research*, 41: 1075–83 (Political Data Yearbook 2001).

Valentinavicius, V. (2003) "Lithuania: A Fragile Democracy on the Road West," *East European Constitutional Review*, 11 (4)–12 (1): 111–15.

de Vallera, J. (2000) "The Negotiating Process," in A. de Vasconcelos (ed.) *Portugal: A European Story*, Cascais: Principia.

de Vasconcelos, A. (2000) "Portugal 2000: the European Way," Groupement d'Etudes et de Recherches Notre Europe, Research and Policy Paper No. 9.

—— and Antunes, L.P. (1996) "Portugal," in D. Rometsch and W. Wessels (eds) *The European Union and Member States: Towards Institutional Fusion?* Manchester: Manchester University Press.

Vaubel, R. (2002) "Die Politische Ökonomie des Europäischen Verfassungskonvents," *Wirtschaftsdienst*, 82: 636–40.

Verney, S. (1994) "Panacea or Plague: Greek Political Parties and Accession to the European Community, 1974–1979," PhD dissertation, Kings College, University of London.

Vida, K. (2003) "National Report Hungary," in C. Franck and D. Pyszna-Nigge (eds) Positions of 10 Central and Eastern European countries on EU institutional reforms. Analytical survey in the framework of the CEEC debate project. Louvain-la-Neuve and Brussels: Université catholique de Louvain. Online. Available at: www.euro.ucl.ac.be (accessed 17 November 2004).

—— (2002) "The management of accession to the European Union: EU-related decision and policy-making in Hungary," in K. Vida and D. Pyszna (eds) The management of accession to the European Union in Poland and Hungary, Budapest: Institute for World Economics, Hungarian Academy of Science, Working Paper No. 128.

Vodička, K. (2004) "Das politische System Tschechiens," in W. Ismayr (ed.) *Die politischen Systeme Osteuropas*, 2nd edn, Opladen: Leske + Budrich.

Wallace, W. (1983) "Less than a Federation, More than a Regime: The Community as a Political System," in H. Wallace, W. Wallace and C. Webb (eds) *Policy Making in the European Community*, 2nd edn, New York: Wiley.

—— (1982) "Europe as a Confederation: the Community and the Nation State," *Journal of Common Market Studies*, 21: 57–68.

Weise, C. (2002) "How to finance Eastern Enlargement of the EU," German Institute of Economic Research (DIW), Discussion paper 287, Berlin: DIW.

Wessels, B. (2002) "Parlamentarier in Europa und Europäische Integration. Einstellungen zur zukünftigen politischen Ordnung und zum institutionellen Wandel der EU," presented at the workshop "Wahlen und politische Einstellungen" of the German Political Science Association (DVPW), Augsburg, 6 June. Online. Available at: www.wz-berlin.de/~wessels/BWDownloads.de.htm (accessed 16 May 2003).

—— (1999) "Institutional Change and the Future Political Order," in R. Katz and B. Wessels (eds) *European Parliament, the National Parliaments and European Integration*, Oxford: Oxford University Press.

Widfeldt, A. (1996) "The Swedish European Election of 1995," *Electoral Studies*, 15 (1): 116–19.

Wincott, D. (2001) "Looking Forward or Harking Back? The Commission and the Reform of Governance in the European Union," *Journal of Common Market Studies*, 39 (5): 897–915.

Xuereb, P.G. (2004) "The Debate on the Future of Europe in Malta: Moving to Centre Stage," *South European Society and Politics*, 9 (1): 142–51.

Yannis, N. (2004) "Greece: On New, European Tracks?" *South European Society and Politics*, 9 (1): 121–41.

Ysmal, C. (2003) "France," *European Journal of Political Research*, 42: 943–56 (Political Data Yearbook 2002).

Zemanek, J. (2003) Making of the European constitution – the Czech view, Prague.

Official documents

Adami, E.F. (2003) Malta's position on the EU Intergovernmental Conference, letter presented by Maltese Prime Minister Dr Eddie Fenech Adami to the Italian EU presidency, 8 September. Online. Available at: www.mic.org.mt/Malta-EU/igc_mltposn.htm (accessed 18 November 2003).

Belka, M. (2004) "Telewizyjne wystąpienie premiera Belki," 19 June. Online. Available at: bip.kprm.gov.pl/bip/index.jsp?artId=913 (accessed 30 January 2005).

Cowen, B. (2003) Opening Remarks by Minister of Foreign Affairs, Dáil Debate on IGC, 15 October 2003. Online. Available at: foreignaffairs.gov.ie (accessed 15 May 2004).

Department of Foreign Affairs (2004) "EU Presidency 2004." Online. Available at: www.eu2004.ie (accessed 15 September 2004).

Department of the Taoiseach (2003) "Ireland and the European Union: Identifying priorities and pursuing goals," 2nd edn. Online. Available at: www.taoiseach.gov.ie/upload/publications/2182.pdf (accessed 15 May 2004).

Draft constitutional treaty (*CONV 850/03*), 18 July. Online. Available at: european-convention.eu.int/docs/Treaty/cv00850.en03.pdf.

European Commission (2003a) "Comprehensive monitoring report on Cyprus's preparations for membership," November. Online. Available at: www.europa.eu.int/comm/enlargement/report_2003/pdf/cmr_cy_final.pdf.

European Commission (2003b) "Allocation of 2002 EU operating expenditure by Member State," September, European Commission Budget. Online. Available at: europa.eu.int/comm/budget/agenda2000/reports_en.htm (accessed July 2004).

European Commission (2003c) "Comprehensive monitoring report on Malta's preparations for membership," November. Online. Available at: www.europa.eu.int/comm/enlargement/report_2003/pdf/cmr_mt_final.pdf.

European Commission (1997) "Agenda 2000: Commission opinion on Slovakia's application for membership of the European Union," Opinion paper No. DOC/97/20, 15 July.

European Commission (1993) "The Challenge of Enlargement. Commission Opinion on Malta's Application for Membership," Bulletin of the European Communities, Supplement 4/93.

Foreign Ministry of Slovakia (2003) "Navrh pozicie slovenskej republiky k hlavnym otazkam prerokovavanych Konventom o buducnosti Europy" (Draft of the official Slovak position on the main questions of the Convention on the Future of Europe), 16 May, MZV SR 3485/2003. Online. Available at: www.rokovania.sk/appl/material.nsf/NezaradenyMat?OpenView (accessed August 2005).

Government of Poland (2003) "Stanowisko Rządu RP na Konferencję Międzyrządową w sprawie Traktatu ustanawiającego Konstytucję dla Europy," Warsaw, 9 September. Online. Available at: www2.ukie.gov.pl/hlp/mointintgr.nsf/0/C7D5631D99C37DC6C126EFC004A0A8D/$file/ME7312.pdf (accessed 30 January 2005).

Groupe "Débat sur l'avenir de l'Europe" (2001) "Ensemble dessinons l'Europe," governmental report on the national debate in France (in French), 30 October. Paris: Cour de cassation.

Kohout, J. (2003) "Non-paper on the reform of EU institutions," Prague: Ministry of Foreign Affairs.

Letter from Ministers of Foreign Affairs of Finland, Ireland, Austria and Sweden to the President of the Council of the European Union "European Security and Defence Policy" (2003) (*CIG 62/03*), 4 December. Online. Available at: ue.eu.int/igcpdf/en/03/cg00/cg00062.en03.pdf.

Österreichische Grundsatzposition, Regierungskonferenz 2003 (Austrian common position, in German), IV-4 der Beilagen zu den Stenographischen Protokollen des Nationalrates XXII. GP, Beratung des Hauptausschusses in Angelegenheiten der Europäischen Union, Dienstag, 30. September 2003. (Auszugsweise Darstellung), 15427/EU XXII.GP.

Roche, D. (2003) Statement from Dick Roche, TD, to the Seanad. The Oireachtas, 22 October. Online. Available at: politics.ie (accessed 15 September 2004).

Roche, D. *et al.* (2003) (*CONV 646/03*), contribution "Reforming the Institutions: Principles and Premises" submitted to the European Convention, 28 March. Online. Available at: register.consilium.eu.int/pdf/en/03/cv00/cv00646en03.pdf.

Secretariat for EU Affairs (2003) "Government Report to Parliament on the outcome of the Work of the European Convention and on the Preparations for the Intergovernmental Conference. A compilations of the positions taken," 29 August (Finnish Government).

Sejm (2004) "Informacja Rządu w sprawie Polskiej polityki wobec Unii Europejskiej," Sejm, Fourth Term, 72nd session, 30 March–2 April. Online. Available at: ks.sejm.gov.pl:8009/kad4/072/40724016.htm (accessed 15 May 2005).

Sejm (2003a). "Resolution of 2 October 2003 on the Treaty establishing the Constitution for Europe," *Sejm Rzeczpospolitej Polskiej, Monitor Polski*, No. 47.

Sejm (2003b) The Roll call vote No. 31, Sejm, Fourth Term, 58th session, 2 October.

Sejm (2003c) "Resolution of 11 December 2003 on the Treaty establishing the Constitution for Europe," *Sejm Rzeczpospolitej Polskiej, Monitor Polski*, No. 58.

Thessaloniki Council Presidency Conclusions, 20 June 2003. Online. Available at: ue.eu.int/pressData/en/ec/76279.pdf.

Wekler, F. (2003) Speech at the Joint Committee on European Affairs, The Oireachtas, Dublin, 5 November (SzDSz deputy, Hungary). Online. Available at: www.irlgov.ie/oireachtas/frame.htm (accessed 1 October 2004).

Databases

Armingeon, K., Careja, R. (2004) "Comparative Data Set for 28 Post-Communist Countries, 1989–2004," Institute of Political Science: University of Berne. Online. Available at: www.ipw.unibe.ch/mitarbeiter/ru_armingeon/CPD_Set_en.asp (accessed July 2004).

Armingeon, K., Leimgruber, P., Beyeler, M. and Menegale, S. (2004) "Comparative Political Data Set, 1960–2002," Institute of Political Science, University of Berne. Online. Available at: www.ipw.unibe.ch/mitarbeiter/ru_armingeon/CPD_Set_en.asp (accessed July 2004).

Bräuninger, T. and König, T. (2001) "Indices of Power IOP 2.0" (computer program), Konstanz: University of Konstanz. Online. Available at: www.tbraeuninger.de/IOP.html.

Catinét (2004) "Flertal for ny EU-traktat," Danish public opinion research (in Danish). Online. Available at: www.catinet.dk/vis_nyhed.asp?nid=273.

CBOS (2005a) "About referendum on the EU constitution," Centrum Badania Opinii Społecznej, Warsaw, 1–2, 9–10 April.

CBOS (2005b) "Opinions on the ratification of the EU constitution," Centrum Badania Opinii Społecznej, Warsaw, 3–6 June.

CIA World Fact Book. Online. Available at: www.worldfactbook.org.

Emor (2005) Emor agency (Estonian public opinion research), 14 March, cited by CIDEL project. Online. Available at: www.unizar.es/euroconstitucion/Treaties/Treaty_Const_Rat_Estonia.htm (accessed 25 April 2005).

Eurobarometer (2005) "The Future Constitutional Treaty – First Results," EB Special No. 214, January. Online. Available at: europa.eu.int/comm/public_opinion/archives/ebs/ebs214_en_first.pdf (accessed 27 April 2005).

Eurobarometer (2004a) "The Future European Constitution," Flash EB No. 159, January. Online. Available at: europa.eu.int/comm/public_opinion/flash/fl159_fut_const.pdf.

Eurobarometer (2004b) Standard EB 62, autumn. Online. Available at: europa.eu.int/comm/public_opinion/archives/eb/eb62/eb_62_en.pdf.

Eurobarometer (2003a) Standard EB 59, spring. Online. Available at: europa.eu.int/comm/public_opinion/archives/eb/eb59/eb59_rapport_final_en.pdf.

Eurobarometer (2003b) Standard EB 60, autumn. Online. Available at: europa.eu.int/comm/public_opinion/archives/eb/eb60/eb60_rapport_standard_en.pdf.

Eurobarometer (2003c) Central and Eastern EB 2003.4, autumn. Online. Available at: europa.eu.int/comm/public_opinion/archives/cceb/2003/cceb2003.4_full_report.pdf.

European Forum (2004) European Forum for Democracy and Solidarity Country Updates. Online. Available at: www.europeanforum.net.

Eurostat (2004) Structural indicators. Online. Available at: europa.eu.int/comm/eurostat.

Eurostat (2003) *Eurostat Yearbook 2003: the Statistical Guide to Europe.* Online. Available at: europa.eu.int/comm/eurostat (accessed 1 August 2004).

IIES (2004) Institute for International Economic Studies. Online. Available at: www.iies.su.se (accessed March 2004).

Inter-parliamentary Union, Parline Database. Online. Available at: www.ipu.org/parline-e/parlinesearch.asp.

Martin, A.D. and Quinn, K.W. (2004) "MCMCpack 0.4–8," (tool for use with the *R* computer program). Online. Available at: mcmcpack.wustl.edu.

MEGAFON (2005) "Måling: Dansk ja ved EU-valget," Danish public opinion research for TV 2/NYHEDERNE (in Danish). Online. Available at: nyhederne.tv2.dk/baggrund/article.php?id=2225352.

OECD (2004) "Economic Surveys: Netherlands," Vol. 2004/9, Paris: OECD.

OECD Economic Outlook (2002). Online. Available at: www.oecd.org/document/18/0,2340,en_2649_201185_20347538_1_1_1_1,00.html.

World Bank (2004) World Development Indicators, Washington DC: World Bank. Online. Available at: www.worldbank.org/data/.

Press sources

Ceska Tiskova Kancelar (CTK) and *BBC Monitoring European*, 3 July 2003, "Czech Christian Democrats disagree with proposed preamble to EU constitution."

Ceska Tiskova Kancelar (CTK) Business News, 7 October 2003, "The government will submit to parliament a draft bill on a general referendum."

Corriere della Sera, 30 November 2002, "Ciampi ai paesi fondatori dell'Europa – 'Riforme entro il 2003'."

Corriere della Sera, 28 February 2003, "La Costituzione Europea pronta prima dell'estate."

Die Presse, 16 November 2002a, "Voggenhuber bricht grünes Tabu. Beistands pflicht für gesamte EU."

Die Presse, 16 November 2002b, "Pilz für Sicherheitsunion."

Die Presse, English edition, 5 December 2002, "Ferrero-Waldner favours the end of neutrality."

Die Presse, 3 October 2003, "EU. Schüssel beharrt auf Kommissar."

Die Zeit, 11 March 2004, "Mit Gewürzbier auf die Datenautobahn."

Economist, The, 9 March 2000.

Economist, The, 19 April 2003, "Hungary and EU membership: An unpersuasive referendum."

Economist, The, 7 June 2003, "Poland's EU Referendum: Try getting excited."

Economist, The, 3 July 2004, "One more defenestration – The Czech Republic."

EUbusiness, 22 April 2005, "Estonia will vote on EU constitution regardless of French result."

EUbusiness, 3 June 2005, "Estonia postpones European treaty ratification."

EUobserver, 18 March 2004, "Brussels defends controversial budget plans." Online. Available at: www.euobserver.com.

EUobserver, 2 August 2004, "German referendum on EU may be legally possible." Online. Available at: www.euobserver.com.

EUobserver, 29 April 2005, "Schröders clears path for EU Constitution." Online. Available at: www.euobserver.com.

EUobserver, 2 May 2005, "Latvia, Malta and Cyprus in the euro pipeline."

Financial Times, 21 June 2003, "New Treaty of Rome agreed."

Frankfurter Allgemeine Zeitung, 16 January 2004, "Dzurinda ohne Mehrheit/Minderheitsregierung in der Slowakei/Simko winkt ab."

Gazeta Wyborcza, 7 May 2004. Online. Available at: www.wyborcza.pl (accessed 15 September 2004).

JEF Europe (2003) Interview with Peter Balázs. Online. Available at: www.constitutional-convention.net (accessed 7 October 2004).

La Stampa, 31 May 2003, "L'italia fa pressioni affinche' le radici cristiane siano ricordate nel preambolo. Il vaticano chiede una modifica 'Menzione esplicita del cristianesimo'."

Le Figaro, 16 January 2003, "Paris et Berlin font cause commune sur l'Europe."

Le Monde, 3 September 2002, "Recherche Europe forte, désespérément."

Le Monde, 16 January 2003, "Paris et Berlin proposent une double présidence de l'UE, avec un président de la commission élu par le Parlement Européen."

Le Monde, 10 July 2003a, "A la convention, Paris préserve in extremis 'l'exception culturelle'."

Le Monde, 10 July 2003b, "Des concessions de dernière minute pour préserver le projet de constitution."

Libération, 14 February 2000, "Pierre Moscovici, ministre délégué aux affaires européennes."

Libération, 22 January 2003, "L'allant franco-allemand relance la convention."

Libération, 2 March 2004, "La France terre d'incroyance."

Libération, 23 April 2005, "Le non affole les sondages."

Magyar Hírlap, 27 January 2003, Rockenbauer, N. "Az eurorealisták felelőssége" [The Responsibility of Euro-realists].

Neue Zürcher Zeitung, 1 October 2003, "Aufbegehren der 'Kleinen' in der Europäischen Union."

Neue Zürcher Zeitung, 2 October 2003, "Unklare Kräfteverhältnisse im slowakischen Parlament. Regiert Dzurinda in der Minderheit?"

NRC, 28 November 2003, "Schending komt VVD goed uit."

NRC Handelsblad, 20 August 2002, "Van Mierlo moet mogelijk Europese conventie verlaten."

NRC Handelsblad, 5 November 2003, Van Straten, "Senaat bromt over geloofsverwijzing."

Slovenska Tlacova Agentura, 14 October 2003, "Austrian–Slovak Symposium on Future of the EU held in Bratislava."

Süddeutsche Zeitung, 12 December 2003, "Machtkampf in der EU gefährdet Verfassung."

Tlacova Agentura Slovenskej Republiky and *BBC Monitoring European*, 1 April 2003, "Slovak opposition leader warns against keeping rotating EU presidency."

Tlacova Agentura Slovenskej Republiky, 14 September 2003a, "National Convention meets ahead of EU constitution conference."

Tlacova Agentura Slovenskej Republiky, 14 September 2003b, "Mečiar – SR should support France and Germany on EU constitution."

Tlacova Agentura Slovenskej Republiky, 17 September 2003, "Kukan presents cabinet's position on draft EU constitution to MPs."
The Irish Times, 1 April 2005, De Bréadún, D. "Anti-EU treaty group launched."
The Malta Independent, 6 November 2003.
The Times of Malta, 6 November 2003.

Index

Made in the USA
Las Vegas, NV
31 January 2025

17299942R00188